From the God
to the Glass Ceiling

From the Goddess to the Glass Ceiling

A Dictionary of Feminism

Janet K. Boles
Diane Long Hoeveler

with the assistance of
Rebecca Bardwell

Jon Woronoff, Editor

MADISON BOOKS

Lanham • New York • London

Published by Madison Books
4720 Boston Way
Lanham, Maryland 20706

3 Henrietta Street
London WC2E 8LU, England

Library of Congress Cataloging-in-Publication Data

From the goddess to the glass ceiling : a dictionary of feminism [edited by]
Janet K. Boles, Diane Long Hoeveler, with the assistance of Rebecca
Bardwell.
p. cm.
Includes bibliographical references.
1. Feminism—History—Dictionaries. I. Boles, Janet K., 1944– .
II. Hoeveler, Diane Long. III. Bardwell, Rebecca.
HQ1115.F77   1996   305.42'03—dc20   95-42618   CIP

ISBN 1-56833-072-3 (pbk.: alk. paper)

Distributed by National Book Network

♾™ The paper used in this publication meets the minimum requirements of
American National Standard for Information Sciences—Permanence of
Paper for Printed Library Materials, ANSI Z39.48–1964.
Manufactured in the United States of America.

This book is dedicated to our three daughters:

Christine Elaine Evans
Emily Ann Hoeveler
Asasys Hope Braaksma

CONTENTS

PREFACE

Feminism as a social, political, and intellectual movement has a very long history. Although the present-day activities and organizations are most familiar, they build on actions, pioneers and role models that reach back through the centuries and even into Antiquity and the biblical era. Over this time, the movement has undergone many changes and mutations, focusing on different goals at different times and adopting different tactics and strategies to attain them under different circumstances. Although much of the news still comes from the United States and Europe, there are activists and participants in every country on every continent, often working out their own solutions to their own problems, but well aware that they have comrades around the world.

The length, depth and breadth of the feminist movement is such that even those most deeply involved may not know some of what has gone before or has been done elsewhere. They may not even realize the extent and diversity of what is being achieved now. These are good reasons for a reference work like *From the Goddess to the Glass Ceiling: A Dictionary of Feminism* which brings together, in a compact form, many of the strands of historical and contemporary feminism. The volume provides background on persons, organizations, campaigns and court cases, goals and achievements. Despite some emphasis on the United States and Europe, where much of the action has been concentrated, there are many entries on other parts of the world. The movement is summed up in an introduction and traced in a chronology. And further sources of information are provided in an extensive bibliography.

Unlike most historical dictionaries, this book was not written by one or two persons but a wide array of authors, all working within their fields of specialization. All of them are or were on the faculty of Marquette University of Milwaukee, Wisconsin. The team was coordinated by Janet K. Boles,

Associate Professor of Political Science, who contributed the Chronology and wrote over 300 entries, and Diane Long Hoeveler, Associate Professor of English, who wrote the Introduction and over 100 entries. Rebecca Bardwell, Associate Professor of Educational and Counseling Psychology, wrote seven entries and was responsible for providing clerical assistance and electronic documentation in the preliminary stages of the project.

As far as we know, this is the first dictionary of feminism written as a collaborative effort by faculty of one university. Although women's studies has traditionally been associated with the principle of collaboration, the other dictionaries on the subject are not collaborative projects, and do not attempt the same sort of interdisciplinary enterprise that we do. By tapping the expertise of faculty in social work, management, engineering, law, nursing, education, communication, history, theology, languages, classics, English, philosophy, political science, anthropology, sociology and psychology, we gain the many different voices that we know make up the contemporary feminist movement.

As co-editors we wish to thank our colleagues in all the above fields for their contributions: Nicholas Abraham, Raquel Aguilú de Murphy, Bonnie Birk, Patricia Bradford, Lori Dillard, Lance Grahn, Carla Hay, Jeanne Herzog, Christine Firer Hinze, Justin Hoffman, Susan Hopwood, Sharon Pace Jeansonne, Rebecca Kasper, Alice B. Kehoe, Christine L. Krueger, Courtney L. Marlaire, Patricia Marquardt, Kathleen McInnis-Dittrich, Rebecca Moore, Maria Okuneva, Georgia Pappanastos, Anne Pasero, John S. Pustejovsky, Belle Ragins, Krista Ratcliffe, Susan Riedel, Eufemia Sánchez de la Calle, Mary Anne Siderits, Gladys Simandl, Nancy Snow, Helen Sterk, Terry Tobin, Rose Trupiano, Lynn Turner, Carolyn Wells, Phoebe Williams, Hollyn Wilson, and Christine M. Wiseman.

Finally, we offer *From the Goddess to the Glass Ceiling: A Dictionary of Feminism* to our readers as a useful and succinct handbook of information about the history of the feminist movement. In doing so, we wish to pay tribute to the struggles of all those who have gone before us, individually or collectively, to change and improve the living conditions for women in the world.

LIST OF ACRONYMS

AAUW	American Association of University Women
ABC	Act for Better Child Care
ACDWF	All-China Democratic Women's Federation
ACLU-RFP	American Civil Liberties Union Reproductive Freedom Project
ACLU-WRP	American Civil Liberties Union Women's Rights Project
AERA	American Equal Rights Association
AFDC	Aid to Families with Dependent Children
AIDS	Acquired Immune Deficiency Syndrome
AIWC	All-India Women's Conference
ANC	African National Congress
ATWS	Attitudes Towards Women Scale
AWSA	American Woman Suffrage Association
AWSA	Arab Women's Solidarity Association
BFOQ	Bona Fide Occupational Qualification
BPW/USA	National Federation of Business and Professional Women's Clubs
BSRI	Bem Sex Role Inventory
BWTA	British Women's Temperance Association
CAC	Citizens' Advisory Council on the Status of Women
CAWP	Center for the American Woman and Politics
CCWI	Congressional Caucus for Women's Issues
CEDAW	Committee on the Elimination of Discrimination Against Women
CEW	Committee for the Equality of Women
CLUW	Coalition of Labor Union Women
CNM	Certified Nurse Midwife

COMADRES	Comité de Madres (Committee of Mothers and Families of Prisoners, the Disappeared, and Victims of Political Assassination of El Salvador, Monsignor Oscar Arnulfo Romero)
C-R	Consciousness-Raising
CRA	Civil Rights Act
CSW	Committee of Soviet Women
CSWI	Committee on the Status of Women in India
CU	Congressional Union
CVS	Chorionic Villi Sampling
CWA	Concerned Women for America
CWLU	Chicago Women's Liberation Union
DES	Diethylstilbestrol
ECOA	Equal Credit Opportunity Act
EEOC	Equal Employment Opportunity Commission
EFU	Egyptian Feminist Union
EGE	Enosis Gynaikon Elladas (Union of Greek Women)
EMILY	Early Money Is Like Yeast
EOC	Economic Opportunities Commission
EPA	Equal Pay Act
ERA	Equal Rights Amendment
ERISA	Employee Retirement Income Security Act
FACE	Freedom of Access to Clinic Entrances
FACT	Feminist Anti-Censorship Taskforce
FBN	Feminist Bookstore News
FFQ	Fédération des Femmes du Québec (Quebec Women's Federation)
FR	Féministes Révolutionnaires (Revolutionary Feminists)
GAM	Grupo de Apoyo Mutuo (Mutual Support Group for the Appearance, Alive, of Our Children, Spouses, Parents, and Brothers and Sisters)
GFWC	General Federation of Women's Clubs
IAW	International Alliance of Women

ICW	International Council of Women
IUD	Intrauterine Device
IWRAW	International Women's Rights Action Watch
IWY	International Women's Year
JOBS	Job Opportunity and Basic Skills Program
KOWANI	Kongres Wanita Indonesia (Congress of Indonesian Women)
LDF	Ligue du Droit des Femmes (Women's Rights League)
LEAF	Women's Legal Education and Action Fund
LWV	League of Women Voters
MFPF	Mouvement Français pour le Planning Familial (French Movement for Family Planning)
MLD	Movimento di la Liberazione della Donna (Woman's Liberation Movement)
MLF	Mouvement pour la Libération des Femmes (Women's Liberation Movement)
NAC	National Abortion Campaign
NAC	National Action Committee on the Status of Women
NACW	National Association of Colored Women
NARAL	National Abortion and Reproductive Rights Action League
NAWSA	National American Woman Suffrage Association
NBFO	National Black Feminist Organization
NCL	National Consumers League
NCNW	National Council of Negro Women
NFIW	National Federation of Indian Women
NIH	National Institutes of Health
NOW	National Organization for Women
NRLC	National Right to Life Committee
NSWS	National Society for Women's Suffrage
NUSEC	National Union of Societies for Equal Citizenship

NUWSS	National Union of Women's Suffrage Societies
NWAF	National Women's Aid Federation
NWHN	National Women's Health Network
NWP	National Woman's Party
NWPC	National Women's Political Caucus
NWRO	National Welfare Rights Organization
NWSA	National Woman Suffrage Association
NYRF	New York Radical Feminists
NYRW	New York Radical Women
OR	Operation Rescue
OWAAD	Organization of Women of African and Asian Descent
OWL	Older Women's League
PAC	Political Action Committee
PC	Politically Correct
PCSW	President's Commission on the Status of Women
PFUF	Parti Féministe Unifié Français (French Unified Feminist Party)
PMS	Premenstrual Syndrome
PPFA	Planned Parenthood Federation of America
RCAR	Religious Coalition for Abortion Rights
RCSW	Royal Commission on the Status of Women in Canada
REAL	Realistic, Equal, Active, and for Life Women
RICO	Racketeer Influenced and Corrupt Organizations Act
SCSW	State Commissions on the Status of Women
SPUC	Society for the Protection of the Unborn Child
TSS	Toxic Shock Syndrome
TWLM	Toronto Women's Liberation Movement
UDI	Unione delle Donne Italiane (Italian Women's Union)

UFCS	Union Française Civique et Sociale (French Civic and Social Union)
UFSF	Union Française pour le Suffrage des Femmes (French Union for Women's Suffrage)
UFV	Unabhängiger Frauenverband (Independent Women's Association)
WAA	Women's Action Alliance
WAC	Women's Action Coalition
WAP	Women Against Pornography
WCF	Women's Campaign Fund
WCTU	Woman's Christian Temperance Union
WEAL	Women's Equity Action League
WEEA	Women's Educational Equity Act
WISH	Women in the Senate and House
WITCH	Women's International Terrorist Conspiracy from Hell
WJCC	Women's Joint Congressional Committee
WLM	Women's Liberation Movement
WNC	Women's National Commission
WOI	Women's Organization of Iran
WREI	Women's Research and Education Institute
WSPU	Women's Social and Political Union
WTUL	Women's Trade Union League
WWC	Women Workers' Council
ZPG	Zero Population Growth

INTRODUCTION

by Diane Long Hoeveler

Feminism as a social, political, economic, and intellectual movement has been defined variously over the past two hundred years. The current consensus is that there is no one feminism, but, in fact, many traditions within a larger movement dedicated to securing equity for women. The overview below of the history of feminism, with some emphasis on the United States and British contexts, is intended to explain the causes for these different feminisms within the larger movement.

I. ORIGINS OF THE MOVEMENT

The feminist movement is sometimes said to have originated in the writings of the Greek poet Sappho, but this seems a pedantic claim given the thousands of years between Sappho's life and any active organized effort to improve living conditions for women. Other scholars claim that the modern feminist consciousness began during the Renaissance, when writers like the Frenchwoman Christine de Pizan wrote for the first time for women and about women. Pizan's *The Book of the City of Women* (1405) argues that women need to build their own city, apart from men, where they will not be attacked and slandered by men. Although Pizan, like a very few other exceptional women, managed to publish her writings, she was very distinctly a singular voice. Another early feminist manifesto was the broadside published in 1589 by one Jane Anger, either an actual historical woman or an "agent provocateur." This piece of pre-feminism is typical of the litany of grievances published by women against men at this time: "We are the grief of man, in that we take all the grief from man: we languish when they laugh, we sit sighing when they sit singing, and sit sobbing

1

when they lie slugging and sleeping" (*Jane Anger, Her Protection for Women*, 1589).

The modern feminist movement, although it may recognize a kindred spirit in these early women writers, actually grew out of the intellectual, social and political milieu that produced the French and American Revolutions. The word "feminism" is of even more recent vintage, having been coined in 1882 by Hubertine Auclert, the organizer of the first female suffrage society in France. By the 1890's these terms--*feminisme* and *feministe*--appeared in their anglicized forms in England and migrated to the United States in the 1910's. Women in the nineteenth century framed their movement not as "feminist," but in terms of "woman suffrage," "the woman movement," and "woman's rights." The popular convention, however, has been to apply "feminism" retroactively to include these earlier struggles for women's advancement.

II. THE INDIVIDUAL RIGHTS TRADITION

A seminal document in the development of the individual rights movement was John Locke's *Two Treatises of Government* (1690), which argued that all individuals have a natural right to the freedom of life, liberty, and possessions that no government can suppress. His ideas were seized by a number of writers over the next century to agitate for political and social change, particularly in France and America, and they were finally adapted and modified by Mary Wollstonecraft in her *Vindication of the Rights of Woman* (1792). Wollstonecraft had begun her writing career by publishing a book on the education of women, and this concern recurs in her *Vindication*. She also wrote two novels in the sentimental and gothic traditions, both of which provided her with the ideology of woman as the innocent victim of oppressive forces beyond her control. For Wollstonecraft women were human beings and individuals in the same way that men were human beings and individuals. She did not believe that women should be defined by their sexual identities nor that their sexuality should be used to deny them access to full personhood with all of the individualist rights that men possessed. Wollstonecraft was very much a product of the Enlightenment, however, and her highest values were Reason and Rationality. She argued that if women were educated to develop fully their faculty of reason then they would have the same qualities that men have. In other words, she condemned the enfeebling and trivial educations that women received as producing physically weak, vacuous, and sensual creatures not fit for any serious work or responsibility. Although she believed that women must escape the gilded cage of marriage and sexual parasitism, she also recognized that only the exceptional woman also would be able to have a career as a teacher or midwife perhaps. For most women, she admitted, the problem was how to make the roles of wife and mother more palatable. Wollstonecraft recommended that women be recognized by the law as equals to their husbands, both in owning property and in the right to earn their own livings. A properly educated woman will make a superior wife and mother, one who will approach her responsibilities with reason and rationality as her guiding forces.

John Stuart Mill was the other leading spokesman for the early British feminist tradition of equal rights. His treatise *The Subjection of Women* (1869) condemns the legal subordination of women to men, and advocates the position that women and men are equal in "privileges and power." He too condemns the existing educational system that produces women who are encouraged to cultivate artificial natures in order to ensnare men as a means of financial support. But like Wollstonecraft, Mill also concludes his treatise by saying that educated women will best serve society by working in their homes as reasonable and companionate wives and mothers.

Other early British leaders in the feminist equal rights movement were Unitarian women like Barbara Leigh Smith Bodichon and her friend Bessie Parkes, Harriet Martineau, author of *On Female Education* (1823), and William Fox, editor of the *Monthly Repository*, which published articles written by Fox advocating reform of the divorce laws and female suffrage. Bodichon and Parkes were instrumental in getting the Married Women's Property Bill before Parliament in 1856, and they later founded the *Englishwoman's Journal* and the Society for Promoting the Employment of Women. These women, along with Emily Davies, Elizabeth Garrett Anderson, and Mrs. Anna Jameson, formed the nucleus of woman suffrage activists in Britain around 1860.

In the US the equal rights tradition of feminism formally began with the "Declaration of Sentiments," a document produced by the Women's Rights Convention held at Seneca Falls, New York, in 1848. This document paraphrases the United States Declaration of Independence by asserting that "all men and women are created equal." It then condemns the socially sanctioned forms of discrimination against women that occurred throughout America: no property rights, no access to divorce, no guaranteed child custody, no access to education or the professions, no right to serve as a religious or political leader, no code of morality that applied to men and women equally.

Prominent leaders in the US wing of equal rights feminism include Lucretia Mott, Susan B. Anthony, Victoria Woodhull, Lucy Stone, the Grimke sisters, and Elizabeth Cady Stanton; all are women who were originally galvanized by their work in the anti-slavery movement. Bitterly stung in the post-Civil War era by black leader Frederick Douglass, who they felt rejected women in order to ensure the vote for black men, Stanton and Anthony formed in 1869 an organization for women only, the National Woman Suffrage Association, a then-radical group that advocated the inclusion of women in the Fifteenth Amendment to the US Constitution. Six months later, the American Woman Suffrage Association, open to both sexes, was formed by Lucy Stone and her husband, Henry Blackwell. The AWSA was a more moderate group that drew its members from civic and professional ranks and adopted the gradualist strategy of state referenda for women's suffrage.

The equal rights feminist tradition of the Enlightenment era believes that the so-called differences between men and women are caused by the social environment, and that if social, educational, and financial opportunities were identical the sexes would also be identical. It emphasizes freedom of rights and responsibilities, self-determination, autonomy, and control over one's fate. This tradition sparked the fight for suffrage and now spearheads the abortion rights campaign.

III. THE EVANGELICAL TRADITION

Another major influence on the feminist movement has been the Protestant and specifically the Evangelical tradition. It is no coincidence that the vast majority of women involved in the early feminist movement were either Unitarians or Quakers. Both are religions that advocate strong individualist positions in regard to every believer's personal relationship to God. Both religions also fostered the belief that women were human individuals before they were sexual creatures, and as such were deserving of the same political rights as men. Also not coincidentally, the feminist movement flourished in countries that were primarily Protestant and highly industrialized. In countries with no strong middle class, no tradition of education, and no professional opportunities for women, feminism did not develop or thrive.

Organizations like the New York Female Reform Society, founded in 1834 to convert prostitutes, formed the nucleus of the female purity crusade that was to culminate in the temperance movement in America (and now undergirds the anti-feminist movements in the US). In England the feminist purity campaign crystallized around the Contagious Diseases Acts in the 1870's. This campaign, largely led by Josephine Butler, sought to repeal a law that required prostitutes to have regular medical examinations for venereal diseases. Designed to protect males and military personnel, feminists believed that it encouraged, indeed that it promoted, a double sexual standard for men and women.

Temperance was the other major goal of reform efforts in the nineteenth and early twentieth centuries for women in both England and the US The British Women's Temperance Association and the Women's Christian Temperance Union both held that women would continue to be victimized as long as men drank. Both organizations believed that there was a direct connection between alcohol and deviant sexual practices, and both groups claimed that men corrupted by alcohol were abusive of their wives and children and wasteful of the family's earnings.

The Evangelical tradition of feminism believes that women are essentially different from men, physically, spiritually and emotionally. Because of these differences between the sexes women are seen, paradoxically, as physically inferior and spiritually superior. Their physical weakness requires that they be "protected," and thus the Evangelical tradition has often been in the forefront of pushing for protective legislation for women.

They have also been involved in institutionalizing what became known in the nineteenth century as the doctrine of "separate spheres" and the "cult of domesticity." The "separate spheres" doctrine maintained that women were naturally suited to the family and private realm of the hearth and home, while men were naturally suited to the working world and the public domain. The two sexes were then naturally complementary in their roles and functions, rather than in competition with each other. The "cult of domesticity" was the literary and artistic expression of the separate spheres doctrine. In innumerable poems, paintings, and novels women were encouraged and lauded for their angelic ministrations as devoted wives and mothers of triumphant capitalists.

IV. THE SOCIALISTIC TRADITION

The third major influence on the development of the early feminist movement was socialism, or a variety of intellectual movements that we now recognize as socialistic. Early socialist theorists such as Robert Owen, founder of the Owenite community at New Harmony, Indiana, was an advocate of radical change in the family. Owen, like John Humphrey Noyes, Charles Fourier, and the Saint-Simonians, all advocated a communal style of living, with women to be shared among the men of the group. Child-raising was to be done by the community at large, and women and men were not to assume individual parental ownership of children. Group marriage, equal sexual freedom for women and men, and the rejection of traditional marriage as a type of property ownership made socialistic theories attractive to a number of feminists, particularly Frances Wright, Victoria Woodhull, and Anna Wheeler.

The writings of Karl Marx and Friedrich Engels on the family, the role of women under capitalism, and equality for women under socialism have also had a major impact on feminism. Engels's *Origin of the Family, Private Property and the State* (1884) states that women are the true bearers of the world's moral future. In other words, women already embodied the values that men would possess only when they lived under the conditions of socialism.

The most influential socialist work of the period was August Bebel's *Woman and Socialism* (1879), which included a long discussion of the oppression of women under capitalism. Bebel claimed that the sex/cash nexus corrupted bourgeois marriage, led to the prevalence of prostitution, and created the factory system that devoured so many proletariat women. The only solutions according to Bebel were equal rights for women, including the vote, equal training for the professions, and equal legal protection against financial exploitation.

The socialistic tradition within feminism can also be seen in the writings of Charlotte Perkins Gilman, who advocated group living in cooperatives where all housework and childrearing would be done through a collective group effort. The socialistic tradition can also be seen, in somewhat muted form, in the work of Jane Addams of Hull House, Chicago, and the larger social work movement which sought to bring humane living conditions to the rapidly increasing urban neighborhoods in both England and the US In England the Fabian Movement, and specifically the Fabian Woman's Group, saw itself as leading the reform movement. The Fabian Mabel Atkinson wrote in 1914, "it becomes clear that the only path to the ultimate and most deep lying ends of the feminist movement is through socialism, and every wise feminist will find herself more and more compelled to adopt the principles of Socialism" ("Economic Foundations of the Women's Movement," Fabian Tract #175, June 1914). Other British women involved in the social movement were: Mary Carpenter, who sought to reform the Ragged Schools; Louisa Twining, of the Workhouse Visiting Societies; Mary Ann Baines, of the Ladies National Association for the Diffusion of Sanitary Knowledge; and Florence Nightingale, who worked for the construction of hospitals.

Socialist feminism continued throughout the nineteenth and twentieth centuries in the formation of "welfare socialism." This movement seeks free abortions for poor women and other government-supported services that help to equalize living and working conditions for working class women and their children. Welfare feminism, with its roots in a strong labor union movement and an organized socialist tradition, is much more prevalent in Britain than it is in America, where the middle-class origins of feminism are still a dominant influence on the character of the movement.

V. ZENITH OF THE MOVEMENT, 1870-1928

Generally considered the heyday of the modern feminist movement, the period of 1870-1928 is characterized by extremely active suffrage activity and parallel educational and social reform movements. Women from all walks of life, but particularly those involved in the anti-slavery and temperance movements, combined forces to push for votes for women in England and the US In England the suffragists were opposed by the ruling Liberal Party, largely because the Liberals believed that votes for women would increase the Conservative voter base. Ironically, the Conservative Party itself offered a good deal of opposition, largely because it was suspicious of any movement that aimed to broaden the voter base. The suffragists were also opposed by prominent women themselves, most notably those writing in the *Nineteenth Century* magazine (1889). One famous article was signed by women like the Fabian Beatrice Webb and the writer Mrs. Humphrey Ward, among others, who claimed that they had no need for the vote because they were already represented by their husbands or fathers. For such women the idea of female suffrage was simply a form of plural voting, redundant, because women would always vote as their men instructed. Suffragists were accused of advocating free love, overthrowing traditional female roles as wives and mothers, and wanting to impose strict moral codes of behavior and temperance on men.

Two factors turned the tide for the suffrage movement in the late nineteenth century. The first was the growth of the settlement movement led by women like Eleanor Rathbone, Alice Crompton, and Emmeline Pethick-Lawrence, all of whom turned their energies to the suffrage issue after realizing its importance in changing social conditions for women. The other factor was the growing labor movement, which linked women's suffrage with work and pay concerns. The catalysts for the successful passage of universal women's suffrage in Britain were the Pankhurst family, Richard, Emmeline, and their daughter Christabel. The British suffragists faced innumerable obstacles before they won full and universal suffrage in 1928, not the least of which came from brewing interests that feared the association between feminism and temperance.

Although the situation in the US was somewhat different, the issue was resolved in an almost identical fashion. The US suffrage movement was complicated not just by the class issue, but also by the race issue. In America, also, the vote had to be won state by state before a federal amendment could be passed, as was the case for the amendment that had given African-American men the vote earlier. A major victory was won when Frances Willard, head of the Woman's Christian Temperance Union, brought the group into support of female suffrage in 1883. But by breaking down the churches' opposition to suffrage, the WCTU mobilized the brewery interests against votes for women. Another complicating factor was the large number of immigrant women who also wanted the vote. Feminists like Elizabeth Cady Stanton supported suffrage for "educated" women only, and by 1903 this was a common view held by a number of women's organizations. In the South support for suffrage was complicated further by the large numbers of African-American men enfranchised by the Fifteenth Amendment. Factions within a number of women's groups advocated votes for white women only, as an attempt to retain the vestiges of white supremacy as long as possible. Carrie Chapman Catt took control of the mainstream and unified National American Woman Suffrage Association in 1915. But two years later the movement again split over tactics when the more radical National Woman's Party, led by Alice Paul, organized picketing around the White House. Although not as militant as the most extreme activists in Britain, the pickets were effective in frightening the government, which saw in them the threat of large-scale social disorder. Suffrage for women in the United States was finally secured in 1920.

There were also well-developed women's movements in almost every other nation in Europe during the late nineteenth and early twentieth centuries. Women's rights activity also emerged in many other parts of the world, particularly in the early twentieth century. These latter campaigns were often initially led by male intellectual reformers (e.g., Qasim Amin in Egypt, Yukichi Fukuzawa in Japan, and K'ang Yu-wei in China) as part of a larger quest for modernity and/or national independence.

In Western Europe the women's movements were often small, elite-based groups led by well-educated middle-class women residing in the largest cities. Because Protestantism places a greater emphasis on universal education than other religions, the strongest women's movements during this period were in the Protestant nations of Western Europe. And even in Asia, many feminist leaders were Christian converts.

First wave feminism worldwide was rooted in moral reform; both abolition (in Brazil) and the Woman's Christian Temperance Union (in many nations, including the anglophone democracies of Canada, New Zealand, and Australia plus Norway, China, Japan, and Egypt) played major roles in movement-building. The first issue to emerge in almost all countries was women's education (access to higher education in Western Europe, Canada, and the United States and literacy elsewhere). Often feminist demands were channelled through a traditional-sounding women's club (e.g., the Bluestocking Society of Japan, the Club Femenino de Cuba, and the Women's Reading Circle of Chile). Next followed demands for legal reform in the status of women (e.g., property rights, divorce reform, and employment rights). In non-European nations the focus was often on cultural or religious issues such as purdah, suttee, foot-binding, veiling, child marriage, polygamy, and concubinage.

Woman suffrage eventually was adopted as a goal in almost all nations as a means to these social and legal ends. The concept of the modern nation-state at that time legitimized the extension of formal legal equality to women and undercut the power of religious rulers. Two coalitions of United States origin, the International Alliance of Women and the International Council of Women, facilitated the exchange of feminist ideas across national boundaries and pressed for the female vote.

VI.   THE LULL, 1928-1960

A major transformation (and fragmentation) of the women's movements in both England and the US occurred shortly after the vote was won. Attention clearly shifted to improving women's educational opportunities, and women began to enter the professions in record numbers during these years. Women like Mary Harris, widely known as "Mother" Jones, were involved in labor unions and in improving the working conditions and pay scales for women workers. Another major concern during this period was the development and distribution of birth control information and devices. Marie Stopes in Britain and Margaret Sanger in the US were the major forces here. Women also began political careers; Edith Summerskill in England entered Parliament in 1938 and founded the Married Women's Association, a group designed to improve the economic position of the wife in the home.

One major issue that confronted feminism during this period was protective legislation, laws that enacted different treatment for women because they were generally recognized to be weaker. A number of professional women's groups, including the American Medical Woman's Association, realized that such legislation worked to protect some women while it hampered others. The Business and Professional Women's Clubs opposed protective legislation that hurt the interests of white-collar women. In 1927 in California the group successfully blocked the imposition of an eight-hour day on all female workers except nurses, maids, and cannery workers. But for women in low paid, unskilled fields, protective legislation continued to be the best hope they had for improving their working and living conditions.

Another major concern during this period was the fight to end the practice whereby women lost their teaching and civil service jobs once they married. White-collar unions within Britain fought throughout this period for equal pay and against the marriage bar, as well as an end to the "family wage," which gave married men with children preferential pay and employment opportunities.

There is no doubt, however, that women's status was tied to the economic and military conditions of this period. During the Depression working women were viewed with contempt and suspicion, largely because they were seen as taking away employment from a man who needed it to support a family. World War II saw women working outside the home in large numbers, largely because of the extreme manpower shortage. Once the war ended and the soldiers returned, however, women were quickly relegated to domesticity again, this time in the newly constructed suburbs, the dumping ground for women and the ever-increasing number of children they were encouraged to bear. Powerful social forces and the new medium of television encouraged women to quietly accept their new homes, identities, and roles as wives and mothers. "The problem that had no name," as Betty Friedan called it, began to emerge as women, once active and contributing to their societies, gradually named their boredom. Many emerged from the 1950's with only the vaguest memory of work outside the home, equal pay, educational opportunities, and professional careers.

VII. MODERN FEMINISM, 1961 TO THE PRESENT

The US contemporary women's movement, 1961 to the present, is characterized by a number of historical events that have largely been mythologized as media happenings: the failure of the Equal Rights Amendment (ERA); the marches on Washington, D.C.; the so-called "bra burnings"; the high visibility of such prominent feminists as Betty Friedan, Gloria Steinem, Kate Millett, and Germaine Greer. For all the media hoopla, however, the basic issues facing women have remained remarkably constant and unchanged. In many ways the contemporary struggles the feminist movement faced mirrored the legacy from the 1790's. The fights to pass the ERA and secure abortion rights were based in the concerns of the individual rights tradition; the fight against the ERA, also led by women, recalled the Evangelical tradition within the feminist movement; and the social critique, the consciousness-raising activities, and the concern with child care facilities reflected the socialistic tradition that has been such a dominant part of the movement.

One branch of this contemporary feminist movement, popularly known as the Women's Liberation Movement, grew out of the radical political protest activities of the 1960's. Women who committed themselves to opposing the war in Vietnam and the racism in the American South found themselves also treated like second-class citizens. They realized that they had much in common with colonized people or people of color vis-à-vis their white, middle-class male comrades. Many leaders in the women's movement recalled their own experiences in these earlier movements. Radical male students, occupying deans' offices on college campuses, sent dispatches to the press while the women among them brought in food (inspiring the later slogan: "Women make policy, not coffee."). Stokely

Carmichael, leader of the Student Nonviolent Coordinating Committee (SNCC) and the larger "black power" movement, made it known that "the only position for women in SNCC is prone" (quoted in Winifred D. Wandersee, *On the Move: American Women in the 1970's*, 2).

Beginning in 1967, numerous independent women's liberation groups began to emerge in US cities. The groups were small, informally organized, and committed to exploring women's common experiences through consciousness-raising (C-R). Because of internal organizational problems, most of these groups had disbanded by 1975 and their participants had either joined the parallel women's rights movement or had become involved in providing alternative services to women, such as health care, rape crisis counseling, and shelter from domestic violence.

The second branch, the liberal women's rights movement, began with the founding of the National Organization for Women (NOW) in 1966. This branch is deeply rooted in earlier government policies to study the status of US women (through a 1961 President's Commission on that topic) and to assure racial equality under the law. The expectation arose that gender equality would also be addressed. Building on the inspiration of Betty Friedan's classic manifesto, *The Feminist Mystique* (1963), and with Friedan as its first president, NOW would prove to be the most visible, largest, and most durable of the US feminist political groups. NOW quickly gained an impressive membership and had formed some 600 affiliate chapters by 1973. It also organized more than two dozen national task forces, addressing issues from poverty, to education, to sports, to day care and other matters judged to be critical to improving the quality of women's lives. NOW and the many other women's rights groups that subsequently have been organized focus on political and legal improvements for women, in accordance with an adherence to the individual rights tradition. But it could not escape political problems of its own, the price of any successful organization. Friedan herself, it must be admitted, pursued an agenda less radical than most of NOW's membership. She never admitted to a patriarchal system in American society or asserted that women, as a class, were oppressed by men. In fact, she did not oppose "the system" as such, and wanted mostly to bring more American women into it. She did not want to join NOW to the militant leftist critique that had become so pronounced by the end of the 1960's. In 1968, however, Ti-Grace Atkinson proclaimed "feminism is the theory; lesbianism is the practice" (*Amazon Odyssey*) and led a splinter group out of the organization. Friedan denounced the dangers of this militancy and the "infantile deviants" who advocated abolition of marriage and the family. She warned: "We cannot have these, our brightest and most spirited young women, turning their backs on society. This is an awfully old-fashioned hang-up" (quoted in Winifred Wandersee, *On the Move: American Women in the 1970's*, 42).

The abortion issue also produced tensions. At its second meeting in 1967, NOW formulated a very strongly libertarian statement on the repeal of laws governing abortion, echoing the feelings of its membership that complete discretion of women in matters of abortion must have a standing in law. But although it was most certainly true that at that time, and since, a clear majority of American women supported such freedom of choice, it was also a fact that within NOW many women considered the issue too radical a demand for a fledgling movement. When the strong pro-choice resolution passed, some conservative women broke from the organization and formed the Women's Equity Action League (which, ironically, soon came to support reproductive rights).

An even more thorny controversy had emerged by the end of the 1960's--lesbianism. Betty Friedan, ever the political strategist, feared that any embracing of this cause would identify the woman's movement, and the NOW organization itself, as radical and far removed from public sentiments and norms of conduct. She did, however, give a cautious and token support for lesbian rights. And at its 1971 convention NOW declared its support of a woman's right to her own sexuality. Lesbian spokeswomen by the middle 1970's had convinced some doubtful feminists that female same-sex love belonged to a historical continuum dating back at least to the Victorian era and that it held a viable place in any movement that stressed the unity of women against the dominating structures of patriarchal power. Adrienne Rich, poet and critic, offered her own celebration in her *Of Woman Born* (1976), praising motherhood, creativity, female bonding, and the lesbian experience collectively as the ingredients of the common female self.

NOW's growth accompanied significant changes for women in American life during the 1970's. By the end of the decade a record 51 percent of women were holding jobs outside the home. But one had to read the statistics cautiously. Most women said they worked because of financial necessity, an unwelcome fact of a more uncertain economy. And only one in seven women held employment in the professions; over half of these women were nurses or teachers. On the other side of the ledger, by the early 1980's women held half the seats in the nation's law schools. By the middle 1980's, they constituted more than half the nation's college students.

Demographics redefined the "normal" pattern of American life in the 1970's and 1980's, and although it was not clear to what extent the feminist movement influenced the changes, none should dismiss it as a negligible contributor. Greater independence for women caused many to think skeptically about following traditional life patterns. Women were now choosing to marry later in their lives than previously. And they were less anxious to have children. Outstanding among the statistical data was the dramatic drop in fertility rates in the United States, from 3.7 births per woman in 1955-59 to 1.8 births in 1975-80. "The Cult of True Womanhood" had clearly lost its mystique.

More disturbing yet was the growing phenomenon of single-parent families. The end of the 1970's counted 7.7 million of them. They owed something to the increase of the divorce rate at the same time, for by 1975 there was almost one divorce in the United States for every two marriages. Divorce lowered the income for women while it increased it for men. Now sociologists began to talk about the "feminization of poverty." One of three single-parent families (and they were overwhelmingly female-headed) lived below the poverty line as opposed to only one of eighteen among two-parent families. By the end of the 1980's single-parent families constituted about 20 percent of all, but the ratio for black families had grown to more than half.

One divisive issue within the women's movements of the industrial democracies is a concern that the feminist movement is producing gains primarily for middle- and upper-class white women. NOW itself appeared to many, including some of its own members, as insufficiently attentive to minority and blue-collar women. Karen DeCrow led an effort to address this problem in 1974, hoping also to involve more men in the organization. Some of the charges of feminist elitism came from black women. Novelist Alice Walker expressed the frustrations of this group when she addressed a convocation at Sarah Lawrence College in 1972. But black feminism confronted problems too as it addressed black females' grievances against black males, as in the novels of Toni Morrison and in the highly controversial book by Michelle Wallace, *Black Macho and the Myth of the Superwoman* (1979).

Another branch of contemporary feminist theory known as radical feminism believes that the source of women's oppression can be found in the "patriarchy," the systemic control and domination by males of all power and capital in society. While most contemporary feminists will agree with that statement, they differ on strategies for addressing the problems that plague women.

Another radical group of feminists, led by Shulamith Firestone, took the position that biology is destiny and that as long as women gave birth to children they would always be discriminated against economically and sexually. Firestone advocated that technology take over the role of childbearing, thereby freeing women from the indignities of pregnancy and lactation, and making them economically independent and as free as men from the consequences of their sexual activities. Firestone's theories served as the catalyst for the fiction of Marge Piercy (*Woman on the Edge of Time*, 1976), in which babies are developed in test tubes and breastfed by their fathers, and Joanna Russ (*The Female Man*, 1979), who envisions a future all-female utopia in which all men have been exterminated.

Other contemporary radical feminists have also condemned marriage, romantic love, and the sexual games that are played between men and women, advocating instead a communal arrangement of free love relationships (à la the Oneida community or New Harmony), celibacy or all-female communities based on a lesbian separatist ethos.

Another avenue of escape from gender polarities has been the movement toward androgyny. Here men and women both recognize that gender is a limiting and constricting force that pushes them into sex-typed roles and behaviors. Both sexes renounce the artificiality of these roles and agree to a shared sexual identity based on the "best" that either gender offers. Thus men are both strong and emotional; women are both intuitive and rational. Both sexes assume equal responsibility for child care and household obligations, regardless of their employment responsibilities or status. The popularity of this ethos can be seen in the number of novels and art works celebrating androgyny that proliferated throughout the 1970's, particularly Ursula Le Guin's *Left Hand of Darkness* (1969).

Another aspect of the contemporary feminist movement is an extreme exaltation of the mother and a fixation on the mother-child relationship. Paradoxically, while some feminists would seek to release women from their biological tie to maternity, others try to find a lost period of history known as the matriarchy, ruled over by mother-queens. Feminist historical revisionism led to the claim that the patriarchy was created only after the overthrow of the reign of the great mother (for an early pre-feminist account of this theory, see Robert Graves's study *The White Goddess*). Such feminists see a radical form of separatism, a rejection of all men as colleagues and friends, as the only way out of the current sexual warfare.

Yet another form of contemporary feminism is concerned with the "second stage" of feminism, as Betty Friedan called it. This second stage began when women, mostly middle-class and well-educated, tried to combine marriage and children with the demands of a full-time professional career. The result for these "superwomen" was exhaustion and depression that most could not accept. For many women the agenda for the feminist movement now is how to make society more hospitable for women with children. This has led to a challenge to the individual rights preference for policies that focus on gender equality under law. Now it is argued that women can only be treated equally through policies that recognize gender differences and the special needs of women for child care and family leave.

Despite the inner dilemmas of feminism in the 1970's and early 1980's, the movement was able to congeal around one dominant cause--the proposed Equal Rights Amendment to the United States Constitution. A simple statement to prevent sexual discrimination in law and social practice, the amendment seemed to be so much aligned with American values that it was irresistible. Both the Democratic and Republican Parties officially endorsed it at their presidential convention, the House of Representatives passed it 354-23, in October 1971, the Senate approved it, 84-8, on March 22, 1972. From there, the measure passed easily through state legislatures across the country and was nearing two-thirds majority of these endorsements by the end of the decade.

But few had counted on the opposition of a remarkably effective opponent of the ERA--the indomitable Phyllis Schlafly. She might have been the perfect example of the 1970's liberated woman--articulate, intelligent, self-confident, and in her own way, courageous. She was a devout Roman Catholic and long-time Republican Party activist, on the far right side of the party's constituency. As early as February 1972 Schlafly had established the National Committee to Stop ERA. It began to sign on a series of allies--the National Council of Catholic Women, the Daughters of the American Revolution, the Ku Klux Klan, and, yes, the Communist Party of the United States. Furthermore, the National Right to Life Committee, especially after the Supreme Court decision of *Roe v. Wade* in 1973, also fueled the countermovement. So did Jerry Falwell's religious organization, the Moral Majority, help to make anti-ERA seem a pro-family issue.

Schlafly did succeed in making the feminist cause in ERA seem elitist and privileged. She charged that victims of ERA would be divorced mothers who would lose their privileges under the law, while women in all classes would be susceptible to the military draft. In a dramatic reversal, states now voted against endorsing the ERA. Some attempted to reverse their earlier approvals. Despite Congress' extension of an earlier deadline, the ERA could not muster the needed state approvals in order to find its way into the Constitution.

These events, however much they helped make the feminist movement a major political story of the 1970's and 1980's, probably had little effect. Women's gains under the law continue to grow, from Affirmative Action programs in the 1970's to the family leave legislation of 1993. What many see as a "backlash" against feminism is due in large part to the successes and gains women have made in all aspects of American life.

The British feminist movement, like those in the United States, became visible in the late 1960's and was led by young women formerly active in student, international peace, and

Marxist politics. Although British feminism shares the dual origins--women's rights and liberation--of the US movement and the same liberal, socialist, and radical feminist traditions, its subsequent development has been distinctive. Britain has no overarching national organization comparable to NOW. Instead, the proliferating local Marxist feminist groups moved directly into instrumental projects such as the world's first shelters for battered women. The context of British politics has facilitated effective feminist participation inside labor unions and the Labour Party. British feminists have also been successful in constructing national coalitions around a single issue such as abortion and violence against women.

Although contemporary feminism has been strongest in the Western industrial democracies with their tradition of liberal civic rights, virtually every nation now has some type of women's movement. But the studies of the UN's Commission on the Status of Women (established in 1947) made clear that in no country are women politically or legally equal to men. The UN International Women's Year (1975), its Decade for Women (1976-85), and its world conferences for women have served as important catalysts and resources for these movements, particularly in poor nations. And the adoption of the UN's Convention on the Elimination of All Forms of Discrimination Against Women in 1979 created the expectation that change for women would occur.

By the mid-1990's only the feminist movements of the United States, Canada, the Netherlands, and Italy had a genuine national mass base. Although women in Scandinavia have served as a vanguard in achieving almost complete formal legal equality, autonomous women's movements have been limited there. No broad-based feminist movement exists in an Islamic society today or in Asia, outside of Japan. Likewise, there are only weak feminist movements in Latin America, where women are more likely to form neighborhood-based groups that combine human rights and traditional gender interests (e.g., El Salvador's Comité de Madres, Argentina's Mothers of the Plaza de Mayo, and the work of Nobel laureate Rigoberta Menchu of Guatemala).

In most nations "women's movement" is less precise than "women's committee/caucus/network." Second wave feminist activity is often confined to an advantaged class sector of middle-class, well-educated professional women or young leftists residing in one to four large cities and operating through a large number of small, local short-lived groups rather than a large national organization. Universal feminist issues include education, employment and equal pay, legal equality, reproductive freedom, child care, health care, protection from violence and sexual harassment, homemaker rights, and political power.

Particularly in Western Europe, feminist projects and strategies strikingly parallel those in the United States: consciousness-raising, women's centers and shelters, collectives, cultural groups, and magazines such as *EMMA* and *Spare Rib*. Feminist protests have been especially global (e.g., Canada's abortion caravan, Australia's Anzac Day Parade Movement, the Mathura Rape Case of India, and groups such as Chupiren in Japan, the Dolla Mina of the Netherlands, and Féministes Révolutionnaires of France.

The global feminist movement was another major political story of the 1970's and 1980's. Women's gains under the law continue to grow although the past 30 years have not brought uniform success. The Equal Rights Amendment failed in the United States. The neo-conservatism of Reaganism in the US and Thatcherism in the United Kingdom presented a new resistance to feminist change. The challenge to women's newly won reproductive freedom has been worldwide, particularly in the ex-communist nations. The organized anti-feminist movement is but one of several backlashes.

Autonomous women's movements have faced great difficulties in authoritarian communist, religious, and military regimes. Reversals in the legal and social status of women in Chile, Egypt, and Iran followed the rise of repressive regimes; the Women's Organization of Iran and the Arab Women's Solidarity Association have been particular targets of Islamic fundamentalists who view the preservation of women's traditional role as a barrier against Westernization, imperialism, and secular society. Weaker fundamentalist movements against feminism are also found in the Jewish, Catholic, Protestant, and Hindu faiths (e.g., the move to permit the heavily Catholic Republic of Ireland to retain a more restrictive abortion policy than allowed by the European Community). It is also not uncommon for a nation's women's movement to be closely linked with or sponsored by a ruling political party (e.g., the Peronist Women's Party of Argentina, the Union of Greek Women, the All-India Women's Conference, the Committee of Soviet Women, and the All-China Democratic Women's Federation). This allows male-dominated regimes to co-opt potential women's leaders and channel feminist activity through the public bureaucracy. Even so, during the past two decades, "sisterhood is global" has moved from brave slogan to at least partial reality.

The contemporary feminist movement has many different voices. The movement is composed not by any one group with one clear agenda, but by a number of different groups, each with their own ideologies and concerns. Basic questions focus on whether women and men are inherently and intrinsically different from each other and whether those differences justify different treatment in employment and before the law. Those questions have been answered variously and contradictorily over the past two hundred years. Feminism has sought to shape and reflect how women have viewed themselves, as wives, mothers, or workers. It has considered how and why women have accepted or rejected their roles within society and their own individual families. And it has tried to improve and reform society to fit its own best imaginings of what a just society for all people should, and would, be.

CHRONOLOGY OF FEMINISM

1405   Completion of Christine de Pizan's *The Book of the City of Women.*

1589   Jane Anger publishes a pamphlet that advances the idea of female superiority.

1622   Frenchwoman Marie de Gournay publishes *The Equality of Men and Women.*

1692   Witch trials charge and execute 31 persons in Salem, Massachusetts.

1791   Etta Palm d'Aelders of the Netherlands asks for equal rights for women and equal education for girls in her address to the National Assembly of France.

1791   Olympe de Gouges's *The Declaration of the Rights of Woman and the Female Citizen* is published.

1792   Publication of *A Vindication of the Rights of Woman* by Mary Wollstonecraft.

1810   Women in Sweden are given access to trade and sales occupations.

1825   William Thompson and Anna Wheeler in *Appeal of One Half of the Human Race Against the Pretensions of the Other Half* advocate woman suffrage.

1829   Suttee is criminalized in India.

1840   Conflict about women's public role emerges at the World Anti-Slavery Convention in London.

1845   *Women in the Nineteenth Century* by Margaret Fuller is published.

1848   A women's rights convention is held at Seneca Falls, New York.

1851   Sojourner Truth delivers her "Ain't I a Woman" speech at an Ohio abolition convention.

1866   John Stuart Mill presents a woman suffrage petition to the House of Commons.

1868   King Mongkut of Thailand gives women the right to choose their marriage partners and prohibits a husband from selling his wife without her consent.

1868   The National Society for Women's Suffrage is founded in England.

1869   Elizabeth Cady Stanton becomes the first woman to testify at a US Congressional hearing (on woman suffrage).

1869   Publication of *The Subjection of Women* by John Stuart Mill (England) and *The Rights of Women* by Léon Richier (France).

1869   The American Woman Suffrage Association and the National Woman Suffrage Association are formed in the United States.

1871   Paragraph 218 of the German Penal Code makes abortion punishable by up to five years' imprisonment and prohibits the sale and use of contraceptives.

1873   US Supreme Court (in *Bradwell v. Illinois*) upholds the exclusion of women from the practice of law, using "separate spheres" ideology.

1874   Frances Willard founds the Woman's Christian Temperance Union.

1877   The trial of Annie Besant and Charles Bradlaugh for distribution of a birth control pamphlet opens in London.

1878   An International Women's Rights Congress is held in France.

1879   *Woman and Socialism* by August Bebel is published.

1882   The Married Women's Property Act is passed in England.

1882   Dr. Aletta Jacobs opens the world's first birth control clinic in Amsterdam.

1884   Friedrich Engels's *The Origin of the Family, Private Property and the State* is published.

1886   *The High Caste Hindu Woman* by Pandita Ramabai analyzes the oppression of women in India.

1892   K'ang Yu-wei establishes the first "Unbound-Feet Society" in Canton.

1893   New Zealand becomes the first nation to enfranchise women.

1895   *The Woman's Bible* is published.

1897   In Japan, Yukichi Fukuzawa in *The New Greater Learning for Women* challenges Confucian teaching about women.

1898   Charlotte Perkins Gilman publishes *Women and Economics*.

1899   Qasim Amin publishes *Tahrir al-Mar'a* (The Emancipation of Women) in Egypt.

1900   *The Woman Worker* is published by Nadezhda Krupskaya in Russia.

1900   Marguerite Souley-Darque teaches the first women's studies course in Paris.

1904   The International Alliance of Women is formed.

1906   Finland becomes the first European nation to adopt woman suffrage.

1908   Norway passes an equal pay law.

1908   The All-Russian Conference of Feminists attracts 1,045 delegates.

1911   The first celebration of International Women's Day is held in Europe.

1913   The National Woman's Party is founded in the United States.

1913   British suffragist Emily Davison is killed when she throws herself under the horse of King George V.

1918   Women in England and Canada receive the vote.

1919   Pope Benedict XV endorses woman suffrage.

1919   The Sexual Disqualifications (Removal) Act allows Englishwomen to be lawyers, jurors, judges, and members of Parliament.

1919   The Versailles Peace Treaty promises French women equal pay for equal work.

1920   The Nineteenth Amendment grants US women suffrage.

1920   The Union of Soviet Socialist Republics becomes the first European nation to legalize abortion.

1920   France bars contraceptive devices and abortion and gives a medal to women having at least five children.

1920   The League of Women Voters is established in the United States.

1923   Huda Sha'rawi founds the Egyptian Feminist Union.

1923   The Equal Rights Amendment is introduced in the US Congress.

1924   María Jesús Alvarado Rivero of Peru is exiled because of her campaign for married women's rights.

1925   Elvia Carrillo Puerto is elected to the Mexican legislature but is denied the seat on the basis of sex.

1929   The Privy Council rules that women are persons in the Canadian Persons case.

1929   Publication of *A Room of One's Own* by Virginia Woolf in England and *The Women's Question* by Phan Boi Chau in Vietnam.

1931   German women begin an "I have aborted" campaign against Paragraph 218.

1931   Pope Pius XI calls for a ban on the employment of married women to protect women and the family.

1936   Iran becomes the first Muslim country to ban the veil.

1937   Filipino women approve woman suffrage in an all-female plebiscite.

1944   France enfranchises women.

1944   The Italian Women's Union is founded.

1947   The United Nations Commission on the Status of Women is established.

1947   The daughter of Morocco's king unveils and reads a feminist speech.

1948   The new Italian Constitution grants women equality and the right to work.

1949   Simone de Beauvoir publishes *The Second Sex*.

1957   The Treaty of Rome establishes the European Economic Community and endorses equal pay.

1961   India outlaws the practices of brideprice and dowry.

1961   John F. Kennedy establishes the President's Commission on the Status of Women.

1963   *The Feminine Mystique* by Betty Friedan is published.

1963   The US Equal Pay Act is passed.

1964   Title VII of the Civil Rights Act prohibits sex discrimination in US employment.

1964   Ruby Doris Smith Robinson presents a paper critical of the status of women in the Student Non-violent Coordinating Committee.

1966   The National Organization for Women is formed.

1967   The Abortion Act is passed by the British Parliament.

1967   The first local radical feminist groups form in New York and Chicago.

1967   The Royal Commission on the Status of Women in Canada is established.

1968   Psych et Po is organized in France.

1968   A protest of the Miss America Pageant is held.

1968   The first national women's liberation conference is held in Chicago and draws women from 37 states and Canada.

1969   The National Association for Repeal of Abortion Laws is founded in the United States.

1969   Anne Koedt challenges Freudian concepts of female sexuality in her essay "The Myth of the Vaginal Orgasm."

1969   The Redstockings hold the first speak-out (on abortion) in New York City.

1970   These classics of new feminism are published: *Sexual Politics* by Kate Millett; *The Female Eunuch* by Germaine Greer; *Sisterhood Is Powerful* by Robin Morgan; *Our Bodies, Ourselves* by the Boston Women's Health Collective; and *The Dialectic of Sex* by Shulamith Firestone.

1970   The first national women's liberation conference in Great Britain is held at Ruskin College (Oxford).

1970   Dutch feminists demonstrate at a medical convention by displaying slogans written across their stomachs.

1970   Canadian feminists organize an abortion caravan.

1970   French feminists dedicate a wreath to the wife of the unknown soldier honored at the Arc de Triomphe.

1970   The British Parliament passes the Equal Pay Act.

1970   The Women's Strike for Equality brings demonstrations in most major US cities.

1971   A manifesto is signed by 343 prominent Frenchwomen who acknowledge having had one or more illegal abortions; in West Germany, 374 women sign a similar letter, published in *Der Stern*.

1971   The US Supreme Court (in *Reed v. Reed*) invalidates a law on the basis of sex discrimination.

1971   The National Women's Political Caucus is formed in Washington, D.C.

1972   The National Action Committee on the Status of Women is formed in Canada.

1972   *Ms.* (United States) and *Spare Rib* (Great Britain) begin publication.

1972   The trial in Bobigny, France, of a teenage girl builds public support for reform of abortion laws.

1972   Erin Pizzey establishes the first shelter for battered women (in Chiswick, England).

1972   The Equal Rights Amendment is passed by the US Congress and sent to the states for ratification.

1972   Women protesting the exclusion of women from major art gallery exhibits hold the first National Conference for Women in the Visual Arts.

1972   Title IX of the Education Amendments bans sex discrimination in all federally assisted education programs in the United States.

1973   Billie Jean King beats Bobby Riggs in a tennis match.

1973   The US Supreme Court (in *Roe v. Wade*) establishes a woman's right to an abortion.

1973   The trial of "the three Marias" opens in Portugal.

1974   The first National Women's Music Festival is held at the University of Illinois.

1974   Italy defeats a referendum to abolish divorce.

1974   The Royal Canadian Mounted Police admit women.

1974   Girls are allowed to play Little League Baseball in the
          United States.

1975   The United Nations' first Conference on the Decade
          for Women is held in Mexico City.

1975   The British Parliament passes the Sex Discrimination
          Act.

1975   *Signs* begins publication in Chicago.

1975   The first `US women's health conference is held at
          Harvard Medical School.

1975   These groups are formed: the National Women's
          Health Network (United States); the Eagle Forum
          (United States); the National Women's Aid Federation
          (Great Britain); and the National Abortion Campaign
          (Great Britain).

1975   Ninety percent of all Icelandic women go on strike
          against sex discrimination.

1976   Feminists protest "snuff films" that portray the torture
          and murder of women as pornographic entertainment.

1976   "Take Back the Night" marches are held in the major
          cities of Italy.

1976   Janet Guthrie becomes the first woman driver in the
          Indianapolis 500.

1976   An article in an American Psychiatric Association
          journal declares male chauvinism a certifiable
          psychiatric illness.

1976   The International Tribunal on Crimes Against Women
          opens in Brussels.

1977   The National Women's Conference in Houston sets an agenda for women in the National Plan.

1977   The National Women's Studies Association is founded in the United States.

1977   *EMMA* begins publication in West Germany.

1977   South Australia becomes the first government in the world to criminalize marital rape.

1977   Australian Women Against Rape stage their first Anzac Day Parade action.

1977   Princess Misha of the royal family of Saudi Arabia is publicly executed for wedding a man of her choice.

1978   The first Women's History Week is celebrated in Sonoma County, California.

1978   The first national feminist conference on pornography is held in San Francisco.

1978   Five women employees at American Cyanamid are sterilized as a condition of employment under a fetal protection policy.

1979   The Mathura Rape Case decision is announced by the Supreme Court of India.

1979   The US Treasury issues the Susan B. Anthony coin.

1979   Judy Chicago's *The Dinner Party* opens at the San Francisco Museum of Art.

1979   Sonia Johnson is excommunicated by the Mormon Church for her support of the Equal Rights Amendment.

1979   Fifteen thousand Iranian women seize the Palace of Justice and demand the restoration of rights lost after the overthrow of the Shah.

1979   The first feminist samizdat *Women and Russia* appears.

1979   The UN General Assembly adopts the Convention on the Elimination of All Forms of Discrimination Against Women.

1981   Sandra Day O'Connor appointed to the US Supreme Court.

1981   The Ministry of Women's Rights is created in France.

1981   Portugal passes a law prohibiting the use of a female image as an advertising device.

1981   The women's peace camp at the Greenham (England) missile base is established.

1982   The Women's Rights National Historical Park opens in Seneca Falls, New York.

1982   The deadline for ratifying the Equal Rights Amendment expires.

1982   Sicilian women, widowed by the Mafia, form a group to oppose the culture of male violence and female submissiveness.

1982   Carol Gilligan publishes *In a Different Voice*.

1982   Women in Algeria present a petition with 10,000 signatures to the National Assembly and demonstrate against a proposed Family Code that would weaken women's rights.

1982   Pakistani women protest the exclusion of women athletes from the Asian Games.

1983   The Minneapolis City Council passes a feminist anti-pornography ordinance, which is vetoed by the mayor.

1983   The chador is made compulsory in Iran.

1984   Geraldine Ferraro receives the Democratic Party's nomination for vice-president of the United States.

1985   The world's first feminist university (the Kvinneuniversitetet) is established in Norway.

1985   Tracey Thurman of Connecticut is awarded $2.3 million in the first civil suit won by a battered wife.

1985   The first pay equity raises are announced by the state of Washington.

1986   The US Supreme Court rules (in *Meritor v. Vinson*) that workplace sexual harassment is illegal.

1986   The *New York Times* accepts "Ms." as a courtesy title.

1986   The last of the Playboy clubs closes.

1988   RU 486 is marketed in France.

1988   The New Jersey Supreme Court invalidates the surrogacy contract in the "Baby M" case.

1989   Fourteen women engineering students at a university in Montreal are killed by a man who resented feminists in the school.

1989   The National Organization for Women announces its interest in forming a new US political party.

1990   The Arab Women's Solidarity Association is dissolved by the Egyptian government and its assets seized.

1990   The US Act for Better Child Care is signed into law.

1990   The Des Moines (Iowa) *Register* fights the stigma of rape by publishing the survivor's name (with her permission).

1990   Forty-seven Saudi Arabian women drive a few blocks in Riyadh to protest the ban on women drivers.

1991   Anita Hill charges US Supreme Court nominee Clarence Thomas with sexual harassment.

1991   At the Tailhook Convention, US Navy and Marine Corps pilots allegedly assault 26 women in a hotel hallway.

1991   The US Supreme Court (in *International UAW v. Johnson Controls*) rules that employers cannot exclude fertile women from jobs to protect potential fetuses.

1991   Four hundred thousand Swiss women strike for equal pay.

1992   The Canadian Supreme Court (in *Regina v. Butler*) rules that pornography is defined by the harm it does to women's pursuit of equality.

1992   The Women's National Coalition forms for the inclusion of women's rights in the new South African constitution.

1992   Over 500,000 participate in the pro-choice "March for Women's Lives," the largest demonstration in Washington, D. C. history.

1992   China implements the "Law for the Protection of Women's Rights and Interests" that guarantees sex equality in political, economic, cultural, social, and family affairs.

1992   Irish voters approve free access to abortion information and the right to travel abroad for an abortion.

1993   The United Nations' Conference on Human Rights defines violence against women as a human rights violation.

1993   Female heads of government are chosen in Burundi, Canada, Pakistan, Rwanda, and Turkey; a woman speaker is elected in the parliament of Japan.

1993   New Zealand women begin a petition drive for equal representation in parliament on the 100th anniversary of woman suffrage.

1993   The US Family and Medical Leave Act is signed into law.

1993   More than one million girls around the world participate in the first Take Our Daughters to Work Day.

1993   Pope John Paul II issues an encyclical that continues the Catholic Church ban on artificial birth control, divorce, abortion, and homosexuality.

1994   A Michigan judge revokes the child custody of a single mother who was attending college and had placed her daughter in a day-care center; he awards custody to the biological father whose homemaker mother could care for the child.

1994   The US Academy Award for Best Short Documentary is won by *Defending Our Lives*, a film about women imprisoned for killing their batterers.

1994   The US Freedom of Access to Clinic Entrances Act becomes law.

1994   The victorious Social Democratic Party of Sweden offers an equal number of male and female parliamentary candidates and then appoints women to half of the cabinet positions.

1994   The Vatican permits girls to become altar "boys."

1994   Canada grants refugee status to a Somali woman based partially on her fears of female genital mutilation.

1994   Delegates to the Cairo international population conference support women's reproductive rights and safe abortions in nations where the procedure is legal.

1994   A Virginia jury acquits Lorena Bobbitt, charged with cutting off her husband's penis in retaliation for earlier sexual assaults.

1995   The US Glass Ceiling Commission reports that women and minorities are extremely underrepresented in senior management posts.

1995   Opening arguments in the murder trial of former football star O. J. Simpson are heard; alleged batterer Simpson is charged with the fatal stabbing of his ex-wife and her friend.

1995   Bangladesh's high court denies a petition to drop blasphemy charges against feminist author Taslima Nasreen, who had angered Muslim fundamentalists over her critique of the Koran.

1995   The UN's Fourth World Conference on Women is held in Beijing, China.

THE DICTIONARY

ABC BILL, ACT FOR BETTER CHILD CARE. Omnibus legislation, popularly called the ABC bill, passed by the US Congress in 1990 in response to a widely perceived crisis in day care (q.v.) services for children. The law provided for tax credits for the child care expenses of low-income working parents, grants to provide child care for families on welfare, funds to the states to increase the quality and quantity of child care services, health and safety standards for programs receiving federal support, and authorization for vouchers that could be used at centers run by religious organizations. Feminists had strongly supported federal funding for child care since the early 1970's. They were concerned, however, that the bill threatened the legal doctrine of separation of church and state and could lead to greater influence for the anti-feminist (q.v.) religious right.

ABOLITIONIST MOVEMENT. A nineteenth-century political movement to abolish slavery in the United States and Great Britain. Historians of the US women's movement have noted strong links between this drive and women's suffrage. Early American feminists were active in both organizations, and although racism and sexism (q.v.) within the ranks of both movements led to their eventual split, the abolitionist movement provided invaluable experience in political organizing. For example, in 1840, at the World Anti-Slavery Convention in London, women were permitted to sit in the galleries but not allowed to speak. Among them was Elizabeth Cady Stanton (q.v). In Britain, some female abolitionists eventually became involved in woman suffrage but the two movements were not similarly joined.

ABORTIFACIENT *see* RU 486

ABORTION. The termination or loss of pregnancy before the fetus is viable or able to live outside the uterus. Feminist movements throughout history have viewed a woman's control over her own reproduction as a core issue. The new feminist movement (q.v.) views safe and legal abortion as a central goal, just as earlier movements embraced family planning (q.v.). At a minimum, an elective abortion should be a choice for women for personal or therapeutic (medical/health) reasons and the incidence of septic abortions, in which an infection occurs, should be extremely low. (*See also* Back-Alley Abortion; Hyde Amendment; *Roe v. Wade*; *Webster v. Reproductive Health Services*.)

ABORTION CARAVAN. A 1970 direct action by Canadian feminists who drove from Vancouver to Ottawa to focus public attention on the issue. Speak-outs on back-alley abortions (qq.v.) and the need for legalization were held at each stop. Once in Ottawa, some women chained themselves to seats in the House of Commons. The action followed a 1969 amendment to the federal Criminal Code that legalized the distribution of birth control information and abortions, if approved by a therapeutic abortion committee (TAC). In 1988, the Supreme Court declared TACs unconstitutional.

ABZUG, BELLA SAVITSKY (1920-). An American lawyer and feminist politician. She was a founder and national legislative director of Women Strike for Peace (1961-70) and a founder of the National Women's Political Caucus (q.v.). Abzug served in the US House of Representatives from New York City, 1971-77. In Congress she was an outspoken exponent of feminism and was criticized for her aggressive style, one that might have been viewed as an asset in a man. She was noted both for her large hats and the amendment barring sex discrimination that she commonly attached to every possible piece of legislation during debate. After several electoral defeats and a brief term as co-chair of President Jimmy Carter's National Advisory Committee on Women, Abzug has become active in the international women's environmental movement and serves as a commentator and writer on politics and women's issues. She is the author of *Gender Gap: Bella Abzug's Guide to Political Power for Women* (1984).

ACCOMMODATING. A speech process in which one's speaking style is shifted to resemble the conversational style of one's partner. Research generally indicates that women accommodate to men rather than the reverse. In traditional societies, particularly in Asia, women use specific self-demeaning words for themselves and exalting ones for men, as well as different speech forms and honorifics. Feminists suggest that this finding may be explained by a power differential between the sexes.

ACQUAINTANCE RAPE, see DATE RAPE

ACQUIRED IMMUNE DEFICIENCY SYNDROME (AIDS). An often fatal viral infection caused by the retrovirus human immune-deficiency virus (HIV). It is transmitted through the blood or other bodily fluids and thus is often contracted through sexual contact. While the incidence of the disease in the United States has been highest in gay men, its occurrence in women is increasing at a rapid rate due to drug use with shared needles and unprotected sex. The HIV virus is transmitted to the fetus in approximately 30 percent of pregnancies of infected women. Because of its early association with gay men, women often fail to see their vulnerability to the disease and fail to protect themselves from it. The women's movement is also concerned that medical researchers have largely ignored women with AIDS.

ACTION COUNCIL FOR WOMEN'S LIBERATION (AKTIONSRAT FÜR DIE BEFREIUNG DER FRAUEN). One of the first organizations of the new German women's movement, founded in Berlin in 1968 to challenge the "comfortable path of dependence" articulated by men of the New Left as an option for women. Its politics aimed to end the exploitation of women in the family and in society. Its programs were based on the needs of mothers; it established alternative children's and mothers' support centers in Berlin. Ultimately the programs failed because of opposition and indifference within the Left itself, and the group disbanded after two years.

ADAM, JULIETTE LAMBER LA MESSINE (1836-1936). A French author, educated by her feminist father. Adam was a firm believer in female autonomy. She responded to Proudhon's theory of women's inferior social value with "*Idées anti-proudhoniennes sur l'amour, la femme et le mariage*" (Anti-Proudhonian Ideas of Love, Women, and Marriage). She argued that employment frees adults of both sexes, that the distinction between "masculine" and "feminine" virtues is not significant, and that women have their own intrinsic value not based on their associations with men.

ADAMS, ABIGAIL SMITH (1744-1818). The wife of the second US President, John Adams. She was a spokesperson for women's rights and education in the new democracy and expressed her views in famed letters like her 1776 admonition to her husband to "remember the ladies." She demonstrated political insight about the value and inclusion of women in democracy, and advised her husband and her son John Quincy Adams, the sixth President.

ADDAMS, JANE (1860-1935). The co-founder, with Helen Starr, of Hull House of Chicago (1889), one of the earliest settlement houses (q.v.) in the United States. Ms. Addams also helped organize the National Progressive Party in 1912 and the Women's Peace Party, of which she became president in 1915. She was elected president of the Women's International Peace Congress, which later became the Women's International League for Peace and Freedom, at The Hague in 1915. She was awarded the Nobel Peace Prize in 1931. Addams was one of the leading exponents of social feminism (q.v.) in the United States.

ADVISORY COUNCIL ON THE STATUS OF WOMEN (CANADA) *see* ROYAL COMMISSION ON THE STATUS OF WOMEN IN CANADA (RCSW)

AFFIRMATIVE ACTION. The organizational policies and practices involved with the selection, retention and promotion of qualified women and minorities in the United States. Affirmative action is concerned with numerical balance in the workforce and uses hiring goals and timetables. In 1965 President Lyndon Johnson signed Executive Order 11246, which required federal contractors to take affirmative action on behalf of racial and ethnic minorities. In 1968 Executive Order 11375 also included sex. (*See also* Reverse Discrimination.)

AFRICAN-AMERICAN FEMINISM. An approach that stresses the interactive effects of sex, gender, class, race, and sexuality and the error of analyzing the oppression of women in isolation from their race. African-American women are more supportive of feminist issues than are white women, but have been hesitant to embrace a movement that defines the experience of white, middle-class women as universal. Black feminists focus on racial self-affirmation and the building of black community and institutions, but they have also been active in support of many feminist movement goals. (*See also* National Association of Colored Women; National Black Feminist Organization; National Council of Negro Women; Womanist Theology.)

AFRICAN-AMERICAN FEMINIST CRITICISM. The effort to illuminate the unique qualities of the African-American female experience in American life and culture as they are reflected in literature. Prominent theorists and publications include the following: Barbara Christian, *Black Women Novelists: The Development of a Tradition 1892-1976* (1980) and *Black Feminist Criticism* (1985); Hazel V. Carby, *Reconstructing Womanhood: The Emergence of the Afro-American Woman Novelist* (1987); Henry L. Gates, Jr., *Reading Black, Reading Feminist: A Critical Anthology* (1990); Erlene Stetson, *Black Sister: Poetry by Black American Women, 1764-1980* (1981); and Roseann Bell, *Sturdy Black Bridges: Visions of Black Women in Literature* (1979).

AFRICAN NATIONAL CONGRESS (ANC) WOMEN'S LEAGUE *see* WOMEN'S NATIONAL COALITION

AGEISM. Negative and prejudiced attitudes directed toward the elderly. Feminists note that older women are subject to both ageism and sexism (q.v.) in a society that values women for their sexual, reproductive, and nurturing capacities, all of which peak during one's youth or middle years.

AGORAPHOBIA. A condition defined by the Diagnostic and Statistical Manual of Mental Disorders (DSM-IV) as a fear of being in places or situations from which escape is difficult or in which help is not available. Due to this fear an individual often restricts personal activities severely, rarely or never leaving home or doing so only with a companion. It is one of the most commonly diagnosed phobias seen clinically in females. It typically begins in early adulthood in women who have been married about five years and have chosen a traditional lifestyle. They also have typically been overprotected by their parents. An original attack is often preceded by a developmental crisis such as leaving home or the breakup of a relationship. The behaviors typically exhibited by an agoraphobic are similar to the behaviors traditionally taught to women such as dependency, unassertiveness, fear of being alone and fear of functioning autonomously. This leads to the suggestion that agoraphobia may be a reaction to stress which follows from the training girls have had and may also enhance the masculinity of the men around the agoraphobic female since these men can be left with a feeling of caretaker and protector.

AGUSTINI, DELMIRA (1886-1914). A Uruguayan poet. Her brief career began with the publication of *El libro blanco* (The White Book, 1907), followed by *Cantos de la mañana* (Songs of the Morning, 1910) and *Los cálices vacíos* (The Empty Chalices, 1913). Agustini was tormented by her longing for an ideal love, which she thought would produce a new human race. This was unattainable because of the contrast between male and female passion, the one predatory and brutal, the other aesthetic and intellectual. Her poetry shows her rebellion against the submission of woman to man. The essential element in all her poetry is erotic exaltation. Her obsession is love, and love becomes the central theme of her passionate poetry.

AID TO FAMILIES WITH DEPENDENT CHILDREN (AFDC). A means tested US public assistance (welfare) program established under the Social Security Act of 1935 (q.v.). AFDC provides cash benefits to children and their caretakers, usually women, when one or both parents are unable or unwilling to provide economic support. Feminist critics of the program cite the failure to bring its recipients above the poverty line as an example of how the program substitutes dependency on the government for dependency on men.

"AIN'T I A WOMAN?" The title of the most famous speech given by the African-American slave and abolitionist Sojourner Truth (q.v.). In the speech, Truth confronts her white audience with the black woman's claims to humanity. Like the white woman, she too has borne children, worked for their survival, and, unlike the white woman, seen them sold into slavery. She then asks her audience why they do not give blacks and women equal rights, when, as she points out, Christ himself was born of a woman. Although Truth was illiterate and left no written records of her speeches, we have them reconstructed and reprinted in *History of Woman Suffrage* (1881-1902). The term is now used in general parlance to suggest that all women, regardless of race or class, share a common experience of discrimination.

ALIMONY *see* SPOUSAL SUPPORT

ALL-CHINA DEMOCRATIC WOMEN'S FEDERATION (ACDWF). The official women's organization within the Chinese Communist Party (CCP), formed at a national congress of representatives of local women's associations on April 3, 1949. Thereafter, all other women's groups in China were absorbed into the organization. The goals were to unify women, advance their status, and implement the new legal rights of women after national liberation. By 1952 branches of the federation were active in 80 percent of local government units. During the Cultural Revolution (1966-69), the CCP suspended the Federation. In 1979 the ACDWF was re-established and has become active in a government campaign for women's and children's rights. The ACDWF has been particularly responsive to wife abuse and infanticide stemming from the policy limiting a couple to one child.

ALL-INDIA WOMEN'S CONFERENCE (AIWC). A group formed in 1928 that was active in the independence movement and spearheaded the Indian women's movement of the 1930's and 1940's for education, legal equality, and abolition of child marriage. The organization originally attracted members from many ideologies, classes, and religions. Later the AIWC, with its connections to the Congress Party of Gandhi and Nehru, became more elite-based. By the 1970's the group had become primarily a reformist social service and lobbying agency. However, its extensive network of local branches made it a valuable participant in new feminist coalitions against rape and dowry deaths (qq.v.).

ALPERT, JANE *see* "MOTHER RIGHT"

ALTERNATIVE BIRTH MOVEMENT. An alliance growing out of the feminist critique of the medicalization of childbirth (q.v.), loosely coordinated efforts to inform patients about the benefits and availability of home births, midwifery, birthing centers and rooms, natural childbirth (qq.v.), and other family-centered birth techniques. Those involved are particularly critical of obstetrical interventions such as fetal monitoring, caesarean sections, induced labor, and routine use of drugs and episiotomies. Feminists have been concerned both with returning decision-making power to women in childbirth and lowering the high rate of infant mortality and birth injury in the United States, in comparison with other industrial nations.

ALTERNATIVE INSTITUTIONS *see* COUNTER-CULTURE, FEMINIST

ALTERNATIVE WORK SCHEDULES *see* FLEXITIME

ALVARADO RIVERO, MARÍA JESÚS. The first modern champion of women's rights in Peru and founder in 1914 of Evolución Femenina (Feminine Evolution), Peru's first women's organization. In 1923 she helped organize the National Council of Women, an affiliate of the International Woman Suffrage Alliance (q.v.), and served as its first secretary. In 1924 she was jailed as a political prisoner and later exiled to Argentina for 12 years for printing political pamphlets that supported Indians' and women's rights and for her attempt to involve the National Council in a project to give married women certain legal rights.

AMAZONS. A race of warrior women who lived in Asia Minor on the boundaries of the civilized world. Independent of men, they practiced a radical gynocracy and kept men only for the purpose of procreation or to serve as slaves. In Greek mythology the Amazons were a nation, apparently in Africa, entirely of women who permitted men only a brief annual visit to impregnate them. This is a myth affirming the Athenian society by describing an inverted society overcome by the Greeks. There is no historical evidence for a matriarchal nation in contact with Classical Greece, and the trait-by-trait inversion of Greek society in the description of the Amazons strongly implies a purely mythical construct. Some anthropologists have suggested that Greek traders' encounters with distant nations where men were customarily absent for months on hunting or trading expeditions, leaving women to manage villages, may have lent credence to the myth of the Amazons. The Amazons' loss to the Athenians in battle was widely celebrated in Greek art as the defeat of female anarchy by the forces of male ordered civilization. The Amazons are seen by the Greeks as the mythological projection of the male fear of female dominance and militancy.

AMERICAN ASSOCIATION OF UNIVERSITY WOMEN (AAUW). A US organization of female college graduates, established in 1881 as the Association of Collegiate Alumnae, to advance educational and employment opportunities for women. A supporter of social feminism (q.v.) in the post-suffrage era, the AAUW shifted to a women's rights position in the 1960's and has played a major role in lobbying for feminist issues. The group has been a strong advocate for sex equity in education; their 1992 report on this topic, "How Schools Shortchange Girls," refocused national attention to gender bias in the classroom, sexual harassment (q.v.), and the increasing gender gap in science.

AMERICAN CIVIL LIBERTIES UNION WOMEN'S RIGHTS PROJECT (ACLU-WRP) AND REPRODUCTIVE FREEDOM PROJECT (ACLU-RFP). Two feminist litigation groups formed within the ACLU. The ACLU-WRP was formed under the leadership of Ruth Bader Ginsburg (q.v.) as a result of *Reed v. Reed* (1971) (q.v.) to use the equal protection (q.v.) clause to expand women's rights. The ACLU-RFP was created in 1974 to defend the decision in *Roe v. Wade* (1973) (q.v.) against the pro-life movement (q.v.) and has become a center of legal and litigation expertise on the subject of abortion (q.v.) rights. Janet

Benshoof led the ACLU-RFP for 15 years, before resigning to form the Center for Reproductive Law and Policy. Both projects have been parties to many of the major court cases in their respective areas during the past two decades.

AMERICAN EQUAL RIGHTS ASSOCIATION (AERA). A group founded in 1865 to promote the interests of both blacks and women. Under the leadership of Wendell Phillips and Horace Greeley, it shifted to a focus on passage of the Fourteenth Amendment, with its introduction of the word "male" into the Constitution. In 1869 the AERA split on the issue of including the word "sex" in the Fifteenth Amendment (and thus enfranchising both black males and women); this led to the formation of the National Woman Suffrage Association (q.v.) by AERA members Elizabeth Cady Stanton and Susan B. Anthony (qq.v.).

AMERICAN WOMAN SUFFRAGE ASSOCIATION (AWSA). An organization founded in 1869 by Lucy Stone (q.v.) to focus exclusively on the suffrage issue in contrast to the National Woman Suffrage Association (NWSA) (q.v.), which was concerned with a broad-based women's rights agenda. The AWSA was a more conservative organization, open to both men and women, and accepted the state-by-state enfranchisement of women through state referenda, as opposed to passage of a national constitutional amendment. This split between the AWSA and the NWSA continued until their merger in 1890.

AMIN, QASIM (1863-1908). A French-educated Egyptian lawyer and judge, recognized as the first Arab feminist and called "the Liberator of Egyptian Women." His *Tahrir al-Mar'a* (The Emancipation of Women, 1899) called for liberalizing the veil, a primary-school education for girls, and reform of polygamy and divorce laws. The book was the center of the first major controversy in the Arab press and sparked the formation of an Arab feminist movement. Scholars today criticize Amin's Eurocentric bias in that he accepted the superiority of Western civilization and expressed contempt for Muslim society and Egyptian women in particular. At root, Amin supported a patriarchal Western-style system of male dominance (q.v.). His second book *al-Mar'a al Jadda* (The New

Woman, 1901) was written as a rebuttal to his critics and included support for women's rights to higher education and professional careers.

AMNIOCENTESIS. A procedure commonly performed on pregnant women to obtain a sample of amniotic fluid from the uterus to assess fetal health, genetic abnormalities, and maturity. Chorionic villi sampling (CVS) is another prenatal test to detect genetic birth defects and can be performed during the first trimester, as early as the eighth week of pregnancy. This permits prompt diagnosis, earlier fetal treatment, and earlier and safer abortions (q.v.). Since sex can also be determined, female infanticide is a potential problem in cultures where male babies have greater value. One United Nations study found that of approximately 8,000 abortions performed in Bombay after amniocentesis, only one involved a male fetus. Bills to curb the use of the procedure are supported by feminists.

ANARCHIST FEMINISM. A theory, derived from Emma Goldman (q.v.), that argues that the state and man-made law, based on violence and coercion, are responsible for gender inequality. Legal equality for women in such a system cannot advance the status of women. Anarchist feminists envision a society without hierarchical structures of domination, one that respects the individual and maximizes cooperative social relations.

ANATOMY IS DESTINY *see* BIOLOGICAL DETERMINISM

ANDROCENTRISM. The masculine bias within Western scholarship. Feminists note that histories, ethnographies, social science and literature are largely written by men, who focus on topics based on their socialization as males in Western societies. Androcentrism may also be seen as an instrument to enforce the ideology of patriarchy (q.v.) by excluding the points of view, and experiences, of women.

ANDROGYNOUS. Representing a balance of stereotypically feminine and stereotypically masculine characteristics. Some feminists have seen androgyny as a new ideal of psychological functioning. Others have some reservations about the use of the term insofar as it incorporates reference to gender stereotypes.

ANGEL IN THE HOUSE. The title of a four-part poem published by the English poet Coventry Kersey Dighton Patmore (1823-96). The poem's four sections--"The Betrothal" (1854), "The Espousals" (1856), "Faithful for Ever" (1860), and "The Victories of Love" (1862)--celebrate married love as the closest man and woman can come to heaven on earth. In an age that had seen the decline of belief in a traditional God, marriage and heterosexual love became the substitute religion embraced by a growing number of intellectuals and their followers. The role of women in this scheme, however, was less than attractive. She was supposed to enshrine the family hearth, like a spotless goddess of domestic purity. As the guardian of her husband's status, her lack of employment outside the home ensured the public perception of his success as a capitalist.

ANGELOU, MAYA (1928-). An African-American poet, screenwriter, actress, and novelist. Angelou has had a checkered career, working as a Creole cook, a street-car conductor, waitress, dancer, madam, singer and editor for an English-language magazine in Egypt. She is best known among feminists as a civil rights activist and as the author of the autobiographical series: *I Know Why the Caged Bird Sings, Gather Together in My Name, Singin' and Swingin' and Gettin' Merry Like Christmas, The Heart of a Woman,* and *All God's Children Need Traveling Shoes.* In addition, she has published four collections of poetry and read her poem "A Rock, a River, a Tree" for President Bill Clinton's inauguration in 1993. She teaches American Studies at Wake Forest University.

ANGER, JANE (circa late sixteenth century). An English pamphleteer who argued, in her pamphlet *Jane Anger, her Protection for Women. To defend them against the Scandalous Reports of a late Surfeiting Lover, and all other Venetians that complain so to be overcloyed with women kindnesse* [sic] (1589), that the biblical story of creation offered proof that Eve was superior to Adam, as she was created from flesh and given the ability to procreate, while he came from dust. Therefore, by extension, all women were superior to men. Jane Anger may have been a pseudonym, though this point remains unclear.

ANIMA AND ANIMUS. The terms used by Carl Jung to denote the feminine aspect of the male personality and the masculine aspect of the female personality, respectively. Both were described as fundamentally unconscious perceptual predispositions underlying the collective images of one sex of the other. Feminists have pointed out that in his use of these terms Jung was heavily influenced by the prevailing Western gender stereotypes.

ANOREXIA NERVOSA. An eating disorder most commonly afflicting young women. Refusal to eat leads to severe weight loss, malnutrition, and sometimes cessation of menstruation. The disorder involves distortion of body image such that an emaciated person may view herself as fat, a misperception that can lead to death by self-starvation. The recent increase in the prevalence of anorexia has been credited to the media's representation of feminine beauty as being thin and the association of happiness with beauty. (*See also* Bulimia Nervosa.)

ANTHONY, SUSAN BROWNELL (1820-1906). The best-known of the early US women's rights and suffrage leaders and present at the first women's rights convention at Seneca Falls (1848) (q.v.). Anthony was active in the temperance and abolitionist movements (q.v.), but during the 1850s she also worked for equal pay (q.v.) for women in the New York State Teachers' Association and organized canvassing and petitions for suffrage and for the passage of the New York Married Women's Property Act (q.v.) (1860). After the Civil War she concentrated on women's rights. From 1868 to 1870 she edited *The Revolution*, a radical journal demanding suffrage, equal education, equal employment opportunities, and trade unions for women. In 1869, with Elizabeth Cady Stanton (q.v.), she formed the National Woman Suffrage Association (q.v.), and in 1888 she convened the meeting which founded the International Council of Women (q.v.). In 1892 she became the president of the National American Woman Suffrage Association (q.v.); in 1904, with Carrie Chapman Catt (q.v.), she founded the

International Woman Suffrage Alliance (q.v.) in Berlin. She was also the co-editor of *History of Woman Suffrage*, four volumes (1881-1902). (*See also United States v. Anthony.*)

ANTI-FEMINISM. Opposition to female equality because of its perceived threat to the model of the traditional family composed of a male wage earner supporting a homemaker wife and children. The anti-feminist position, based on a natural law of biological determinism (q.v) and religious principles, dictates separate, but complementary, spheres for the sexes. Women are to be confined to the domestic sphere (q.v.) of homemaking and child care while men work outside the home and act as head of the household. Stable family life requires that women have limited choices regarding divorce, abortion (qq.v.), and a demanding profession within the paid labor force. During the 1980's the New Right pro-family movement (q.v.) was the leading proponent of anti-feminism in the United States.

ANTI-FEMINIST MOVEMENTS. The organized opposition to feminist goals, in particular those of woman suffrage (q.v.), the Equal Rights Amendment (q.v.), and legalized abortion (q.v.). These countermovements have a largely female constituency and seek to defend the traditional family and the full-time homemaker. Anti-feminists believe that gender-neutral policies (q.v.) will deny women long-established protection under the law: exemption from combat, domestic support in marriage, and special benefits in the workplace. (*See also* Anti-feminism; Concerned Women for America; Eagle Forum.)

ANTIGONE. The strong-willed daughter of Oedipus of Thebes. In defiance of the edict of Creon, she performed funeral rites for her slain brother Polynices, who was regarded as an enemy of the state. Entombed alive as a punishment for her disobedience, she hung herself. She was a courageous and eloquent champion for the rights of the family against the dictates of the state.

ANTI-PORNOGRAPHY MOVEMENT *see* MINNEAPOLIS PORNOGRAPHY ORDINANCE

ANZAC DAY PARADE MOVEMENT. An action by Australian feminists to protest rape (q.v.) in war, staged during or before the traditional ceremony for the nation's veterans. The demonstrations began in 1977 and participation steadily increased until, in 1981, 61 women were arrested. The marches are well-publicized, effectively raise the issue of rape, and have provoked the government to repress the actions.

APHRODITE. The goddess of love, beauty, and sexuality. She was associated with the sea from which, according to Hesiod, she arose from the severed genitals of Uranus. Although Aphrodite was married to Hephaestus (Vulcan), she took Ares (Mars) as her lover and had affairs of short duration with other gods and heroes. With her son Eros (Cupid), she promoted the love affairs of many figures in mythology. The embodiment of sensual beauty and unfettered sexuality, she remained emotionally independent and complete unto herself. These qualities are symbolized by the ritual bath she regularly took to renew her virginity. She was called Venus by the Romans.

APPROPRIATION. A term used in feminist literary criticism to refer to either women's use of traditionally masculist (q.v) forms of discourse, or to male writers' use of female voices, as in the "ventriloquizing" effect of a female narrator.

ARAB WOMEN'S SOLIDARITY ASSOCIATION (AWSA). A Pan-Arab feminist organization (Jam'iyya Taddamun lil-Mar'a al-Arabiyya) formed in 1985 in Cairo with Nawal al-Saadawi (q.v.) as president. The AWSA has chapters in several Arab countries and in some ethnic communities outside the Middle East. As a consequence of its challenge to fundamentalist Islamic teaching on women, the group was ordered by the Egyptian government to cease publication of its journal *Nun* in 1989. In 1990 the AWSA itself was dissolved by the government and its assets were seized and given to the government-sponsored Women of Islam. This abolition was upheld in May 1992 by an administrative court that noted the group "threatens the peace and political and social order."

ARCHAEOLOGY OF GENDER. The concern with pruning scholarly disciplines of androcentric (q.v.) bias which stimulated archaeologists in the late 1980's to examine their practices and interpretations for this flaw. It was apparent that the majority of archaeologists accepted a convention that stone artifacts were made and used primarily by men, in spite of ethnographic data (and commonsense observation) to the contrary. Although there were exceptions, most pictures of Paleolithic and Neolithic societies placed men in the foreground and tended to overlook activities or signs of women. The question of methods to elicit data relevant to gender roles (q.v.) has become increasingly discussed. Many anthropologists now take issue with the emphasis on "man the hunter"; the counterposition is to focus on the critical subsistence role played by vegetable foods and small animals gathered by women. This latter position sees cooperative activities of women fostering selection for nurturant human groups.

ARDENER, SHIRLEY. An English anthropologist who initiated and led an influential ongoing colloquium in women's studies (q.v.) at the Center for Cross-Cultural Research on Women at Queen Elizabeth House, Oxford University, in the 1970's. Ardener has presented women as a "muted class," a group whose discourse is not heard by members of the dominant class.

ARIZONA GOVERNING COMMITTEE V. NORRIS, 463 US 1073 (1983). An opinion of the US Supreme Court that considered whether an employer's deferred compensation plan violated the sex discrimination prohibition of Title VII of the Civil Rights Act of 1964 (q.v.). Under the plan the employer offered its employees the option of receiving retirement benefits from one of several private companies, all of which paid the female employee a lower monthly retirement benefit than the male employee who had made the same contributions. The Court ruled that this policy violated the Act. Restating the principle it had previously enunciated in *Los Angeles Department of Water and Power v. Manhart* (q.v.), the Court concluded that Title VII does not permit an employer to classify employees on the basis of sex when predicting their longevity.

ARMAND, INESSA FYODOROVA (1875-1920). A Russian and international communist, born in Paris of an English father and French mother and brought up in Moscow. In 1904 she joined the Bolshevik Party. Later she met Lenin in Paris and in 1917 she returned with him to Russia and settled in Moscow. From

1918 to 1920 she was in charge of implementing women's rights in the Soviet Union and was the first head of the Zhenotdel (Women's Department). She organized the first school for the wives of workers in Petrograd and Moscow, wrote several articles on women's role in politics, and was in charge of organizing the participation of women in the Bolshevik Party.

ARTEMIS. A virgin huntress and goddess of the mountains, woods, and untamed nature. Fiercely vindictive, she punished those who invaded her domain or intruded upon her space. Cool and distant, she was identified with the moon and, thereby, with the female reproductive cycle and childbirth. The sudden death of women, particularly in childbirth, was attributed to her arrows. Particularly hostile to men, she avoided populated areas and preferred the haunts of animals and the companionship of her nymphs, female spirits of nature. She was called Diana by the Romans.

ASHLEY, JO ANN (1939-). A pioneer of contemporary feminism in nursing. She studied misogyny in the hospital and published *Hospitals, Paternalism, and the Role of the Nurse* in 1979, in which she exposed the patriarchy (q.v.) of the hospital system.

ASKING THE WOMAN QUESTION. A feminist legal methodology which poses a set of questions formulated to uncover the gender implications of rules and practices which might otherwise appear neutral or objective. First referenced by Simone de Beauvoir (q.v.) in *The Second Sex*.

ASPASIA (c. 470-410 B.C.). The mistress of Pericles and said by Socrates in Plato's dialogue *The Menexenus* to have taught him rhetoric. Because of her learning and wisdom, even wives were brought to listen to her, though she ran a house of prostitution (q.v.).

ASSERTIVENESS TRAINING. Training designed to teach people, especially women, how to communicate their wants, needs, and feelings directly rather than indirectly. The purpose is to help habitual nurturers of others to meet their own needs, through appropriate verbal and nonverbal expression.

Assertiveness training took hold in the 1960's and 1970's as modern feminism was gaining ground. Often assertiveness training classes were a first step for a woman to break out of the traditional roles she had been in and begin to redefine her life in more personally satisfying ways.

ASTELL, MARY (1666-1731). A British woman of letters, called the "Philosophical Lady." Astell was a strong defender of women's rights. In *A Serious Proposal to the Ladies*, she condemns the stifling of women's intelligence and proposes a school for women with a similar curriculum to men's schools. In *Christian Religion*, she argues that if God had not wanted women to use their reason, he wouldn't have given them any. And in her work, *Some Reflections Upon Marriage*, Astell argues that marriage should be between equals, not a man oppressing his wife into slavery. She supported education for women and outlined controlling facets of patriarchal society in works such as *A Serious Proposal to the Ladies* (1694), *A Letter to a Lady Written by a Lady* (1696), and *An Essay in Defence of the Female Sex* (1696).

ATALANTA. According to Greek mythology, the legendary huntress and runner who rejected (and, in some accounts, killed) her suitors after defeating them in a footrace. She was eventually outdistanced by Hippomenes (or Milanion) who diverted her attention during the race by throwing aside the three golden apples given to him by Aphrodite (q.v.). The consummate female athlete, Atalanta distinguished herself in several well-known exploits of men, notably the Calydonian boar hunt and the Argonautic expedition.

ATHENA. A Greek mythological goddess of defensive warfare, wisdom, weaving, and arts and crafts in general. She sprang fully grown in military attire from the head of Zeus, who had swallowed her mother Metis, an earlier goddess of wisdom. A strong, independent goddess who never married, Athena, nonetheless, played an active role in the affairs of men and took a maternal interest in a number of Greek heroes, especially Odysseus, Bellerophon, and Perseus. She considered herself motherless and generally exhibited a marked hostility to women. Her association in art with the owl, serpent, and olive tree, however, suggest an origin among the pre-Hellenic goddesses of nature before she was "masculinized" by the patriarchal Mycenaeans. She was called Minerva by the Romans.

ATKINSON, TI-GRACE (1939-). A founding member of the New York chapter of the National Organization for Women (NOW) and The Feminists (qq.v.). Atkinson left NOW in 1968 in protest against its hierarchical structures. In 1970 she left The Feminists after being trashed (q.v.) by the group for her prominence in the media and prohibited from contact with the press. A collection of her writings, *Amazon Odyssey*, was published in 1974.

ATTITUDES TOWARDS WOMEN SCALE (ATWS). A questionnaire devised by Janet Spence and Robert Helmreich to assess views on issues related to economic, political, and social gender equality.

ATWOOD, MARGARET (1939-). Canadian woman poet and novelist who has published a series of novels that have meditated on the role and identity of contemporary Canadian women: *The Edible Woman* (1969), *Surfacing* (1972), *Lady Oracle* (1976), *Life Before Man* (1979), *Bodily Harm* (1982), and *The Handmaid's Tale* (1985). The latter book is best known among feminists as a fictional recreation of the theories of the radical feminist (q.v.) Andrea Dworkin (q.v.), author of *Womanhating: A Radical Look at Sexuality* (1974) and *Our Blood: Prophecies and Discourses on Sexual Politics* (1981). *The Handmaid's Tale* presents itself as science fiction, but it is actually a feminist critique of the reproductive system in place now under the patriarchy (q.v.). In her poetry Atwood has explored the myths and stereotypes that have confined and dehumanized women throughout history. Her thesis can be summed up in the words of one of her heroines, in *Surfacing*: "That above all, to refuse to be a victim."

AURORA LEIGH. A book-length verse-novel published in 1856 and generally considered to be one of the most influential protofeminist documents published in England before the rise of an organized feminist movement. The heroine, an orphaned poet, becomes the vehicle for her author Elizabeth Barrett

Browning's (q.v.) expression of her own social, literary, and ethical beliefs. Aurora, who bears a number of similarities to that other extremely popular Victorian heroine Jane Eyre (q.v.), also voices a creed that Jane shared: "I too have a vocation--work to do ... most serious work." The poem attacks the inferior education most women receive, and it goes on to defend the right of women to intellectual self-determination.

AWAKENING, THE. A novel by Kate Chopin (q.v.), published in 1899, that was violently denounced in the press as "an essentially vulgar story" about a married woman's decision to leave her husband and children, have an adulterous affair, and kill herself. The action of the novel, set in New Orleans, explored the gilded cage of marriage, the stifling effects of marriage and maternity on a woman's creativity, and the essentially deadening social conventions that kept a woman tied to a loveless marriage. Although the novel was vilified at its publication and then "lost" for almost 75 years, it was rediscovered by feminist literary critics in the 1970's and has been widely reprinted and taught during the past 20 years.

-B-

BABY M *see IN RE BABY M*

BABY-SELLING. The legally prohibited practice of selling children for profit. Some contend that surrogacy (q.v.) and adoptions are a form of baby-selling since the parents must "pay" adoption agencies and lawyers to adopt a child; however, current laws prohibit any compensation to the mother other than reimbursement of her medical and legal expenses, which may be another form of female oppression and control. (*See also In Re Baby M.*)

BACHOFEN, JOHANN JAKOB (1815-1887). A German Professor of Roman Law at the University of Basel. He was a pioneer in the comparative study of ancient law, customs and ritual, carried out in the speculative and romantic traditions popular in those days. His studies of ancient culture, with its matriarchy, emphasis on female goddesses and the mother-figure of the Earth, caused him to conclude that the social and political position of women should be improved. His seminal study was *Myth and Mother Right*.

BACK-ALLEY ABORTION. An illegal, unsafe, and expensive abortion (q.v.) performed outside the traditional medical system by (often) unlicensed personnel. By keeping abortions in "back alleys," feminists argue that the social problem can be ignored and the woman held responsible. Although such procedures were most common before the modern era of legalized abortion, feminists today point to evidence that women are again resorting to these alternatives in the belief that legal abortions are no longer available in their area because of governmental regulations.

BACKCHANNEL CUES. Saying "uh-huh," "mmm," "go on" while others are speaking. Deborah Tannen argues that these cues function differently for men and women. Women use and expect to receive these cues as evidence of involvement in the speaker's comments. Men send and receive these cues to express specific agreement with what is being said. Tannen asserts that conversational problems between women and men result from this type of communication misperceptions. Some feminists take issue with Tannen's argument. They state that the power differential between men and women is not accounted for in this misunderstanding explanation. For example, withholding backchannels may be a dominance strategy on men's part rather than a manifestation of a different style.

BACKLASH, FEMINIST. A counterassault on women's rights that attempts to reverse the achievements of the feminist movement. The current movement is portrayed as having seriously harmed women through its advocacy for gender-neutral (q.v.) child custody and alimony (q.v.) laws, no-fault divorce (q.v.), and the interests of career women rather than the needs of pink-collar (q.v.) mothers. Feminists have also been accused of encouraging women to postpone marriage and motherhood until the opportunities for either become remote. These reactions against women's rights historically have been triggered by the perception that the status of women is rapidly improving.

BAMBARA, TONI CADE (1939-). An African-American novelist and leading voice of black literary feminism. She was born Toni Cade, but she took the name "Bambara" from a name she found in her great-grandmother's trunk. Bambara has edited the anthology *The Black Woman* (1970), and published the short story collections *Tales and Stories for Black Folks* (1971), *Gorilla, My Love* (1972), and *The Sea Birds Are Still Alive* (1977). All of her works deconstruct the stereotypes about black women and generally focus on the struggle between the generations in black culture. Specifically, she is concerned with depicting the clash between the accommodationist generation of blacks and the more militant African centrist blacks.

"BAREFOOT AND PREGNANT." A short-hand expression for the subjugation of women, restricted to a domestic role with limited mobility. In the early history of the National Organization for Women (q.v.), local chapters frequently gave "Barefoot and Pregnant Awards" to men for acts of egregious sexism (q.v.). *(See also Kinder-Küche-Kirche.)*

BARRETT, MICHELE (1949-). The author of *Woman's Oppression Today* (1980), a seminal document in the contemporary Marxist feminist movement (q.v.) in Britain. Barrett argues that capitalism uses processes of stereotyping, compensation, collusion, and recuperation in order to culturally produce women as commodities for a market economy. For Barrett the main goal of Marxist feminism is "to identify the operation of gender relations as and where they may be distinct from, or connected with, the processes of production and preproduction understood by historical materialism" (see her "Ideology and the Cultural Production of Gender," in *Feminist Criticism and Social Change*, ed. Judith Newton and Deborah Rosenfelt, 65-85). Barrett's more recent publications are *The Anti-Social Family* (1982), *The Politics of Diversity: Feminism, Marxism, and Nationalism* (1986), and *The Politics of Truth: From Marx to Foucault* (1991).

BARRY, KATHLEEN *see* INTERNATIONAL TRAFFIC IN WOMEN.

BARTHES, ROLAND (1915-1980). A leading French structuralist and semiotician. Barthes published numerous works that analyzed the underlying *langue* beneath such popular culture icons as advertisements, wrestling matches, and photographic exhibitions. Barthes sought to analyze functions rather than substances, and as such he tried to locate objects as objects for study by what he called the new "human sciences." Feminist applications of structuralist principles rely on analyses of semiosis, or signs of meaning, analyses of women as objects in advertising or media like television. By focusing on the interplay of objects as the only access we have to meaning, feminist structuralists seek to understand how women have been objectified and commodified in a capitalistic culture.

BATHSHEBA. In the Hebrew Bible, the wife of Uriah and later the wife of King David and the mother of King Solomon. Some commentators assumed she was a seductress because David has intercourse with her, but feminists point out that it is more likely that she was raped. She suffers for David's sin; the king has Uriah killed, and her baby, fathered by David while she was still Uriah's wife, dies as a result of God's punishment.

BATTERED WOMAN SYNDROME. A pattern of behaviors of women suffering from repeated abuse by a significant other, usually a husband or boyfriend but sometimes an older child. The batterer is usually but not always male. It consists of three phases: 1) tension, followed by minor abuse; 2) more serious violence, followed by the woman's "learned helplessness" (q.v.) to remedy the situation; 3) a temporary lull in abuse, during which the woman forgives her assailant. In some states, testimony on this pattern is admissible as a defense in cases where women have injured or murdered their abusers. It is argued that a consistent pattern of abuse inflicts damage that prevents a woman from protecting herself according to the usual self-defense (q.v.) standards of reasonable force only when death or serious injury is an imminent danger. Feminists argue that battered women fear for their lives from an unarmed man and may legitimately use a weapon against his fists and kicks or wait until he is asleep or otherwise vulnerable to retaliate.

BEALE, DOROTHEA (1831-1906). The English founder of Cheltenham Ladies College (circa 1858) at a time when secondary education for girls was a radical act. She sought education for girls comparable to boys even though education was thought then to inhibit the reproductive capacity of women.

BEARD, MARY RITTER (1876-1958). An American historian, author, feminist and political activist who advanced women's rights. She helped form the Women's Trade Union League (q.v.) in New York and edited "The Woman Voter" of the New York Women's Suffrage League. She authored *Women as a Force in History* and *America Through Women's Eyes*.

BEAUVOIR, SIMONE DE (1908-1986). French existential philosopher and author of the influential *The Second Sex* (1953), a seminal document in the history of feminist thought. At one time the student and lover of Jean-Paul Sartre, de Beauvoir's book has been seen as a response to his existential masterpiece *Being and Nothingness*. De Beauvoir seeks in her work to understand why women have been constructed as the "Other" (q.v.) by men. She notes that traditionally the sources for this oppression have been seen in biology, psychoanalysis, and history. But de Beauvoir reviews these three areas and says instead that the reason for women's relegation to "otherness" can be found in her being: "It is not in giving life but in risking life that man is raised above the animal; that is why superiority has been accorded in humanity not to the sex that brings forth but to that which kills" (see her *Second Sex*). Because men were free from the reproductive burdens that women faced, they were free to become subjects capable of shaping their own futures and going to war. This has raised their status above women, who are defined by the limitations of their bodies.

BEBEL, AUGUST (1840-1913). A prominent German socialist leader, founder of the Social Democratic Party in 1869. He was also the author of a number of books that examined the roles of women and socialism in German history, of which the best known is *Die Frau und der Sozialismus* (Woman And Socialism, 1879).

BECKER, LYDIA (1827-1890). A British suffragist leader of the Manchester Women's Suffrage Committee and the National Society for Women's Suffrage (q.v.). Convinced that women should study science, she spoke at Liverpool girls' schools and published *Botany for Novices* (1864) and *Elementary Astronomy* (1866). Strongly influenced by the writings of Barbara Bodichon and Richard Pankhurst (qq. v.), she published her own article "Female Suffrage" in the *Contemporary Review* in 1867. In 1868 she became the first British woman to speak publicly on women's suffrage. In 1868, with Richard Pankhurst, she prepared the test case, *Chorlton v. Lings*, which argued that women had the right to vote under older English law, because they were included under the generic term "men." It was ruled that custom outweighed the letter of the law, and that new legislation would be required. During the last 20 years of her life Becker edited the *Women's Suffrage Journal*, reporting on all Parliamentary speeches and events related to the cause.

BEECHER, CATHERINE ESTHER (1800-1878). An American writer and educator. Beecher's best known text, *A Treatise on Domestic Economy, for the Use of Young Ladies at Home and at School* (1856), demonstrates her interest in elevating the character of women's service in the domestic sphere. The Christian virtues of service and self-denial were the foundation for Beecher's appraisal of the sacred nature of women's labor in the home. In order to instruct women in their holy mission, Beecher established several colleges and wrote extensively on the need and practical means for educating women.

BEGUINES. A women's communal religious movement originating in northern Europe at the end of the twelfth century. A very popular movement (there were reportedly over 2,000 Beguines in the city of Cologne alone), these communities afforded women a degree of personal autonomy and opportunity for public service without the vows of life-long commitment intrinsic to monastic religious orders. By the fourteenth century, however, Church authorities ordered these women to either marry or join established orders for women, and the Beguine movement gradually dissolved.

BEHN, APHRA (1640-1689). England's first professional woman writer and also a spy, traveller, and middle-class widow who wrote to support herself after King Charles II failed to pay her for the spying she did for him in Antwerp. Her first play, *The Forced Marriage*, was produced in London when she was 30 years old. She went on to write and produce 13 more plays and a poem entitled "The Disappointment." After the theaters in London were closed, she took up writing in a new form and produced what is considered by many to be the first novel, *Oroonoko* (1688), an emotional denunciation of slavery. Although her memory was buried for hundreds of years, she has recently been rediscovered by feminist literary critics and is frequently taught in women's literature classes.

BELL, REBECCA (1971-1988). The first minor in the United States known to have died because of a parental consent (q.v.) law. The 17-year-old Indianapolis girl sought a legal abortion (q.v.) only to be told she would need her parents' permission. She died from complications of an infection stemming from attempts to induce an illegal abortion.

BELMONT, ALVA ERSKINE SMITH VANDERBILT (1853-1933). An American women's suffrage leader, speaker and author who provided the National Woman's Party (NWP) (q.v.) Mansion in Washington, D. C., where she served as NWP President from 1921 to 1933. She was the US representative to the International Woman Suffrage Alliance (q.v.) Conventions in 1926 and 1930. After divorcing William Kissam Vanderbilt, she used her wealth to support women's causes.

BEM SEX ROLE INVENTORY (BSRI). A psychological measurement developed by Sandra Bem. It permits assessment of the relative strength in the individual personality of (stereotypically) feminine and (stereotypically) masculine characteristics. Test takers can be classified into one of four types: "feminine," "masculine," "androgynous," or "undifferentiated." There has been some feminist criticism of the test insofar as the labels "feminine" and "masculine" relate to stereotypic assumptions regarding the traits in question.

BESANT, ANNIE (1847-1933). An English feminist challenger, with Charles Bradlaugh, of legal barriers to the promulgation of birth control information. In 1877 they reissued Charles Knowlton's contraceptive manual, *Fruits of Philosophy*. Besant's action cost her the custody of her daughter. Also in 1877 Besant helped found the British Malthusian League to disseminate contraceptive information.

BIBLE, FEMINIST EXEGESIS. The nineteenth-century use of biblical texts which were supportive of women to counter the passages used by those who wished to keep women in the domestic sphere (q.v.), especially in the women's suffrage debate. Also, specific biblical women were held up as models for women. By the end of the nineteenth century, feminists such as Elizabeth Cady Stanton (q.v.) began to view the biblical text as sexist and thoroughly androcentric (q.v.). In the twentieth century a second stage of feminist exegesis recognized that women in the Bible cannot serve unambiguously as role models (q.v.) for women seeking empowerment (q.v.) and social change. Feminist biblical exegetes of the late twentieth century, while not necessarily completely rejecting the authority of biblical texts, do not recognize sexist texts as authoritative. Many acknowledge ways the Bible has been used as a source of empowerment for women. Using methods developed by feminist historians, many feminist exegetes argue that women and their stories need to be written back into the biblical texts. (*See also* Feminist Theology; *Woman's Bible*.)

BIBLICAL WOMEN *see* BATHSHEBA; DEBORAH; DINAH; ESTHER; GOMER; HANNAH; JAEL; JEPHTHAH'S DAUGHTER; JUDITH; LEAH; LEVITE'S CONCUBINE; MAGDALENE, MARY; MANOAH'S WIFE; MARY OF NAZARETH; MIRIAM; RACHEL; RAHAB; REBEKAH; RUTH; SARAH; SHIPHRAH AND PUAH; SUSANNA; TAMAR; WOMAN OF VALOR; WOMAN WISDOM

BILLINGTON-GRIEG, TERESA (1877-1964). A suffragist from Manchester, England, who helped to found the Women's Social and Political Union (WSPU), the militant wing of the movement. She linked working-class women to the suffrage movement, organized the Women's Freedom League, refused to pay taxes, and boycotted the census as a nonrepresentative tool of the patriarchy (q.v.).

BIOLOGICAL CLOCK. A term that suggests that women who delay childbirth until after age thirty to concentrate on careers face a "now or never" choice complicated by greater infertility. According to figures from the US National Center for Health Statistics, American women, 30-34, have only a three percent higher risk of infertility than women in their early twenties. Even so, the feminist movement has been criticized for encouraging women to pursue career fulfillment as their chances for motherhood expire.

BIOLOGICAL DETERMINISM. An explanation of women's subordinate status based on physiological differences, in particular women's unique reproductive role and lesser physical strength. Anti-feminists (q.v.) thus see male dominance (q.v.) as natural. Most feminists believe that women's oppression is not rooted in biology per se but in gender roles (q.v.) based on these biological differences. However, some radical feminists (q.v.) such as Shulamith Firestone (q.v.) espouse a version of biological determinism.

BIOLOGY IS DESTINY *see* BIOLOGICAL DETERMINISM

BIRTH CONTROL *see* FAMILY PLANNING

BIRTH CONTROL PILL. A daily oral form of estrogen and progesterone that inhibits ovulation and thereby prevents conception. Birth control pills have been available since 1960 in a variety of forms and are intended for long-term use. Although feminists initially welcomed a medical innovation that was convenient and effective, by the late 1960's usage had been linked with fatal blood clots, strokes, cancer, and other less serious side-effects. The high-dose estrogen pills were removed from the European market in the early 1970's and, under prodding from the women's health movement (q.v.), they were banned in the US market in 1988.

BIRTHING CENTER. A freestanding primary care center providing homelike birthing experiences and access to acute care hospital services and specialist consultation as needed. These centers emphasize a family-centered approach with minimal use of technology. Advantages include cost savings and reduced caesarean delivery rates. Birthing centers are a part of the alternative birth movement (q.v.) supported by many feminists.

BIRTHING ROOM. A room in a hospital or birthing center (q.v.) in which the mother experiences labor, delivery, and recovery. It may also be used for the entire postpartum stay. The atmosphere is homelike in furnishings and decor. Ideally, there is greater decisionmaking power for the woman experiencing an uncomplicated birth, and support persons and siblings may be present. (*See also* Alternative Birth Movement.)

BIRTHNAME *see* LUCY STONE LEAGUE; NAMING CONVENTIONS

"BITCH MANIFESTO." An essay, written by Chicago Women's Liberation Union (q.v.) founder Joreen (political scientist Jo Freeman), to redefine the common pejorative used against "unfeminine" women to that of a feminist ideal: an assertive, ambitious, and self-determined woman. The article was reprinted in the New York Radical Women's (q.v.) *Notes from the Second Year* (1970).

BLACK FEMINISM *see* AFRICAN-AMERICAN FEMINISM

BLACK MATRIARCHY. A stereotypical image cultivated by social scientists to characterize, and thus denigrate, the role of black women in relationship to their children and black men. The myth has perpetuated the belief that domineering and aggressive women have weakened men, thus leading to the general deterioration of black family life.

BLACKWELL, ALICE STONE (1857-1950). An American feminist and a supporter of women's suffrage, abolition, peace, and the women's trade union movement. In 1887 she began editing the "Women's Column," a collection of suffrage items sent to newspapers around the country. She assisted in establishing the bond between the American Woman Suffrage Association (q.v.) and Susan B. Anthony's (q.v.) rival organization, the National Woman Suffrage Association (q.v.). Blackwell became the recording secretary of the new National American Woman Suffrage Association (q.v.) in 1890 when the two groups merged. She was the author of *Lucy Stone: Pioneer in Women's Rights*, the biography of her mother. She was also the niece of Elizabeth Blackwell, the first woman physician, and Antoinette Blackwell (q.v.), the first woman minister ordained in America.

BLACKWELL, ANTOINETTE BROWN (1825-1921). The first woman minister to be ordained in America and an active speaker for women's suffrage. She supported the right of women to be paid for work outside the home and called for the equality of women in a harmonious universe. She reinterpreted the Bible to reconcile feminism with Christianity and argued against Darwin and Spencer who claimed that males were mentally and physically superior.

"BLAMING THE VICTIM." A phrase coined by William Ryan in 1976 to describe the process of attributing personal fault for social problems to those persons who are the victims of socio-economic and political forces beyond their control or, in other words, placing the responsibility of an event on the person who was the recipient of the damage. The victim is usually disempowered to the extent that she feels incapable of defense or retaliation. For example, women are often blamed for irresponsible childbearing yet simultaneously are denied access to comprehensive reproductive health care. Another example is blaming women for being raped.

BLATCH, HARRIET EATON STANTON (1856-1940). The daughter of Elizabeth Cady Stanton (q.v.) and a leader of the American woman suffrage movement, especially in New York. In 1907 she organized the Equality League of Self-Supporting Women, a suffrage group that was the first to include working-class members and to utilize parades and outdoor rallies as tactics. Blatch was also a member of the National Woman's Party (q.v.) and a supporter of the Equal Rights Amendment (q.v.)

BLOOMER, AMELIA JENKS (1818-1894). The publisher and editor of the first prominent women's rights newspaper, *The Lily*, in 1849. A suffragist and temperance leader, she introduced and popularized a new garment, the Bloomer costume, a tunic belted at the waist and a short skirt about knee length over Turkish pantaloons which took the weight of long skirts off women's backs. Intended to give women greater freedom of movement than their restrictive, corseted dress, the "Bloomer" became an object of derision. Advocates of equal rights for women were often ridiculed as "bloomers."

BLUE-COLLAR WOMEN *see* NONTRADITIONAL OCCUPATIONS, WOMEN IN

BLUESTOCKING SOCIETY (SEITOSCHA). A Japanese women's literary group founded in 1911 by Hiratsuka Raicho. Its journal, *Seito*, addressed such issues as abortion (q.v.), motherhood, prostitution (q.v.), and woman suffrage and published Western feminists, including Emma Goldman and Olive Schreiner (qq.v). It was on occasion censored by a government concerned with corruption of traditional feminine virtues and stopped publication in 1916. The Bluestocking group gradually disbanded after having raised feminist consciousness (q.v.) and presented a model for the "new woman" in Japan.

BLY, ROBERT (1926-). An American poet, translator, editor, and author of *Iron John: A Book About Men* (1990), an examination of the psychology of masculinity and men in America that established Bly as a leader of the new men's movement (q.v.). Bly advocates a return to male metaphors such as war, hunting, and strength to sustain the traditional male archetype. His volume of poems, *The Light Around the Body*, won the National Book Award in 1968 and gained him a reputation as a political poet when its earnings were given to draft-resistance groups.

BOARD OF DIRECTORS OF ROTARY INTERNATIONAL V. ROTARY CLUB OF DUARTE, 481 US 537 (1987). A US Supreme Court decision that resolved a First Amendment (freedom of association) challenge to a California law that provided that all persons are entitled to full access to business establishments. Despite an international rule restricting membership to males, a local chapter of the Rotary Club in California admitted women to the chapter, was expelled, and challenged that expulsion. The Court concluded that relationships among Rotary Club members are not of the "kind of intimate or private relation that warrants contitutional protection [and that the] compelling interest in eradicating sex discrimination justified any incidental restrictions by the states on the club members' rights of expressive association." This case is one of the landmark decisions against male-only clubs that restrict the professional opportunities of excluded women.

BOBIGNY TRIAL, THE. A 1972 trial held in a Paris suburb where a poor 17-year-old girl, raped by a schoolboy, received an abortion (q.v.). Her mother and two of her mother's friends were charged under a 1920 law that prohibited obtaining or aiding in abortion. The defense argued that, in arranging for her daughter's abortion, the mother was performing a maternal duty. As a result of the national dialogue arising from the case, abortion was made legal in France in 1975.

BODICHON, BARBARA LEIGH-SMITH (1827-1891). A British aristocrat who argued in the pamphlet "A Brief Summary in Plain Language of the Most Important Laws Concerning Women, Together with a Few Observations Thereon" (1854) that married women had precious few legal rights. In 1855 she, along with others, organized a committee to petition Parliament to increase married women's control over their property and earnings.

BODY POLITICS. A term used to suggest that the human body is a social and ideological product constructed to conform to or reinforce prevailing attitudes toward "women's appropriate place" in society. Building on the theories of Michel Foucault (q.v.), this concept sees the human body as perceived, interpreted, and represented differently in different historical periods because of differing material cultures, technologies, and means of control. What Foucault has called "the discourse of the body" emerged in the late eighteenth and early nineteenth centuries as a response to a new set of social, political, and cultural meanings that gave new significance to both male and female bodies. The obsessive biologization of femininity can be seen in the nineteenth century's need to equate women's bodies with reproduction and the forces of nature, and to claim that women were uniquely prone to various new diseases, like hysteria, that originated in their bodies.

BOGUS CLINICS *see* FAKE CLINICS

BONA FIDE OCCUPATIONAL QUALIFICATION (BFOQ). A term referring to a justification of what would otherwise constitute unlawful sex discrimination. Section 703 (e)(1) of Title VII of the US Civil Rights Act of 1964 (q.v.) allows individuals to be hired on the basis of sex when that characteristic is reasonably necessary to the normal operation of a particular business or enterprise. Even while upholding the exclusion of women from being hired as guards in a state prison for men, the Supreme Court indicated that the BFOQ exception is subject to an "extremely narrow" interpretation.

BOSTON WOMEN'S HEALTH BOOK COLLECTIVE. A non-profit group, founded in 1970 as an advocate for accessible information about women and health. In 1970 the New England Free Press published a newsprint edition of what would become the best-selling commercial book entitled *Our Bodies, Ourselves* (1973). The collective has continued to operate according to egalitarian principles and has published other editions and other projects. Profits are used to fund other women's health projects.

BOSTONIANS, THE. A novel published in 1866 by Henry James, the American expatriate author who spent most of his life in England and France. The novel presents a very unflattering portrait of feminists as man-hating and frustrated women, neurotically attracted to other women as a way of avoiding mature heterosexual relationships.

"BOTTLE BABY DISEASE." A health crisis among children stemming from the practices of infant formula manufacturers to encourage use of their product in developing countries. In using the free samples, new mothers become dependent on formula as their breast milk dries up from disuse. Because of the cost of the product (world average: $550 annually), women in developing nations dilute it and also use unsafe water or unsterilized containers. It is estimated that one million babies die annually from the misuse of formula. In 1984 a seven-year international boycott of Nestlé, widely publicized by women's groups, forced some reforms and in 1993 all infant-food manufacturers agreed to stop providing free samples in developing countries that prohibited this practice (less than a dozen in 1992).

BOURGEOIS FEMINISM. A term used by Marxist feminists (q.v.) to describe those who support equal rights for women but deny or ignore the need for system-transforming change in society. According to this critique, these middle-class reformers are counter-revolutionary dilettantes, who dabble in politics as an avocation.

BOYER, ELIZABETH see WOMEN'S EQUITY ACTION LEAGUE

BRA-BURNERS see MISS AMERICA PAGEANT PROTEST

BRADLAUGH, CHARLES see BESANT, ANNIE

BRADWELL V. ILLINOIS, 83 US 130 (1873). A decision of the US Supreme Court that upheld the exclusion of women from the practice of law. It is perhaps best known for Justice Bradley's expression of the "separate spheres" ideology, in which the male spouse was the breadwinner and the couple's representative for public purposes, while the woman's role dominated the family and the home. The separate spheres ideology became the basis for upholding many laws limiting women's rights; it was finally rejected by the Supreme Court in the early 1970's.

BRAUN, LILY (1865-1916). A German writer and member of the Social Democratic Party. Her strong feminist views, expressed in *Die Frauenfrage* (The Women's Question, 1901), alienated party leaders who believed that women's issues should be subordinated to those of the working class as a whole. Braun was forced to leave the party, but she continued to work for the radical, militant wing of German feminism.

BREAD AND ROSES. A Boston women's liberation (q.v.) network formed in 1969 by Meredith Tax and Linda Gordon to link through weekly meetings small local feminist collectives (q.v.) engaged in their own projects. Women were involved in women's studies (q.v.), anti-war efforts, arts groups, zap actions (q.v.), and consciousness-raising (q.v.). The group was politico (q.v.) in approach and lasted into the mid-1970's.

BREAST CANCER. A form of cancer that occurs in breast tissue. It can be treated by surgical removal of the breast and all adjoining lymph tissue (radical mastectomy), removal of just the breast tissue (mastectomy), or more recently, removal of just the cancerous tumor (lumpectomy). Surgery is usually followed by radiation and chemotherapy. Feminists have questioned the standard use of radical mastectomy, despite evidence that in the early stages a lumpectomy has similar survival rates. More recently, US feminists have succeeded in greatly increasing the amount of government money allocated for research on this common disease among women.

BREAST IMPLANTS. Elective cosmetic surgery to augment (increase) the size of women's breasts or for reconstruction following mastectomy. The procedure has become controversial due to complications resulting from the use of silicone gel implants. The feminist movement has been vocal in its concerns about the safety of implants. It has also been critical of the importance placed on the female breast that causes women to be dissatisfied with their bodies.

BRIDEPRICE/BRIDEWEALTH/BRIDESERVICE. A practice in many societies whereby a bridegroom demonstrates respect for his bride and her family by presenting them with gifts or assisting them with his labor. Elopement without such formal presentations may be judged disrespectful of the bride and bring opprobrium upon the bridegroom. Missionaries and colonial agents often misunderstood "brideprice" gifts, interpreting them as purchasing the woman from her family. Brideprice is not the inverse of dowry. *Dowry* classically meant the endowment of the bride so that she should have some means of support should she be widowed or deserted; *brideprice* established the bridegroom's capacity to support a wife.

BRITISH WOMEN'S TEMPERANCE ASSOCIATION (BWTA). A group formed in 1876 to eliminate drunkenness in England through both political means, through pressure on Parliament to eliminate grocers' liquor licenses, and evangelical means, through the use of missionaries among the poor. By 1892 the BWTA had some 577 branches with approximately 45,000 members. Under the leadership of Lady Henry Somerset, the BWTA became actively involved in woman suffrage.

BROWN, RITA MAE (1944-). A contemporary American lesbian (q.v.) novelist and poet. She joined the National Organization for Women (q.v) in 1968 and insisted that the group confront the issue of lesbian rights. As one of the Radicalesbians, she wrote "The Woman-Identified Woman" (q.v) (1970) and has been active as a lecturer on feminism and gay liberation. She has published widely, from collections of poetry--*The Hand that Cradles the Rock* (1971), *Songs to a Handsome Woman* (1973)--to collections of essays--*A Plain Brown Rapper* (1976)--to *Rubyfruit Jungle* (1973), one of the first works to present the lesbian "coming-out" experience, and *Six of One* (1978). Her poetry was published in a complete edition (1987).

BROWNING, ELIZABETH BARRETT (1806-1861). A British poet, translator, abolitionist, feminist, and political activist for Italian unification. Browning's importance for feminism lies in her publication of a number of poems that plead for women's rights, her need for an equal education, and intellectually rewarding employment. She also published "The Runaway Slave at Pilgrim's Point" (1850), a poem that explored the moral degradation and inhumanity of slavery, "The Cry of the Children" and "A Song for the Ragged Schools of London," both early denunciations of the mistreatment of poor urban children. (*See also Aurora Leigh.*)

BULGARIAN WOMEN, THE COMMITTEE OF. An organization within the Communist Party, in operation 1944-

1990 as the sole women's group in Bulgaria. Although lacking influence within a totalitarian one-party regime, the group's journal *Zhenata dnes* (Woman Today) was a popular and liberal journal. Official goals included: improving the status of women, public education, and lobbying for needed policy changes. In 1990 a splinter group, the Women's Democratic Union, emerged. It has embraced both feminist and traditional roles for women.

BULIMIA NERVOSA. An eating disorder, akin to anorexia nervosa (q.v.), most commonly found in women. The sufferer binges or gorges on food and may then, in an effort to avoid gaining weight, purge herself by self-induced vomiting. Other means of purging commonly include laxatives, diet pills and diuretics. The pattern of binging and purging frequently begins in an attempt to diet for weight loss. The condition is seen most frequently in high achieving women, or women who have come from families where achievement is expected.

BURNS, LUCY (1879-1966). An American feminist, participant in the British suffrage movement, and leader of the militant wing of the American suffrage movement. The Women's Social and Political Union (WSPU), led by the Pankhursts (q.v.), bestowed a special medal for valor on Burns, who was arrested numerous times and joined in the prison hunger strikes in 1909. In 1912 Burns returned to the United States and organized the immense suffrage parade the day before Woodrow Wilson's inaugural. That same year she helped form the Congressional Union for Woman Suffrage (CU). With Alice Paul (q.v.), Burns shaped the major policies of the CU and of its successor organization, the National Woman's Party (NWP) (q.v.). Imprisoned in 1917 for picketing the White House, she was sentenced to prison in the notorious Occoquan Workhouse, where she joined hunger strikers and was force fed, which brought the suffrage cause to national attention.

BUTLER, JOSEPHINE GREY (1828-1906). A British moral reformer and feminist. Butler was one of the leaders of the Ladies' National Association for the Repeal of the Contagious Diseases Acts (q.v.) and the founder of the first international moral reform society, the British, Continental and General Federation for the Abolition of Government Regulation of

Prostitution. She viewed woman suffrage as an instrument for social reform.

-C-

CALIFANO V. GOLDFARB, 430 US 199 (1977). A US Supreme Court decision that addressed the constitutionality under the Equal Protection (q.v.) Clause of a provision of the Social Security program. The provision at issue permitted a widow to collect survivor benefits based on her husband's earnings. However, a widower could not collect a survivor's benefit based on his wife's earnings unless he established that he had been receiving one-half of his support from his wife prior to her death. A majority of the Court decided that this aspect of the Social Security program was unconstitutional. The *Goldfarb* decision was viewed by some as a "feminist triumph." Others felt that the decision did not focus on the true victims of discrimination.

CALIFORNIA FEDERAL SAVINGS AND LOAN ASSOCIATION V. GUERRA, 479 US 272 (1987). A US Supreme Court decision that determined whether a California fair employment law, which created for pregnant employees a qualified right to reinstatement after maternity leave (q.v.), was valid. The petitioners argued that Title VII of the Civil Rights Act of 1964 (q.v.) forbids the state of California from legislating practices that favor pregnant women. The Court concluded that Congress did not intend to prohibit preferential treatment of pregnant women. Feminists are split on the importance of this case. Those committed to the equal treatment of women fear the revival of protective labor laws (q.v.) that may make employers less willing to hire women. Others argue that preferential treatment of pregnancy simply recognizes the differential burden of childbearing.

CAMPBELL, CARLYN KOHRS. A contemporary American feminist rhetorical historian, theorist, and author of a two-volume critical work on women's public address, called *Man Cannot Speak for Her*. Campbell is known for her thorough reconstruction of women's historical situations and their unique strategic responses to the situations. Her work is one of the few which critiques women in terms appropriate to them, thereby fostering feminist rhetorical criticism.

CANADIAN CHARTER OF RIGHTS AND FREEDOMS, SECTION 28. A provision of the federal Constitution adopted in April 1982 which guarantees the equal rights and freedom of males and females. The provision was the product of a two-year campaign primarily by anglophone feminists, including the National Action Committee on the Status of Women (NAC) (q.v.). Women's groups were also successful in gaining an exemption of Section 28 from a provision allowing provinces to ignore charter guarantees in special limited circumstances. The Fédération des Femmes du Québec (FFQ), unable to support the federal charter because of issues of provincial autonomy, withdrew from the NAC over this issue.

CANON OF LITERATURE AND FEMINIST CRITICISM. A major goal of feminist literary critics, to critique and revise standards by which texts are deemed "major" in ways that will valorize women's writings previously neglected or disparaged. Feminist criticism has substantially revised curricula, literature anthologies, and publication lists as well as scholarly research.

CAREER FEMINISM. A tradition based on individual self-determination and achievement in the labor force, assertive resistance to male-imposed barriers, and a willingness to help other women through networking and mentoring (qq.v.).

CARPENTER, MARY (1807-1877). An English pioneer in the reformation of juvenile delinquents and a founder of "ragged schools" for the children of the poor. She was also an activist in the abolition movement and the movement to stop the abuses of prostitutes' civil rights through reform of the Contagious Diseases Act (q.v.).

CARRILLO PUERTO, ELVIA. A Mexican socialist politician who, with her brother Felipe, formed feminist leagues in Yucatan to combat immorality and illiteracy and to advocate birth control. She was elected to the Yucatan legislature in 1923 and to the national Chamber of Deputies from San Luis Potosi in 1925, a seat she was denied on the grounds that suffrage and office-holding were restricted to males. Returning to Yucatan, she organized the Liga Orientadora de Acción Femenina (Orienting League of Feminine Action) to lobby for woman suffrage.

CARTER, ANGELA (1940-1992). A British novelist and essayist, best known in the United States as a feminist reteller of traditional fairy tales. In *The Bloody Chamber* (1979) she presents a postmodern version of a number of traditional tales, Red Riding Hood and the Bluebeard story, in order to reverse the power in the texts. In "The Company of Wolves" she presents Red Riding Hood as calmly seducing the wolf, while eating the lice off his body. A profound interest in the Marquis de Sade motivates much of her vision, as does her conviction that the mysterious permutations of desire control most of human behavior.

CASA DELLA DONNA. A house for women founded in Rome by the Movimento di la Liberazione della Donna (MLD) (q.v.), which simply occupied a vacant church on October 2, 1976. At various times the house was a birth-control clinic, a day-care center, and an office coordinating anti-violence and reproductive freedom (q.v.) activities. The house also functioned as a women's center for other feminist groups and projects.

CATT, CARRIE CHAPMAN (1859-1947). An American suffrage leader and founder of the League of Women Voters (q.v.). She is credited with bringing a strong organization to the National American Woman Suffrage Association (q.v.) as its president, 1900-1904 and 1915-1920. She also served as president of the International Woman Suffrage Alliance (q.v.), 1904-1923. In 1912 Catt took control of the New York suffrage movement, organizing two major campaigns which eventually won the state vote for women in 1917. After national suffrage was won in 1920, Catt became active in the peace movement and founded the National Committee on the Cause and Cure of War.

CELIBACY. A conscious decision by some feminists to conserve energy that otherwise would be spent on men and sex. The Feminists (q.v.) advocated celibacy as an alternative lifestyle choice. Such abstinence could be permanent or for a limited period to permit women to discover themselves. Most feminists do not consider celibacy as a realistic solution to inegalitarian relations between the sexes.

CELL 16. An early Boston radical feminist (q.v.) group formed by Roxanne Dunbar in 1968. Originally known as the Female Liberation Front, the group pioneered self-defense (q.v.) by studying karate, advocated celibacy (q.v.) and separatism (q.v.), and published *No More Fun and Games*. In 1970 the group and its journal were the targets of an attempted takeover by the Socialist Workers Party, a conflict that weakened the group and led to its demise in 1973.

CENTER FOR THE AMERICAN WOMAN AND POLITICS (CAWP). A research center founded in 1972 as part of the Eagleton Institute of Politics, Rutgers University, to examine the status and impact of women in public office in the United States. Through its publications and conferences, the CAWP has been central to the formation of a network of female officials and in introducing many of these women to the feminist agenda.

CERTIFIED NURSE MIDWIFE (CNM). A registered nurse with advanced education and training to assist women through pregnancy, childbirth and the postpartum period and to provide care of the newborn infant and general well woman care. The majority of CNMs are women. They apply a patient centered holistic approach and emphasize education. Historically, women have given birth at home, with a midwife in attendance. In industrialized nations outside the United States, midwives continue to manage most normal deliveries in hospitals. US feminists have strongly supported the greater reliance on midwives. (*See also* Alternative Birth Movement; Medicalization of Childbirth.)

CHICAGO, JUDY (JUDY COHEN, 1939-) *see THE DINNER PARTY*

CHICAGO WOMEN'S LIBERATION UNION (CWLU). The first, largest, and most enduring of the socialist feminist (q.v.) unions, formed in 1969. In the early 1970's the CWLU had around 500 dues-paying members, more than the local chapter of the National Organization for Women (q.v.), and a number of projects, including the Jane Collective (q.v.). It disbanded around 1977, a victim of leftist sectarian disputes.

CHICANA. A woman of Mexican origin residing in the United States, who has had to fight oppression both within her own culture and from outside. Her struggle is threefold: to overcome repression by colonialism, by the Anglos and by men. She has sought to forge her own identity on gender, race and culture issues simultaneously. This effort is manifested not only in political action but also in artistic endeavors such as literary, theatrical and other diverse cultural presentations.

CHICANA POLITICS. Refers to the awareness by women within the Chicano movement of integral issues especially related to them and needing to be viewed from a feminist perspective. During the 1970's Chicanas (q.v.) began to examine their role not only as Mexican-Americans within US society, but also their position in the Chicano movement itself. They confronted *machismo* from within and without; they looked anew at racial and gender stereotyping of Chicanas; they studied the role of the Chicana in the family and the workplace, and they attempted to define the nature of Chicana feminism and its relevance to the general feminist movement. During the past couple of decades, numerous national conferences have dealt with issues of general concern to Chicanas: education, employment, gender and race discrimination, health care. Chicana feminist writings have proliferated. Chicana feminists emphasize the interstructuring of oppressions (q.v.): race, class, and gender. Only when these issues are viewed together and as interconnected can the experience of the Chicana be adequately understood and appreciated.

CHILD CARE *see* DAY CARE

CHILD SUPPORT ENFORCEMENT. A legal and philosophical commitment on the part of government and the courts to award and collect financial support from a child's non-custodial parent, usually the father, regardless of the legal relationship of the parents. Forty-two percent of US women with children do not receive any child support from absent fathers and less than one-quarter receive the full amount stipulated by the court. Although feminists see enforcement as helpful in terms of providing economic support, such efforts also reinforce a woman's economic dependency on the father of her children. (*See also* Family Support Act of 1988.)

CHISHOLM, SHIRLEY (1924-). The first African-American woman to serve in the US Congress (1969-1983, from New York) and a candidate for the Democratic nomination for president in 1972. She has documented her experiences in *Unbought and Unbossed* (1970) and *The Good Fight* (1973). One of her major accomplishments was coverage of (mostly female) domestic workers in the minimum wage law. She also worked for the rights of women and racial minorities, for the improvement of employment and educational opportunities, and for reforms in inner-city living conditions. After retiring from Congress, she has held the Purington Chair at Mount Holyoke College.

CHODOROW, NANCY (1944-). An American sociologist whose publications have challenged the traditional view that females are biologically predisposed toward nurturing infants. Mothering, she has argued, fulfills a woman's psychological need for reciprocal intimacy that originates during her own babyhood when she and her own mother perceived each other as extensions of each other. Mothers are also close to their infant sons, but they view their male children as different and do not share with them the same sense of "oneness" that they experience with their daughters. Mature males, unaccustomed to a psychologically intimate relationship, are, therefore, content to leave mothering to women. This theory, developed in *The Reproduction of Mothering: Psychoanalysis and the Sociology of Gender* (1978) and *Feminism and Psychoanalytic Theory* (1989), argues for a change in traditional parental roles.

CHOISIR (TO CHOOSE). A liberal feminist (q.v.) group especially prominent in the French abortion (q.v.) and rape (q.v) reform movements, led by lawyer and Parliament member Gisèle Halimi and organized in 1971 to defend the signers of the *Manifeste des 343 femmes* (q.v.). In 1974 the group helped to form a feminist political party, the Parti Féministe Unifié

Français (PFUF), which has not been successful in national elections. Choisir uses litigation, lobbying, and electioneering as main strategies and in 1978 issued its platform for legal and social change, the Common Program for Women.

CHOPIN, KATE (1851-1904). An American novelist and local-colorist, best known for writing the protofeminist novel *The Awakening* (q.v.). Born in St. Louis, Missouri, to a prosperous family, Chopin was educated at home and married a Creole cotton trader, with whom she had six children. After 13 years of marriage Chopin was widowed and began to write stories to supplement her income. Influenced by Darwin, Huxley, Zola, Flaubert, and de Maupassant, Chopin began to write tales set in New Orleans that attacked marriage as an institution, that questioned racism, classism, and sexism (q.v.).

CHORIONIC VILLI SAMPLING (CVS) *see* AMNIOCENTESIS

CHORLTON V. LINGS (1868) *see* BECKER, LYDIA

CHUPIREN (PINK PANTHERS). A Japanese women's liberation (q.v.) organization founded by Misako Enoki in 1972. The pink-helmeted group received much media attention for their direct actions against male adulterers and batterers and for legalization of abortion and birth control pills (qq.v.) in Japan. Enoki retired from public life and Chupiren was disbanded after her Japan Woman's Party failed to win a seat in the legislative elections of 1977.

CINDERELLA COMPLEX, THE. The pattern of pathological female dependence on men described by Colette Dowling in her 1981 popular book with the same name. While feminists join Dowling in her concern about those women who look to men to rescue them, they have objected to the book's implication that, as a whole, women are more dependent than men.

CIRCE. According to Greek mythology, a seductive sorceress who kept a menagerie of male victims whom she had transformed into wild boars, lions, and other beasts. She met her match in the hero Odysseus who, by wielding a magical herb, was able to counter her malevolent power and free his comrades from her spell. Subsequently, she lived amiably with Odysseus for one year and gave birth to a son, Telegonus. Ever the alchemical goddess, Circe directed Odysseus' journey to the land of the dead and thus accomplished a spiritual, if not physical, transformation of the hero.

CIRCUMCISION, FEMALE see FEMALE GENITAL MUTILATION

CITIZENS' ADVISORY COUNCIL ON THE STATUS OF WOMEN (CAC). A body established in 1963 by US President John F. Kennedy to continue the work of the President's Commission on the Status of Women (q.v.). The Council was continued until 1977, when President Jimmy Carter appointed a similar body. Composed of 20 private citizens, the CAC played an important role in implementation of subsequent anti-discrimination policies through its research and publication program and its sponsorship of four national conferences of State Commissions on the Status of Women (q.v.). Anti-feminists (q.v.) charged that the Council's private citizen membership allowed it to publish feminist propaganda and lobby for feminist causes at government expense. CAC support for the Equal Rights Amendment and the International Women's Year (qq.v.) was especially criticized.

CIVIL RIGHTS ACT OF 1964, TITLE VII (CRA). A US law making it unlawful to discriminate against individuals in employment because of sex, race, color, religion or national origin. The law covers private employers with more than 15 employees, unions, employment agencies and federal, state and local government. Although the CRA was primarily directed toward racial equality and was passed before the revival of a feminist movement, sex discrimination was included because of the interest of many members of Congress and women's groups. (*See also Phillips v. Martin Marietta Corporation.*)

CIVIL RIGHTS ACT OF 1991. A US law that extends and restores coverage of the Civil Rights Act of 1964 (q.v.) after a number of Supreme Court rulings had eroded the 1964 Act. It requires employers to either show that practices or policies do not have an adverse impact on protected minorities or that the practices are related to successful performance on the job. It also allows for jury trials and compensatory and punitive damages for employees receiving intentional discrimination.

CIVIL RIGHTS MOVEMENT, THE. The movement begun by African-Americans in the US South in the 1950's to challenge racial prejudice and segregation. Its importance with respect to the women's movement is similar to the nineteenth-century abolitionist movement (q.v.). Even though the leadership was male dominated, for the black and white women who took part in numerous sit-ins and demonstrations during the 1960's, it fostered "consciousness raising" (q.v.) on issues of inequality, injustice, and oppression, while at the same time providing experience in political mobilization. However, sexual and racial politics within the movement eventually led to exclusion of whites from some civil rights groups in the mid-1960's. According to feminists, the resulting separation along racial lines (e.g., the "black power" movement and the "white" anti-war movement) culminated in the formation of groups that were typically male dominated. However, the leadership for the new feminist movement (q.v.) eventually emerged from the ranks of these other activist groups.

CIVIL RIGHTS RESTORATION ACT OF 1988 *see GROVE CITY COLLEGE V. BELL*

CIXOUS, HÉLÈNE (1937-). A leading French postmodern feminist (q.v.) and author of a number of feminist works that explore the relation between language and culture. Cixous's theories are not easy to summarize, but she is basically concerned with the distinction between women as biological and social and "female," "feminine" or "other," where these terms refer metaphorically to the condition of being other in a relation of difference rather than in opposition. Cixous has tried to create a feminine language and female society outside of and apart from male language and society, and has been criticized for doing so by other French feminists like Julia Kristéva (q.v.). Generally speaking, Cixous is concerned with how the politics of language controls the social roles assigned to women. Most of her early writings have been translated into English and published in this country as *The Newly-Born Woman*

(1986) and *Inside* (1986). Cixous is most accessible through her much-reprinted essays, "The Laugh of the Medusa" and "Castration or Decapitation?"

CLAFLIN, TENNESSEE CELESTE *see* WOODHULL, VICTORIA CLAFLIN

CLASSISM AND FEMINISM. The critique that feminist discourse, historically the domain of white middle-class women, has often occluded or ignored the systematic harms of class segregation, disparity, and exploitation. Some feminists now explore the complex interactions of classism, defined by Audre Lorde (q.v.) as "the belief in the inherent superiority of one class over the other and thereby the right to dominance," with sexism and racism (qq.v.). Both the compounded sufferings of women caused by class and the feminists' own unacknowledged classism are exposed, and transformative responses are sought. (*See also* Oppressions, Interstructuring of; Racism and Feminism.)

CLEOPATRA VII (69-30 B.C.). A Macedonian princess and the last of the Ptolemaic dynasty to rule Egypt (51-30 B.C.). A highly intelligent, ambitious, and alluring woman, she had intimate relationships with both Julius Caesar and Mark Antony, who bestowed upon her the title "Queen of Kings." Together with Antony, she suffered defeat in the naval battle of Actium in 31 B.C. against the fleet of Octavian. Too proud to appear as a prisoner of war in Octavian's triumphal procession in Rome, she committed suicide by submitting to the bite of a poisonous serpent. A formidable woman in every respect, she fought against the might of Rome and competed with men at the highest levels of power.

CLICK! A term referring to a moment of feminist insight triggered by a personal experience (e.g., a woman suddenly conscious of having repeatedly thanked her husband for cleaning a common living area). These experiences lead some women to develop a feminist consciousness (q.v.) that exposure to abstract feminist political theory (q.v.) would not produce.

CLINIC PROTECTION. The protection from harassment of women who enter clinics where abortions (q.v.) are performed. People are trained in nonviolent tactics, such as escorting women or forming human barriers to prevent pro-life (q.v.) activists from blocking access to the clinic. US clinic protectors have also had to deal with bombings, arson, and other attacks upon abortion facilities and death threats (and several murders) directed against clinic personnel. In 1994 feminists received permission from the US Supreme Court to charge pro-life militants under the Racketeer Influenced and Corrupt Organizations Act (RICO) and the Freedom of Access to Clinic Entrances Act (FACE) was passed. This law makes it a federal crime to injure, intimidate, or interfere with someone trying to enter or leave an abortion clinic.

CLINTON, HILLARY RODHAM (1947-). The wife of US President Bill Clinton and since 1993, America's "first lady." As a nationally acclaimed Yale-educated attorney who had always been her husband's policy partner, she has been a feminist role model (q.v.) for the nation. Some of her comments during the 1992 presidential election campaign ("I suppose I could have stayed home and baked cookies." and "I'm not some little woman standing by her man.") raised controversy as did her direction of the president's national health care proposal, 1993-1994. Mrs. Clinton has also focused on women's and children's issues such as mammography and TV violence and on a new book about children.

CLITORIDECTOMY *see* FEMALE GENITAL MUTILATION

CLUB FEMENINO DE CUBA. A Cuban women's club, formed in 1917, to advance social issues such as children's courts, prostitution (q.v.), women's prisons, and women's rights. In 1923 the Club formed an association of women's groups that organized the First National Women's Congress in Havana (1923) to discuss a broad range of social reform and women's issues. In 1925 the Club held a second congress, where a split developed between the radical feminists of the Club and conservative and religious feminists, who supported suffrage but also the traditional family and a class-based society. In 1928 the Club was supplanted by the newly formed Alianza Nacional

Feminista (National Feminist Alliance) as the leading feminist group. Suffrage was granted in 1934.

CLUB WOMAN'S MOVEMENT. The involvement of middle-class American women during the last two decades of the nineteenth century in voluntary associations. These early groups were committed to literary study and self-improvement but also social, economic, and political reforms such as temperance, suffrage, child labor, conservation, and health care. This period marked the first widespread public role for women in their communities. In 1890 the club movement formed the General Federation of Women's Clubs (q.v.). Black women's clubs, excluded from this federation, formed the National Association of Colored Women (q.v.).

CLYTEMNESTRA. According to Greek legend, the notorious wife of Agamemnon who, according to the tragedians, murdered her husband upon his return from the Trojan War, together with Cassandra, his Trojan concubine. She ruled forcefully in Mycenae for seven years with her lover Aegisthus until she, in turn, was murdered by her son Orestes. Her legend, for the Greek male, became a nightmare of the extremes of a wife's treachery and aggression against her husband, although Clytemnestra had suffered extreme emotional abuse from Agamemnon who had sacrificed their daughter, Iphigeneia, at the outset of the war to gain a favorable wind for the fleet and earlier had murdered her first husband and two other children.

COALITION OF LABOR UNION WOMEN (CLUW). A women's caucus within the American Federation of Labor-Congress of Industrial Organizations (AFL-CIO), established in 1974 to seek equality for women within the union movement and in the larger society. The CLUW has urged greater union efforts to organize women in service occupations, inclusion of women in union leadership, and more active support of women's issues by the AFL-CIO. In 1980 CLUW President Joyce Miller became the first woman elected to the AFL-CIO Executive Council. Under pressure from the CLUW, the AFL-CIO has vigorously lobbied on feminist issues such as child care, comparable worth, the Equal Rights Amendment, family leave, and pregnancy discrimination (qq.v.). Its 16,000 members constitute approximately one percent of female union members, primarily those already within the leadership ranks of union committees and local office. Despite this upper-status bias, the CLUW effectively serves as a network for female union members and a liaison with other women's groups and the AFL-CIO.

CODE NAPOLÉON DE 1804. The civil code of France establishing the family, not the individual, as the basic unit of society and giving the husband as "head" control over all family property. It stated that the wife owed obedience to her husband and was barred from public life unless her husband permitted or required such involvement. The code was amended during the late nineteenth and early twentieth centuries to extend certain rights to married women and between 1965 and 1975 the Napoleonic family code was almost completely rewritten to give married women equal rights in the family.

CODE SHIFTING. The ability of women to speak and think like men. Since women are socialized within a male-defined culture, women develop the skill of understanding and using language like men do. A hazard exists for women when code shifting becomes code switching and women internalize the male code and can no longer identify with women's ways of speaking and thinking.

CODEPENDENCY. A relationship between two people that includes excessive dependency upon one another, so that each is expected to meet unhealthy emotional needs of the other. This term is often used to describe the relationship between an alcoholic and his or her partner, where not only is the partner's life consumed in meeting the needs of the alcoholic, but the alcoholic also meets the needs of the partner to be needed. As codependency became increasingly defined as a female neurosis, some feminists became wary of a possible cult of the victimization of women (q.v.).

COIGNET, CLARISSE (1823-?). A leader of La Morale Indépendante, a French movement that wanted to establish the independence of morality from both religion and science. Her major work is *La Morale Indépendante dans Son Principe et Son*

Objet (The Independent Morality in Its Principal and in Its Object), in which she argues that human beings are the creators of morality. Part of that morality involves the transformation of women's roles so that they are no longer the property of their husbands. They can remain wives and mothers but have respect as human beings.

COLLECTIVE, FEMINIST. An organization based on principles of radical participatory democracy and equality characterized by lack of hierarchy and consensual decision-making. These communities operate with only minimal specialization of labor and rules and an equal sharing of profits and rewards. Many women's liberation movement (q.v.) groups were organized as collectives, as were the first feminist counter-culture (q.v.) institutions.

COLONIZATION, EFFECT UPON WOMEN. A feminist critique of the deleterious effect of colonization upon women. Colonization usurps the political-economic structure of the colonized nation and imposes a regime often based on conscripted male labor. Families must accommodate the loss of able-bodied men who may be furloughed only long enough to impregnate their wives again (reproducing the labor force). The women are left in rural areas to raise crops and maintain homes alone for most of the year. Market enterprises are restricted by the colonial agents, curtailing women's independent incomes. Political and religious structures that may have provided complementary governance with female officials are usually ignored or replaced with a hierarchical patriarchal government. Racist policies sometimes encourage colonial agents to co-habit with local concubines (whom they were forbidden to marry) and sometimes encourage them to bring wives from the home country and establish homes in government compounds where local women serve as domestics and nannies. The imposition of the colonial government's culture denigrates colonial peoples and frequently devalues their arts, especially those practiced by women. Independence movements have encouraged revivals or development of indigenous arts, but global economics have prevented restoration of pre-conquest political-economic patterns. (*See also* Development, Women in.)

"COLONIZATION OF THE FEMALE." A phrase used in feminist literary criticism to refer to a male author's appropriation of female subjectivities or experiences, such as the equation of masculine literary production with giving birth.

COLOR, WOMEN OF. A phrase used in the United States to describe women who are of African, Asian-Pacific, Hispanic, or Native American heritage. This umbrella term recognizes that common experiences of racism and sexism (qq.v.) unite these women across vast differences of culture and language. The intersectionality (q.v.) of race, class, and gender in their daily lives is the principal framework for discussing racial-ethnic women. (*See also* Oppression, Interstructuring of.)

COMBAT EXCLUSION RULE. The traditional policy of the US government barring women from all military service with combat and field exposure despite the fact that combat duty accelerates military promotions. (*See also Rostker v. Goldberg.*)

"COMFORT WOMEN." A term used to describe Asian women forced into prostitution (q.v.) by the Japanese Army during World War II. As many as 200,000 women from six Asian nations were sent to military bases, where they were daily raped and beaten by soldiers. Although many women died in captivity, some by murder, survivors began to speak out in the early 1990's and three Korean women filed a compensation suit in Japan in 1991. After demonstrations by Korean women, Japanese Prime Minister Kiichi Miyazawa publicly apologized for the episode.

COMMISSION FOR RESPONSIVE DEMOCRACY. Group formed by the National Organization for Women (NOW) (q.v.) in 1989 to investigate the feasibility of a new US political party. After two years of hearings held throughout the country, the 21st Century Party, the Nation's Equality Party, was established and was endorsed at NOW's 1992 National Conference. The new party hopes to attract individuals from groups traditionally underrepresented within the political system: feminists, racial and ethnic minorities, peace and environmental activists. This initiative has received virtually no support from the media, women in elected office, and other liberal feminist (q.v.) groups.

COMMITTEE FOR THE EQUALITY OF WOMEN *see* ROYAL COMMISSION ON THE STATUS OF WOMEN IN CANADA (RCSW)

COMMITTEE OF MOTHERS AND FAMILIES OF PRISONERS, THE DISAPPEARED, AND VICTIMS OF POLITICAL ASSASSINATION OF EL SALVADOR, MONSIGNOR OSCAR ARNULFO ROMERO (COMITÉ DE MADRES, COMADRES). A Salvadoran human rights organization established on December 24, 1977, by 12 mothers with the support of Archbishop Oscar Romero. Its purpose was to protest against political violence and death squad activity in El Salvador. In 1978 its members staged their first public demonstration. By the mid-1980's, as the violence grew, its membership increased to 400. Like other mothers' organizations in Latin America, this Committee of Mothers utilized the traditional sexual roles of mother and wife as the basis for national and international political and human rights activism. CoMadres received the 1984 Robert F. Kennedy Human Rights Award. Its leadership, including Maria Teresa Tula, however, was denied entry into the United States to receive the honor. Tula was later detained and tortured by Salvadoran security forces after the United States embassy in San Salvador labeled the group a Communist front.

COMMITTEE OF SOVIET WOMEN (CSW). The official women's group of the Communist Party of the Soviet Union. It was a successor of the sponsored women's movement active in the post-revolutionary period but disbanded in 1930 when female equality had, in theory, been achieved. With the resurgence of feminism in the West, members of the CSW, chaired by the first woman astronaut, Valentina Tereshkova, represented the nation at international women's conferences.

COMMITTEE ON THE ELIMINATION OF DISCRIMINATION AGAINST WOMEN (CEDAW) *see* CONVENTION ON THE ELIMINATION OF ALL FORMS OF DISCRIMINATION AGAINST WOMEN

COMMITTEE ON THE STATUS OF WOMEN IN INDIA (CSWI). A body established by the Indian government in 1971. In 1975 it released its influencial report, *Towards Equality*. Its data on women's status in religion and the family, in health care, and under law were new to many well-educated citizens and led to pressures for new public policies and heightened interest in empowering women through community organization and cultural change.

COMMUNAL. A term introduced into the psychological literature by David Bakan to denote an orientation toward affiliation, a quality of personality, or a lifestyle that emphasizes human relationship and concern for others. Motivation theorists find women more frequently display this motivation style which is exemplified by an orientation toward working together and feeling a sense of motivation or satisfaction with goals if the persons one is working with are successful. This motivational style difference is cited as a reason women are more likely to pursue the helping professions.

COMMUNES *see* SEPARATISM

COMMUNITY PROPERTY *see* MARITAL/COMMUNITY PROPERTY LEGISLATION

COMMUTER MARRIAGE. A union in which both husband and wife are employed in different locales, thus requiring the maintenance of two residences and co-habitation only during work holidays. Such arrangements have become increasingly common as women have attained professional and managerial positions that are not easily coordinated with a spouse in a similarly demanding career.

COMPARABLE WORTH. The principle that men and women should receive equal compensation when employed in positions that require comparable, rather than identical, skill, responsibility, and effort. The concept evolved from the equal pay for equal work (q.v.) doctrine in response to the fact that traditionally female occupations receive lower compensation than traditionally male occupations. This results in positions such as mechanics, janitors, and bus drivers receiving higher wages than primary school educators, nurses, and child-care workers. In the mid-1970's, US feminists adopted pay equity as a goal and were successful in gaining comparable worth policies in several states and local governments. The opposition of the Reagan administration, the loss of a federal appeals court case in 1985, and a perceived conflict with market-set wages prevented further adoption of the policy. (*See also* Occupational Segregation.)

COMPLIANCE GAINING STRATEGIES. A term for stereotypically feminine strategies of persuasion. Compliance gaining strategies include undirectional ones such as asking for help, withdrawing, or telling of a need and also indirect ones such as hinting, setting a mood, or diversion. These strategies are understood as characteristic of people who are in a less powerful position than their conversational partner. These strategies grow out of the situational intersection of power and gender.

COMPULSORY STERILIZATION *see* STERILIZATION ABUSE

CONCERNED WOMEN FOR AMERICA (CWA). A religious fundamentalist anti-feminist (q.v.) women's organization founded in 1979 by Beverly LaHaye (q.v.). The group, with its almost 2,500 local chapters and a mailing list of 600,000 names, claims to be the largest women's organization in the United States. The CWA is actively opposed to abortion (q.v.), secular humanism in the schools, and homosexuality and often uses litigation as a tactic.

CONGRESS TO UNITE WOMEN. A regional conference of women's liberation (q.v.) groups held in New York City, November 21-23, 1969. The Congress was the first large meeting of local feminist groups and over 500 women attended. A press conference held at the conclusion announced the movement to the nation. Later Congresses were held in other cities and parts of the country.

CONGRESSIONAL CAUCUS FOR WOMEN'S ISSUES (CCWI). A group formed in 1977 as the Congresswomen's Caucus within the US House of Representatives. Its purpose was to facilitate the exchange of information on women's policy issues between female members of Congress, the bureaucracy, and feminist organizations and to organize support for pending legislation and monitor implementation after enactment. In 1981 the name was changed and membership was opened to Congressmen. Only Congresswomen, however, may serve on the executive committee that sets policy. The Women's Research and Education Institute serves as a separately incorporated but associated policy center.

CONGRESSIONAL UNION *see* PAUL, ALICE

CONGRESSWOMEN'S CAUCUS *see* CONGRESSIONAL CAUCUS FOR WOMEN'S ISSUES

CONSCIOUSNESS-RAISING (C-R). Activities concerned with increasing a victim's awareness of discrimination, oppression, and sexual harassment (q.v.). A key component of feminist therapy and the early women's liberation groups (qq.v.), C-R is tied to the notion that many of the stumbling blocks for women are social in origin. C-R has been most often associated with groups in which women could share their experiences.

CONTAGIOUS DISEASES ACTS. English legislation of 1864, 1866, and 1869 which authorized the police to detain and subject to a medical examination any woman suspected of being a prostitute (q.v.) in order to guard the health of military personnel. Earlier attempts to subject male soldiers to such examinations had been rejected; instead, the policy sought to assure that male sexual needs could be safely met. Under strong opposition from a Victorian feminist group led by Josephine Butler (q.v.), the acts were suspended in 1883 and repealed in 1886. From their participation in this and other moral reform movements, British women began to demand the vote.

CONTEMPORARY FEMINIST MOVEMENT *see* NEW FEMINIST MOVEMENT

CONTRACEPTIVES *see* BIRTH CONTROL PILL; FAMILY PLANNING

CONVENTION ON THE ELIMINATION OF ALL FORMS OF DISCRIMINATION AGAINST WOMEN. An international treaty adopted by the United Nations General Assembly on December 18, 1979 and ratified or acceded to by over 115 nations. An additional 11 nations, including the United States, are signatories. The Women's Convention is a statement of women's human rights and a framework for women's participation in the development process. Ratifying governments are obligated to eliminate sex discrimination and to file periodic reports on that effort with the Committee on the Elimination of Discrimination Against Women, an independent group of experts established under the Convention.

CONVERSATIONAL STYLE. A habitual mode of interpersonal communication. Feminist scholarship in communication has shown that women and men differ in their approach to conversation. Men tend to view conversation as an opportunity to compete, while women tend to converse cooperatively. Women use direct eye contact, face their partners, give nonverbal support (such as "yes," "uh huh" and smiling) and chain from one topic to another. Women's conversational style initiates, develops, and maintains relationships.

COUNTER-CULTURE, FEMINIST. The alternative women-owned institutions that provide services to other women and help to create a women's community. The myriad of such enterprises include bookstores and publishing houses, restaurants and coffee houses, churches, record companies and music festivals, theater groups, day care centers, credit unions and banks, art galleries, and professional and business services such as health care, legal aid, and car repair. These institutions offer a refuge from a male-dominated world, a challenge to the legitimacy of this system, and a promise of a women's culture based on female values. (*See also* Cultural Feminism.)

COUNTERFEIT CLINICS *see* FAKE CLINICS

COURTESY TITLES *see* MS.

COVERTURE. The common law doctrine that, with marriage, a woman's separate status disappeared and she became the legal responsibility of her husband. She had no right to own property, control her own wages, sue or be sued, or sign contracts. The first break with this doctrine came in England and the United States with the adoption of Married Women's Property Acts (q.v.).

CRAIG V. BOREN, 429 US 190 (1976). A decision of the US Supreme Court that established a new standard for evaluating laws that make distinctions on the basis of sex. At issue in this case was the constitutionality of an Oklahoma statute prohibiting the sale of non-intoxicating beer to males under the age of 21 and females under the age of 18. The Court concluded that Oklahoma's scheme failed to satisfy the new intermediate standard: that it be "substantially related" to "important" governmental objectives. The issue before the Court was whether the differential treatment of males and females violated the Equal Protection (q.v.) Clause in the Fourteenth Amendment. Some have criticized the failure of the Supreme Court to justify the intermediate standard it applied and questioned why a classification burdening males, who are hardly a disadvantaged or disempowered group, should for the first time be subject to a heightened measure of constitutional scrutiny. The intermediate standard recognizes the legitimacy of some gender classifications without a theory about which are legitimate and why.

CROSS, AMANDA *see* HEILBRUN, CAROLYN

CULT OF DOMESTICITY OR TRUE WOMANHOOD. A concept that emerged in the nineteenth century, particularly in England and the United States, extolling motherhood and the domestic sphere (q.v.) as a woman's appropriate and important areas of activity. Advocates often talked about the moral superiority of women and frequently argued that the "hand that rocks the cradle rules the world." This bourgeois movement idealized the domestic femininity of women, glorified women's role as homemaker, and spirited thinking from religion to science. Central virtues of piety, purity, and domesticity were considered by-products of nurturance and resulted in women's "natural" moral and spiritual superiority. Coinciding with the shift to extradomestic production, this view also described women as physically and cognitively "weaker" and less fit for the world of work. Feminists claim that these ideas contributed to the devaluation of women's labor and economic dependence on men and that they ignored the need (and reality) of women who performed wage labor (especially women of color [q.v.] and of the working class).

CULT OF FEMININITY *see* CULT OF DOMESTICITY OR TRUE WOMANHOOD

CULT OF VICTIMIZATION *see* VICTIMIZATION OF WOMEN

CULTURAL FEMINISM. A later branch and transformation of radical feminism (q.v.) that celebrates female differences and advocates the creation of a separatist feminist counter-culture (q.v.) in which women's superior nurturing and pacific values can transform society. In contrast to difference feminism (q.v.), this tradition is non-political and focuses instead on individual change. The theory is rooted in the writings of Margaret Fuller and Charlotte Perkins Gilman (qq.v.) and is partly responsible for the renewed interest in matriarchy and the goddess (qq.v.).

CYCLE OF ABUSE. A term used by theorists who study domestic violence (q.v.) to describe a pattern in which a batterer commits violence, repents, and is forgiven. A peaceful honeymoon phase ensues, followed by a period of escalating tension. Finally, tension increases to the point where battery occurs again and the cycle starts over. The term "cycle of abuse" is also used to describe a behavior pattern in which those who have been battered as children batter their own children in turn, establishing a generational cycle of abuse. (*See also* Battered Woman Syndrome.)

-D-

DALKON SHIELD. An intrauterine birth control device (IUD) marketed by A. H. Robins, 1970-74, and linked with perforated uteri, miscarriages, stillbirths, infections causing permanent sterility, and several deaths. Although the product was taken off the market in 1974, a worldwide recall of the shields still being worn was not begun until 1984 after a ten-year campaign by the National Women's Health Network (q.v.). In 1985 Robins declared bankruptcy after losing several lawsuits brought by injured women. As a part of a reorganization plan, a trust fund of $2.5 billion was established to pay claims to almost 200,000 women.

DALY, MARY (1928-). An American theologian and self-described radical feminist (q.v.) "Nag-Gnostic philosopher." Daly writes and lectures to expose what she sees as lies of the patriarchal "foreground" and to replace them with truths of her radical feminist "background." Her many books explore issues in ethics, religion, and the place of women in Christianity and the church. Daly's critiques of patriarchy's (q.v.) myths and languages have become progressively more radical as her language play becomes more "outrageous." *The Church and the Second Sex* (1968) argues for equality of the sexes within the Catholic Church, while *Beyond God the Father* (1973) envisions a new definition of God that will create a space of "human becoming." *Gyn/Ecology* (1978) calls for a radical feminist meta-ethics with which any woman can begin "re-fusing" patriarchal history and "dis-covering" her own history as well as its connections with other women's histories. *Pure Lust* (1984) suggests an alternative to "phallic lust" that will capture the humor, hope, and harmony of women who challenge patriarchy. Her other books include *Wickedary* (q.v.) (1987) and the autobiographical *Outercourse: The Be-Dazzling Voyage* (1992).

DANAIDS. According to Greek legend, 50 ill-fated sisters who were forced to marry their cousins, the sons of Aegyptus. All but one sister (Hypermnestra) murdered their bridegrooms on their collective wedding night at the urging of their father Danaus, who feared treachery from his nephews. Although the sisters were purified of the murder of their husbands on earth, they paid for this crime in the underworld by forever having to carry water in leaky vessels. Whatever the religious or poetic origins of their curious legend may have been, the Danaids represented to the Greek male the threat of wide-scale female deception and rebellion.

DATE RAPE. Sexual intercourse forced by an acquaintance. Often the incident occurs during a regular social engagement such as a "date," in which the victim is coerced or manipulated into sexual intercourse. The perpetrator ignores protests or interprets them as encouragement. The victim may not interpret such an event as a "real rape" and tends not to report it. Because of feminist consciousness-raising (q.v.) about date rape, many US colleges now hold student orientations on the topic. (*See also* Victimization of Women.)

DAUGHTERS OF BILITIS *see* MARTIN, DEL

DAVIES, (SARAH) EMILY (1830-1921). An English feminist and educational reformer with the Society for Promoting the Employment of Women. In 1861 she became editor of the feminist *English Woman's Journal.* She was active in the suffrage cause and helped to organize the first suffrage petition presented to Parliament by John Stuart Mill (q.v.) in 1866. Her opinions were published in *Thoughts on Some Questions Relating to Women 1860-1908.*

DAVIS, ANGELA (1944-). An African-American radical feminist (q.v.) and member of the US Communist Party. In 1969 she was offered an appointment as lecturer in philosophy at UCLA, but the California Board of Regents refused to confirm the position because of Davis' politics. Davis was also involved with the "Soledad Brothers," imprisoned African-American activists. Both brothers died in a shootout in the Marin County courthouse (August 1970), and the guns used by Jonathan Jackson to attempt to free his brothers were found to be registered to Davis. She was charged with kidnapping, murder and conspiracy, and was eventually arrested in New York. Her trial (1971-72) lasted 13 weeks before she was acquitted of all charges. Davis published her autobiography in 1974 and then returned to teaching ethnic studies at San Francisco University. She is also author of *Women, Race, and Class* (1981) and *If They Come in the Morning: Voices of Resistance* (1971) regarding the situation of political prisoners in the United States.

DAVISON, EMILY WILDING (1872-1913). A British Women's Social and Political Union activist who threw herself in front of the king's horse on Derby Day, May 31, 1913 and was trampled to death. This event has come to epitomize the extremism and escalating violence of the militant wing of the English suffragist movement led by the Pankhursts (q.v).

DAY CARE. Child care facilities for preschool and primary school age children. The current shortage of day care facilities is due to the increase in women's labor force participation and the lack of social policy and planning. Many organizations provide day care services or offer day care vouchers as part of employee benefit packages. In countries such as the United States, without an extensive system for out-of-home child care, new feminists (q.v.) almost immediately made government-subsidized day care a core goal. (*See also* ABC Bill; Work-Family Conflict.)

DE LA CRUZ, MARÍA. An advocate of women's suffrage and emancipation in Chile and founder of the Partido Femenino Chileno (Chilean Women's Party) in 1946. In 1950 de la Cruz was the first Chilean woman to run (unsuccessfully) for national political office. She helped to build a women's movement that was a key to the presidential election of 1952.

DE LA CRUZ, SOR JUANA IRES (1648-1695). The first woman to voice the "feminist protest" in Latin America. Sor Juana defended and affirmed women and thus affirmed herself. Her poetry is an expression of her revolutionary sensibility. She spoke out against traditions and myths that enslave women, such as the cult of virginity and the double standard (q.v.). In her time Sor Juana gained wide recognition, but it was mainly due to attempts to silence her and make her conform. In 1693 she wrote a letter to the Bishop of Puebla that constituted a powerful declaration of the rights of women. She championed the equality of the capabilities of men and women during the seventeenth century in Mexico.

DEBORAH. In the Hebrew Bible, judge and military leader. Feminists stress that unlike her compatriot Barak she displays steadfast authority, courage, and faith in battle.

DECADE FOR WOMEN *see* INTERNATIONAL WOMEN'S YEAR

DECLARATION OF SENTIMENTS *see* SENECA FALLS CONVENTION

DECONSTRUCTION. A theory of meaning in philosophy, literary criticism or other disciplines in the humanities that attempts to describe the limits of understanding. Deconstruction tests the assumptions underlying intellectual arguments in order to question the supposedly "self-evident" claims on which they are based. Instead of trying to find a way of understanding new phenomena and placing them into a "bounded" context, deconstruction seeks to expose the unexamined premises that define the supposedly new phenomena, their paradigms and boundaries. Deconstruction typically critiques unexamined notions of meaning, such as "God," "the center," "origins," "time," "the self," "Nature," the "subject." Feminism has had a stake in deconstruction insofar as the methodology has exploded long-held tenets that have provided the undergirding of the patriarchy (q.v.). Once the subject is decentered and viewed as a social construction, gender itself can be viewed as an artificial construct, a play of signifiers. (*See also* Derrida, Jacques.)

DEFICIT PERSPECTIVE. An argument, developed by Fern Johnson, that this view permeates much of the research done on women's and men's language. Those who adopt the deficit approach posit that women's language is inherently inferior to men's. In other words, women's speech is deficient in comparison to men's. A variant of this perspective, the new deficit approach, takes the position that while women's speech is deficient, it can be remedied and women can learn to speak like men. Johnson and other feminists argue that both these perspectives cause negative interpretations to be applied to women's speech.

DEITIES, FEMALE. Expressions of divinity in female form, including Ishtar, Isis, Gaia, the Hebrew Bible's personification of Wisdom, and the Iroquois Grandmother of the god. Scholars debate how communities' perception of female strength and power in the divine realm has reflected and/or influenced the actual historical status of women. Although many scholars assert that goddesses (q.v) were invented by men for the purpose of exerting control over women, one could challenge this by pondering a second century invocation to Isis that proclaims: "for all time; thou didst make the power of women equal to that of men."

DEL-EM. A simple menstrual-extraction suction device, invented by Californian Lorraine Rothman in 1971, to allow women to perform early abortions (q.v.) for each other. Although never widely used in the US for self-help (q.v.) abortions after legalization in 1973, the device is used for therapeutic reasons and convenience and has been introduced in Latin America as a self-help abortion technique.

DELL, FLOYD (1887-1969). An American novelist, poet and critic who led the New Renaissance movement in Greenwich Village, pre-World War I. He was a male feminist who examined prototypes of women in representing them as world builders. He is the author of *Women as World Builder* (1913), which demanded full equality for women.

DEMETER. According to Greek myth, the venerable goddess of agriculture and the cultivated earth. Her annual separation from and reunion with her daughter, Persephone, the goddess of the seeds and tender shoots, who spends one-third of the year in the underworld with her husband Hades and the remainder of the year on earth with her mother, is a myth of the earth's seasonal fertility. Demeter and Persephone (also known as Kore) were central figures in the Eleusinian Mysteries, which linked the eternal cycle of vegetation with the immortality of the soul. The myth of Demeter and Persephone affirms the life-bestowing role of the female as well as the sanctity of the mother-daughter bond. Demeter and Persephone were called Ceres and Proserpina by the Romans.

DEPENDENT PERSONALITY DISORDER. A diagnosis often given to an individual, usually a woman, who is generally passive in relationships, has low self-esteem, and tends to tolerate abusiveness. Feminists object to this behavior pattern being labeled a "personality disorder" because such a diagnostic label further stigmatizes what many women experience as learned female sex role (q.v.) behavior.

DERANIYAGALA, EZLYNN (1908-1973). The first Sri Lankan woman barrister and long-time president of the All-Ceylon Women's Conference (1944), the core national organization for women's rights. She twice served as president of the International Alliance of Women (q.v.).

DERRIDA, JACQUES (1930-). One of the most influential of living philosophers, generally considered one of the founders of deconstruction (q.v.), a major theoretical movement that has had enormous effects on philosophy, literary criticism, psychoanalysis, theology, linguistics, and art. Born in Algiers and educated in France, Derrida is not a feminist nor is he sympathetic to advancing the feminist agenda, but several of his terms and philosophical strategies have been appropriated by feminist critics--specifically his attack on the notion of a "center" of meaning, the "logos." Derrida denounced this desire for a center as "logocentrism" (in his *On Grammatology*, 1976), and it was this notion that was adapted and modified by the French feminists as "phallogocentrism" (qq.v.). Derrida also coined the term "différance" to explain the divided nature of the sign, while feminist theorists have adapted it to explain the undecidable nature of gender constructions. Characteristic applications of Derrida's theories to feminism include a denunciation of all binary oppositions (culture/nature, male/female), an assault on the notion that there are any determinate bounds, limits or margins to a text (or a gender), and the idea that supposedly literal terms are themselves metaphors whose metaphoric meanings have been forgotten.

DES (DIETHYLSTILBESTROL). A synthetic progesterone prescribed to as many as six million American women, 1941-71, to prevent miscarriage, despite evidence that women taking DES were more likely to miscarry. A link was established in 1971 to unusual vaginal and cervical cancer in young women exposed in utero to DES. Feminist groups mounted an outreach program to warn DES daughters about the need for early cancer screening. Even so, DES use increased in the early 1970's when it was prescribed as a "morning-after pill" to prevent conception. Cases of vaginal and cervical cancer due to DES exposure have declined in the 1990's, but DES continues to be marketed as an abortifacient.

DESPARD, CHARLOTTE FRENCH (1844-1939). A British suffragist who stood apart from the mainstream movement because of her claim that even a partial franchise would be of benefit to both the wealthy class of women and the working classes. Strongly attached to the Labour Party, Despard broke with the Women's Social and Political Union (WSPU) in 1907 and formed the Women's Freedom League. Her views on feminism were colored by her primary concern, the problems of women and children. Her approach to feminism was spiritual rather than materialist; she argued in one of her speeches that spiritual love was at the core of the women's movement because she saw the movement as an expression of women's spiritual nature.

DEVELOPMENT, WOMEN IN. A feminist critique of modernization in the Third World that suggests a decrease in the status of women. Although women there produce most domestically consumed food, development funds for agricultural equipment and training are targeted to men. With the widespread destruction of forests and tillable land, men must migrate to cities, leaving women to engage in even more difficult subsistence farming. Those women who also migrate must accept the lowest-paying of urban jobs. (*See also* Colonization, Effect Upon Women.)

D'HERICOURT, JENNY (1809-1875). A French physician who began publishing feminist articles in 1855. Some of these denounce Proudhon's argument of the "exceptional woman" who does not fit misogynist conceptions. In her work *A Woman's Philosophy of Woman*, she used her medical knowledge to argue areas of morality and social and political philosophy. She refuted Michelet who said that menstruation is proof that women are weak and inferior. She moved to the United States later and worked with the leaders of the women's rights movement.

DIALECTIC OF SEX, THE. Published in 1970, this feminist work by Shulamith Firestone (q.v.), argues that the power of the patriarchy (q.v.) is located in the biological inequality of the sexes. For Firestone, the only way for women to escape their subjugation is to use technology to divorce themselves and their bodies from the tyranny of reproduction. Once the biological family is destroyed as a reproductive unit, it will also be destroyed as an economic unit, thereby freeing women from unpaid labor in the home. Firestone advocated an androgynous (q.v.) culture that would be "more than a marriage, rather an abolition of the cultural categories themselves, a mutual cancellation--a matter-antimatter explosion, ending with a poof! culture itself" (see her *Dialectic of Sex*).

DIETHYLSTILBESTROL *see* DES

DIFFERENCE FEMINISM. A belief that the sexes differ in significant ways and that some women's values are superior and should be celebrated. The writings of Carol Gilligan and Mary Daly (qq.v.) have been especially important in this re-examination of women's traditional role. Some feminists fear that any retreat from equality feminism (q.v.) will only reinforce gender stereotypes (q.v.) and derail the movement for change. Many feminist legal scholars, however, argue for differential treatment of women; without policy accommodations for childbirth and child care, they feel that women can never be equal in society.

DINAH. In the Hebrew Bible, daughter of Leah and Jacob. She is raped by Shechem of the Hivites, which precipitates a skirmish between the sons of Jacob and the Hivites, breaking the tenuous peace in the area. A voiceless victim in the account, feminists stress that she is noteworthy not only because of Shechem's abuse, but because of her neglect by her father and the use of her plight to justify her brothers' revenge.

DINNER PARTY, THE. An artwork unveiled by Judy Chicago in 1979. It traces the history of Western women through 39 carved or sculptured place settings grouped around a (46-foot) triangular banquet table. A tile floor lists 999 women of achievement. Because of Chicago's usage of sexual imagery, the installation has been controversial since its first exhibition. It is currently housed in the Carnegie Library of the University of the District of Columbia.

DINNERSTEIN, DOROTHY (1923-1992). The author of *The Mermaid and the Minotaur: Sexual Arrangements and Human*

Malaise (1977). Dinnerstein argued that the oppression of women is caused by their monopoly of and obsession with the act of mothering. Because women remember their own mothers as so powerful, they themselves spend most of their adult lives trying to reject their own mothers and all things feminine. But because of her sexual similarity to her mother, a girl can never fully escape her mother and thus never achieves the autonomy and power that a male achieves. The only way out of this malaise, according to Dinnerstein, is dual parenting, which will have the effect of breaking down the sexual divisions that now are so rigid and confining to both sexes.

DISADVANTAGES APPROACH. A feminist legal approach which asserts that less attention should be paid to differences and more attention should be given to disadvantages stemming from them in order to further the goal of eliminating disadvantages experienced by oppressed members of society. (*See also* Difference Feminism.)

DISPLACED HOMEMAKER. A woman who, after spending many years as an unpaid family caretaker, has been abandoned, divorced, or widowed. Ineligible for a family support pension because her children are no longer minors, she usually will be qualified only for low-wage work, with few or no benefits. In 1974 Tish Sommers and Laurie Shields formed the Alliance for Displaced Homemakers, which sensitized the US feminist movement to the special problems of full-time homemakers. By the 1990's over 1,000 government-funded programs were providing job training and counseling for displaced homemakers.

DIVORCE *see* NO-FAULT DIVORCE

DIVORCE AND MATRIMONIAL CAUSES ACT (1857). An English law that made civil divorce available, apart from religious courts, and established some property rights for married women, the first break with coverture (q.v.). The separate spheres doctrine was maintained, however, and women could be divorced for a single act of adultery, whereas men had to commit some other offense in addition to adultery to give a wife grounds for divorce.

DOHM, HEDWIG (1833-1919). A German feminist and writer who rejected the contemporary bourgeois feminist view that women were destined for motherhood. Personally acquainted with the major literary figures of her age, she wrote about housework, motherhood, childrearing, and sexuality in works that are both highly insightful and viciously witty, demonstrating the need for economic, intellectual, and political independence of women. Her works include *Jesuitry in the Household* (1873), *The Nature and Rights of Women* (1874), and *The Antifeminist* (1902).

DOLLE MINA (MAD MINA). A direct action socialist feminist (q.v.) group founded in the Netherlands in 1970 and named after the earlier feminist leader Wilhelmina Drucker (q.v.). Its widely publicized protests on abortion (q.v.), education, and public toilets led to its name becoming a generic term for any Dutch feminist.

DOMESTIC FICTION. A predominantly novelistic literary genre dating in Britain and America from the eighteenth century. Domestic fiction advanced tenets of domestic ideology, including separation of spheres, the idealization of motherhood, and the "angel in the house" (q.v.) figure.

DOMESTIC LABOR *see* HIDDEN WORK

DOMESTIC PARTNERSHIPS. Long-term non-marital companion relationships particularly involving, although not limited to, gay and lesbian (q.v.) couples. As of December 1992, 19 American cities had enacted ordinances affording domestic partners certain rights traditionally reserved for legally married couples if they register for licenses at City Hall. The rights are usually limited to visiting privileges at city hospitals and jails, access to school records of partners' children, and qualifying for dependent health care coverage on one partner's employer sponsored insurance program. To obtain a license, generally domestic partners must have lived together for at least six months, not be closely related by blood, and intend to remain in "a relationship of mutual support, caring and commitment."

DOMESTIC SPHERE (PUBLIC/PRIVATE DISTINCTION). One manifestation of the oppositional dualism pervasive in Western cultural tradition, the conventional dichotomy between public and private/domestic. This dichotomy was used in Classical Greece to separate the activities of men (citizens) in the *agora* (public market/meeting space in the center of the *polis*) from the domain inhabited by women and slaves behind the walls of the private dwelling. Men were properly engaged in business and politics, women (and slaves) in nurturing activities to sustain and reproduce men. Feminist theorists today note that the distinction between "public" and "domestic" is neither universal nor necessary to human societies. Its dominance in industrial capitalist nations is linked to the practice of maximizing profits by eliminating homemaking from the category of waged labor.

DOMESTIC VIOLENCE. Abuse that occurs in the home inflicted by family or other household members. Weaker persons such as women, children, and the elderly are most likely to be victims. Perpetrators are likely to be those household members who are physically strongest. Domestic violence is a learned pattern of behavior, so that victims are likely, in turn, to abuse others weaker than themselves. (*See also* Battered Woman Syndrome; Cycle of Abuse; Women's Battery Shelter.)

DOMINANCE *see* MALE DOMINANCE

DOMINANCE APPROACH. A feminist legal theory advanced by Catharine MacKinnon (q.v.) and founded on the premise that it is impossible to know whether there are important differences between the sexes that have not been created by male dominance (q.v.). Advocates assert that any law, practice, or policy that perpetuates the subordination of women should be repealed.

DOUBLE SHIFT. A sardonic feminist reference to the longer workday of a woman who is employed full-time in the paid labor force and continues to perform the bulk of domestic labor. After completing a full day's work outside the home, the woman begins the second shift as a wife and/or mother. In marriages between two full-time employees, the fact that most women earn less than men often means that the women will get no more than minimal assistance with housework from their spouses.

DOUBLE STANDARD. Gender expectations regarding maintenance of virginity, marital fidelity, or other restrictions on sexual behavior. Feminists object to females and males being held to different standards of behavior.

DOWRY see BRIDEPRICE/BRIDEWEALTH/BRIDESERVICE

DOWRY DEATHS. A practice prevalent in India, whereby young married women are abused and then set on fire, poisoned, drowned, or strangled by their husbands or in-laws because their dowry is viewed as inadequate. The deaths are usually classified by police as suicides or accidents. The husband is then free to re-marry and collect a new dowry. India has prohibited dowry since 1961, but the law is poorly enforced. Since the Indian women's movement began to publicize dowry deaths in the late 1970's, local police have established special Anti-Dowry and Crimes Against Women units to investigate domestic violence (q.v.).

DRESS FOR SUCCESS. A clothing style for businesswomen featuring well-tailored suits that allow women to be taken seriously in the workplace. The originator of the term was male fashion consultant John T. Molloy, whose bestseller *The Women's Dress for Success Book* (1977) argued that clothing that emphasizes sexual attractiveness is a deterrent to business success. For the next decade, annual sales of suits rose and dresses declined. Feminists welcomed this trend in that suits were often better-made and remained fashionable for a longer period of time. By the late 1980's, however, female executive-dressing was criticized by fashion writers as boring and masculine.

DRESS REFORM. A nineteenth-century movement to destroy the sexual division of labor by freeing women from restrictive fashions that tied them to the home. US feminist advocates of this new practical attire included Amelia Bloomer, Lucy Stone, and Elizabeth Cady Stanton (qq.v.), who believed that since men and women had a common nature their dress should also be similar.

DRUCKER, WILHELMINA (MINA) ELISABETH. The leading Dutch feminist of the nineteenth century and founder of De Vrije Vrouwenbeweging (Association of Free Women) in 1889. She edited the group's journal, *Evolution.* Her nickname was Dolle Mina (Mad Mina) due to her fervent support of women's rights.

DUAL CAREER COUPLES. Couples in which both spouses individually pursue work and career roles while simultaneously maintaining a family life. It was originally viewed as a nontraditional relationship, but with the increase of women in the labor force, the relationship is now commonplace. (*See also* Mommy Track; Work-Family Conflict.)

DUAL LABOR MARKET. The division of the labor market into the primary sector, which has high paying jobs (usually held by men), and the secondary sector (dominated by women and minorities), which has lower paying jobs. Women and minorities are trapped in secondary labor markets by discrimination, sexism (q.v.), and the inflexibility of the primary labor market to accommodate special employment considerations.

DUAL ROLE *see* DOUBLE SHIFT

DWORKIN, ANDREA (1946-). An American radical feminist (q.v.), called "one of the most compelling voices in the Women's Movement." Her writings are concerned with questions of sexuality, sexual roles that men and women play, ♦nd sexual deviations. She is the author of *Intercourse* (1987), which considers the psychology of sex and sexual roles, and *Letters from a War Zone* (1988), which considers sexual discrimination, pornography (q.v.) and feminism. Her *Our Blood* calls for the abandonment of the quest for sexual equality. Dworkin now believes that more radical solutions are required to achieve a complete social realignment of the sexes. She is also noted for her co-authorship of the Minneapolis Pornography Ordinance (q.v.).

-E-

EAGLE FORUM. An American anti-feminist (q.v.) organization formed by Phyllis Schlafly (q.v.) to continue the work of her Stop ERA movement, which was instrumental in preventing the ratification of the Equal Rights Amendment (q.v.) The group has a membership of 80,000, primarily women, that is heavily drawn from the Republican Party's political right and conservative Catholics. The group has opposed abortion, day care, comparable worth, family leave, and women's battery shelters (qq.v.).

EARNINGS GAP *see* WAGE GAP

EARTH MOTHER. The use, in early theology, of female fertility to view the earth as the source of divine life. In contemporary feminism, the term is applied to women committed to naturalistic processes, such as natural childbirth (q.v.) or nutrition. They are frequently involved in raising children and affirming kindness in motherhood. Many are also concerned about the earth. (*See also* Ecofeminism.)

EASTMAN, CRYSTAL (1881-1928). A US journalist, peace worker, feminist, and labor lawyer. A suffragist, Eastman joined the Political Equality League in 1912 in Milwaukee and led the drive for woman suffrage in Wisconsin. In 1913 she joined with Alice Paul and Lucy Burns (qq.v.) to found the Congressional Union for Woman Suffrage.

EATING DISORDERS *see* ANOREXIA NERVOSA; BULIMIA NERVOSA

ECOFEMINISM. A feminist tradition that emerged in the 1980's to explore relations between environmental issues and women's issues. Born of the accident at the US nuclear power plant at Three Mile Island in Pennsylvania, the ecofeminist movement has spawned many groups such as the WomanEarth Institute and has succeeded in gaining leadership positions for women in mainstream environmental organizations. Ecofeminists view domination--of women, minority groups, animals, the earth--as the basic problem, rather than patriarchy (q.v.). Ecofeminists speak of an interconnected web of life that encompasses all of the earth's residents.

ECONOMIC OPPORTUNITIES COMMISSION (EOC). A British bureaucracy, created in 1975 to enforce the Equal Pay Act and Sex Discrimination Act in the areas of education, housing, and employment. Although the EOC did not initially prove to be a strong advocate for women and, until the late 1970's, women with feminist ties were rejected for membership on the 15-person commission, it has raised public awareness of sex discrimination and has provided grants for many feminist projects and conferences. In the 1990's the EOC began to play a role in organizing the women's lobby and has become a part of these pressure groups.

EDUCATION AMENDMENTS OF 1972 see TITLE IX

EGALITARIAN FEMINISM see EQUALITY FEMINISM

EGYPTIAN FEMINIST UNION (EFU). A group founded by Huda Sha'rawi (q.v.) in 1923 after the ruling Wafd Party and the new national constitution restricted suffrage to men. The goals of the group were: political, social, and legal equality for women; access to education at all levels; and divorce law reform. The EFU provided scholarships to women for foreign study, primary school and vocational training for girls, aid to widows, and health care. Composed of upper- and middle-class women, the EFU remained vital for a quarter century and published two journals, *L'Egyptienne* and *Al-Misriyya*.

ELIOT, GEORGE (1819-1889). The most respected and widely read female author in nineteenth-century England. Born as Marian Evans, Eliot was the author of a number of novels that presented women who tried to break out of their conventional backgrounds and gain an education that would make them equal to men. Eliot employed the theories of Charles Darwin and the German higher criticism of the Bible in her most famous novels: *Adam Bede* (1859), *Mill on the Floss* (1860), *Silas Marner* (1861), *Romola* (1863), *Middlemarch* (1871-72), and *Daniel Deronda* (1874-76).

ELITISM. A charge leveled against a feminist by other feminists due to perceived violation of the anti-leadership ethic and power-seeking behavior. More recently concern about elitism has involved the upper-status bias of participation in the feminist movement. This, it is feared, may lead the movement to place the needs of women of color and pink-collar (qq.v.) women below those of women in careers and the professions. (*See also* Trashing.)

EMILY'S (EARLY MONEY IS LIKE YEAST) LIST. A US political action committee (PAC) founded in 1984 by IBM heir Ellen Malcolm to provide campaign funding and technical assistance to feminist Democratic women running for high political office. In 1992 the group raised $6 million, making it the largest congressional PAC that year.

EMMA. A German bi-monthly feminist magazine and the first in Europe. Founded in 1977 and edited by Alice Schwarzer (q.v.), *EMMA*'s circulation in 1993 was 60,000. Currently *EMMA* is campaigning against *Frauenhass* (woman-hating) in an attempt to get the German government to collect statistics on hate crimes (q.v.) against women.

EMPIRICISM. The use of rational arguments by feminists to claim that the underlying assumptions of existing law are not objective and that by identifying and remedying these assumptions the law can become objective.

EMPLOYEE RETIREMENT INCOME SECURITY ACT (ERISA). A US law enacted in 1974 that applies to employee benefit and pension plans and includes requirements that such plans cover a broad classification of employees, have a low minimum age requirement and a minimal number of years required for participation and vesting. The intent was to assist women, who are clustered in low-paying positions and are more likely to change jobs or leave the labor force for short periods to accommodate family needs.

EMPLOYMENT, SEX DISCRIMINATION IN. Discrimination on the basis of sex in employment decisions relating to compensation, terms, conditions, or privileges of employment.

Discrimination may occur in hiring, promotion, transfers, and training. It may be direct and deliberate or may entail unnecessary policies or procedures that have an unintended adverse impact on women (e.g., height and weight requirements for police officers). (*See also* Civil Rights Acts of 1964 and 1991; *Equal Employment Opportunity Commission v. Sears, Roebuck & Co.; Phillips v. Martin Marietta Corporation.*)

EMPOWERMENT. The process of helping individuals, usually women, minorities and others who have been politically impotent, to increase their personal and socio-political influence in improving their own circumstances. Empowerment for women requires that women identify their own experiences, feelings, and values and that women decide for themselves what is deserving of conversational and public communication. Empowerment must be initiated by women and must be granted by male communication gatekeepers.

EMPTY NEST SYNDROME. The negative feelings experienced by some parents when grown children have left the home and the caretaking aspects of the parental role are accordingly diminished. Women are thought to be especially vulnerable to such feelings if they have perceived motherhood to be the central component of their identity.

ENGELS, FRIEDRICH (1820-1895). The author of *Origins of the Family, Private Property and the State* (1884), one of the most influential Marxist-inspired works published during the nineteenth century. Engels stressed the family's original communistic structure. Private property and the concept of individual, rather than community, ownership arose to alienate humanity from its original state. Engels believed that humanity originally lived in a state of group marriage, with no concept of the incest taboo. Biological descent was determined only through the mother, so mother-right and female supremacy ("gens") were the dominant characteristics of this early society. Engels traced the evolution of the family from savagery to barbarism to gens to herding and the development of slavery. With the development of metal-working, weaving, and finally agriculture it now became profitable to own the labor of other people. The development of private wealth and the paired family transformed societies based on matriarchal gens. The husband now purchased a guarantee of paternity in order to pass on his accumulated wealth. Engels identified the historical defeat of the female sex as stemming from the dominance of patrilineal rather than matrilineal descent. Woman now was a slave in the home, a means of producing children as property for the husband and master. Monogamy applied only to women, not men, according to Engels' vision of the patriarchal family. Engels next traced the development of monogamous and finally modern bourgeois marriages. The latter was supposedly based on a free contract between two equal partners, but Engels claimed that women were analogous to the proletariat in the bourgeois economic system. Real inequality of power and status between proletariat and capitalist caused the worker to sell his labor in order to survive, while his surplus product, the profit he produced over and above his wages, goes to his employer. The same situation held true for the bourgeois wife who labored at home for no wage besides her subsistence. Finally, Engels predicted the eradication of monogamy and the single family unit because the social revolution that was to come would transform the means of production and place all profit into common ownership.

ENGLISH WOMAN'S JOURNAL. A magazine founded in 1858 by Barbara Leigh Smith Bodichon (q.v.) and Bessie Rayner Parkes, sometimes known as the "Ladies of Langham Place," and Mrs. Anna Jameson. This magazine quickly became the major forum for discussing women's issues and problems in Victorian England.

ENOKI, MISAKO *see* CHUPIREN

EQUAL CREDIT OPPORTUNITY ACT OF 1974 (ECOA). A US law that outlaws discrimination on the basis of sex or marital status in any aspect of a credit transaction (such as getting a credit card, a mortgage, a consumer or business loan). Before the ECOA was passed, single women were often required to have a male relative as a co-signer, the incomes of wives of child-bearing age were not fully counted in home mortgage applications, and women had difficulty establishing credit in their own names after divorce or death of a spouse. The Federal

Reserve Board now requires that credit records be maintained in the names of both spouses and that no questions be asked of applicants regarding child-bearing intentions.

EQUAL EMPLOYMENT OPPORTUNITY COMMISSION (EEOC). A US bureaucracy established by the Civil Rights Act of 1964 (q.v.). It is charged with investigating complaints of employment discrimination and providing interpretation of court cases and legislation. The EEOC can act as the employee's attorney or issue the right to sue. It also publishes guidelines on discrimination, sexual harassment (q.v.) and other related topics that are used by employers, legislators and the courts. Feminists charged that the EEOC initially ignored its mandate to investigate charges of sex discrimination in employment, a situation that led to the formation of the National Organization for Women (q.v.).

EQUAL EMPLOYMENT OPPORTUNITY COMMISSION V. SEARS, ROEBUCK & CO., 628 F. SUPP. 1264 (N.D. ILL. 1986) AFF'D, 839 F.2D 302 (7TH CIR. 1988). The opinions of the US district and appeals courts that involved allegations that a department store employer discriminated against female employees when filling the higher-paying commission sales positions. The Commission presented statistics which reflected substantial underrepresentation of women in these positions. Nevertheless, the courts accepted Sears' explanation that female employees preferred lower-paying noncommission positions. The case received unusual notoriety when two noted feminist historians testified on opposing sides. Rosalind Rosenberg noted that women are socialized to be less competitive and that the easier but more secure and congenial sales jobs might be preferred as more compatible with the demands of the home. Alice Kessler-Harris argued that, given the opportunity as during both world wars, women have quickly moved into higher-paying, traditionally male jobs.

EQUAL PAY ACT OF 1963 (EPA). A US law that forbids wage discrimination on the basis of sex. It requires organizations to pay men and women the same wages for substantially equal work. Equal work is defined by skill, effort, responsibility, and working conditions. Gender differences in wages are permitted when there are differences in merit, seniority, or the quality or quantity of work. As originally introduced, the law would have provided equal pay for comparable worth (q.v.), but this language was rejected as too far-reaching.

EQUAL PAY FOR EQUAL WORK. The equal compensation of men and women who occupy essentially the same position. This concept was one of the first raised to remedy sex discrimination in the workplace. Feminists have since enlarged their demands to encompass comparable worth (q.v.) or paying men and women equal wages when occupying comparable positions. (*See also* Equal Pay Act of 1963.)

EQUAL PROTECTION. A US constitutional protection that mandates equal treatment under state, local, and federal laws for all citizens except in those circumstances where distinctions among citizens are justifiable. The concept of equal protection is derived from two sources in the Constitution, the Fourteenth and the Fifth Amendments. The Fourteenth Amendment specifically states that "no State shall...deny to any person within its jurisdiction the equal protection of the laws." The US Supreme Court did not apply the principle to women until 1971. (*See also Califano v. Goldfarb; Frontiero v. Richardson; Kahn v. Shevin; Mississippi University for Women v. Hogan; Personnel Administrator of Massachusetts v. Feeney; Reed v. Reed.*)

EQUAL RIGHTS AMENDMENT (ERA). A proposed US constitutional amendment, first introduced by the National Woman's Party (q.v.) in 1923, that provided, in its final wording, that "equality of rights shall not be denied or abridged by the United States or by any State on account of sex." In 1972, as a result of the mobilization of the new feminist movement (q.v.), the amendment was approved by the US Congress and submitted to the states for ratification. By 1982, the new extended deadline set by Congress, the amendment had only been ratified by 35 of the needed 38 states and it died. During its decade before the states, the ERA assumed an importance to feminists comparable to that of suffrage during the first wave (q.v.) of feminism. It also played a central role in building the anti-feminist movement (q.v.). It continues to be reintroduced in each session of Congress.

EQUAL RIGHTS FEMINISM *see* EQUALITY FEMINISM

EQUALITY DOCTRINE. A principle espoused by liberal feminists (q.v.) who contend that granting full equal rights to women will end their oppression and subordination which are rooted in customary social and legal constraints.

EQUALITY FEMINISM. The belief that, despite biological and social role differences, men and women should be treated exactly the same under the law. During the period 1920-60, these egalitarian feminists supported the Equal Rights Amendment (q.v.) and opposed protective labor legislation (q.v.) in conflict with social feminists (q.v.). By the late 1960's most feminists held an equality perspective and denied that there were any important differences between the sexes. With the rise of a feminist counter-culture (q.v.) in the 1980's, however, some feminists argued that women could be treated equally only by recognizing differences. (*See also* Difference Feminism.)

ESCORT SERVICES *see* CLINIC PROTECTION

ESSENTIALISM. A term used to imply that there is some a priori essence or quality in men and women that is as inherent as their genes. This essential "femininity" or "masculinity" buttresses politically conservative arguments about what can and cannot occur for men and women in our society. Believing that women must assume full responsibility for childbearing because they are naturally nurturing is an example of an argument made on essentialist grounds.

ESTES, CLARISSA PINKOLA *see* WILD WOMAN MOVEMENT

ESTHER. In the Biblical book that bears her name, the Jewish Queen of the Persian King Ahasuerus. She pleads successfully with the king to save the Jews from extermination after they are headed for annihilation at the hands of the wicked Haman. Her traditional female virtues of silence and obedience often are disparagingly compared by feminists to the more independent character, Vashti, the king's first wife. In Jewish history and story, Esther is a paradigm of women's courage in the face of anti-Semitism.

ESTROGEN REPLACEMENT THERAPY. A prescription drug of estrogens for menopausal and post-menopausal women intended to replace the loss of estrogen production by the body as women age. Some feminists express concerns about health risks as well as the possibly underlying motivation, that of maintaining youthful body images for sexist reasons. Aging naturally is offered as an alternative.

ETATS-GÉNÉRAUX DE LA FEMME. A conference of French egalitarian (q.v.) and reform (q.v.) feminists held in 1970 under the sponsorship of the women's magazine *Elle* to consider the status of women. Radical feminists (q.v.) interrupted the conference to protest the high status of those invited to participate. Even so, resolutions were passed on a number of issues and many pre-existing women's organizations shifted their attention to women's rights as a result of the meeting.

EVANGELICAL FEMINISM. A movement of US women in the late eighteenth and nineteenth centuries to spread Christianity and improve the conditions of prostitutes (q.v.), working-class immigrants, children, and the poor. In attacking male drunkenness and the sexual double standard (q.v.), the movement adopted a feminist perspective. (*See also* Social Gospel Movement, Women and.)

EXISTENTIAL FEMINISM. A reference to the work of Simone de Beauvoir (q.v.) and her book *The Second Sex*. This analysis uses existential categories (immanence-transcendence, subject-object, and self-other) to explain the oppression of women. De Beauvoir maintains that women have become the "other" or object of male subjectivity. This is primarily due to women's biology. Women's oppression consists of being denied transcendence and subjectivity.

-F-

FABIAN'S WOMEN'S GROUP. A group of Englishwomen, whose ranks included Beatrice Webb, Olive Schreiner, and Annie Besant (qq.v.). They sought to protect the rights of working women and were also instrumental in forging cross-class alliances in the 1890s and 1900s.

FAKE CLINICS. Anti-abortion counseling services that place advertisements in telephone book Yellow Pages that promise abortion (q.v.) information and problem pregnancy counseling (q.v.), but instead only provide pro-life (q.v.) information. In the United States, it is estimated that 1,500 to 3,000 bogus clinics exist, in contrast to fewer than 600 abortion providers. Because of the non-profit, non-commercial nature of fake clinics, neither national laws against false advertising nor state consumer fraud statutes are always applicable. In 1991 the Yellow Pages Publishers of America recommended that "Abortion" listings be segregated into "Services" and "Alternatives," with the latter clearly identified as not providing services or referrals. The "Clinics" listings remain open to all advertisers, however.

FALWELL, JERRY see MORAL MAJORITY

FAMILY AND MEDICAL LEAVE ACT OF 1993. A US law that allows workers to take up to 12 weeks of unpaid leave with benefits during any 12-month period for birth or adoption, or the care of a child, spouse or parent with a serious health condition. Workers are guaranteed their old job or an equivalent position upon return. The act only applies to employers with more than 50 workers and workers who have been with the same employer for over a year. Although US feminists wanted paid leave and broader coverage of employers (only five percent of employers are included), two earlier vetoes of this bill by President George Bush had made the movement more pragmatic. (See also Family Leave.)

FAMILY LEAVE. A national policy of unpaid or paid leave, with job security, for men and women for personal disability, childbirth, adoption, or to care for ill dependents. By 1990 every Western European nation required paid, job-protected maternity leave (q.v.). In 1993 the US Congress passed the (unpaid) Family and Medical Leave Act (q.v.). Because family leave can be taken by fathers as well as mothers, it was hoped that employers would not view women workers as more expensive and thus less desirable employees and that men would assume a larger role in child care. In countries where parental leave is public policy, however, it is primarily mothers who take the leave because of traditional gender roles (q.v.) and the greater earning power of men.

FAMILY PLANNING. The conscious planning of the number and spacing of one's own children, for the physical health of the mother and the emotional and financial security of the family as a whole. Family planning requires both education about human reproduction and access to birth control information and contraceptive practices. Family planning has been universally supported by feminist movements because it allows women to take control of the reproductive process and permits them to decide to have fewer children and focus on other parts of their life such as a career. (*See also* Reproductive Freedom.)

FAMILY POLICY. A national philosophical and legislative commitment to comprehensive social and financial services that support the family such as child care (q.v.), reproductive health, employment and training, and family social services. Feminists often note that the United States is the only industrialized Western nation which does not have a comprehensive family policy, in part due to the lack of political power of women and children, the primary beneficiaries of a family policy.

FAMILY SUPPORT ACT OF 1988. A US welfare reform law which requires government efforts to collect delinquent child support, involve public assistance recipients in the Job Opportunity and Basic Skills program (JOBS), expand Aid to Families with Dependent Children-Unemployed Parent benefits, and encourage state governments to increase efforts in the area of experimental programs to reduce welfare dependency. It has been criticized for forcing individuals, primarily women, to participate and as being least helpful to women with child-rearing responsibilities and limited employment skills. Feminists fear that the legislation will funnel women into low-paying jobs which do not pay as well as welfare.

FAMILY VIOLENCE *see* DOMESTIC VIOLENCE

FAMILY WAGE. A rate of pay that is adequate to support an entire family. That one wage earner is assumed to be the male head of household. A belief in this "just" wage has also led to hiring and salary preferences for married men on the assumption that they provide the sole economic support for a family.

FARRELL, WARREN (1940-). A college lecturer and author of the male feminist book *The Liberated Man* (1974) and the backlash (q.v.) books *Why Men Are the Way They Are* (1986) and *The Myth of Male Power* (1993). Once active in the early (feminist) men's "liberation" movement and head of the Masculine Mystique Task Force of the National Organization for Women (q.v.), Farrell now argues that feminism has made women too independent and left men powerless.

FAWCETT, MILLICENT GARRETT (1847-1929). An English proponent of women's property rights and suffrage. When previously contentious factions united in 1897 to form the National Union of Women's Suffrage Societies (NUWSS), Fawcett was chosen as its leader. She served as president until 1918 when women received the vote and her group became the National Union for Equal Citizenship. Fawcett eschewed the militant tactics endorsed by the Pankhursts (Emmeline, Christabel and Sylvia) (q.v.), who formed the rival Women's Social and Political Union (WSPU) in 1903.

FEAR OF SUCCESS. A term associated with the work of Matina Horner suggesting that some persons are strongly motivated to avoid occupational or other achievement because of the perceived negative consequences. Horner argued that such motivation was especially prominent in women, but subsequent research has revealed it in a significant number of men as well.

FÉDÉRATION DES FEMMES DU QUÉBEC *see* CANADIAN CHARTER OF RIGHTS AND FREEDOMS, SECTION 28; ROYAL COMMISSION ON THE STATUS OF WOMEN IN CANADA (RCSW)

FELIX, CONCEPCIÓN. A Filipino woman suffrage leader and founder in 1905 of the Asociación Feminista Filipino, a suffrage and social service organization. Until suffrage was extended in 1937, Felix was active in many other groups and often spoke to the legislature on suffrage bills. In 1937, when a plebiscite was called among women on the suffrage issue, she toured the country registering over 500,000 women, of whom 447,725 approved woman suffrage.

FEM/CRITS. Feminists who draw upon the critical legal studies movement as a foundation for their theories. They reject the premise of law's neutrality, oppose the hierarchy in democracy and note how dichotomies such as public/private and form/substance reinforce male dominance (q.v.). Such feminists also reject equality doctrine (q.v.) discourse.

FEMALE CHAUVINISM. The assumption that traditional female values are superior and that patriarchal and male values are responsible for women's oppression, war, racism, and environmental problems. (*See also* Cultural Feminism; Difference Feminism.)

FEMALE CIRCUMCISION *see* FEMALE GENITAL MUTILATION

FEMALE EUNUCH, THE (1972). Major document in the contemporary feminist movement, this book by Germaine Greer, an Australian woman educated in England, elaborated on Simone de Beauvoir's (q.v.) *The Second Sex.* Like Beauvoir, Greer criticized women for being inner-directed, defined by their otherness as "female eunuchs": "The female is to become deformed and debilitated by the destructive action of energy upon the self, because she is deprived of scope and contacts with external reality upon which to exercise herself . . . . When she becomes aware of her sex the pattern has such sufficient force of inertia to prevail over new forms of desire and curiosity. This is the condition which is meant by the *female eunuch*" (see her *Female Eunuch*).

FEMALE/FEMININE PRINCIPLE (RELIGION). A symbolic projection growing out of the social importance of recognizing the role of the female in the perpetuation of the community. Although believed by some devotees of feminist spirituality to be immanent, such a principle is a human cognitive construct, not empirically based. Archaeological data cannot determine how ancient or widespread the concept of a cosmic female principle may have been. Similarly, ethnographic or historic art or practices cannot be assumed to embody such a concept unless this is specifically verified in text. Where such a principle is found, it is usually complementary to a male (or masculine) principle in a dualistic cosmology.

FEMALE GENITAL MUTILATION. The removal of all or part of a young girl's external genitalia (the clitoris and the labia minora), followed by the closing of the vulva with thread or thorns (infibulation) to guarantee virginity, decrease sexual pleasure, and make the future woman marriageable. This Muslim practice (primarily in Africa, but also the Middle East and Southeast Asia) is viewed by Western feminists as torture and a human rights violation that should be outlawed or subject to United Nations' economic sanctions. Alice Walker (q.v.), in her novel *Possessing the Secret of Joy* (1992) and the co-authored *Warrior Marks: Female Genital Mutilation and the Sexual Blinding of Women* (1993), has been active in opposition. Although some nations have banned the practice on health grounds and a group of African and Arab women, the Inter-African Committee, support this movement, other Third World women and Western multi-culturalists either view "female circumcision" as a traditional custom that should be respected or argue that the pressure for abolition must be indigenous to each culture, not externally imposed by the West.

FEMALE-HEADED HOUSEHOLD *see* SINGLE-PARENT FAMILY

FEMALE MAN, THE. A novel published by the American lesbian author Joanna Russ (q.v.) in 1975. This feminist fabulation, sometimes considered a work of science fiction, depicts a variety of women living in the past, present, and future. Perhaps the most shocking aspect of the book is its vision of the future--an all-female utopia that has exterminated all men and reproduces through the merging of two ova, always producing more women.

FEMALE SEXUAL SLAVERY *see* INTERNATIONAL TRAFFIC IN WOMEN

FEMININE MYSTIQUE, THE. A seminal document in the American feminist movement, published by Betty Friedan (q.v.) in 1963. Based on an article she had published originally in 1960 in *Good Housekeeping*, "Women Are People Too!" Friedan went on to amass personal interviews and data from popular culture, sociology, and psychology in order to construct her argument about the malaise striking middle-class, largely suburban wives and mothers. Friedan's book is the first easily accessible work to attribute women's problems to a sex-based society rather than to any personal failures of women themselves.

FEMINIST ANTI-CENSORSHIP TASKFORCE (FACT) *see* PORNOGRAPHY, FEMINIST DEBATE ON

FEMINIST ART AND AESTHETIC THEORY. A recent academic attempt to rediscover and evaluate the artistic productions of lost or marginalized women painters and photographers. Feminist art history is predicated on exposing women's absence from creating dominant art forms. It seeks to build a counter-cultural tradition, frequently avant-garde, that opposes the dominance of patriarchal ideology in the visual arts. It poses the question, What would art that did not oppress or exploit women look like? It seeks to oppose sexism (q.v.) in culture and it frequently seeks to use art for propagandistic purposes. (*See also* Guerrilla Girls.)

FEMINIST BOOKSTORES. A group of more than 100 commercial enterprises in North America that sell pamphlets, newspapers, magazines, and books about women, feminism, and the women's movement. These stores are typically community resources that offer many of the same services as women's centers (q.v.) and, in the early years, were often owned by feminist collectives (q.v.). Today feminist bookstores have sales of $30 million annually and their stock reflects the interest of mainstream publishers in feminist topics. They remain a major sales outlet for feminist publishing houses and for lesbian fiction, anti-racist and nonsexist children's literature (q.v.), and books by and about women of color (q.v.).

FEMINIST CONSCIOUSNESS. A set of attitudes held by women that includes: a recognition of membership in and shared interests with a group called "women"; awareness and rejection of women's unequal status in society; and support for collective action by the group to change their status. Most feminist movement participants have this sense of group consciousness, which is a prerequisite for social change.

FEMINIST ECONOMICS. An approach to the study of economics that rejects the model of rational and self-interested "economic man" and the wisdom of a free market system. Critics argue that this traditional model ignores social and cooperative aspects of economic behavior. They also note that the market neither corrects for inequities such as gender discrimination nor does it result in pay commensurate with the social value of labor. Feminist economics is a method of analysis that focuses on gender and views both gender and economics as socially constructed. The International Association for Feminist Economics was established in 1992.

FEMINIST EPISTEMOLOGY. Generally defined as the concept of knowing through perception, intuition, conceptualization, inference, representation, reflection, imagination, remembrance, conjecture, rationalization, argumentation, justification, contemplation, ratiocination, speculation, meditation, validation, or deliberation. According to feminist theory, feminist epistemology refers to the unique ways women know the world, the way they understand the multiplicity of experiences that all women have undergone. Current feminist thinking emphasizes that there is no one female experience or female nature, but many different ways of knowing that one is a woman. Whereas each school of feminism emphasizes only one aspect of the female condition--class, psychology, otherness--contemporary feminist epistemology tries to grasp the entire picture of race, sexual orientation, class, and age in order to appreciate the differences and validities of how all women know the experiences of femaleness. Major works on this topic include Genevieve Lloyd, *The Man of Reason*; Sandra Harding and Merrill Hintikka, eds., *Discovering Reality*; Sandra Harding, *The Feminist Question in Science*; and Jean Grimshaw, *Philosophy and Feminist Thinking*.

FEMINIST FILM THEORY. A recent conjunction between the women's movement and the film industry. The first stage in feminist consciousness (q.v.) about film resulted in a campaign against sexism (q.v.) within the film industry, including discrimination against female directors and producers. The second stage resulted in analyses of sexism in filmic representation of women as bitch, whore, or femme fatale, while the third stage was the use of film for propaganda purposes such as documentary cinema about the living conditions of women in various countries. These issues have been explored in *Women and Film*, the first journal of feminist film criticism, founded in 1972 and published in California. The first feminist film festivals took place in New York and Edinburgh and began the task of rediscovering the work of lost female directors: Dorothy Arzner, Ida Lupino, Leni Riefenstahl, Leontine Sagen, Maya Deren, Shirley Clarke, Sally Potter, Marguerite Duras, Laura Mulvey, Michelle Citron, Chantal Akerman, and Yvonne Rainer. A useful summary of the history of feminist film can be found in Ann Kaplan's *Women and Film* (1983).

FEMINIST HUMOR. A type of comedy that focuses on gender inequity and sexist assumptions. Oppression on the basis of race, class and sexual orientation are also common themes of this change-oriented approach. Feminist comedy generally does not rely on put-downs, one-liners, and lengthy "jokes." Among the best-known feminist comedians are: Elayne Boosler, Roseanne, Kate Clinton, Whoopi Goldberg, and Lily Tomlin.

FEMINIST JURISPRUDENCE. An examination of the principles underlying partriarchal laws and the adjustment of these principles to include the experiences of women. One goal is to expose legal principles which operate to constrain or limit women.

FEMINIST LEGAL THEORY. An examination of the functions of law by women in which emphasis is placed on the methods the legal system uses to define the female's subordinate role and to advance the power and control of males.

FEMINIST LIBERATION THEOLOGY. Contemporary religious scholarship guided by theoretical and practical commitments to emancipation and justice for women. Reflecting liberation theology's starting point in concrete crises of oppressed peoples, feminist liberation theologians are rooted in the standpoints and experiences of particular communities of women. Patriarchal dimensions of religious traditions and texts are critiqued, and their liberative features interpreted, from vantage points intentionally informed by justice-seeking and solidarity with women. (*See also* Feminist Theology.)

FEMINIST LITERARY CRITICISM, MATERIALIST. An adaptation of the Marxist assumption that subjectivity is socially constructed that focuses attention on literary structures which produce gender ideology. It considers how society causes men and women to identify themselves as "masculine" or "feminine." A materialist feminist literary critic also looks at the material (e.g., economic, racial) circumstances in which texts by and about women and/or gender (q.v.) are produced and read.

FEMINIST LITERARY CRITICISM, NEW HISTORICIST. An examination of literature as a site of the production and enforcement of, as well as opposition to, hierarchical power relations. As in the work of Michel Foucault (q.v.), new historicist feminist literary criticism considers historically specific power struggles, but focuses on gender relations ignored by Focauldian critique.

FEMINIST MORAL THEORY. A newly developing field of inquiry that draws upon women's experiences as a way of refashioning traditional Western approaches to moral theory. Feminist moral theory is both critical and constructive. It seeks to expose and critique the male biases inherent in the concepts and methods of traditional ethical theory, and to reconceive and rearticulate those concepts and methods in ways representative of and congenial to the distinctive features of women's experiences. Although contributions to feminist moral theory are rich and diverse, a central development in this area has been an ethic of care.

FEMINIST MUSIC AND MUSICOLOGY. A cultural movement that developed during the 1970's and is best represented within the folk tradition and at the National Women's Music Festivals held annually since 1974. A feminist musicology has documented sex discrimination in conservatory admissions and the bias against women composers, instrumentalists, and conductors and has attempted to gain some recognition for these early female musicians. Feminists have also protested against the violent and sexist lyrics of popular music and pornographic album art and have founded performance groups, record and promotion companies, festivals, and publications for a new women's music. Prominent feminist musicians include: Meg Christian, Holly Near, and Cris Williamson. Olivia Records and the *Ladyslipper Catalog* of women's music are also important parts of this network.

FEMINIST PEDAGOGY. An instructional strategy that fosters resistance to "masterful meaning" and "reductive appropriations" (q.v.) of women to dominant patriarchal (q.v.) discourses. Feminist pedagogy reintroduces the personal as well as the oppositional into classroom dialogues in order to disseminate authority and deconstruct (q.v.) the false universality of patriarchally institutionalized meanings. The goal of feminist pedagogy is to overthrow the objectifying, hegemonic reduction/appropriation of the "other" in favor of an oppositional practice, one which does not reduce the personal into the generalizable.

FEMINIST PERSPECTIVES IN HEALTH EDUCATION. An attempt to address and integrate feminist concerns specific to the health-related professions. It encompasses curricular inclusion of feminist ideologies to inform students and raise consciousness about the androcentric biases and social behaviors embedded in the male-dominated medical field.

FEMINIST PHENOMENOLOGY. The work of contemporary postmodern (q.v.) feminists, who make use of phenomenological method, i.e., giving precise descriptions of women's lived experiences and providing etymological analysis of linguistic terms that have been used to oppress women. The purpose is not to explain women's oppression but instead to empower women by validating their experience. Some common topics are women's eroticism, bodily comportment, essential difference, and capacities for subversive language use.

FEMINIST POLITICAL THEORY. A variety of traditions and movements that seek to articulate political theories based on women's experiences, especially that of oppression. Liberal feminism (q.v.) seeks to extend the values and ideals of traditional political liberalism to women. Radical feminism (q.v.) seeks to overthrow the system of male domination (q.v.) and to articulate political values and ideals that grow out of women's experiences of gender oppression. Socialist feminism (q.v.) tries to combine the central insights of radical feminism and Marxism.

FEMINIST PRACTICAL REASONING. A feminist approach that combines practical deliberation with an emphasis on identifying and accounting for the perspectives of the excluded by reasoning from contextual frameworks. It focuses on individual fact-finding as opposed to the application of universal rules.

FEMINIST PRESS. A publishing house, established in Old Westbury, New York, in 1970 and specializing in nonsexist children's literature (q.v.) and reissued books by women that attracted little attention on first publication. Before the formation of the National Women's Studies Association, the press published the *Women's Studies Newsletter*.

FEMINIST SCIENCE. The pursuit of scientific knowledge shaped and broadened by feminist ideology. Feminist science may differ from "status quo" science in the types of scientific questions posed, the methods of experimental subject selection, the processes used to acquire data, and the bases for generating results and conclusions.

FEMINIST SOCIAL WORK. The practice of social work using a feminist orientation that acknowledges societal discrimination against women and specifically attempts to help women overcome problems related to this discrimination (e.g., unpaid labor in the home, low-wage work, and prescribed sex-role behaviors such as dependency).

FEMINIST THEOLOGY. The critical reflection upon religious matters, usually from the perspective of a particular faith community, which has its starting point and goal in a concern for the voices, the experiences, and the flourishing of women. It has been defined as "faith seeking understanding." In its Christian and Jewish forms, feminist theology unmasks, critiques, and denounces elements of scripture, tradition and practice that have wreaked or legitimated harm against women. It also attempts constructively to retrieve and reinterpret elements of tradition and scripture that offer liberative paradigms. In its post-Christian, pagan, or goddess (q.v.) centered forms, feminist theology deliberately leaves behind dominant historical religious traditions to seek uniquely female-centered forms of religious interpretation and practice. (*See also* Deities, Female; Feminist Liberation Theology; Neopaganism.)

FEMINIST THERAPY. Therapy practiced from a feminist perspective, in which the client, usually a woman, is assisted to identify and deal with problems that relate to sex discrimination and sex role stereotyping (q.v.) in the family and wider society. Techniques include consciousness-raising (q.v.), education, and assertiveness training (q.v.).

FÉMINISTES RÉVOLUTIONNAIRES (FR). A French radical feminist (q.v.) group, organized in 1970, with a membership that included Simone de Beauvoir and Monique Wittig (qq.v.). The strongly separatist (q.v.) group staged dramatic protests such as the *Manifeste des 343 Femmes* (q.v.) and the dedication of a wreath to the wife of the unknown soldier honored by a tomb at the Arc de Triomphe.

FEMINISTS, THE. A radical feminist (q.v.) group formed in 1968 by Ti-Grace Atkinson (q.v.) and other members of the National Organization for Women and New York Radical

Women (qq.v.) as "The October 17th Movement." In keeping with their commitment to nonhierarchical organization, the Feminists developed the lot system for random rotation of creative and boring tasks within the group and an equitable system for allotting discussion time in meetings. A restrictive set of rules mandating compulsory work and attendance and limiting the percentage of members co-habiting with men led to many resignations in 1969. The group formally disbanded in 1973.

"FEMINIZATION OF POVERTY." A phrase identified by social scientist Diana Pearce in 1978 to describe the growing proportion of the US poor comprised of women and their children. This increase in poverty is due to marital instability and women's inability to successfully participate in the labor market while fulfilling the responsibilities of raising children. Although feminists denounce this trend, they also object to the assumption that poverty would not exist if these women developed and sustained an economic relationship with a man.

FEMINOLOGY. The science of women and used to refer to women's studies (q.v.) programs in other countries, most notably in Scandinavia. It was originally used in Paris to refer to a course taught by Marguerite Souley-Darque (q.v.) from 1900 to 1905 which resembled contemporary women's studies courses in content, institutional innovativeness and diversity of student audience.

FEMOCRAT. A feminist who is employed within a public bureaucracy and works on women's issues. The term is primarily associated with Australian feminists who consciously sought public jobs after the defeat of the supportive Labor Party government in 1975. Elizabeth Reid, Prime Minister Gough Whitlam's advisor on women's affairs, was the first femocrat.

FERRARO, GERALDINE (1935-). The Democratic nominee for Vice President of the United States in 1984 and the first woman to appear on a major political party's ticket in that country. She was selected by presidential candidate Walter Mondale after strong lobbying from feminists. Although she and Mondale were defeated, Ferraro was an outspoken advocate for women's issues during the campaign and a very effective fund-raiser among women. Ferraro, a lawyer, served in the US House of Representatives, 1979-85.

FETAL PROTECTION POLICIES. Employment policies that prohibit women of childbearing years from working in (generally higher paying) positions that may expose them to substances that are harmful to a fetus unless women provide proof of sterility. These policies have been defined as illegal sex discrimination in the United States. (*See also International Union, UAW v. Johnson Controls.*)

FETAL RIGHTS. An emerging area of legal discourse in which a woman and her fetus are viewed as two separate entities with potentially conflicting interests and each with legal rights. This doctrine originates in the pro-life movement (q.v.) that portrays the fetus as a preborn baby and stresses the ability of medical science to treat the fetus in utero and to link infant health problems with a woman's consumption of tobacco, drugs, and alcohol and exposure to toxic chemicals during pregnancy. Some US women, prosecuted for using alcohol or drugs while pregnant, have been jailed or denied custody of their children; others, seriously ill, have been forced to have a caesarean section. Although feminists are concerned that the rights of women are being compromised here, many also urge that rehabilitation programs begin to accept pregnant women. To date, the courts have not upheld involuntary caesareans or fetal protection policies (q.v.). (*See also International Union, UAW v. Johnson Controls.*)

FETAL TISSUE RESEARCH AND TRANSPLANTS. Medical research utilizing fetal remains, usually obtained as a result of abortions (q.v.). There is currently hope that fetal transplants may be effective in the treatment of Parkinson's and Alzheimer's diseases. The Bush administration banned federally funded fetal tissue transplants into humans on the grounds that such procedures would increase the incidence of abortions. Although most feminists supported Bill Clinton's revocation of this policy, there is also concern among some feminists that the altering of abortion techniques in order to obtain usable fetal material may make the procedure more uncomfortable and dangerous for women.

FIRESTONE, SHULAMITH (1944-). Generally considered to be a Marxist feminist (q.v.), Firestone is best known as the author of *The Dialectic of Sex* (1970) (q.v.) and a proponent of a feminist historical materialism. "Historical materialism is that view of the course of history which seeks the ultimate cause and the great moving power of historical events in the dialectic of sex: the division of society into two distinct biological classes for procreative reproduction, and the struggles of these classes with one another, in the changes in the modes of marriage, reproduction and child care created by these struggles; in the connected development of other physically differentiated classes; and in the first division of labor based on sex which developed into the class system" (see her *Dialectic of Sex*).

FIRST WAVE FEMINISM. The worldwide campaign for women's rights waged in the nineteenth and early twentieth centuries. Key demands centered on education, married women's legal rights, employment opportunities, and suffrage. By the late 1930's woman suffrage had been adopted in most nations and a woman's right to equal treatment had been validated. (*See also* Second Wave Feminism; Third Wave Feminism.)

FLEXITIME. An organizational practice that involves alternatives to the 9 a.m. to 5 p.m. work schedule. Flexitime allows employees to choose different hours, such as 7 a.m. to 3 p.m. or 11 a.m. to 7 p.m. This policy is particularly useful for parents in that a child's daily activities can be coordinated with a parent's hours of work. The practice is widespread in Europe and is becoming more available in the United States.

FLIRTING. A behavior described by speech accommodation (q.v.) theorists as an example of divergence. Here speakers exaggerate the differences in their speaking styles. Divergence is usually a way to establish status differences and this may be true in the case of flirting as well, where men adopt masculine (higher status) behaviors and women express feminine (lower status) behaviors. Men's broad stance and protruding chest and women's cocked head and averted eyes are examples of flirting behaviors.

FORMS OF ADDRESS *see* NAMING CONVENTIONS

FOUCAULT, MICHEL (1926-1984). The leading French theorist of discourse, or of how language is formed by social institutions in accordance with institutional rules that make certain kinds of knowledge possible. Foucault's major works focus on how madness and modern medicine were invented through the invention of asylums and clinics. After the failure of the Paris uprising in May 1968, Foucault turned his attention to the exercise of power through social practices, including language, or what he called "discursive practices." His *Discipline and Punish* (1975) examined the evolution of the prison system and its exercise of power over the human body. His final work, the three-volume *History of Sexuality* (1976-86), traced the invention of the notion of the "homosexual." Feminist interest in Foucault centers on how he enunciated issues of power in relation to social institutions and their locus in the human body.

FOUQUÉ, ANTOINETTE *see* POLITIQUE ET PSYCHANALYSE

FOURTEENTH AMENDMENT *see* EQUAL PROTECTION

FOX, WILLIAM (1786-1864). A member of the English Parliament, a Calvinist minister, and the editor of the *Monthly Repository*. He advocated reform of the harsh English divorce laws, the elimination of sacramental marriage with the use of a civil contract in its place, and women's suffrage. (*See also* Divorce and Matrimonial Causes Act.)

FREDRIKA BREMER ASSOCIATION. A Swedish liberal feminist (q.v.) group, formed in 1894 as a suffrage organization. Since the mid-1970's it has concentrated on networking (q.v.) and increasing the role of women in political life.

FREEDMAN, MARCIA (1938-). A US immigrant to Israel, philosophy professor at the University of Haifa, and member of the Israel Knesset, 1973-77. Freedman was one of the founders of the new feminist movement (q.v.) in Israel. During her years in the national legislature, Freedman, as its only feminist, raised many women's issues, including abortion (q.v.) reform and domestic violence (q.v.).

FREEDOM OF ACCESS TO CLINIC ENTRANCES ACT (FACE) *see* CLINIC PROTECTION

FRENCH, MARILYN (1929-). The author of *Beyond Power: On Women, Men and Morals* (1985) and the feminist potboiler *The Women's Room* (1976). French's serious analysis, *Beyond Power*, sees sexism (q.v.) as the root cause of all oppression in society. She condemns the patriarchy (q.v.) for instituting "stratification of men above women [which] leads in time to stratification of classes: an elite rules over people perceived as 'closer to nature,' savage, bestial, animalistic." Because women were identified with nature, men grew to fear and desire to control them. She sees the only solution to this impasse as the cultivation of values such as "love and compassion and sharing and nurturance, as well as control, structure, possessiveness, and status" (see her *Beyond Power*).

FREUD, SIGMUND (1856-1939). An Austrian physician and founder of psychoanalysis, noted for his theory of sexual politics and the concept of "penis envy." According to Freud, girls react to their lack of a phallus by rejecting their clitoris (deficient penis) and their mothers (other women). They gravitate toward their fathers and, later, other men, in order to compensate by giving birth, preferably to a son through whom they then live. Heterosexuality is thus assured, but a struggle between husband and wife continues as she seeks to infantilize her husband in her retreat to the domestic sphere (q.v.). For self-preservation, men are driven to the public sphere and to ignore wife and family. Freud also argued that the sexes are undifferentiated from birth; both are bisexual. The development of adult female sexuality falls within one of three patterns: inhibition or frigidity (q.v.); retention of infantile sexuality, including lesbianism (q.v.); and the "normal femininity" of heterosexuality and vaginal eroticism.

Feminists have viewed Freud as misogynistic and patriarchal (q.v.) and reject the idea of a woman's body as incomplete.

Contemporaries like Karen Horney (q.v.) suggest that "womb envy" may be more powerful than "penis envy" given the effort men have devoted to controlling women's reproduction (q.v.). Horney, among others, notes that what some have interpreted as "penis envy" in adult females is actually a wish for the power routinely available to males in society. Feminists have also pointed out that Freud's thinking was based on his work with emotionally disturbed patients and that there is no evidence that these developments occur inevitably in the lives of normal females. Efforts to validate "penis envy" through non-clinical methods have been unsuccessful. Other feminist theorists like Juliet Mitchell and Nancy Chodorow (qq.v.) have used Freudian theory to explain women's condition in a patriarchal society.

FRIEDAN, BETTY (1921-). The woman viewed as the catalyst of the new feminist movement (q.v.) in the United States. Her description of "the problem that has no name" (q.v.) in *The Feminine Mystique* (1963) (q.v.) brought a critical discussion of women's domestic life to the widespread attention of the public. She was one of the founders of the National Organization for Women (NOW) (q.v.) and served as its first president. She was also one of the convenors of the National Women's Political Caucus (q.v.). Friedan lectures and writes widely on the women's movement and public policy. She has been associated with a number of American universities since founding NOW and has published three additional books: *It Changed My Life* (1976), *The Second Stage* (1981), and *The Fountain of Age* (1993).

FRIGIDITY. An obsolete term to describe women who do not experience sexual desire. Feminists believe that this term is often used as a put-down for women who are well within the normal range of sexual desire and experience but who are perceived by the user of the label as unavailable.

FRONTIERO V. RICHARDSON, 411 US 677 (1973). A decision of the US Supreme Court that found that certain regulations of the armed services violated equal protection (q.v.) guarantees provided by the Constitution. The regulations permitted male members of the armed forces to automatically receive dependent benefits such as increased quarters allowance and medical and dental coverage. In order to receive benefits for their dependents, female members of the armed forces were required to prove that they provided over one-half of the family support. *Frontiero* was a landmark case in the development of the Supreme Court's sexual equality doctrine because four justices agreed that the most stringent test, "strict scrutiny," should be applied to laws based on sex.

FUKUZAWA, YUKICHI (1834-1901). A Meiji period reformer who opposed the traditional Confucian views of women. His *Essay on Japanese Women* (1879) and *The New Greater Learning for Women* (1897) criticized the status of women in Japan and advocated equal rights and education for women.

FULLER, MARGARET (1810-1850). An American journalist and reformer, best known as author of *Woman in the Nineteenth Century* (1845). After brief stints as a teacher, translator, and an editor of *The Dial*, a transcendentalist magazine, she began a career as America's first self-supporting woman journalist. She used transcendentalist philosophy and Kantian epistemology in her *Woman in the Nineteenth Century*, the first major feminist manifesto in America, and applied them to women. Fuller advocated an androgynous (q.v.) consciousness, claiming that there was "no wholly masculine man," just as there was "no purely feminine woman." She believed in the primacy of the spirit and urged women to turn inward to find their true natures and strength.

FUND FOR THE FEMINIST MAJORITY. A group organized in 1987 by former National Organization for Women (q.v.) president Eleanor Smeal to increase the number of feminist women in US elective office. Supported by direct-mail fundraising, the organization actively recruits and endorses women candidates but does not provide campaign contributions through a political action committee.

FURIES. According to Greek legend, female powers who punished the shedding of kindred blood and, in particular, crimes committed against the mother. Also called Erinyes, these terrible goddesses (usually three in number) were depicted as bat-winged, snorting, snake-wreathed demons who reside in the underworld and pursue their victims relentlessly. As ancient matriarchal goddesses, they are in sharp contrast to the brilliant, younger generation of deities, such as Apollo and Athena, who reside on Mt. Olympus and uphold the patriarchal order established by Zeus. In their most famous myth, recounted by Aeschylus in the *Oresteia*, the Furies hound Orestes for murdering his mother Clymnestra until they are persuaded to abandon their maternal allegiance and join the new order of gods. They receive the title *Eumenides* ("Kindly Ones") to indicate their new status.

FURIES, THE. The most prominent of the early lesbian feminist (q.v.) collectives (q.v.), founded in 1971 in Washington, D. C., by a dozen women, including Rita Mae Brown (q.v.) and Charlotte Bunch. The group disbanded within a year, but not before providing analyses of heterosexism, lesbian feminist separatism, and political lesbianism (qq.v.).

-G-

GAY AND LESBIAN CRITICISM. An effort to make visible that which has been made invisible in heterosexual culture. This tradition presents itself as a form of rebellion against the sexual norms of the patriarchy and heterosexism (qq.v.). Prominent theorists in the attempt to discuss the power issues implicit in same-sex relationships in literature and culture include Monique Wittig, *The Lesbian Body* (1976); Eve Kosofsky, *Between Men: English Literature and Male Homosocial Desire* (1985) and *Epistemology of the Closet* (1990); Adrienne Rich, *Of Woman Born* (1979); and Lillian Faderman, *Surpassing the Love of Men: Romantic Friendship and Love Between Women from the Renaissance to the Present* (1981).

GAY/STRAIGHT SPLIT. A cleavage within the US women's liberation movement (q.v.), primarily occurring during the period 1970-72. The conflict centered on the role of lesbians (q.v.) as lesbians within the movement and the priority of lesbian issues on the feminist agenda. Underlying the split was much mutual misunderstanding and distrust as lesbians perceived heterosexism (q.v.) within the movement and straight women believed their feminist credentials were being questioned. (*See also* Lavender Menace; Political Lesbianism; "The Woman-Identified Woman.")

GEDULDIG V. AIELLO, 417 US 484 (1974). An opinion of the US Supreme Court that resolved a challenge to the constitutionality of an employee benefits policy. California provided an insurance plan that paid benefits to private (nonstate) disabled workers during periods of unemployment but excluded pregnancy as a disability. The policy was challenged as a violation of equal protection (q.v.). The Court ruled that the policy was based on pregnancy and did not involve the use of a sex classification in that "non-pregnant persons" also included women. By ignoring the impact of pregnancy on the employment of women, this Court decision mobilized the US feminist movement to appeal to Congress for a clarification of Title VII of the Civil Rights Act of 1964 (q.v.). (*See also* Pregnancy Discrimination Act.)

GENDER. A term variously used to denote: the equivalent of sex; those qualities of femaleness and maleness that develop as a result of socialization rather than biological predisposition; and any qualities associated with femaleness or maleness, regardless of their roots in biology or socialization. Although there is a feminist preference for a definition of gender as socially constructed and distinct from the biological term "sex," usage of the terms is interchangable in popular discourse.

GENDER CONSCIOUSNESS *see* FEMINIST CONSCIOUSNESS

GENDER DISCRIMINATION. The differential treatment of those distinguished as male or female. When US courts have interpreted the prohibition against "sex" discrimination in Title VII of the Civil Rights Act of 1964 (q.v.), they have adopted a narrow definition of sex, which basically corresponds to gender discrimination. A broader definition of discrimination is available to the courts. This more expansive construction of sex discrimination includes not only discrimination based on gender but also discrimination based on sexuality, sexual preferences, or sexual practices.

GENDER DISPLAYS. The act of marking one's gender through engaging in sex-specific behavior. Gender displays are a product of culture, not nature. Both women and men engage in gender displays--for example, women by preening their hair, crossing their legs at the knees, dressing in skirts and hose and men by dressing in pants and low-heeled shoes, sitting with legs open, and growing mustaches. Insofar as a woman consciously resists engaging in gender displays, she increases her ability to define herself rather than being defined by her gender.

GENDER GAP. The difference in the proportion of women and men who vote for a candidate. First noted in the United States in the early 1980's, this divergence is based in attitudinal differences between the sexes on a variety of policy issues, including international peace, civil rights, social welfare, and the environment. These differences in voting behavior are important because women are a larger proportion of the eligible electorate and are somewhat more likely to vote than are men in some political systems.

GENDER-NEUTRAL LAW. A law that does not use masculine or feminine references and does not have a differential effect on men and women. Although feminists support the removal of clearly discriminatory statutes based on sex stereotypes and domestic sphere (q.v.) ideology, many also question the wisdom of uniform gender neutrality in areas where men and women are biologically and socially different. Here equality may result in greater burdens on women who experience a work-family conflict (q.v.).

GENDER ROLE. A term that refers to stereotyped behavior prescribed on the basis of apparent or assigned male or female sex. "Gender" is preferred to "sex" because an individual's genetic sex is seldom determined. Instead, the individual's appearance is the basis for prescribing role. This means that infants are assigned to male or female gender on the basis of external genitalia, and children and adults are assigned on the basis of costume and mannerisms, both of which are learned social behaviors. Society demands ascription of all individuals to one or the other gender category, man/boy or woman/girl.

GENDER STRATIFICATION. A condition usually discussed in relation to issues of inequality between men and women and the (stratified) distribution of social and economic resources of society along gender lines. Although men have more access to these resources in most societies, there is variation historically and cross-culturally. Central determinants are the division of labor along gender lines and the degree to which women's labor is more or less socially valued. As power and status relates to the production of goods in any society, women's status is related to their contribution to the production of valued goods. It is high where women produce most of the food supply (as in hunting and gathering societies) and low where production of valued goods occurs outside the household (as in industrialized societies).

"GENDERLECT." A term coined by Cheris Kramarae (q.v.) that refers to the concept of two distinct language styles for men and women.

GENERAL ELECTRIC CO. V. GILBERT, 429 US 125 (1976). An opinion of the US Supreme Court that narrowly construed the scope of the prohibition of Title VII of the Civil Rights Act of 1964 (q.v.) against sex discrimination in employment. The Court concluded that the Act did not forbid discrimination based upon pregnancy and that employers could exclude pregnancy from the illnesses for which employees could receive disability compensation. In 1978 Congress responded to this decision by enacting the Pregnancy Discrimination Act (q.v.).

GENERAL FEDERATION OF WOMEN'S CLUBS (GFWC). An international organization linking women's clubs in around 35 countries. Founded in 1890 in the United States to encourage literary and social activities, the GFWC quickly became active in Progressive reforms such as protective labor legislation (q.v.) and abolition of child labor and in 1914 endorsed woman suffrage (q.v.). Although in the 1920s it again became more social and apolitical, the GFWC did endorse the Equal Rights Amendment (q.v.) in 1944 and was active in the campaign for ratification. State federations have also been supportive of contemporary feminist issues such as rape and domestic violence (qq.v.).

GENERIC PRONOUNS. Traditionally, "he" and "him," now "they." Before the eighteenth century, "they" served as the generic pronoun for both singular and plural antecedents. In 1746 "he/him" were codified as the pronouns for humans in "Eighty-Eight Grammatical Rules" by grammarian John Kirkby. Since English-speaking people continued to use "they," an Act of Parliament was required in 1850 to institute the male pronoun as the generic. Recently, alternatives have been suggested, such as s/he, but the plural pronoun remains the most felicitous choice. (*See also* Nonsexist Language.)

GENLET. A word coined to name an experience or object which is meaningful for women. Examples include: "pseudostudliness," lying about conquests men have had with women; "lavagaggle," the propensity of women to go to bathrooms in large groups; and "piglabelphobia," eating before going out so your date won't think you're eating too much; "perchaphonic," sitting by the phone waiting for a man to call; "Brinkleymirror," the paranoia felt when compared to an airbrushed model; and "lidomania," the rage a woman feels when she discovers she is sitting on porcelain.

GERMAN WOMENS' COUNCIL (DEUTSCHER FRAUENRAT). An umbrella organization founded in 1969. It encompassed roughly one hundred women's groups and ten million members, including women trade unionists, women in the two largest political parties, and members of women's church guilds. Rooted as it was in the first German women's movement and cumbersome as an organization, it never achieved more than marginal political influence and was overshadowed by the new, autonomous women's movement almost as soon as it was formed.

GILBERT, SANDRA (1936-) AND SUSAN GUBAR (1944-). The authors of *Madwoman in the Attic* (1979) and *No Man's Land,* 2 vols. (1988 and 1989), co-editors of *The Norton Anthology of Literature by Women: The Tradition in English* (1985) and prominent American literary historians and critics. As co-authors and co-editors, they have produced some of the most important texts in the American feminist literary revival. They are credited with exploring the psychodynamics of

Anglo-American women in the nineteenth and twentieth centuries, specifically that the "anxiety of authorship" that plagues women authors resulted from the stereotyped notion that literary creativity is exclusively male. This anxiety produced in women writers a tendency to create female characters who are monstrous or dangerous, "usually in some sense the author's double, an image of her own anxiety and rage" (see their *Madwoman in the Attic*).

GILLIGAN, CAROL (1936-). A professor of education, Harvard Graduate School of Education. Her research interests are adolescence, moral reasoning and conflict resolution, identity development, and the contribution of women's thinking to psychological theory. She has written numerous articles, but her most important work concerns her revisions of Kohlberg's theories of moral development in males. Gilligan's research, done with females, proved that women make moral decisions on different bases than men do. Women, she found, value community and "an ethic of care" that men do not possess. Her books include *In a Different Voice: Psychological Theory and Women's Development* (1982), *Making Connections: The Relational Worlds of Adolescent Girls at Emma Willard School* (co-edited with Nona P. Lyons and Trudy J. Hanmer, 1989), a collection of essays entitled *Mapping the Moral Domain: A Contribution of Women's Thinking to Psychological Theory and Education* (1988), and with Lyn Mikel Brown, *Meeting at the Crossroads: Women's Psychology and Girls' Development* (1992).

GILMAN, CHARLOTTE PERKINS (1860-1935). A prominent American feminist writer and theorist, author of one of the most famous Gothic short stories ever published, "The Yellow Wallpaper" (1892). Based on her own experience, the story depicts the disastrous consequences on a young mother of a treatment for postpartum depression prescribed by the well-respected nerve specialist, Dr. S. Weir Mitchell. After her own breakdown and divorce, Gilman remarried her cousin and gained custody of her daughter. She spent the rest of her life lecturing, writing, and editing a feminist newspaper, *The Forerunner* (1909-16). Her major feminist works include *Women and Economics* (1898) and *The Home: Its Work and*

Influence (1903); both were denunciations of what she called "androcentrism" (q.v.), and both advocated communal cooperation over masculine aggression and possessiveness.

GINSBURG, RUTH BADER (1933-). A member of the US Supreme Court since 1993 and pioneering litigator of women's rights cases during the 1970's as a founder of the American Civil Liberties Union's Women's Rights Project (q.v.). Before being appointed to the Supreme Court, she was a law professor at Rutgers University and Columbia University and a widely acclaimed legal scholar. She served on the US Court of Appeals, 1980-93.

GIOVANNI, NIKKI (1943-). A contemporary African-American poet, author of over 40 books of poetry, including *The Women and Men* (1975) and *My House* (1981). She has also published the essay collection *Sacred Cows and Other Edibles* (1988). Giovanni tours and lectures throughout the US, and teaches at Virginia Polytechnic Institute and State University.

GLASS CEILING. The discriminatory barriers affecting women in mid-management positions that prevent their advancement to higher ranks. Although women are advancing to middle-level managerial positions, they are infrequently found in top-level positions and directorships. The glass ceiling is invisible but powerful and may reflect overt or covert forms of discrimination.

GLOBAL FEMINISM. An international women's movement that emerged in the mid-1970's as an outgrowth of the International Women's Year (q.v.) and is rooted in the commonalities of women's lives: low economic status and the burden of the double shift (q.v.). Broadly defining all issues as women's issues, this international network has critically examined the impact of development (q.v.), patriarchal religions, international traffic in women (q.v.), and the Westernization of the Third World.

GODDESS (RELIGION). The recognition within most religions of one or more manifestations or embodiments of "female" qualities associated with reproduction and nurturance.

Projection of "feminine" qualities upon a cosmic symbol is a projection and legitimation of social qualities important to the survival and well-being of a social group. Veneration of a goddess does not indicate matriarchal rule or even particular respect for women, as is illustrated by the Virgin Mary (q.v.) in European societies. Contemporary belief and feminist interest in a Goddess religion are twentieth-century creations reflecting the increased opportunities for women to live independently and work in a variety of fields. Goddess religion legitimates and reinforces such contemporary women by projecting a cosmic dimension to their lives. Claims are made for great antiquity of this religion, to legitimate it through a myth of a primordial origin. Goddess religion in America and Europe is a real contemporary religion but not a survival of ancient religion.

GOESAERT V. CLEARY, 335 US 464 (1948). A decision of the US Supreme Court that upheld the constitutionality of protective labor legislation (q.v.) enacted by the state of Michigan to prohibit the licensing of women as bartenders unless related to male bar owners. As equality feminists (q.v.) had long argued, women could be "protected" from being employed by such statutes.

GOLDMAN, EMMA (1869-1940). A Russian immigrant to the United States, anarchist, feminist, and pioneer advocate of birth control. She introduced the concept of the "New Woman," a woman who attacked conventional marriage and advocated "free love." In 1916 she was arrested and jailed for 15 days for distributing birth control information. She worked as a nurse and midwife in New York City when not involved in writing or cross-country lecture tours advocating voluntary motherhood and family limitation. Goldman, however, opposed woman suffrage as a "fetish."

GOLDSTEIN, VIDA (1869-1949). An Australian leader of the United Council for Women's Suffrage and owner and editor of the feminist paper *The Australian Woman's Sphere*. In 1901 she was elected Secretary of the International Woman's Suffrage Society (q.v.) and was one of the founders of the Women's Political Association. She was the first woman candidate for the

Australian Parliament in 1903. In 1909 she began the periodical *The Woman*.

GOMER. In the Hebrew Bible, the wife of Hosea the prophet. A promiscuous woman, her relationship with Hosea is a metaphor for the sins of Israel. Stereotyped by some commentators as a temptress and adulteress who should be punished, feminists point out that such an image is taken out of context and that this interpretation is often used to justify violence against women.

GOSSIP. A negative term for a form of talk women use to indicate their concern about and for other people. When men gossip, it is called catching up on local news. But men are allowed to engage in gossip because they have a higher status in the social group. When women gossip such talk is viewed as uncontrolled or disruptive of the social harmony that men have a stake in preserving. Gossip is concerned with the actions of people which affect others, with relationships, and with character. In a positive sense, gossip reinforces community because it values people and the social codes and mores that the group believes are necessary for harmony. By labeling such talk negative or trivial, men attempt to marginalize the concerns and visions of women in social organizations.

GOTHIC NOVEL. A work generally recognized as a distinctly female art form that depicts the struggles of an orphaned young female heroine under siege by evil relatives, usually a corrupt uncle or aunt, to regain her rightful inheritance. In its emphasis on property rights, inheritance, and family dynamics, the Gothic novel explored the changing political and social ambience of Anglo-American women from the 1790s through the 1860s. Major practitioners of the Gothic novel were Mrs. Ann Radcliffe, Jane Austen, and Charlotte and Emily Brontë in England, and Charlotte Perkins Gilman (q.v.) in America. The tradition continues in the novels of Joyce Carol Oates and Anne Rice in America and Angela Carter (q.v.), Iris Murdoch, and Muriel Spark in England.

GOUGES, MARIE OLYMPE DE (1748-1793). A French playwright and pamphleteer who wrote a *Declaration of the*

Rights of Woman (1791) in Paris in response to the "Declaration of the Rights of Man" written for the French Revolution. An activist in the time of the revolution, she attempted to establish women's clubs for intellectual and political discussion, but they were outlawed. In her *Declaration* she argues, based on natural law assumptions, for full equal rights for women and equal opportunity of employment, education, and public office. Part of the treatise includes a social contract to serve as a replacement for marriage vows and calls for married women to be able to own property. In *The Call of the Wise by a Woman*, she urges people not to assume that the interests of women are included in those of their male relatives. She was sentenced to death by Robespierre and guillotined.

GOURNAY, MARIE LE JARS DE (1565-1645). A French author of poetry, essays, political works, and translations of classics. Her mentor was Michel de Montaigne and she was known as his spiritual daughter. Gournay was a staunch supporter of the rights of women to be educated and, in *Grief des Dames* (Women's Complaint), she expresses anger that men would not converse seriously with a woman. In *Égalité des Hommes et des Femmes* (The Equality of Men and Women), she argues that women are equal to men and that the essence of a human being is the soul, not his or her sex.

GRAFENBERG AREA (G-SPOT). An area located within the anterior wall of the vagina, along the course of the urethra, which is highly sensitive to erotic stimulation. Studies of women's sexual responses in the 1980's were based on earlier work by Ernest Grafenberg. The existence of the G-spot remains controversial and has given rise to the theory of a second type of female orgasm, the vaginal orgasm, rather than just a clitoral orgasm.

GRAHN, JUDY (1940-). A contemporary American lesbian poet, author of *The Work of a Common Woman* (1978), one of the first poetry collections to be published by and about working-class lesbian women. Grahn herself has worked as a waitress, in a meat-packing factory, as a maid and a secretary. Her poetry directs a good deal of anger at men at the same time that it celebrates women's survival skills.

GRASS-ROOTS FEMINISM. The branch of the movement based in local communities and focused on organizing, consciousness-raising (q.v.), and services to women. Generally radical and socialist feminists (qq.v.) are of this type. In nations with well-developed women's movements (e.g., Canada, Europe, India, the United States), both grass-roots and institutionalized feminism (q.v.) are active.

GREEN PARTY see KELLY, PETRA

GREENHAM COMMON WOMEN'S PEACE CAMP. A permanent British feminist collective (q.v.) of over 30,000 women, established in 1981 to protest the installation of Cruise missiles at a US airbase there. The encampment attracted an extensive support network in the United Kingdom and provided the model for the Seneca Women's Peace Encampment in Romules, New York. Both camps combine feminist spirituality with non-violent direct action and civil disobedience against militarism.

GREER, GERMAINE see FEMALE EUNUCH, THE

GRIFFIN, SUSAN (1943-). A contemporary American feminist poet and theorist, best known for her two works of feminist theory, *Woman and Nature: The Roaring Inside Her* (1978) and *Pornography and Silence: Culture's Revenge Against Nature* (1981). Her poetry collection, *Like the Iris of an Eye* (1976), contains the much-anthologized poem "I Like to Think of Harriet Tubman," a meditation on one woman's efforts to "make right / what is wrong."

GRIMKÉ, SARAH (1792-1873) AND ANGELINA (1805-1879). Sisters who were abolitionists and women's rights advocates in the United States. Born into a wealthy family in the US South, they were among the first women to lecture in public in the United States. They viewed women's rights and anti-slavery as related human rights issues. In 1838 Sarah wrote *Letters on the Equality of the Sexes and the Condition of Woman*, one of the first essays on women's equality by an American. It detailed the unscriptural and unchristian spirit of men and advised women to look to other women, not ministers, for religious validity.

GRISWOLD V. CONNECTICUT, 381 US 479 (1965). A decision of the US Supreme Court that found that a Connecticut law that prohibited the use of contraceptives by married couples violated constitutional rights to privacy (q.v.). The *Griswold* decision was one of the two cases that laid the foundation for the Supreme Court's decision in *Roe v. Wade* (q.v.) on abortion (q.v.).

GROUP CONSCIOUSNESS *see* FEMINIST CONSCIOUSNESS

GROVE CITY COLLEGE V. BELL, 456 US 555 (1984). A decision of the US Supreme Court that addressed two important issues regarding both the scope and the coverage of Title IX (q.v.), which forbids any educational program or activity receiving federal financial assistance from discriminating against persons on the basis of sex. The Court held that Title IX did not apply to the entire institution but only to the isolated program receiving federal funds. The Court, however, expansively interpreted the coverage of Title IX, holding that the statute could apply to institutions if only the students rather than the institution received federal financial assistance. Congress responded to this decision by enacting the Civil Rights Restoration Act of 1988. In amending Title IX, Congress explicitly provided that institution-wide coverage is required with the receipt of federal funds in a single program. Congress also extended the coverage of Title IX to include not only educational institutions, but also all of the operations of state or local government units and enterprises principally engaged in providing housing, health care, parks, or social services.

GUBAR, SUSAN *see* GILBERT, SANDRA

GUERRILLA GIRLS. A New York-based collective of anonymous women artists and gallery professionals who challenge white male dominance of the art world. The group was formed in 1985, in response to the underrepresentation of women artists (15 out of 166 artists) in an international survey show at New York's Museum of Modern Art. The women wear gorilla masks and fishnet stockings when staging their zap actions (q.v.) and plastering the city with witty posters. (*See also* Feminist Art and Aesthetic Theory.)

GYNOCRITICISM. A term coined by the literary critic Elaine Showalter (q.v.) in her seminal essay "Feminist Criticism in the Wilderness." Showalter defines "gynocriticism" as the study of women's writing and the processes and manifestations of female creativity. She distinguishes it from the early emphasis in feminist literary criticism (q.v.), which examined the stereotyped images and representations of women in literature primarily written by male authors. Gynocriticism is a criticism which concerns itself with developing a specifically female framework for analyzing works written by women, from their production to their motivation and interpretation.

-H-

HALE, SARAH JOSEPHA (1788-1879). A US opponent of enfranchisement for women and editor of the first major magazine for women, the *Ladies Magazine*, later the *Godey's Lady's Book*. Although she never endorsed the women's rights movement, Hale was an advocate of higher education for women, admission to the medical professions for women, and dress reform (q.v.).

HALIMI, GISELE *see* CHOISIR

HAMILTON, CICELY (1872-1952). A British feminist writer who advocated women's psychological and financial independence from men. She wrote *Marriage as a Trade* (1909), the play *How the Vote Was Won* (1909), history books, travel books, and critiques of male power and aggression.

HANNAH. In the Hebrew Bible, the wife of Elkanah and the mother of the prophet Samuel. Feminists emphasize that her insistence on having a child and dedication to God's service ensured the future of Israel in a troubled time.

HARASSMENT *see* SEXUAL HARASSMENT; STREET HARASSMENT

HARPER, FRANCES ELLEN WATKINS (1825-1911). An African-American lecturer, author, and reformer. She delivered her first anti-slavery speech, "Education and the Elevation of the Colored Race," in 1854 in New Bedford, Massachusetts. She travelled throughout the country for the next six years, varying her lectures with recitations from her *Poems on Miscellaneous Subjects* (1854), her volume of anti-slavery poetry. She stressed the need for education, temperance, and a higher standard of domestic morality among African-Americans. She also denounced racism within the suffrage movement. In 1896 she helped to organize the National Association of Colored Women (q.v.) and in 1897 became its president.

HARRIS V. FORKLIFT SYSTEMS see MERITOR SAVINGS BANK V. VINSON

HATE CRIMES. A term encompassing illegal speech or behavior directed toward others on the basis of their race, color, creed, religion, sex, or sexual orientation. In 1993 the US Supreme Court upheld (in *Wisconsin v. Mitchell*) a state law that assessed longer sentences for violent crimes motivated by bias. Some state and local legislatures have criminalized biased verbal or written insults, but in 1992 the Court struck down (in *R.A.V. v. St. Paul*) a local ordinance of this type on the grounds that constitutionally protected free speech was being prohibited. Critics charge that this legal approach requires politically correct (q.v.) speech and behavior. Supporters argue that hate speech is a violation of equal protection (q.v.) if it creates a hostile environment for women and minorities.

HAYS, MARY (1760-1843). A British feminist and author of the anonymously published *Appeal to the Men of Great Britain on Behalf of the Women* (1798). A close friend of Mary Wollstonecraft (q.v.), Hays also advocated greater freedom for women in marriage and ownership of property. Also a novelist, Hays published *The Memoirs of Emma Courtney* (1796), the story of an independent and educated woman; *The Victim of Prejudice* (1799), about an illegitimate orphan girl; and the *Dictionary of Female Biography*, six volumes (1803).

HEALTH MOVEMENT *see* WOMEN'S HEALTH MOVEMENT

HECATE. An ancient Greek goddess associated with prosperity, the underworld, and the occult. Regularly depicted as a crone, she was closely associated with Artemis in her role as moon-goddess and with Persephone, whom she attended in the underworld. According to Hesiod, Hecate was a beneficent and fostering goddess, powerful throughout all realms of nature to confer on mortals wisdom, victory, and good fortune. Small statues, called Hecataea, which depicted her in triple form, were erected at the entrances to houses and at the crossroads to ward off evil. Her strong association with black magic began in the Hellenistic Age (after 300 B.C.). Hecate represents the female life-cycle at its maturity, endowed with wisdom and mystic power.

HEILBRUN, CAROLYN (1926-). A prominent American literary critic, for many years professor of English at Columbia University. Best known as a scholar for her *Towards a Recognition of Androgyny* (1973), *Reinventing Womanhood* (1979) and *Hamlet's Mother and Other Women* (1990). She has also published a series of feminist detective novels under the name of Amanda Cross.

HELEN. According to Greek legend, the world's most beautiful woman whose elopement with Paris, a Trojan prince, was the poetic cause of the Trojan War. Her origins as a pre-Hellenic goddess of fertility, associated with trees, was reflected in the mythological details which portrayed her as the daughter of Zeus and favorite of Aphrodite with whom she was closely identified. Her mother was Leda, a mortal woman. After the Trojan War, Helen was reunited with her husband Menelaus, the king of Sparta, who forgave her infidelity because, as the husband of a demi-goddess, he was entitled after death to spend a blessed eternity at her side in the Elysian Fields. An alternate tradition, reflected in Euripides' *Helen*, absolves Helen of blame for causing the Trojan War and places her in Egypt for the duration of the war. In this version, only a "phantom" Helen went to Troy. The popular story of her elopement with Paris and the subsequent war to win her back is typical of Bronze Age feuds which regularly began with cattle-theft or bride-theft.

HERA. The Greek mythological queen of the gods and goddess of marriage and the family. Although her worship flourished in Greece before the Indo-European invaders brought Zeus, she was incorporated into the Olympian hierarchy as Zeus' sister and wife. In mythology, she plays the demeaning role of the frustrated, vindictive wife who punishes the unwilling partners and illegitimate offspring of her philandering husband. Her own offspring are Hephaestus, Mars, Hebe, and Eileithyia, goddess of childbirth, who is probably another manifestation of Hera herself, as guardian of the family. Hera's tempestuous union with Zeus reflects the fundamental clash of two religious systems--the goddess-oriented religion of the pre-Greek inhabitants and the patriarchal religion of the Indo-European invaders, which came to dominate in Greece. She was called Juno by the Romans.

HERETICAL RELIGIOUS SECTS, WOMEN IN. The movements such as the Gnostics and Montanists in the Patristic era, Cathars and Albigensians in the Middle Ages, and the followers of Anne Hutchinson in seventeenth-century America, in which women played significant roles. Although differences in doctrinal matters were decisive in assessing the orthodoxy of a given sect, feminists suggest that many of these groups were declared heretical expressly because of the high status and responsible positions of the women within them.

HERLAND. An early feminist novel written by Charlotte Perkins Gilman (q.v.) in 1915 depicting an all-woman utopia. Reprinted in 1979, it has become a standard text taught in women's literature classes. The sequel, *With Her in Ourland* (1916), continues the story and takes the protagonists back into civilization.

HETEROSEXISM. The tendency to regard heterosexuality more positively than other sexual orientations. The term is sometimes used as the equivalent of "homophobia."

HEWLETT, SYLVIA ANN (1946-). An economist and author of *A Lesser Life: The Myth of Women's Liberation in America* (1986), a revisionist view that charges that feminism is an elite-dominated movement that has ignored the needs of working mothers for child care, maternity leave, and protective labor laws (qq.v.). She also attacks the movement for championing no-fault divorce (q.v.) and gender-neutral (q.v.) domestic support laws.

HIDDEN WORK. A term used to describe women's work. To the extent that much of women's contributions are not (have not been) in the paid labor force and because our concept of work is tied to paid employment, women's work remains "hidden." Some suggest that the development of paid labor has resulted in the devaluation of women generally. Feminist scholars have emphasized women's essential and distinctive contributions: within the household (e.g., the provision of food, shelter, and clothing); in maintaining ties to the extended family and community (e.g., family and social networking, volunteer work and ties to school and community activities); and in support of employers (e.g., by caring for workers in the paid labor force and providing an available pool of cheap labor). For these reasons, feminists stress that every mother is a working mother.

HILL, ANITA (1956-). An African-American law professor and former government attorney who accused African-American Supreme Court Justice nominee Clarence Thomas of sexual harassment (q.v.) in a case that received national publicity during televised confirmation hearings. Professor Hill's credibility was sharply questioned, but no conclusion was reached about whether her charges were true. The Senate voted, 52-48, to confirm Thomas. In the aftermath, Hill became a powerful symbol for the feminist movement of the treatment of women who speak out against harassment. Feminist media were used to raise funds to endow a chair in her name at her institution, the University of Oklahoma Law School.

HOLTBY, WINIFRED (1898-1935). A British feminist, writer, and journalist. Author of *Women and a Changing Civilization* (1934), she wrote novels, short stories, and essays, and was a contributor to newspapers and women's publications. She argued that equality demanded mental and social transformation far beyond suffrage only. Her novels include *Anderby Wold* (1923), *The Land of Green Ginger* (1927), *Poor Caroline*

(1931), *The Astonishing Island* (1933), *Mandea! Mandea!* (1933), and *South Riding* (1936), her most popular book.

HOLYOAKE, GEORGE JACOB (1817-1906). An English male feminist who is known as the "father" of feminism. He published his own newspaper, *The Oracle of Reason*, where he advocated his secularist, liberal, and feminist beliefs. He recorded his support of women's equality in *The Workman and the Suffrage* (1858) and *Sixty Years of an Agitator's Life* (1893). A vigorous supporter of socialist society, education for women, and atheism, he called for a women's movement in the United States as well as England.

HOME BIRTH. The delivery of an infant within the home. The birth may be attended by a physician, certified nurse midwife (q.v), lay midwife or no one except family or friends. In reaction against the medicalization of childbirth (q.v.), feminists have expressed interest in and support for the home birth movement. (*See also* Alternative Birth Movement.)

HOMOSEXUALITY *see* LESBIANISM

HOOKS, BELL [pseudonym of GLORIA WATKINS] (1952-). An African-American feminist writer and cultural critic. Her books include *Yearning: Race, Gender and Cultural Politics, A Woman's Mourning Song, Black Looks: Race and Representation, Breaking Bread: Insurgent Black Intellectual Life,* and *Ain't I a Woman: Black Women and Feminism.* hooks, who uses only lower-case letters in her pseudonym, teaches English and women's studies at the City University of New York.

HORNEY, KAREN (1885-1952). A German-American psychoanalyst trained in Freudian analysis, but who went on to question Freud's (q.v.) assumptions about female sexuality. Most notably Horney claimed that rather than women experiencing "penis envy," men envied women's ability to give birth. Further, Horney understood "penis envy" as women's envy for man's superior status in society. She published extensively on the reasons for the distrust between the sexes, the development pattern of young girls, and the roots of conflict with the mother. Later in her life Horney developed a theory of female personality that posited three stages: moving toward others, against others, and withdrawal. She considered the integration of all three patterns to be normal behavior. After she published *New Ways in Psychoanalysis* (1930), she was forced to resign from the New York Psychoanalytic Society because she so threatened traditional Freudian truisms. In 1941 she founded the Association for the Advancement of Psychoanalysis and served as editor of the *American Journal of Psychoanalysis*.

HOSTILE ENVIRONMENT. A working or educational environment filled with unwelcome sexual attention. A hostile environment is created by communication practices which demean women through objectifying and sexualizing them. Such practices include invasion of personal space, touching, comments on appearance, sexual propositions, and sexual expletives. These practices reinforce male dominance (q.v.) through overt and covert intimidation. A hostile environment is the product of one type of illegal sexual harassment (q.v.). (*See also Meritor Savings Bank v. Vinson.*)

HOWE, JULIA WARD (1819-1910). An American author and lecturer best known for the "Battle Hymn of the Republic," first published in the *Atlantic Monthly* in February 1862. Howe was also a suffrage leader who helped found the New England Woman Suffrage Association and was active in the American Woman Suffrage Association (q.v.). A frequent speaker at conventions and legislative hearings, she was a founder of the *Women's Journal* (1870) and edited *Sex and Education* (1874). In 1873 she joined in founding the Association for the Advancement of Women, an organization that tried to advance the cause of equal education and professional and business opportunities for women. Howe was one of the founders of the General Federation of Women's Clubs (q.v.) as well as the first president of the Massachusetts Federation.

HOYT V. FLORIDA, 368 US 57 (1961). A decision of the US Supreme Court that upheld a statute which automatically exempted women from jury pools unless they volunteered their names. The Court based its decision on the separate spheres ideology first articulated in *Bradwell v. Illinois* (q.v.) in 1873. The Court stated that "woman is still regarded as the center of home and family life" and therefore a woman should be free to decide if jury duty was consistent "with her own special responsibilities."

HUMAN LIFE AMENDMENT *see* PRO-LIFE MOVEMENT

HUNT, HARRIOT KEZIA (1805-1875). An American physician, feminist reformer, and the first woman to practice medicine in the US She set up a medical clinic for women and children in Boston after studying privately with a physician. Harvard Medical School accepted her in 1850, the same year black men were admitted, but men students protested and she was forced to withdraw. The Female Medical College of Philadelphia awarded her an honorary degree of Doctor of Medicine in 1853. Hunt's medical theories were based on physiology, natural laws, and the science of disease prevention. She advocated attention to diet, bathing, rest, exercise, and sanitation, and in 1843 founded the Ladies Physiological Society in Charlestown, Massachusetts, a center for medical reform for working-class women and children.

HURSTON, ZORA NEALE (c. 1901-1960). An African-American novelist, essayist, and folklorist. She is the author of the classic feminist text, *Their Eyes Were Watching God* (1937), a novel about life in an all-black town in Florida, modelled on Hurston's own childhood home in Eatonville. After a brief stint at Howard University, Hurston made her way to New York City, where she moved on the fringes of the Harlem Renaissance and worked with artists like Langston Hughes. A genius at garnering financial support, Hurston studied anthropology at Barnard College and gathered folktales with the financial support of wealthy white donors. She had two Guggenheim fellowships to travel in the Caribbean (1936-37), and worked for a time for the Federal Writers' Project in Florida. Hurston observed that "de nigger woman is de mule uh de world," but her novels and essays celebrate the strength and tenacity of black women, all of them, like Hurston "jumping at de sun."

HYDE AMENDMENT. A provision, named for its sponsor US Representative Henry Hyde of Illinois, passed in every session of Congress since 1976 to restrict the use of federal Medicaid funding for abortions (q.v.). Although the exceptions have varied, federal money as of 1995 can be used when pregnancies are life-threatening or result from rape (q.v.) or incest. The US Supreme Court in *Harris v. McRae* (1980) upheld the amendment as reflecting a "legitimate congressional interest in protecting potential life." The annual renewal of the provision is highly contested by the pro-life and pro-choice (qq.v) forces. It is an important symbol for both movements, even though its impact on reducing abortion has proven negligible.

HYPATIA. A journal founded in 1983 by members of the Society for Women in Philosophy to provide a forum for the discussion of philosophical issues raised by the new women's movement.

HYPHENATED NAMES *see* NAMING CONVENTIONS

-I-

ICHIKAWA, FUSAE (1893-1981). Organizer, with Hiratsuka Raicho and others, of the equal rights Association of New Women (1919) and the Women's Suffrage Alliance (1924) in Japan. In 1946 she was instrumental in gaining General Douglas MacArthur's support for the women's vote; that same year, she founded the Women Suffrage Center. While a member of the Diet's House of Councillors during the United Nations' Decade for Women (q.v.), Ichikawa formed a coalition of 48 women's groups that gained parliamentary approval of the U. N. Convention on the Elimination of All Forms of Discrimination Against Women (q.v.).

IDENTITY POLITICS. An attempt to make feminist theory and action coherent with one's personal life. This may involve viewing lesbianism (q.v.) as a political definition, not a clinical sexual identity, and addressing questions of class, race, and sexual practices such as sadomasochism and their legitimacy within the feminist community.

"I'M NOT A FEMINIST BUT" SYNDROME. A set of beliefs that includes support for an equal role in society for women but rejects the efforts of the feminist movement. Even among many who support gender equality, the term "feminist" evokes negative connotations from which they seek to disassociate themselves.

IMPOSTOR PHENOMENON. The notion that one's achievements are spurious or that one is overly well regarded. This is accompanied by a fear of being discovered or unmasked as undeserving of recognition. This reaction is believed to occur more commonly among females who are not socialized to an achievement ethic or suffer from low self-esteem (q.v.).

IN A DIFFERENT VOICE. A book, published by Carol Gilligan (q.v.) in 1982, that suggests that women's moral development and moral reasoning are distinctively different from those of men and introduces the notion that women's moral experience gives rise to an "ethic of care." She presents data based on social scientific studies to support a new conception of women's moral development as consisting of three stages: self-oriented, other-oriented, and, at the highest stage, an appropriate balance between the concerns of self and others. Gilligan argues that care is the distinguishing hallmark of women's moral experiences. The ethic of care provides an alternative to traditional Western conceptions of ethics that are based on such notions as virtue, rights, duty, justice, and respect.

IN RE BABY M. A 1988 New Jersey Supreme Court case that ruled that surrogacy (q.v.) is illegal in that it constitutes baby-selling. The parties to the suit were William and Elizabeth Stern, a married couple, and Mary Beth Whitehead, who for a fee of $10,000 agreed to be inseminated with Stern's sperm and to turn over that child to the Sterns for adoption. Whitehead refused to surrender Baby M after birth. The court upheld a lower court's custody award to William Stern but restored Whitehead's parental rights, including visitation privileges. Feminists were deeply divided on the case. Equality feminists (q.v.) believed that women are competent to enter into contracts involving their bodies; difference feminists (q.v.) viewed surrogacy as victimization of both infertile women and those who, in reality, signed over control of their bodies in entering these contracts. The issue of class exploitation was also an underlying concern in a case involving two affluent well-educated scientists and a high school dropout with a history of domestic violence (q.v.) and welfare dependency.

INCLUSIVE LANGUAGE *see* NONSEXIST LANGUAGE

INDEPENDENT WOMEN'S ASSOCIATION (UNABHÄNGIGER FRAUENVERBAND, UFV). A group formed in 1989 by women from the German Democratic Republic (East Germany) as a feminist group committed to the emancipation of women in the new Germany. In adopting the title "Independent," the founders differentiated themselves from the Communist Party's official women's group, the Democratic League of Germany. The UFV has established women's centers (q.v.) and services for women in the larger cities. Since 1991 memberhip has been open to all German women.

INDIRECTNESS. The process of refraining from saying directly what is really meant. Instead of stating exactly what is meant, people hint, speak obliquely, or explain only part of their meaning. In so doing people establish a sense of rapport (a partner understands a veiled reference) and protect themselves as well (rejection is impossible without a direct request). Convention has it that women are more indirect than men. This often carries with it a negative connotation, that women should simply say what is on their minds. Gender communications scholar Deborah Tannen points out that both women and men speak indirectly because it is basic to communication and provides a pay-off.

INDIVIDUALIST FEMINISM *see* LIBERAL FEMINISM

INFIBULATION *see* FEMALE GENITAL MUTILATION

INNUMERACY. The lack of expected proficiency in tasks involving numbers, particularly when attributable to low social encouragement of these skills. Some feminists maintain that innumeracy has been inculcated in women. (*See also* Mathique/Feminine Mathique.)

INSANITY PLEAS (DEFENSE). A successful criminal defense that results in the commitment of the defendant to a mental institution until sanity has been restored. Acceptance of such a defense in a jury trial is usually noted by a jury finding of "not guilty by reason of insanity." In recent years, a substantial minority of states has adopted the Model Penal Code approach, which allows that a defendant is not responsible for the crime if, at the time, because of mental disease or defect, that person lacked substantial capacity either to appreciate the criminality (wrongfulness) of that conduct or to conform to the requirements of the law. Victims of domestic violence (q.v.) who have killed or mutilated their batterers in self-defense have been acquitted on the grounds of temporary insanity, a defense strategy that feminists usually support. Use of this defense in cases of premenstrual syndrome (PMS) (q.v.) are more controversial in that there is an implication that all menstruating women are irrational and victims of biology.

INSTITUTIONALIZED FEMINISM. The branch of the movement based within traditional political institutions such as legislatures, political parties, and public bureaucracies and focused on the legal rights of women. Generally liberal feminism (q.v.) is of this type. In nations with well-developed women's movements (e.g., Canada, Europe, India, the United States), both institutionalized and grass-roots feminism (q.v.) are active.

INSURANCE, SEX DISCRIMINATION IN *see ARIZONA GOVERNING COMMITTEE V. NORRIS; LOS ANGELES DEPARTMENT OF WATER AND POWER V. MANHART*

INTERMEDIATE STANDARD OF CONSTITUTIONAL SCRUTINY *see CRAIG V. BOREN*

INTERNATIONAL ALLIANCE OF WOMEN (IAW). A group founded in 1904 as the International Woman Suffrage Alliance, under the leadership of Carrie Chapman Catt (q.v.), to press for the female vote in all countries with representative forms of government. By 1925 around 25 national suffrage societies had become members. The group had a more radical and activist perspective than the International Council of Women (q.v.) and met biennially in congress.

INTERNATIONAL COUNCIL OF WOMEN (ICW). An organization founded by the Elizabeth Cady Stanton and Susan B. Anthony (qq.v.) branch of the American suffrage movement in 1888, at a conference to celebrate the fortieth anniversary of the Seneca Falls Convention (q.v.). Only national women's councils could be affiliates, and by 1914 more than 20 nations, including Australia, South Africa, and Argentina, had established these councils. The ICW was moderately feminist and its congresses, held at five-year intervals, provided for the exchange of ideas across national boundaries. Its agenda included most women's rights issues of the time, except, for a long period, suffrage on which unanimity did not exist. In many European countries, these national councils of women remain as important lobbying groups.

INTERNATIONAL FEMINIST NETWORK AGAINST FEMALE SEXUAL SLAVERY *see* INTERNATIONAL TRAFFIC IN WOMEN

INTERNATIONAL TRAFFIC IN WOMEN. The sexual exploitation of women through sex tours (q.v.) and prostitution (q.v.) on a global scale. Women from poorer Asian countries are also promised service jobs in richer nations like Japan but are instead forced into prostitution. In 1983 Kathleen Barry formed the International Feminist Network Against Female Sexual Slavery to combat these practices.

INTERNATIONAL UNION, UAW V. JOHNSON CONTROLS, 111 S.CT. 1196 (1991). A decision of the US Supreme Court that considered whether a fetal protection policy that excluded only fertile female employees from certain jobs violated Title VII of the Civil Rights Act of 1964 (q.v.). Finding that the policy was not neutral but sex-specific, the Court concluded that the policy did not fall within the bona fide occupational qualification (q.v.) exception. Fertile women were able to perform the essential functions associated with the manufacturing positions in question as well as anyone else. The Court concluded that Title VII "forbids sex-specific fetal protection policies." Feminists generally hailed the decision as one that gave women the right to weigh the risks and choose high-paying, dangerous jobs, but they also urged that the workplace be made safe for all workers.

INTERNATIONAL WOMAN SUFFRAGE ALLIANCE *see* INTERNATIONAL ALLIANCE OF WOMEN

INTERNATIONAL WOMEN'S DAY. An event celebrated annually on March 8, particularly in countries with a strong socialist movement. In 1910 Clara Zetkin (q.v.) and Luise Zietz of the Socialist Women's International (q.v.) led the drive to designate a day for a celebration of women as a recruitment device for the socialist movement and as a way to support woman suffrage. The first event was held on March 18, 1911, and continued on that date until Lenin adopted March 8 to coincide with the anniversary of the 1917 Russian Revolution. With the rise of the new feminist movement (q.v.) in the late 1960's, nonsocialist nations have joined this feminist celebration.

INTERNATIONAL WOMEN'S RIGHTS ACTION WATCH (IWRAW). A global network of several thousand individuals and organizations, begun in 1985 to monitor implementation of the Convention on the Elimination of All Forms of Discrimination Against Women (q.v.). The Women, Public Policy and Development Program in the Humphrey Institute of Public Affairs at the University of Minnesota serves as the clearinghouse for the network. The IWRAW publishes a newsletter, *Women's Watch*.

INTERNATIONAL WOMEN'S YEAR (IWY) (1975). An event proclaimed in 1970 by the United Nations, which sponsored a world conference that year in Mexico City. Conferees adopted a World Plan of Action for the improvement of the status of women within the legal, economic, political, social, and cultural system of each country. The International Women's Year was extended to a Decade for Women (1976-85) by the United Nations and three more world conferences were held in Copenhagen (1981), Nairobi (1985), and Beijing (1995). Although delegations to all three conferences were selected on the basis of official position or personal connections, rather than feminist ideology or policy expertise, these events helped to establish an international feminist network.

INTERRUPTION. A competitive use of language by which one person stops another from talking, either by challenging, changing the subject, or terminating the conversation. In mixed sex conversation, studies have shown that men interrupt 75 percent of the time. In practice, interruption may look like cooperative overlapping, but in function, it short-circuits rather than manages conversation. (*See also* Conversational Style.)

INTERSECTIONALITY. The legal requirements noted by law professor Kimberle Crenshaw that minority women base their discrimination claims on either evidence of sex discrimination or race discrimination, but not both. These requirements permit employers to invidiously discriminate against minority women as long as they do not discriminate against minority men or white women.

INTRAUTERINE DEVICE (IUD) *see* DALKON SHIELD

INVOLUNTARY STERILIZATION *see* STERILIZATION ABUSE

IRIGARAY, LUCE (1930-). Contemporary French feminist and theorist, best known as the author of *The Sex Which Is Not One* and *The Speculum of the Other Woman* (both 1985). The latter is a study of the phallocentric (q.v.) bias in Freud (q.v.) and cost Irigaray her teaching position at the University of Paris (Vincennes). Irigaray argues that women are distinctively different from men and that this difference is biologically based. Only when women assert their *jouissance* (q.v.) can they subvert phallocentric oppression and speak in their own voices. Irigaray proposes a "woman's writing" which defies male monopoly and the risk of appropriation (q.v.) into the existing patriarchal system by establishing as its originating principle the diversity and fluidity of the female sexual organs. Irigaray argues that woman's problematic relationship to masculine language is caused by her sexuality: "Woman has sex organs just about everywhere. She is infinitely other in herself. That is undoubtedly the reason she is called temperamental, incomprehensible, perturbed, capricious--not to mention her language in which she goes off in all directions and in which he is unable to discern the coherence of any meaning. Contradictory words seem a little crazy to the logic of reason, and inaudible for him who listens with ready-made grids, a code prepared in advance. In her statements--at least when she dares to speak out--woman retouches herself constantly" (see her *Speculum of the Other Woman*). (*See also L'Écriture Féminine.*)

ISIS. According to Egyptian mythology, the great mother-goddess and embodiment of the life-bestowing principle of nature. She restored her murdered husband, Osiris, to life after a long search for his body, and subsequently became the mother of Horus, the sun-god. Called *myrionymia* ("of countless names"), she was believed to have dominion over the seas, the earth, and the underworld, where she was powerful to bestow immortality on the souls of her believers. Through the process of syncretism, she was identified with several deities in the Greco-Roman world, notably Demeter and the Virgin Mary. Apuleius' novel, *The Golden Ass*, contains moving testimony to her broad powers and beneficent nature and to the ethical nature of her worship.

IT TEST. A test devised by Daniel Brown to assess gender identity in children, who were asked to make choices on behalf of a purportedly sex neutral stick figure ("It"). The actual neutrality of the figure has been questioned by feminists, among others. The test was riddled with stereotypic assumptions and has fallen out of favor.

ITALIAN WOMEN'S UNION (UNIONE DELLE DONNE ITALIANE, UDI). A group formed in liberated areas in 1944 to work for the political and economic rights of women. After the end of World War II, the UDI became associated with the Communist Party, which caused Catholic women to withdraw. The large (upwards of a quarter million members) organization now represents the reform (q.v.) branch of the movement and has successfully worked for day care (q.v.), divorce law reform, equal pay (q.v.), maternity leave (q.v.), and spousal benefits. In 1982 the UDI ended its formal links with the Communist Party.

-J-

JACOBS, ALETTA (1854-1929). The first female doctor in the Netherlands, credited with opening the world's first birth control clinic in 1882 in Amsterdam. She advocated shorter working hours, protective labor legislation (q.v.), venereal disease education, the abolition of regulated prostitution (q.v.), and reform of the marriage laws. She was a prominent suffragist as well. In 1883 her attempts to register to vote led the government to formally restrict the voting rolls to men. She was a founder and president of the Dutch Suffrage Association and active in the International Alliance of Women (q.v.). In 1911 she toured the world for suffrage with Carrie Chapman Catt (q.v.). During World War I she led the peace movement with Jane Addams (q.v.).

JAEL. In the Hebrew Bible, the woman who elicits the trust of Sisera, Israel's enemy, in order to slay him. The account stresses her unique position as a woman and as a foreigner in this unusual role.

JAMESON, ANNA (1794-1860). An Irish feminist and writer whose travel books, art books, and literary criticism included protests against women's position in society. Among her most successful works are *Characteristics of Women* (1832), essays on the women characters in Shakespeare's dramas, and *Sacred and Legendary Art* (1848-60).

JANE COLLECTIVE. A Chicago Women's Liberation Union (q.v.) project that performed around 11,000 illegal abortions (q.v.), 1969-73. After 1970 the women of the collective began to perform abortions themselves and had a safety record for first-trimester procedures comparable to clinics in states with legalized abortions. Counseling, birth control information, and a Pap smear were part of the abortion services provided for an average cost of $45.

JANE EYRE. A British novel published by Charlotte Brontë in 1848. Jane Eyre, like so many earlier domestic and Gothic heroines, was an orphan forced to prove herself and regain her rightful social class and inheritance. The novel, published under a male pseudonym, was attacked at the time of its publication for its feminist undertones; indeed, its heroine at one point in the novel demands meaningful work and to be treated with respect and equality by the hero. Generally considered to be a classic in women's literature, *Jane Eyre* established many of the standard devices now recognized as staples of women's literature.

JEPHTHAH'S DAUGHTER. In the Hebrew Bible, the young woman who greets her father after a victory for which he promised to sacrifice the first person or thing he saw upon his return. Feminists demonstrate that Jephthah's vow was unnecessary and irresponsible. In contrast to her father, who has no other children to remember him, she is honored each year by a four-day ceremony by the women of Gilead.

JEWISH FEMINISM. A type of feminism in which ethnicity and religion intersect with gender. Religious Jewish women seek greater participation for women in religious and community life and the inclusion of feminist ideals (and the exclusion of sexist practices) within Judaism. The survival of Jews and Israel is a major goal but a feminist commitment to peace and democracy is also reflected in concern for the rights and humanity of the Palestinians and Middle East peace.

JIU JIN (QUIU JIN) (1875-1907). A nationalist and feminist, who revolted against the Manchu dynasty and supported the emancipation of Chinese women. Born into the gentry and classically educated, Jiu Jin left her husband and children to study in Japan for two years. She challenged the traditional Confucian role for women by riding horseback, fencing, drinking wine, and adopting Western male dress. In 1906 she published the *Chinese Women's Journal* and formed a women's army. She was executed in 1907 for her role in a plot to overthrow the government.

JOB RETENTION. A provision that guarantees employees the right to return to their jobs or a comparable position after taking time off for the birth or adoption of a child, to care for a seriously ill family member, or to recover from their own illness or disability. Such policies reduce work-family conflict (q.v.), particularly for women. (*See also* Family and Medical Leave Act of 1993; Family Leave.)

JOB SHARING. The division of job responsibilities of one full-time position between two employees, typically to permit them to fulfill child-rearing responsibilities. Ideally both employees will be eligible for fringe benefits and promotions. In practice, both supervisors and colleagues may view these workers as less committed to the organization.

JOHNSON V. TRANSPORTATION AGENCY OF SANTA CLARA COUNTY, CALIF., 480 US 616 (1987). A decision of the US Supreme Court that upheld the use of gender preferences in affirmative action (q.v.) plans. The case involved a charge of reverse discrimination (q.v.) by a man who was denied a supervisory position given to a woman, despite his longer work experience and a slightly higher score on an oral interview. Because of the gender imbalance in the agency workforce (not one of the agency's 238 skilled positions was held by a woman), the court ruled that Title VII of the Civil Rights Act of 1964 (q.v.) permits some discretion to end discrimination.

JOINT CUSTODY. A legal arrangement between a child's parents, who no longer have (or never had) a legal relationship with each other. Joint custody stipulates that both parents be involved in the physical care and/or major decisions about the child's well-being rather than granting specific legal custody to one or the other of the parents. In most of these arrangements, the child remains under the primary care of the mother. For this reason, some feminists have expressed concern that fathers may threaten to ask for joint custody as a way of receiving a more favorable division of marital property (q.v.) and lower child support awards.

JOKING-HUMOR. The suggestion that men and women have different styles of humor. Men's humor is generally found in specific jokes with punch lines. Women's humor is often embedded in stories and situations and is more contextual. Joke telling is often used by men to make a point or criticize women while at the same time being able to deny their negative message (i.e., "I was only joking.") (*See also* Feminist Humor.)

JONES, "MOTHER" MARY HARRIS (1830-1930). A teacher and dynamic labor activist, who was an official organizer for the United Mine Workers and co-founder of the Industrial Workers of the World. Jones' first association with a labor organization was with the Knights of Labor in 1871. Thereafter she travelled throughout the United States working on behalf of various labor groups. She was actively involved in Socialist Party politics and was arrested on numerous occasions for her support of striking miners. Jones was critical of her feminist contemporaries whom she felt were too removed from the realities of poor women. New feminists (q.v.), however, have embraced her feisty spirit that urged women to raise more hell and fewer daisies.

JONG, ERICA (1942-). An American poet and novelist, best known for her feminist potboilers, *Fear of Flying* (1973), *How to Save Your Own Life* (1977), and *Fanny, Being the True History of the Adventures of Fanny Hackabout-Jones* (1980). Less a serious feminist theorist than an adventuress with a sexually explicit imagination, Jong's poetry is taken more seriously by feminist literary critics.

JOUISSANCE. The direct reexperience of the physical pleasures of the female body. There is little agreement among the new French feminists (q.v.) about what this *jouissance* consists of or how it can be articulated in language that is itself a product of patriarchal culture.

JUDITH. In the Apocrypha, the woman in the book which bears her name. Without the help of any men she assassinates the general of the Assyrian army, Holophernes, demoralizing the troops and saving a strategic Judean city from attack. Judith is a timeless example of the piety and faith of women and embodies the respect that some independent women of means enjoyed in Israel.

-K-

KAHN V. SHEVIN, 416 US 351 (1974). A decision of the US Supreme Court that involved an equal protection (q.v.) challenge to a Florida law which entitled widows but not widowers to a $500 property tax exemption. Accepting the state's claim "that the purpose of the law was to reduce 'the disparity between the economic capabilities of a man and a woman,'" the Court approved the widows-only tax exemption. For some feminists, the decision merely reinforced the image of women as permanently needy in upholding a law that offered very meager benefits.

K'ANG YU-WEI (1858-1927). Prominent Chinese leader of the reformist movement of the 1890s to expand women's rights. His *Book of the Great Community* (1903) described the inferior status of women and an egalitarian society where marriage is a renewable contract and men and women wear unisex (q.v.) clothing. In 1892 he formed the first "Unbound-Feet Society" in Canton.

KARTINI, RADEN AJENG (1879-1904). A founder of the women's rights movement in Indonesia. Both a product of and a party to polygynous marriages, she opposed the practice and forced marriage generally. Denied the right to study beyond age 12, she supported women's education by forming a girls' school. After her death in childbirth at age 25, her letters (*Through Darkness Into Light*) were published in Holland and translated into Indonesian in 1923. Kartini later became a cult figure who is recognized as a national heroine.

KELLY, PETRA (1947-1992). A founder of the Green Party and activist in the peace, ecology, and feminist movements in West Germany. Kelly served in the German Parliament (Bundestag), 1983-90. The circumstances surrounding her gun-related death continue to be controversial. She correctly predicted that the reunification of Germany would diminish the legal rights of women in both East and West Germany.

KENNEDY, FLORYNCE (FLO) (1916-). An African-American lawyer, civil rights activist, feminist lecturer and writer, and founder of the Feminist Party and the Coalition Against Racism and Sexism. Kennedy led one of the first legal challenges (in 1971) to the use of tax-exempt funds by the US Catholic Church in its anti-abortion activities. Kennedy was among the relatively few women of color (q.v.) who participated in the women's liberation movement (q.v.) and was among the founders of the National Organization for Women (q.v.).

KESSLER-HARRIS, ALICE *see EQUAL EMPLOYMENT OPPORTUNITY COMMISSION V. SEARS, ROEBUCK AND CO.*

KINDER-KÜCHE-KIRCHE (CHILDREN, KITCHEN, CHURCH). A phrase used in the same way as the English "barefoot and pregnant" (q.v.). The National Socialist Party in Germany during the 1930's and 1940's attempted to link national economic problems and working women. The Nazis largely succeeded in reviving the traditional role of German women as the ideal. In the first volume of *EMMA* (q.v.), editor Alice Schwarzer (q.v.) suggested that the materialist thinking of the postwar period had in fact replaced "church" with "consuming" (*Konsum*).

KISHIDO, TOSHIKO (1863-1901). A Liberal Party lecturer for women's issues and suffrage in Japan. In 1883 she was arrested and jailed after a speech attacking the Japanese family system. Kishido supported education and job training for women, legal equality, and identical sexual codes for men and women. She founded the Kyoto Women's Lecture Society and was a frequent contributor to women's magazines.

KNIGHTS OF LABOR, WOMEN. A US Catholic labor organization, founded in 1869, that achieved national recognition under the leadership of Terrence V. Powderly and Leonora Barry, who was appointed to the Knights' executive board as general investigator for women's labor. In 1886 women members received approval to set up a women's association, the Lady Knights of Labor. Chartered "ladies locals" brought women together from every sphere of labor (including domestic) for cooperative organizing. Comprising up to ten percent of the union's membership by the late 1880s, the Lady Knights worked for equal pay (q.v.), women's suffrage and the temperance movement.

KOEDT, ANNE *see* "MYTH OF THE VAGINAL ORGASM"

KOLLONTAI, ALEXANDRA (1872-1952). The foremost feminist socialist in the Russian Social Democratic Party, with responsibility after 1905 for organizing working-class women. The only female commissar (of charities and public welfare) in Lenin's government, she subsequently headed the Women's Department, the Zhenotdel. Through influential essays, such as "The Social Basis of the Woman's Question" (1908), she promoted communal housework, free maternity care, the legalization of abortion (q.v.), and egalitarian marriage easily terminated by divorce. Her advocacy of a woman's right to control and enjoy her own sexuality and her personal sexual behavior ultimately cost her Lenin's support. She was removed from office in 1922 and exiled to minor diplomatic posts.

KONGRES WANITA INDONESIA (CONGRESS OF INDONESIAN WOMEN, KOWANI). A coalition of more than 50 women's groups that, since independence was declared in 1945, has worked for women's legal rights, including suffrage under the new constitution of 1949.

KRAMARAE, CHERIS (1938-). A US feminist communications scholar and author of the landmark book *Women and Men Speaking* (1981). Kramarae is well-known for her development of muted group theory as it applies to women's communication. She published *The Feminist Dictionary* (1985) with Paula Treichler and teaches in the Department of Communication at the University of Illinois-Urbana.

KRISTÉVA, JULIA (1941-). Contemporary French feminist, novelist, theorist, and essayist, best known for her semiotic and psychoanalytic writings: *Revolution in Poetic Language* (1984), *Tales of Love* (1987), *Powers of Horror* (1982), *Black Sun* (1989), *About Chinese Women* (1977). Born in Bulgaria, Kristéva has conducted a critique of structuralism and advocated instead what she calls "semanalysis," a poststructuralist approach to literature that sees the text as a dynamic "working" of language through the desires of the speaking subject as she reacts to the social and economic forces we know as history. In literature writers take the ideologies of their culture and displace or decenter them by using linguistic signifiers in unusual or shocking ways. The result is polyvalence, or multiple meanings that undermine or suspend all oppositional meanings. Kristéva posits a "chora," or prelinguistic, pre-oedipal signifying process centered on the mother that she calls the "semiotic." This original voice is repressed when we gain patriarchal language which she labels the "symbolic." The semiotic can always break out in revolutionary ways--particularly in avant-garde poetry--as a "heterogeneous destructive causality" that assaults the stable "subject." This assault undermines the rationality of phallic discourse and the power of the "law of the Father," the patriarchal system that keeps women in a marginal status. Kristéva sees women as "hysterics," outsiders to male-dominated discourse, largely because of their ability to bear children and their marginality in relation to masculine culture: "If women have a role to play it is only in assuming a negative function: reject everything finite, definite, structured, loaded with meaning, in the existing state of society. Such an attitude places women on the side of the explosion of social codes: with revolutionary movements" (see her *Polylogue)*.

KRUPSKAYA, NADEZHDA (1869-1939). The wife of V. I. Lenin and editor of *The Working Woman* (1913). Krupskaya's *The Woman Worker* (1900) was only a small brochure but was extremely popular and influential in the socialist women's movement. It was both an accessible Russian Marxist analysis on women and the first revolutionary statement to women written by a Russian since the 1870s (and the first by a Russian woman).

KVINNEUNIVERSITETET. The first feminist university, founded in 1985 in Loten, Norway. A bylaw states its goal as "building a center for education based on feminist values and feminist methods of instruction." The university is small (around 1,500 students), offers degrees recognized by the ministry of education, and emphasizes off-campus and adult education.

-L-

LABARCA HUBERTSON, AMANDA (1886-1975). A feminist leader in Chile and founder in 1915 of the Círculo de Lectura

(Women's Reading Circle) that in 1919 helped to form a National Council of Women to work for woman suffrage. In 1944 Amanda Labarca was chosen to lead the newly formed Federation of Women's Organizations and in 1949 Chilean women received the vote.

LABOR FORCE PARTICIPATION. A reference to paid employment in the labor force. Women's labor force participation in the United States has been steadily increasing; in 1949 26 percent of married women between the ages of 25 and 44 held jobs, by 1989 it was 67 percent. Women accounted for more than three-fifths of the labor force growth between 1984 and 1995. The increase in labor force participation among women corresponds to the increase in dual-career couples (q.v.) and the need for more day care (q.v.) and family-friendly organizational policies and practices such as flexitime and job sharing (qq.v.). (*See also* Family Leave; Work-Family Conflict.)

LACAN, JACQUES (1901-1981). A French psychoanalyst whose writings have been collected in the large volume *Ecrits* (1977), best known among feminists for his revision of traditional Freudian theory. According to Lacan, the true subject of psychoanalysis and language was the unconscious mind, rather than the ego. Lacan claimed that the unconscious was structured like a language and could only reveal its meanings through the connection of its signifiers. Lacan reformulated Freud's (q.v.) theories about psychosexual development by seeing them as stages in the use of language. The prelinguistic stage he called the "imaginary" and the stage after the acquisition of language he called the "symbolic." In the first stage he claimed that there was no clear distinction between the subject and the object, or between self and others. But in the second stage the child assimilates the inherited system of linguistic differences, and then learns to accept its pre-determined "position" in such linguistic oppositions as male/female, father/son, mother/daughter. Lacan saw the symbolic realm of language as the realm of the law of the father, in which the "phallus" (the symbol of the father's power) was the "privileged signifier" for all discourse. Lacan further claimed that all discourse was driven by a "desire" for a lost and unachievable object, as if moving incessantly along a chain of unstable signifiers without any possibility of coming to any final point of meaning of fixed significance.

LADY KNIGHTS OF LABOR *see* KNIGHTS OF LABOR, WOMEN.

LAHAYE, BEVERLY (1930?-). A US anti-feminist (q.v.) spokesperson, author, and founder of Concerned Women for America (q.v.). LaHaye is the wife of Baptist minister Tim LaHaye, himself a co-founder of the New Religious Right group, the Moral Majority. LaHaye is well-known in religious circles for her book *The Spirit-Controlled Woman* (1976) and a sex manual for evangelicals, *The Act of Marriage* (1976), co-written with her husband.

LANGE, HELENE (1848-1930). An activist in the first German women's movement. Lange overcame strong resistance to earn a teaching license and then became an advocate of education for women. In 1894 she founded the Federation of German Women's Associations. As its leader until 1930, she resisted the influence of more radical feminists, even to the point of refusing admission of Social Democrat groups. She did, however, support the easing of Germany's abortion (q.v.) laws.

LATINA FEMINISM *see* CHICANA POLITICS

LAVENDER MENACE. A term used to describe the threat that some feared lesbians (q.v.) presented to the legitimacy of the new feminist movement (q.v.) as opponents attempted to equate feminism with lesbianism. In response, at the second Congress to Unite Women, held in New York City in May 1970, about 20 radical feminists (q.v.) wearing T-shirts bearing the words "Lavender Menace" read a position paper presenting lesbianism as a political choice. As a group, the Lavender Menace later changed their name to Radicalesbians. (*See also* Political Lesbianism.)

LEAGUE OF WOMEN VOTERS (LWV). A group formally organized in 1920 as the US post-suffrage successor of the National American Woman Suffrage Association (q.v.) in order to integrate women into the political system. The League was a participant within the early social feminist (q.v.) coalition, the Women's Joint Congressional Committee (q.v.), but withdrew in the 1950's and ignored feminist issues until its endorsement of the Equal Rights Amendment (q.v.) in 1972. The group has since become a major force within state and national women's rights lobbies. Despite its preference during much of its history to be classified as a "public interest" group rather than a "women's" group and its strict policy of nonpartisanship, the League has trained and motivated many women to seek elective office.

LEAH. In the Hebrew Bible, daughter of Laban, sister of Rachel (q.v.), and wife of Jacob. Usually ignored by past commentators, feminists stress that Leah suffers from her father's scheme to have Jacob unwittingly marry her. Jacob disregards her, and God responds to her plight by blessing her with six sons, eponymous ancestors of tribes of Israel. She also has a daughter, Dinah. Along with Rachel, Leah severs the ties with her treacherous father and permits Jacob to return to Canaan, thus ensuring the clan's inheritance of the land of God's promise.

LEARNED HELPLESSNESS. A term used by Martin Seligman to refer to subjective estimates of low probability of success in one's undertakings as a consequence of a history of low reinforcement for--or active discouragement of--achievement. Such an attitude may lead to depression when the helplessness is attributed to relatively permanent and pervasive personal deficits. Women, by dint of their socialization, may be more vulnerable to learned helplessness than are men.

L'ÉCRITURE FÉMININE. A term coined by the leading French contemporary theorists, Julia Kristéva, Luce Irigaray, Hélène Cixous, and Monique Wittig (qq.v.) to mean writing that is based on female objectivity and the physiology and bodily instincts of women as distinct from men. This writing seeks to resist the patriarchal system by which man has sought to objectify the external world in relation to his power. *L'Écriture féminine* takes as its source the mother, or the mother-child relation before the child gains male-dominated verbal language.

It is this prelinguistic potentiality in the unconscious that reveals itself in women's writings that seek to undermine fixed meaning, and defy the "closure" of phallocentric (q.v.) language. The new French feminists (q.v.) emphasize as a form of rebellion a quality that they term *jouissance.*

LE GUIN, URSULA KROEBER (1929-). America's most prominent female science fiction (SF) author. LeGuin is credited with introducing a number of feminist themes in mainstream SF works like *The Left Hand of Darkness* (1969), *The Dispossessed* (1974), and the award-winning Earthsea trilogy (1968-72). The daughter of prominent anthropologists, LeGuin takes an almost anthropological approach to the creation of new civilizations on other planets, exploring her interest in androgyny (q.v.) and empathy.

LEILA KHALED COLLECTIVE *see* TORONTO WOMEN'S LIBERATION MOVEMENT

LEMNIAN WOMEN. According to Greek legend, a murderous community of women who exterminated the entire male population on the Island of Lemnos. Only the princess Hypsipyle spared the life of her royal father and helped him to escape the massacre. Legend says that the women were enraged by the rejection of their husbands, who were repelled by the bad odor Aphrodite inflicted on the women as a punishment for neglecting her rites. Eventually cured of their affliction, the women warmly welcomed the Argonauts, who stayed on Lemnos for a year and fathered a new generation of males. The Lemnian Women are another manifestation of Amazonian (q.v.) hostility to men in Greek mythology. The phrase "Lemnian Deed" came to mean a heinous and utterly despicable act.

LERNER, GERDA (1920-). An American historian instrumental during the 1960's and 1970's in legitimizing women's history and women's studies (q.v.) in the academic curriculum. An author who examines American women, Afro-American women, and feminists in history as well as the effect of patriarchy (q.v.) on civilization, her works include *Black Women in White America* (1972), *The Majority Finds Its Past:*

Placing Women in History (1979), *The Creation of Patriarchy* (1986), and *The Creation of Feminist Consciousness* (1993).

LESBIAN FEMINISM. A tradition that links institutionalized heterosexuality to women's subordinate status and stresses the social, rather than the biological, construction of sexuality. Lesbian feminists have variously presented lesbianism as a viable option and as a political imperative for feminists. Rejecting the idea of a universal female experience, lesbian feminists focus on the differences between gay and straight women. (*See also* Gay/Straight Split; Lavender Menace; Political Lesbianism; Separatism; "The Woman-Identified Woman.")

LESBIAN MORAL THEORY. A reflection on the unique ethical experiences and ethical needs of "the woman-identified woman" (q.v.) and all women. This often means a critique of the traditional philosophical emphasis on ethical rules and principles, in addition to a valorization of what enables women to develop individual integrity and agency in relation to others. In general, this tradition believes that father-centered ethics diminish women's capacity for moral action while women-centered ethics empower women as moral agents.

LESBIAN MOTHERHOOD. The condition of being both a lesbian (q.v.) and a mother, whether within a heterosexual marriage or through adoption, artificial insemination, or heterosexual intercourse outside marriage. These women often face legal challenges to child custody, difficulties in obtaining artificial insemination services, and disqualification as an adoptive parent. The feminist movement has become increasingly supportive of the rights of lesbian mothers.

LESBIANS. Female homosexuals who relate to other women as sexual partners, either as a biologically determined response or a consciously chosen political statement as a "woman-identified woman" (q.v.). Lesbian couples, denied the right to marry, lack survivor's benefits, group insurance coverage for partners, and rights of guardianship. In some cities and states, domestic partnership (q.v.) policies extend these benefits. Lesbians are not covered under most laws barring domestic violence (q.v.) and discrimination in housing, employment, and public accommodations nor is lesbian sexual activity protected under the US Constitutional right to privacy (q.v.). Lesbians have played major roles as leaders and participants in feminist movements and in the modern gay liberation movement. Despite early tensions between feminists of different sexual orientations, the feminist movement currently supports the gay political agenda. Lesbians have been especially active in building cultural institutions such as feminist bookstores (q.v.), women's centers (q.v.), and music groups.

LESSING, DORIS (1919-). An author, born in Iran, raised in Rhodesia, and a resident of England for most of her adult life. She is the author of a number of feminist literary classics: the five-volume *Children of Violence* series (1950-69), *The Golden Notebook* (1962), *The Four-Gated City* (1969), *The Summer Before the Dark* (1973), *Briefing for a Descent into Hell* (1971), and *The Memoirs of a Survivor* (1975). Lessing's female characters portray the stultifying effects of social conditioning and limited aspirations. More recently she has written a series of science fiction novels that explore alternative life forms on other planets.

LÉVI-STRAUSS, CLAUDE (1908-). A French anthropologist who did fieldwork in Brazil among Amazonian Indians during the 1930's. From his analysis of their social structures and from extensive surveys of American Indian mythologies, Lévi-Strauss concluded that the statuses of men and women form a central problem in human thought. In an early monograph on marriage relationships in small lineage-structured societies, he presented women as a form of communication passed between lineages; this excessively androcentric (q.v.) viewpoint was abandoned in his later works. Lévi-Strauss has asserted what appears to be a vulgar formula--man:woman:/culture:nature--but in fact he reflects on the theme "To what larger realms do men, and women, belong?"

LEVITE'S CONCUBINE, THE. In the Hebrew Bible, the woman who is raped by the Gibeahites and whose welfare is disdained by the Levite. The account underscores the anarchy that existed in the days of the judges; feminists point out that a priest, a man of voice and station, so completely fails to protect such a voiceless victim.

LIBERAL FEMINISM. Also termed "mainstream feminism" and based on traditional political liberalism, which accepts a positive view of human nature and the ideals of liberty, equality, justice, dignity, and individual rights. There is also confidence that society, properly reformed, can maximize individual autonomy and ensure equality of opportunity. Liberal feminists believe that women should enjoy the same rights and treatment as men.

Prominent liberal feminists include Mary Wollstonecraft, John Stuart Mill, Elizabeth Cady Stanton, and Susan B. Anthony (qq.v.). In the contemporary United States feminist movement, groups such as the National Organization for Women and the National Women's Political Caucus (qq.v.) are primarily composed of liberal feminists, in contrast with those of the women's liberation (q.v.) branch, and pursue their goals through conventional political activities of lobbying, litigation, and legislation.

LIGUE DU DROIT DES FEMMES (WOMEN'S RIGHTS LEAGUE, LDF). A group formed in 1974 by members of the Féministes Révolutionnaires (q.v.) to seek changes in French laws that oppress women. The group is registered as a formal association and serves as a link between radical (q.v.) and egalitarian (q.v.) feminists.

LONDON WORLD ANTISLAVERY CONVENTION (1840). The catalyst for the 1848 Seneca Falls Women's Rights Convention (q.v.). The conference's refusal to seat American women delegates on the convention floor, relegating them instead to the visitor's gallery as observers, focused the attention of delegates Lucretia Mott and Elizabeth Cady Stanton (qq.v.) on the inequitable treatment of women.

LORDE, AUDRE (1934-1992). An African-American lesbian feminist poet and founder, with Barbara Smith, of Kitchen Table: Women of Color Press. The author of 13 books of poetry and essays, Lorde served as poet laureate of New York State and helped form Sisterhood in Support of Sisters in South Africa. Her works include *I Am Your Sister: Black Women Organizing*

Across Sexualities (1985), *Sister Outsider* (1984), and *Our Dead Behind Us* (1986).

LOS ANGELES DEPARTMENT OF WATER AND POWER V. MANHART, 435 US (1978). Opinion of the US Supreme Court that examined an employer's policy that required female employees to contribute greater sums than the male employees in order to receive the same retirement benefit. As a justification for this discriminatory policy, the employer argued that women as a class enjoyed greater longevity. However, the Court focused on the fairness of the employer's policy to the individual employees, rather than the fairness of the policy to the classes of male versus female employees and found the employer's policy unlawful under Title VII of the Civil Rights Act of 1964 (q.v.).

LUCY STONE LEAGUE. A movement to encourage women to retain their birthname after marriage. The group is named for suffrage and abolition leader Lucy Stone (q.v.), who kept her own name rather than assume her husband's name at the time of her marriage. (*See also* Naming Conventions.)

LUTZ, BERTHA MARIA JULIA (1894-1976). A Sorbonne-educated biologist and lawyer, who helped to organize the women's suffrage movement in Brazil. In 1918, in reponse to a newspaper columnist's attack on US and British feminists, Lutz wrote an article calling for the establishment of a Brazilian women's rights league. In 1922 she founded the Brazilian Federation for the Advancement of Women, an affiliate of the International Woman Suffrage Alliance (q.v.). After the vote was won in 1932, Lutz remained active in the international women's movement and attended the International Women's Year (q.v.) conference in Mexico City in 1975.

LUXEMBURG, ROSA (1870-1919). A revolutionary socialist born in Russian Poland, where she helped found the Polish Social Democratic Party. After moving to Berlin in 1899, she became a leader of the German Socialist Party. She typified those socialists who supported working women's movements but distanced themselves from the feminist agenda advocated by other socialists like Clara Zetkin (q.v.). A founder with Karl

Liebknecht of the Spartakus League which promoted a working-class revolution, she was executed in 1919 for her role in the abortive Spartacist Revolt in Berlin.

LYSISTRATA. A Greek fictional heroine of Aristophanes' anti-war comedy of the same name. She successfully masterminds a sex-strike among the women of Greece to force a truce between the Athenians and Spartans during the Peloponnesian War. Her activism and militancy are uncharacteristic of real Greek women, who lived in virtual seclusion in the home and were politically powerless. Even attendance at the theater was denied to them. Lysistrata's feminist actions were the product of wishful thinking and pure comic fantasy--the absurdity of women dictating political policy through sexual bribery.

LYTTON, LADY CONSTANCE (1869-1923). A British aristocrat and member of the Women's Suffrage and Political Union. Lady Lytton was imprisoned in 1910 for her suffrage protests and was force fed, which attracted much publicity and sympathy for the suffrage cause.

-M-

MACAULAY-GRAHAM, CATHARINE SAWBRIDGE (1731-1791). A British historian and political pamphleteer who together with her brother, John Sawbridge, was an influential figure in the late eighteenth-century English parliamentary reform movement. She criticized the political philosophy of Hume, Burke, and Hobbes, and in her *Letters on Education* (1790), she refuted Rousseau's arguments on the complementary roles of men and women and his claims that women are inferior. She recommended that boys and girls be educated together in similar subjects.

MCCLUNG, NETTIE LETITIA (1873-1951). Canada's most prominent proponent of social feminism (q.v.) as a member of the Alberta Assembly, 1921-26, where she sponsored bills on children's health care, mothers' pensions, and married women's property rights (q.v.). McClung was an early advocate of birth control, a temperance leader, and one of the litigants in the

Persons case (q.v.). She was also a best-selling novelist and with other members of the Canadian Women's Press Club formed the Political Equality League in 1912 to work for woman suffrage.

MCCORVEY, NORMA *see ROE V. WADE*

MACHO. A word of Spanish origin meaning "male" and having come to represent exaggerated displays of maleness or *machismo*, with emphasis on excessive virility and dominance of and superiority over women, physically, psychologically, and emotionally. *Machismo* carries with it a set of attitudes that automatically relegate woman to an inferior position and justify an abuse of power, force, and position. A *macho* is by association considered a sexist. (*See also Marianismo.*)

MACKINNON, CATHARINE (1946-). A prominent US legal theorist and advocate against violence against women. In her writings on feminist jurisprudence (q.v.), she has cautioned that the law should not be viewed as an effective agent for social change; instead, she argues in *Only Words* (1993) that lawyers and judges have redefined pornography (q.v.) as "political speech." She is known for co-authoring the Minneapolis Pornography Ordinance (q.v.), for developing the distinction between *quid pro quo* and "hostile environment" (q.v.) sexual harassment (q.v.) (in *Sexual Harassment of Working Women*, 1979), and for her statement that "radical feminism (q.v.) is feminism" (in *Feminism Unmodified*, 1987). According to MacKinnon, all other feminisms are only modified attempts to integrate women into a man-made system.

MAGDALENE, MARY. A figure mentioned in all four gospel accounts as a witness to the crucifixion, death, burial, empty tomb, and the first to encounter the risen Jesus, a tradition most scholars believe to be ancient. As the first resurrection witness and the first to proclaim the Easter message to the disciples, she has been called "apostle to the apostles." Extra-canonical and gnostic literature portray Mary and Peter in disagreement over Mary's authority in the early community and her special relationship to Jesus. Later identification of Mary Magdalene as a prostitute is without textual or historical basis and is linked by feminist scholars to tendencies to deny her status as apostle in later Christian tradition.

MAINSTREAM FEMINISM *see* LIBERAL FEMINISM; WOMEN'S RIGHTS MOVEMENT

MAKIN, BATHSUA PELL (1608-1675). A tutor to Princess Elizabeth at the court of Charles I. Her *Essay to Revive the Education of Gentlewomen* supports education for women in law, commerce, and military strategy as well as in the liberal arts. She believed that the better educated women are, the less likely they are to be poverty-stricken or dependent on males.

MALE CHAUVINIST. A widely used new feminist movement (q.v.) term denoting a man who believes in the natural superiority of his sex and in the restriction of women to a traditional role. Viewed as a "man-hating" expression by its critics, the term is seen by feminists as a neutral shorthand concept that identifies the target and facilitates movement unity.

MALE DOMINANCE. The tendency for men to be allotted social roles giving them ascendancy over women. This is not universal in human or primate groups and has been linked to situations where men are frequently called upon to defend the community. Because most historic and ethnographic accounts deal with societies at war, our data are biased toward heavy representation of male dominance. When this possible bias has been considered, the finding is that social relations are complex even in simply structured small societies. Men may assert dominance in hopes of persuading others, while women ignore these overtures and quietly proceed with their tasks. Or one sex may be allowed a more decisive voice according to the activity involved.

"MALE GAZE, THE." A phrase that describes the dominant feminist film theory (q.v.). According to Laura Mulvey (in "Visual Pleasure and Narrative Cinema"), the male gaze defines and dominates women as erotic objects in films, rendering them absent, silent, or marginal or omnipowerful in the discourse of the film. The voyeuristic pleasure of looking at someone lies at the heart of film, and women have functioned for the male gaze as perfect objects onto which the male has projected his own fantasies about women--by seeing them either as mothers, whores, bitches, or castrating femme fatales.

MALE ONLY CLUBS *see BOARD OF DIRECTORS OF ROTARY INTERNATIONAL V. ROTARY CLUB OF DUARTE; NEW YORK STATE CLUB ASSOCIATION V. CITY OF NEW YORK; ROBERTS V. UNITED STATES JAYCEES*

MALINCHE, LA (1504-1529). A woman known as the "Mexican Eve," the Indian noblewoman offered to Cortez upon his arrival in Veracruz in 1519. She served him as guide, interpreter, and lover. She has been perceived negatively for supposedly "selling out" both herself and her country and is often referred to pejoratively as *la chingada* or the "fucked one." For the most part, her name implies sexual passivity and exploitation, by men and by a white society. Recent feminist revisionism is attempting to reverse this perception.

MAMONOVA, TATIANA *see WOMEN AND RUSSIA*

MAN-MADE LANGUAGE. A book title and a term coined by Dale Spender (q.v.), British feminist linguist, to refer to the current state of the English language. When women's meanings are not encoded into the language used in public discourse, such as dictionary definitions, published literature, and public speech, the language which dominates the culture is language made by men. Currently, feminist scholarship is expanding the resources of the English language to include women's meanings.

MANAGING DIVERSITY. An administrative approach that focuses on understanding and valuing employee differences related to gender, race, religion, disability, sexual preference, and other differences. This perspective was partially a result of projections that white males will make up only 15 percent of the increase in the workforce in the year 2000.

MANIFESTE DES 343 FEMMES. A public acknowledgement published in the weekly newsmagazine *Le Nouvel Observateur* on April 5, 1971, and signed by 343 Frenchwomen, including Simone de Beauvoir (q.v.), actress Catherine Deneuve, writer

Françoise Sagen, Gisèle Halimi (q.v.), and Yvette Roudy (q.v.), that they had had at least one abortion (q.v.). In 1973 a number of French doctors issued a letter acknowledging their own participation in abortions. These actions are credited with placing abortion on the public agenda in France.

MANN ACT. The popular name for the White Slave Traffic Act passed by the US Congress in 1910. It prohibited interstate transportation of women for any "immoral purpose" despite a lack of evidence of any national organized syndicate. Under expansive Supreme Court interpretations, it became a vehicle for prosecuting women for extramarital or premarital sex as well as prostitution (q.v.).

MANOAH'S WIFE. In the Hebrew Bible, the mother of Samson. Feminists point out that unlike her husband, she comprehends the message of God's angel. She keeps the ascetic vows of the Nazirite, usually undertaken only by men, in order to ensure her son's service to God.

MAQUILADORA. The factories owned by multinational corporations in which work many young unmarried Third-World women still living in their parental home. These workplaces employ local women at wages and under working conditions that local men and Western workers would not tolerate. Feminists argue that this exploitation of young women in the global factory affects the economies of both the Third-World nations and the older industrial nations from which the factories moved in their owners' search for cheaper labor. (*See also* Development, Women in.)

MARIANISMO. A reference to the divinization of the powers of the Virgin Mary (q.v.), her spiritual superiority, and inspirational nature. Rather than being a reference to the repression of women, from a feminist perspective *Marianismo* lends credence to the notion of female supremacy as a counterbalance to *machismo*. (*See also Macho.*)

MARITAL/COMMUNITY PROPERTY. A legal principle that gives both spouses vested rights (such as ownership, management and control) in all property acquired during marriage by the personal efforts of either spouse. This recognizes that marriage is an economic partnership to which both spouses contribute, with household or wage labor or both, and in which each has an equal share. This affects the division of property upon the death of one spouse and/or dissolution of the marriage. US feminists have strongly supported adoption of the model Uniform Marital Property Act in the states because of the protections extended to traditional housewives and women who have taken low-paying jobs in order to support their husbands in graduate and professional training.

MARITAL RAPE. Sexual intercourse forced on one spouse by the other, generally involving the assault of the wife. Many men incorrectly believe that intercourse is their right in marriage and refuse to honor their wife's communication that she does not desire it at a particular time. Marital rape is now against the law in most US states as a result of a feminist campaign to reform state laws on rape (q.v.). Even so, marital rape may be treated differently and the penalty may be less than other types of rape.

MARKET INALIENABILITY. A term used to refer to sales which should be legally barred or regulated in order to prevent commerce that adversely affects people. These include baby-selling (q.v.) and, perhaps, surrogacy and prostitution (qq.v.).

MARRIED WOMEN'S PROPERTY ACTS. Statutes enacted in the nineteenth century in the United States and England to "emancipate" wives from feudalistic concepts in the common law which prevented wives from owning property free from their husband's control. The Acts also gave women control over the choice of their domicile and the right to enter into contracts and to sue and be sued.

MARTIN, DEL (1921-). The co-founder in 1955 of Daughters of Bilitus, a support and social group for lesbian women, and its first president. An advocate of homosexual rights, she and her partner Phyllis Lyon joined the National Organization for Women (q.v.) in 1968 at the special rate for couples and Martin later served as an officer of her local chapter. Her books include *Lesbian/Woman* (with Lyon, 1972), *Battered Wives* (1976), and *The Male Batterer: A Treatment Approach* (co-authored, 1985).

MARTINEAU, HARRIET (1802-1876). A British writer, best known for a series of articles that agitated for the improvement of women's lives. Her article "On Female Education" (1823) denied the inferiority of the female mind and demanded a formal system of education for women that would allow them to reach their potentials as wives and mothers. A 1859 article inspired a group of feminists to found the Society for Promoting the Employment of Women. She also wrote *Illustrations of Political Economy*, which clarified the subject for the general public and sold over 160,000 copies. She was one of the first sociologists to advocate field observation as a method of study and is known as the "mother of sociology."

MARVIN V. MARVIN, 18 CAL.3D 660, 134 CAL.RPTR. 815, 557 P.2D 106 (1966). A celebrated decision from which the term "palimony" arises. It involved Michele Triola, a nightclub singer, who gave up her career for six years to become a full-time homemaker for actor Lee Marvin. Although she had changed her last name to Marvin, she did so without benefit of marriage. When Lee Marvin left her for another woman and discontinued voluntary support payments for which he had no obligation under applicable divorce statutes, Michele Marvin sued him for half of the $3.6 million in property accumulated during their relationship. According to a majority of the California Supreme Court, courts could promote equity in such circumstances through various legal doctrines. Although Marvin could not prove that the property was acquired through "mutual effort," she was awarded $104,000 for re-education. Feminists, although sympathetic to her plight, urge that women protect themselves in such relationships through a written contract.

MARX, KARL (1818-1883) The founder of Communism and a socialist reformer. Both Marx and Friedrich Engels (q.v.) believed that socialism would bring about a profound change in gender relations and the relief of women's economic repression. Although Marx rarely discussed feminist issues at length or in specific terms, he appointed English school teacher Harriet Law to the General Council of the International Workingmen's Association, or First International.

MARXIST FEMINISM. A branch of feminism that examines the connection between gender status and production methods, applies Marxist theories to the role of families in society, and asserts that the burdens of physical and social reproduction in the home operate to reinforce a male-dominated economic and political order. This tradition also notes that since women work in the home, unlike men they have no place to escape from material alienation. Marxist feminists support wages for housework (q.v.) and have recently begun to examine the impact of the welfare state upon women. (*See also* Aid to Families with Dependent Children; Engels, Friedrich.)

MARY OF NAZARETH, FEMINIST INTERPRETATIONS. The examination of scripture, doctrine, and popular piety concerning Mary, the mother of Jesus, to expose the degree to which, especially in the Catholic West, Mary came to be a symbol for maternal or feminine features of divinity, operating alongside dominant imagery for God to, in turn, support or indirectly subvert patriarchal symbolism and practice. By disentangling the poor Jewish villager, Miriam of Nazareth, from the near-divine "Mediatrix, Theotokos, Queen of Heaven and Earth," feminist theologians seek to reinstate the former as a genuinely inspiring woman of faith and courage, and the latter as revealing feminine dimensions of deity that patriarchy (q.v.) had obscured. (*See also* Deities, Female; Feminist Theology; *Marianismo*.)

MASCULIST/MASCULINIST. The tendency to define all value and meaning in male-defined terms. The masculinist impulse reads history as a series of wars, political events, and male-dominated episodes and reads literature as a series of texts written by male authors.

MASHAM, DAMARIS CUDWORTH (1659-1708). A British philosopher who objected to the inferior education allowed women and believed men felt threatened by educated women. She argued that women needed to be knowledgeable in order to understand Christianity and rejected the virtue of women being reduced to chastity. Her works include *A Discourse Concerning the Love of God* and *Occasional Thoughts in Reference to a Virtuous or Christian Life.*

MATER/MOTHER (IN RELIGION). The projection of human community structure into a legitimating cosmology that tends to create a Mother figure who may be the consort of a Father. Contemporary feminist mythology sees a Great Mother (*Mater*) primal Goddess (q.v.) worshipped by peaceful, nurturing matriarchal societies that are then overthrown by rapacious patriarchal conquering male warriors, who subordinate the Goddess to their own wrathful God. There is slight support for this myth. In the Late Bronze Age wars of conquest and displacement, invaders frequently symbolized themselves as followers of a Storm God heard in the thunder. Their Lord of Storms superseded the conquered peoples' indigenous deities, which likely included a Mother figure. The parallel for this Bronze Age phenomenon is the European post-Roman elevation of a conquering Christ over pagan deities when a battle victor believed his triumph had been secured through the intervention of Christ. It is important to note that the conquered nations were not matriarchies (q.v.) and their Mother deities were aspects of pantheons.

MATERNAL FEMINISM *see* SOCIAL FEMINISM

MATERNAL INSTINCT. The presumption that women have a biological readiness, ability, and desire to be mothers. This "instinct" has been linked to other characteristics with which women have been credited such as their emotionality, their preference to work communally, and their care taking. While researchers have failed to find concrete evidence of such an instinct in humans, the concept continues to have consequences for women. Feminists believe that it creates pressure on women to have children and often elicits guilt in women who do not wish to have children. It also suggests that women should have a greater role in the raising of children.

MATERNAL THINKING. A perspective from difference feminism and social feminism (qq.v.) presented by philosopher Sara Ruddick. She suggests that an ethic of care and concern is developed by the act of mothering and that this way of thinking must not be restricted to the domestic sphere (q.v.) in that maternal thinking challenges the prevailing impersonal and amoral public order. Emphasis is on the positive achievements of maternal practices, not the victimization of women (q.v.).

MATERNITY LEAVE. Release time from work for a pregnant woman. In the United States, the time allowed is usually only the period directly surrounding birth and a short period for physical recovery. This results in distress for many women and children and inadequate time for bonding. (*See also California Federal Savings and Loan Association v. Guerra*; Family Leave; Pregnancy Discrimination Act.)

MATH ANXIETY. A term coined by science writer Sheila Tobias to explain the lack of mathematical competence exhibited by a disproportionately large percentage of women. The use of the term "anxiety" refers to the observation that the lack of mathematical competence is usually not due to lack of ability, but rather is due to a societally imposed lack of expectation of mathematical ability based on gender.

MATHTIQUE/FEMININE MATHTIQUE. A term originating with mathematician Lynn Osen to denote stereotypes about women and mathematics, particularly those that involve expectations of poor mathematical performance in women, without any concern for remediation.

MATHURA RAPE CASE. A decision of the Supreme Court of India, issued in September 1979, that is linked with the rapid growth of the women's movement in India. The case involved the alleged rape of a young untouchable orphan in 1972 while in police custody after her brother had reported her kidnapping by her boyfriend. In reversing a decision of guilty by an intermediate appeals court, the Supreme Court interpreted her lack of physical injury as denoting consent, not submission. An outraged "Open Letter to the Chief Justice of India" from four (two male and two female) law professors was widely circulated as women demonstrated and formed new women's groups throughout the nation.

MATRIARCHY. The rule by women. Despite the concept's importance in the current feminist revival, there is not one soundly documented instance, in history, ethnography, or archaeological recovery, of a society truly ruled by women as a class. Those Classical societies that elevated goddesses (q.v.) to highest status in their pantheons were patriarchal (like Western societies idealizing the Virgin Mary). Pre-Classical Western societies and non-Western societies with female images prominent in their art or pantheons may similarly be masking patriarchy (q.v.) through manipulating images of the subordinated class or may reflect societies with more complementary roles for men and women. (*See also* Bachofen, Johann Jakob.)

MATRIFOCAL. Families headed by women, in which men are marginal. Matrifocal families are common in impoverished areas where there is little employment for men but women can subsist on government welfare or have somewhat better opportunities for employment. Matrifocal families appear to be a strategy for dealing with endemic poverty, not a cultural tradition.

MATRILINEAL. Tracing descent or inheriting through female links. Matrilineal societies may claim that the bond between mother and child is the strongest or least equivocal bond, but anthropological theory suggests that matrilineality is most often correlated with a political-economic structure built upon corporate (as opposed to individual) landowning units. Women and their brothers are the basic workgroup in these societies; men either live during marriages in their wives' homes or maintain principal residence in their matrilineal house. It is not unusual for societies to designate certain rights and privileges as being inherited through the mother and others through the father. In such cases, residence and farmland may be obtained through the mother's lineage, religious roles through the father's.

MEAD, MARGARET (1901-1978). The best-known American anthropologist of the twentieth century. Mead aimed most of her publications, including a monthly column in the women's magazine *Redbook*, at a general readership. Mead is best known for her work on personality and culture, based on fieldwork in Samoa, New Guinea, and Bali. Mead championed women, especially encouraging mature women to return to college and prepare for professional careers. She was particularly interested in the interaction of women with their children, a topic generally ignored by male fieldworkers. Mead saw herself not only as a feminist but also as an advocate for the general liberalization of American society. She endorsed the Equal Rights Amendment (q.v.) in the 1940's, at the request of Alice Paul (q.v.), and in 1965 she edited a commercial version of the report of the President's Commission on the Status of Women (q.v.).

MEDEA. According to Greek myth, the sorceress-princess of Colchis who helped Jason steal the golden fleece from her father's kingdom. She dwelt in Greece with Jason for a number of years and bore him several children before returning alone to her native land. According to Euripides, she killed her own children in a jealous rage to punish Jason for abandoning her and used her magical arts to destroy Jason's new bride and father-in-law, the king of Corinth. Although Euripides paints a sympathetic picture of the wronged wife and women's lot in general through his portrayal of Medea, the older tradition which absolves Medea of the murder of her children is kinder to her and more accurate.

MEDIA STARS *see* TRASHING

MEDICALIZATION OF CHILDBIRTH. A feminist critique of how the birthing process has been removed from women, both physically and emotionally, since the advent of modern medicine and hospital births. Specific objections involve the definition of pregnancy as abnormal, the overuse of technology and drugs, and the use of overt professional power to exert control over women's birthing decisions. (*See also* Alternative Birth Movement.)

MEDICALIZATION OF MENOPAUSE. A feminist critique of how menopausal women's bodies have been and are being used for medical experimentation. It rejects the view that menopause and its related symptoms are abnormal and thus require rigorous drug and other treatment. Feminist studies have revealed a range of medical responses from denial that women's symptoms exist to excessive treatment with estrogen replacement therapy (q.v.) and other drugs, such as antidepressants.

MEDICALIZATION OF WOMEN'S BODIES. A feminist critique of the ways in which women's bodies have been used historically and presently for medical experimentation. Included are explorations of the misogynist contributions of Freud (q.v.) and certain medical diagnoses and procedures such as schizophrenia, hysteria, depression, breast cancer (q.v.), birthing, uterine cancer, contraception, infertility treatments, and menopausal treatments. (*See also* Women's Health Movement.)

MEDICINE WOMAN. Colloquial English for women religious practitioners, particularly those who are American Indian. The preferred term is "native (or, indigenous tradition) doctor." As in other societies, American Indians generally employed women practitioners to deal with events related to the female reproductive system, such as births. It is also common for women practitioners to specialize in herb medicines, in contrast to more strictly spiritual (psychological) therapies, partly because collecting, processing, and administering herb medicines can more easily be fitted into child care and homemaking, whereas strictly spiritual (psychological) therapies tend to require protracted interactions between healer and patient.

MEDUSA. In Greek myth the snake-haired Gorgon whose hideous appearance and penetrating gaze turned mortals to stone. After she was decapitated by Perseus, her severed head became the possession of the virginal goddess Athena, who displayed it regularly on her shield or breastplate to immobilize her enemies in battle and to prevent an assault on her person. According to Freudian (q.v.) interpretation of this myth (e.g., Philip Slater, *The Glory of Hera*), Medusa's head is the symbol of the mature female genitalia (the "vagina dentata"), and Perseus' act of decapitation is a symbolic "castration" (i.e., clitoridectomy) of the sexually intimidating female by the Greek male who is ambivalent about his own sexuality.

MENCHU, RIGOBERTA (1960-). A Quiché Mayan political activist from Guatemala and recipient of the 1992 Nobel Peace Prize. Propelled into a position of human rights and indigenous leadership, including a prominent role in the Committee of Peasant Unity (Comité de Unidad Campesina) in the early 1980's by the murder of her parents and brother, she became a leading spokesperson for Guatemalan Indians. Her outspoken criticism of government policies and vivid accounts of the Indians' plight in the country's civil war prompted her exile in 1981. Life abroad, however, led to publication of her memoirs and the international recognition of her feminist, indigenist, and Christian critique of social injustice. She remains a leading proponent of rights for women, native peoples, and peasants.

MENOPAUSE. The permanent cessation of menstrual periods, defined as when a woman has not had a period in one year. The average age is 51 but can be surgically induced by the removal of the uterus. (*See also* Estrogen Replacement Therapy; Medicalization of Menopause.)

MEN'S MOVEMENT. A term encompassing a variety of responses to the feminist movement, ranging from support for gender equality and changing men's roles to the "men's rights" and New Age masculist movements that are in direct opposition to the feminist movement and seek to regain men's power and entitlement. In the 1970's the National Organization for Women (q.v.) sponsored consciousness-raising (q.v.) groups for feminist men who believed that the male role imposed costs on men and on male-female relationships and contributed to rape and domestic violence (qq.v.). Warren Farrell (q.v.) and Marc Feigen Fasteau (*The Male Machine*, 1974) were prominent spokespersons for this movement. The spiritualist/cultural movement associated with Robert Bly (q.v.) encourages men to get in touch with the "wild man within." This separatist movement arose in reaction to the prominence of sensitive men in the entertainment industry like Alan Alda and Phil Donohue and the fear that men have lost their identities in a female-dominated world. The backlash (q.v.) men's rights movement originated in changes in domestic relations law involving marital property (q.v.), child custody, and child support enforcement (q.v.) that were perceived as denying equal rights to men and fathers. More recent issues have involved complaints concerning reverse discrimination (q.v.) in employment and false charges of sexual harassment (q.v.), child abuse, and incest.

MENSTRUAL CYCLES AND BEHAVIOR. Research linkages between the menstrual cycle and behaviors such as violence, suicide, admission to psychiatric hospitals, accidents, and eating patterns. Even though much of this research contains methodological flaws and often the menstrual phase has not been well established, this research has been used as the basis for a legal defense and women have been acquitted for crimes as serious as murder because of their menstrual cycle. These findings have also given rise to the argument that women are not reliable employees and should not hold responsible positions. (*See also* Premenstrual Syndrome.)

MENSTRUAL EXTRACTION *see* DEL-EM

MENSTRUATION AND CULTURAL ASPECTS. A topic of interest to feminists because of the negative connotations of menstruation and menopause (q.v.) in Western societies. Western cultural tradition has considered menstruation a "curse" linked, after the establishment of Christianity, to Eve's sin. Premenstrual syndrome (q.v.) has been considered evidence of the debilitating effect of this female "handicap." Other cultural traditions see menstruation as a boon to women, assumed to regularly cleanse their bodies; the American Indian sweatlodge is generally used to cleanse men by sweating, a compensatory means for those denied the blessed regular cleansing through menstruation (women of childbearing age traditionally do not participate in sweatlodges). Many societies consider menopausal women to have passed into a social role unconstrained by child care responsibilities or the accompanying spiritual practices fostering fecundity and health. The "hag" or crone image stereotyped in Western culture is foreign to many societies; menopausal women are considered to merit respect. Anthropologists have found that the supposed physical symptoms of menopause (hot flashes, depression) are not recognized in many societies. Whether this is because they do not occur due to non-Western diet and activity patterns or because they are ignored as idiosyncratic (only a minority of Western women report the symptoms) has not been established.

MENTORING. A developmental relationship between senior mentors and junior protégés. The relationship may be informally developed or formally assigned. Mentors are usually senior, higher-ranking organizational members with advanced experience and knowledge who take an active interest in the career and well-being of the protégé, who is usually younger and at an earlier career stage. The establishment of such a relationship is related to the protégés' mobility, career satisfaction, and compensation, and to the mentors' sense of life satisfaction and fulfillment. Feminists have been concerned that men in organizations are less likely to mentor women (and thus retard women's mobility); special mentoring programs for women have been developed and high-ranking women have been encouraged to participate in these programs.

MERITOR SAVINGS BANK V. VINSON, 477 US 57 (1986). A decision of the US Supreme Court that resolved the nature of the prohibition of Title VII of the Civil Rights Act of 1964 (q.v.) against workplace sexual harassment (q.v.). The court rejected the bank's claim that only sexual harassment that resulted in an economic loss (as opposed to purely psychological harm) was covered under Title VII. The Court held that the creation of a hostile environment (q.v.) may violate Title VII. In *Harris v. Forklift Systems* (1993), the Court unanimously agreed that there need not be evidence of extreme psychological harm to prove sexual harassment.

METAMESSAGES. Information that is communicated nonverbally and contextually and reflects the relationship between the speakers, their attitudes toward each other, the situation and what is said. When a doctor calls patients by their first name and they respond with "Dr. Smith," a metamessage of status difference is conveyed. When men refer to women acquaintances as "honey" or "babe," a metamessage of condescension may be received. Women are believed to be more attuned to metamessages and men to messages. However, feminists point out the contradiction that occurs in date rapes (q.v.) when men claim they ignored the message -- "no" -- and concentrated on the perceived metamessage -- "yes."

MICHAEL M. V. SUPERIOR COURT, 450 US 464 (1981). A decision of the US Supreme Court that upheld a California statutory rape (q.v.) law that punished only adult men who had sexual intercourse with a female child. The statute placed no liability on underage females or females who had attained the age of 18 who engaged in sexual intercourse with underage males. Acknowledging that at least one of the statutory purposes appeared to be the prevention of pregnancy, Justice Rehnquist, writing for a plurality of the court, emphasized that men and women were "not similarly situated" with respect to that purpose. "Because virtually all of the significant harmful and inescapably identifiable consequences of teenage pregnancy fall on the young female, a legislature acts well within its authority when it elects to punish only the [male] participant who, by nature, suffers few of the consequences of his conduct." This case exemplifies those instances where the Court has upheld sex-based classifications because a majority of the justices believe that the classification reasonably advances a significant state interest.

MIDWIFE. A person, usually a woman, trained to assist women during childbirth. (*See also* Certified Nurse Midwife.)

MIFEPRISTONE *see* RU 486

MILL, HARRIET HARDY TAYLOR (1807-1858). A British feminist, libertarian philosopher and author of "The Enfranchisement of Women," an article published in the *Westminster Review.* As the wife of John Stuart Mill (q.v.), she influenced him to write his classic feminist treatise, *The Subjection of Women,* in accordance with her own views on the subject, and she very likely co-authored *On Liberty and Principles of Political Economy.* Her essay on marriage and divorce calls for equal access of women to education and employment while married and states that divorce should be available with no grounds required (i.e., "no-fault divorce" [q.v.]).

MILL, JOHN STUART (1806-1873). British philosopher, best known among feminists for his *The Subjection of Women* (1869), generally considered to be a classic example of the individualist school in nineteenth-century feminist thought. Mill tried in his work to demonstrate that "the existing relations between the sexes, the legal subordination of one sex to the other is wrong in itself, and now one of the chief hindrances to human improvement, and that it ought to be replaced by the principle of perfect equality admitting no power or privilege on the one side nor disability on the other" (see his *The Subjection of Women*). Mill was concerned with the legal barriers to women's equality, arguing that female subordination was a type of slavery imposed on the weaker by the stronger. He goes on, like Mary Wollstonecraft (q.v.), to claim that we cannot know the true nature of women because they have been corrupted and further weakened by an inferior system of education. Mill wanted women to enter marriage as equal partners and to have the right to earn their own support after marriage.

MILLETT, KATE (1934-). Best known as author of *Sexual Politics* (1969), an early text in the contemporary radical feminist (q.v.) movement. Millett argued that all sex is political because male-female relationships are based on power: "Social caste supercedes all other forms of inegalitarianism: racial, political, or economic, and unless the clinging to male supremacy as a birthright is finally forgone, all systems of oppression will continue to function simply by virtue of their logical and emotional mandate in the primary human situation" (see her *Sexual Politics*). Millett based a number of arguments on a literary critique of male authors like D. H. Lawrence and Henry Miller, but she finally recommended the elimination of gender (q.v.) as the only means of improving women's condition in the patriarchy (q.v.). Millett's publications since *Sexual Politics* include *Flying* (1974), *The Prostitution Papers* (1976), *Sita* (1977), *The Basement: Meditations on a Human Sacrifice* (1979), *Going to Iran* (1982), and *The Politics of Cruelty* (1993).

MINISTÈRE DES DROITS DE LA FEMME. The French ministry of women's rights, created in 1981 by President François Mitterrand to help eliminate discrimination against women and broaden support for women's rights. Yvette Roudy, the first Minister of Women's Rights, became a full minister with cabinet status in 1985, making France the first modern nation to create a large-scale executive agency dealing with women's rights.

MINNEAPOLIS PORNOGRAPHY ORDINANCE. An ordinance written by Andrea Dworkin and Catharine MacKinnon (qq.v.) and twice vetoed by the mayor after passage by the Minneapolis city council in 1983. It would have allowed women, harmed by pornography (q.v.), to sue the makers and distributors for sex discrimination. It was adopted in 1984 in Indianapolis and overturned by a federal court as an unconstitutional abridgement of free speech. The ordinance defined pornography as the "sexually explicit subordination of women, graphically depicted in words or pictures" that debased women. Among the contexts specified were women "enjoying" pain, rape (q.v.) or humiliation; serving as sexual objects for domination, conquest, exploitation, and possession; or appearing in positions of servility or submission or display. The ordinance was criticized by some feminists; others suggested that legislatures prohibit sexually explicit visual portrayals of force or violence that lack redeeming literary, artistic, political, or scientific value.

MINOR V. HAPPERSETT, 88 US (21 Wall.) 627 (1875). A decision of the US Supreme Court that concluded that the Fourteenth Amendment to the Constitution did not enfranchise women. The suit involved a woman who had unsuccessfully attempted to register to vote in Missouri, which restricted the suffrage to men. The Court ruled that suffrage was not a right of national citizenship protected by the Fourteenth Amendment. Nor did that amendment add the right of suffrage to the privileges and immunities of citizenship. Since the Constitution did not confer the right of suffrage upon anyone, the constitutions and laws of the various states which reserved the right of suffrage to men alone were not void.

MINORITY WOMEN *see* COLOR, WOMEN OF

MIRIAM. In the Hebrew Bible, sister of Moses and Aaron. Although "the Song of the Sea," the victory anthem of the Israelites after their escape from Egypt, has two superscriptions, one crediting Moses and the other Miriam, most scholars agree that Miriam's is older and original to this famous poem. Feminists conclude that the account of her punishment for challenging Moses and her praise in the book of the prophet

Micah indicates that she once was credited with an important leadership position in ancient Israel.

MISS AMERICA PAGEANT PROTEST. A demonstration staged in 1968 against the annual beauty contest in Atlantic City to dramatize the impact of male-imposed standards of personal appearance upon women. Organized by New York Radical Women (q.v.), the action involved around 200 women who crowned a live sheep Miss America and tossed symbols of women's status as sex objects into a trash can. Although the items--brassieres, high-heeled shoes, fashion magazines, hair curlers--were never ignited, the press reported a fire and feminists thereafter were termed "bra-burners."

MISSISSIPPI UNIVERSITY FOR WOMEN V. HOGAN, 458 US 718 (1982). A decision of the US Supreme Court that involved an Equal Protection (q.v.) challenge brought by a man to a nursing program at a state university for women. Although the state provided other opportunities for coeducational education, the male student sought admission to this program because it was more conveniently located near his home. The Supreme Court, in a closely divided opinion, held that the nursing program must open its doors to men. According to the majority, "there was no evidence that women suffered from discrimination in nursing..." The state's policy only served to maintain the "stereotypical image of nursing as a female occupation."

MITCHELL, JULIET (1940-). A prominent contemporary British feminist, best known as the author of *Woman's Estate* (1971), *Psychoanalysis and Feminism* (1974), and *Women, the Longest Revolution: Essays on Feminism, Literature and Psychoanalysis* (1984). Mitchell's first book argues that women's condition has been "overdetermined" by the structures of production, the socialization of children, and the realities of reproduction (q.v.) and female sexuality. Before women can improve their condition they must radically reform all three areas of their lives. In shaping such a theory, she seeks to combine the perspectives of the Marxist feminists, the liberal feminists, and the radical feminists (qq.v.). In her later books Mitchell argues that women must finally radically reshape their interior lives, their psyches, before they can be fully free from patriarchal thought patterns.

MOMMY TRACK. A controversial term that refers to the differential treatment and tracking of women with children in organizations. The term did not appear in, but grew out of, a 1989 article by Felice N. Schwartz in *Harvard Business Review*. The practice can result in positive outcomes, such as providing women with the option of taking low-pressure positions while raising a family. However, it can also lead to women being relegated against their will to positions with low power, authority, and responsibility. (*See also* Employment, Sex Discrimination in; Flexitime.)

MONTAGU, LADY MARY WORTLEY (1689-1762). A famous English letter writer and poet in an age when learned women were treated with ridicule and contempt. Her almost 900 letters present a vivid picture of a number of issues that concerned upper-class women in the eighteenth century: the importance of gaining an education, access to medical care, and the sexual politics of love and marriage.

MONTREAL MASSACRE. The murder of 14 women at an engineering school of a Montreal university in 1989 by an armed man shouting "I hate feminists." From December 1 to 6, Canadian men annually mark the anniversary of these shootings by pinning white ribbons to their lapels as a symbol of their opposition to male violence against women (q.v.).

MOON (GODDESS). The embodiment of a female principle complementary to a male principle that may be embodied in the sun. These projections are not universal. Where the moon is a deity, she may be wife to the sun. The Moon Goddess may be the patron of women, of childbirth, of weaving (a major occupation of women), and of sexual relations. She may be portrayed as young and round-faced, or as among the Maya, sometimes as young, sometimes as a bent old woman. The coincidence that menstrual and moon cycles are each approximately a month is assumed to promote an association between women and the moon, but actual myths do not lend this much support. The association of the moon and feminine power seems due to the common structure of complementary dualism, through which men and women are paralleled by the (stronger) sun and (less strong, but enduring) moon.

MORAL MAJORITY. A conservative pro-family (q.v.) political organization founded by US Baptist minister Jerry Falwell in 1979 to combat the decline of public morality. The group was strongly anti-feminist (q.v.) in its opposition to abortion (q.v.) and the Equal Rights Amendment (q.v.) and had close ties to Concerned Women for America (q.v.). The group disbanded after its failure to influence the 1986 congressional elections.

MORAL REFORM FEMINISM. Based on religious beliefs in social justice, world peace, and non-violence. Nineteenth-century US feminists within this tradition fought urban vice and slavery and participated in the settlement house (q.v.) and temperance movements. Contemporary feminist critiques of violence against women (q.v.), international traffic in women (q.v.), and workplace exploitation also stem from this tradition.

MORGAN, ROBIN (1941-). A radical feminist (q.v.) author, editor, and poet. Morgan was a founding member of New York Radical Women, Women Against Pornography, and WITCH (qq.v.), and a long-time contributing editor and editor of *Ms.* (q.v.) Her best-known works include *Sisterhood Is Powerful* (1970), an anthology of new feminist writings, *Going Too Far* (1977), a collection of her essays, including the influential "Goodbye to All That," and *Sisterhood Is Global* (1984), one of the earliest attempts to document the international women's movement. Morgan is also noted for her evolution from "politico" to cultural feminist (qq.v.) and for her role in the Miss America Pageant protest (q.v.) and in shaping Jane Alpert's "Mother Right" (q.v.).

MORNING-AFTER PILL. A prescription drug used to prevent pregnancy after intercourse has occurred without the use of contraceptive methods. The series of medication must be started within 72 hours after intercourse to be effective. Because of the high incidence of side effects and the lack of knowledge of long-term effects, women's health advocates urge use only in emergencies. (*See also* DES.)

MORRISON, TONI (1931-). A contemporary African-American novelist, recipient of the 1993 Nobel Prize for Literature, and theorist, best known as the author of a series of novels about African-American women: *The Bluest Eye* (1970), *Sula* (1973), *Song of Solomon* (1977), *Tar Baby* (1981), *Beloved* (1987), and *Jazz* (1992). The first two novels stress the destructive effects that dysfunctional families have on forming a young woman's self-identity and self-esteem (q.v.). The third novel also concerns the maturation process, but in this book Morrison sketches its development over four generations of one family. The more recent novels stress the influence that the heritage of slavery has had on African-American families and their self-definition. Most recently Morrison has published theoretical works that attempt to understand the role that African-Americans have played in mainstream American culture: *Playing in the Dark: Whiteness and the Literary Imagination* (1992) and *Race-ing Justice: En-gendering Power: Essays on Anita Hill, Clarence Thomas, and the Construction of Social Reality* (1992).

MOTHER BLAMING. The historical notion of blaming women as sole rearers of children for the problems the children have while young and as they mature into adults.

MOTHER EARTH. The belief that earth is an ecosystem and gives life. It is sometimes argued that many cultures, such as Native Americans, have adopted this notion as is exemplified in their worship of Mother Earth and the accompanying belief in harmony, egalitarian relationships, reverence for life, and pervasive spirituality. It also has been used as a metaphor for the goddess (q.v.) by some feminist theologians to replace or supplant the white male in most Western patriarchal religions. The metaphor has given many women hope and a deeper sense of their spirituality and connectedness to earth and to others. But anthropologists argue that the Mother Earth imagery is either fiction by Euro-American writers or a reference to a female generative principle poorly understood by European observers. The concept of Mother Earth is actually Classical European.

"MOTHER RIGHT." An early cultural feminist (q.v.) essay written in 1973 by Weather Underground fugitive Jane Alpert in which she uses women's reproductive capacity to explain gender differences. She argues that biology is the basis of women's powers and that all women are united by maternal and pacific qualities which empower, not disadvantage. (*See also* Maternal Thinking.)

MOTHERHOOD ENVY/WOMB ENVY. Envy by males of activities unique in motherhood (e.g., pregnancy, childbirth, and nursing). Karen Horney (q.v.) countered Freud's (q.v.) notion of "penis envy" with this possible analogue in males.

MOTHERS OF THE PLAZA DE MAYO (MADRES DE LA PLAZA DE MAYO). An Argentine human rights organization established in 1976 by middle-class women to protest the murder and disappearance of family members in political violence that became known as the "Dirty War." Although not the first political organization of mothers in Latin America, it is largely responsible for defining the mothers' movement in the region. The group held its first weekly public assembly at the Plaza de Mayo, site of the Government House and the national monument to Argentine independence, in Buenos Aires on April 30, 1977. These mothers established the recognized ritual forms of women's protest: public marches, the wearing of white head scarves on which were written the names of disappeared family members, and posters bearing the names and photographs of missing or dead husbands and children. The Mothers numbered only 14 in 1977, but by 1983 they had grown into one of the largest and most vigorous popular movements in Latin America. This group significantly contributed to the fall of the Argentine military government in 1983.

MOTT, LUCRETIA (1793-1880). An American Quaker who founded the first Female Anti-Slavery Society in Philadelphia in 1833. Denied her seat as a delegate to the 1840 World Antislavery Convention in London, she concluded with her fellow delegate, Elizabeth Cady Stanton (q.v.), that the "woman question" required political action. The two women, together with Martha Wright (Mott's sister), Mary Ann McClintock, and

Jane Hunt organized the 1848 Women's Rights Convention at Seneca Falls (q.v.).

MOUVEMENT FRANÇAIS POUR LE PLANNING FAMILIAL (MFPF). The French branch of Planned Parenthood (q.v.), founded in 1956. The movement rapidly expanded nationwide in membership and clinics. Although it opposed a 1920 law prohibiting the availability of contraceptive information and devices, the group long denied any conflict with Catholic teaching on that topic. The Neuwirth law of 1967 authorized the sale of contraceptives.

MOUVEMENT POUR LA LIBÉRATION DES FEMMES (MLF). The generic media-created name for the contemporary feminist movement (q.v.) in France. In 1979, Psych et Po (q.v.) registered MLF as their trademark for operating a chain of feminist bookstores (q.v.), magazines, and a publishing house (all called *des femmes*). The resulting lawsuits over the use of the MLF name, initials, and logo ended the MLF as a national movement.

MOVIMENTO DI LA LIBERAZIONE DELLA DONNA (WOMAN'S LIBERATION MOVEMENT, MLD). A loose network of Roman feminist collectives (q.v.), formed in 1970 and leader of the referendum drive in 1971 to repeal the abortion (q.v.) law and to defeat the anti-divorce referendum in 1974. In 1976 it founded the women's center in Rome, the Casa della Donna (q.v.). The MLD has been associated with the Radical Party, the Socialist Party, and the workers' movement in Italy.

MOZZONI, ANNA MARIA (1837-1920). An author and the most important early socialist feminist (q.v.) in Italy. A frequent contributor to *La Donna*, a feminist newspaper published 1868-88, and the author of books on the emancipation of women, Mozzoni supported divorce and woman suffrage. In 1881 she founded the League for the Promotion of the Interests of Women, a forerunner of the Italian Women's Union (q.v.).

MS. A glossy popular periodical founded in 1972 by a group of New York women, including Gloria Steinem (q.v.), to accurately cover the new feminist movement (q.v.). After several changes of ownership, 1987-89, and a seven-month hiatus from monthly publication, the magazine reappeared in July 1990 as an advertisement-free bi-monthly under the editorship of Robin Morgan (q.v.) and now Marcia Ann Gillespie.

MS. The established term of address when a woman's marital status is unknown. A combination of the courtesy titles "Miss" and "Mrs.," "Ms." has been popularized by feminists who argue that women should be recognized as individuals rather than being identified by their relationship with a man. (*See also* Naming Conventions.)

MULLER V. OREGON, 208 US 412 (1908). A decision of the US Supreme Court that upheld protective labor legislation (q.v.) enacted on behalf of women. The statute in question limited the hours of work for female laundry workers. Although social feminists (q.v.) and some labor reformers strongly supported the decision, laws conferring special benefits only upon female workers made women less attractive to potential employers.

MURRAY, JUDITH SARGENT (1751-1820). An early American author whose writings on the rights and opportunities of women predated those cf Mary Wollstonecraft (q.v.). During the American Revolution (in an essay not published until 1790), she wrote that American women needed education not only to complement their husbands but also to prepare their sons to serve the new democracy. She defined marriage as a republican union of mutual esteem.

MURRAY, PAULI (1910-1987). African-American lawyer who was active in the civil rights movement (q.v.) for women and blacks. She was one of the founders of the National Organization for Women (q.v.) and was one of the first women priests ordained in the Episcopal Church in the 1970's. Her *Autobiography of a Black Activist, Feminist, Lawyer, Priest, and Poet* (1987) recounts her multifaceted life.

MUTING. A consequence of lack of access to a forum for expressing oneself. Muting occurs when a speaker lacks the tools and/or the opportunity to articulate feelings and thoughts.

Muting is generally a consequence of a power differential wherein higher power groups find full expression and lower power groups are silenced. Cheris Kramarae (q.v.) suggests that women are a muted group because the English language does not contain words from a woman's perspective. (*See also* Ardener, Shirley.)

MUTTIPOLITIK (MOMMY POLITICS). An East German feminist critique of public policy addressing only one role of women, that of motherhood. Such policy serves to reinforce traditional gender roles, limit women's professional options, and maintain gender inequity.

MUTUAL SUPPORT GROUP FOR THE APPEARANCE, ALIVE, OF OUR CHILDREN, SPOUSES, PARENTS, AND BROTHERS AND SISTERS (GRUPO DE APOYO MUTUO, GAM). A Guatemalan human rights organization formed by women to protest abuses and state-sponsored terrorism. This group was established in June 1984 by about 25 women who met while searching Guatemala City morgues for disappeared and dead family members. Despite the brutal murder of two of its leaders in March 1985, its membership grew to about 1,000 by 1986. The GAM was the most prominent human rights organization in the country in the mid-1980's. Like that of similar groups in Latin America, the GAM's political activism emerged out of women's traditional family roles of nurture and protection and was sustained by feminist solidarity and mutual support.

"MYTH OF THE VAGINAL ORGASM." A feminist classic published by Anne Koedt in 1970. The essay challenges the linkage between frigidity (q.v.) and vaginal eroticism. According to Koedt, the center of female sexuality (and orgasm) is the clitoris and the vaginal orgasm does not exist. Instead, women have been defined sexually in terms of the male orgasm that requires the friction of penetration. This critique became the center of feminist demands that women define their own sexuality and demand sexual techniques that pleasure them, whether obtained from a man or another woman. (*See also* Grafenberg Area.)

MYTHOLOGICAL AND CLASSICAL FEMALES *see* AMAZONS; ANTIGONE; APHRODITE; ARTEMIS; ASPASIA; ATALANTA; ATHENA; CIRCE; CLEOPATRA VII; CLYTEMNESTRA; DANAIDS; DEMETER; FURIES; HECATE; HELEN; HERA; ISIS; LEMNIAN WOMEN; LYSISTRATA; MEDEA; MEDUSA; PENELOPE; SAPPHO

-N-

NAMING CONVENTIONS. The system for naming people that historically has meant that women use the name of a man, whether father or husband, as a last name. Feminists, in protest against this male-oriented system, have suggested that women: choose a surname that is not related to any male relative; retain their birthname, both before and after marriage; or, with marriage, create a new name or hyphenate the two partners' birthnames. Under the common law, a person has the right to use any name she or he likes so long as there is no intent to defraud. Women have adopted their husbands' names as a matter of social custom and not because the law requires it. One study suggests that whether a woman changes her name, retains her birthname or hyphenates her name with her husband's depends on how she ranks her concerns for self, the relationship, and social conventions. A second aspect to naming conventions concerns courtesy titles (i.e., Miss, Ms. [q.v.], Mr., Mrs., etc.). An examination of their use reveals inequality between men and women. Although "Ms." was introduced to parallel "Mr.", "Miss" and "Mrs." have not dropped out of use and a recent survey showed few respondents understood the term "Ms." and many believed it should be used only for divorced or widowed women.

NATIONAL ABORTION AND REPRODUCTIVE RIGHTS ACTION LEAGUE (NARAL). A US single-issue pro-choice (q.v.) group formed in 1969 as the National Association for Repeal of Abortion Laws. After the legalization of abortion (q.v.) in 1973, the group adopted its present name and added "and reproductive" in 1994 to signal a broader focus. NARAL has over 400,000 individual and organizational members within its affiliates in almost all states. The group has a well-staffed Washington, D. C. headquarters, a political action committee, and a foundation. Executive director Kate Michelman emerged in the 1980's as the leading spokesperson for women's reproductive freedom (q.v.).

NATIONAL ABORTION CAMPAIGN (NAC). A group formed in Great Britain in 1975 to coordinate the abortion (q.v.) rights movement and to defend the 1967 Abortion Act. This non-hierarchical organization loosely links local groups, many of which are a part of trade unions. The NAC focuses on public education through demonstrations as well as lobbying Parliament. In 1983 a new group, the Women's Reproductive Rights Group, split from the single-issue NAC in order to pursue the broader issue of reproductive freedom (q.v.).

NATIONAL ACTION COMMITTEE ON THE STATUS OF WOMEN (NAC). A coalition of approximately 590 Canadian women's organizations, formed in 1972. Representing around five million women, the NAC is the nation's largest feminist lobby group and is notable for its inclusion of women of color (q.v.), aboriginal women, and women with disabilities within its leadership. Despite its heavy reliance on the federal government as a source of operating funds, the NAC successfully opposed the proposed national constitution of 1992 on the grounds that it would weaken women's established rights.

NATIONAL AMERICAN WOMAN SUFFRAGE ASSOCIATION (NAWSA). An organization formed in 1890 when the National Woman Suffrage Association (q.v.) and the American Woman Suffrage Association (q.v.) merged. After suffrage was won, the NAWSA became the League of Women Voters (q.v.).

NATIONAL ASSOCIATION OF COLORED WOMEN (NACW). The African-American counterpart of the General Federation of Women's Clubs (q.v.), formed in 1896 as a feminist, suffragist, and civil rights organization linking local black women's clubs. Under the leadership of its first president, Mary Church Terrell (q.v.), a wealthy suffragist and National Woman's Party (q.v.) member, the NACW also supported the Equal Rights Amendment (q.v.).

NATIONAL BLACK FEMINIST ORGANIZATION (NBFO). Group founded in 1973 to advance the rights of African-American women within the feminist and civil rights movements and to confront sexism (q.v.) and racism through a single organization. Eleanor Holmes Norton and Margaret Sloan were among its founders and early leaders. Within a year of its formation, the NBFO had more than 2,000 members in ten chapters but by the end of the decade sexual orientation and class cleavages had weakened the organization.

NATIONAL COMMISSION ON THE OBSERVANCE OF INTERNATIONAL WOMEN'S YEAR. A body established by US President Gerald Ford in 1975 to coordinate US participation in the International Women's Year (q.v.). Congress extended the life of the commission to March 1978, and provided funding for meetings in every state and territory and for a National Women's Conference. At this conference, held in Houston, Texas, November 18-21, 1977, delegates adopted the National Plan of Action, a 26-plank program addressing major issues affecting women.

NATIONAL CONSUMERS LEAGUE (NCL). A movement founded in 1899 to reform the workplace for women in industrial America. Under the leadership of Florence Kelley, the League argued for child labor laws and protective labor legislation (q.v.) before legislatures and the courts. The group supported woman suffrage (q.v.) in order to enfranchise a more humanistic, reform-oriented constituency but strongly opposed the Equal Rights Amendment (q.v.). Although the organization still exists, it has not been active on women's rights issues since the 1930's.

NATIONAL COUNCIL OF NEGRO WOMEN (NCNW). The largest African-American women's group, founded by Mary McLeod Bethune in 1935 to advance racial equality and the particular interests of black women. As a part of the Women's Bureau (q.v.) coalition, the NCNW long opposed the Equal Rights Amendment (q.v.) but also worked on many women's issues: appointments of black women to federal office, equal pay (q.v.), equal employment opportunity, and sterilization abuse (q.v.). Dorothy Height, the president of the NCNW since 1957, served on the President's Commission on the Status of Women (q.v.).

NATIONAL FEDERATION OF BUSINESS AND PROFESSIONAL WOMEN'S CLUBS (BPW/USA). An organization founded in 1919 to advance the status of employed women and to support legal equality for women. An early (1937) supporter of the Equal Rights Amendment (q.v.), the BPW has also been active on behalf of affirmative action (q.v.), equal pay (q.v.), national and state commissions on the status of women (q.v.), and women in elected and appointed public office. Although the BPW has now become primarily a women's rights organization, rather than a service club, the membership long resisted the feminist label and in 1966 rejected suggestions that it become a civil rights group for women.

NATIONAL FEDERATION OF INDIAN WOMEN (NFIW). A group formed in 1954 with ties to the Communist Party of India. It operates as both a lobby group for women's rights in New Delhi and a provider of services to poor and working-class women. Although the NFIW has joined feminist coalitions opposing rape and dowry (q.v.), it remains aloof from the feminist label, in keeping with its belief in state socialism as the key to women's emancipation.

NATIONAL LIBERATION CONFERENCE. A meeting held at Ruskin College, Oxford, in February 1970, and viewed as the beginning of the new feminist movement (q.v.) in Great Britain. The conference agreed upon four national goals: equal pay (q.v.); equal education and opportunity; 24-hour day care (q.v.) centers; and free contraception and abortion (q.v.) on demand. The conference grew out of the omission of women's history from an earlier history workshop at the college. National conferences were held through 1978, when a split developed between the radical and socialist strands of the movement.

NATIONAL ORGANIZATION FOR WOMEN (NOW). The largest and oldest new feminist organization in the United States, founded by Betty Friedan (q.v.), among others, in 1966. NOW has a dues-paying membership of around 280,000 in almost 700 local chapters in all 50 states. NOW supports a legal defense and education fund and a political action committee and publishes a newsletter, *National NOW Times*. NOW was established by those active in state commissions on the status of women (q.v.) as a civil rights group on the model of the National Association for the Advancement of Colored People. As additional liberal feminist (q.v.) groups have formed, NOW has increasingly taken more radical positions on issues such as abortion (q.v.), lesbian rights, and the need for a feminist party in US politics. (*See also* Commission for Responsive Democracy.)

NATIONAL PLAN OF ACTION *see* NATIONAL COMMISSION ON THE OBSERVANCE OF INTERNATIONAL WOMEN'S YEAR

NATIONAL RIGHT TO LIFE COMMITTEE (NRLC). The largest of the US pro-life (q.v.) groups, established as a separate organization by the Catholic Church in 1973 to coordinate the anti-abortion campaign for a constitutional amendment that would extend full legal rights to an embryo upon conception. The NRLC has not taken a public position on contraception but has threatened a boycott of any drug company marketing RU 486 (q.v).

NATIONAL SOCIETY FOR WOMEN'S SUFFRAGE (NSWS). A coalition of local English suffrage societies, formed in 1868. Beginning in 1870, the monthly *Women's Suffrage Journal*, edited by society president Lydia Becker (q.v.), chronicled their activities. The NSWS used home, ward, and district meetings to educate the public. It organized demonstrations and published letters, articles, and pamphlets. In 1888 a splinter group broke with the NSWS over the latter's refusal to accept political party groups as affiliates; this split within the English movement lasted 12 years. In 1890 Lydia Becker died and was replaced by Millicent Garrett Fawcett (q.v.) as president.

NATIONAL WELFARE RIGHTS ORGANIZATION (NWRO). An organization of public assistance recipients formed in 1966 to empower poor (mostly African-American) women to act as their own advocates within the welfare system and to seek improvements in public assistance programs. Johnnie Tillmon, a welfare mother, was its well-known chairperson, but the group was dominated by paid male staff and financed by middle-class Euro-Americans who agreed that "every woman is just one man away from welfare." The NWRO peaked in 1969 with 22,000 members and 500 local chapters. In 1972 poor black women took over the group and aligned it with the feminist movement. When funding dried up in 1975 in the backlash against welfare, the NWRO disbanded.

NATIONAL WOMAN SUFFRAGE ASSOCIATION (NWSA). An exclusively female organization, founded in 1869 by Elizabeth Cady Stanton and Susan B. Anthony (qq.v.) to secure a woman suffrage amendment to the US Constitution. The group formed in the wake of the split in the American Equal Rights Association (q.v.) over the suffrage issue, a circumstance Stanton and Anthony attributed to the preponderance of men in that organization. The NWSA was considered the radical wing of the suffrage movement in its insistence on a constitutional amendment and its commitment to other women's rights issues. In 1890 the group merged with the American Woman Suffrage Association to form the National American Woman Suffrage Association (qq.v.).

NATIONAL WOMAN'S PARTY (NWP). US group founded by Alice Paul (q.v.) in 1913 to promote woman suffrage and, after suffrage, to advance equality feminism (q.v.). In 1923 the NWP proposed the Equal Rights Amendment (q.v.), which became its sole domestic issue for many years. The NWP maintained a feminist presence, 1920-60, in Washington, D. C., at a time when the movement was largely in abeyance. It also worked for the inclusion of "sex" in Title VII of the Civil Rights Act of 1964 (q.v.) and for a provision on sex equality in the U. N. Charter.

NATIONAL WOMEN'S AID FEDERATION (NWAF). A non-hierarchical coalition, established in 1975, to link local anti-violence groups and shelters in Great Britain. In addition to supporting these member organizations, the NWAF has also worked on national and local reforms for battered women (q.v.) services and treatment under the law. One achievement is the

Domestic Violence Act of 1976 giving a battered woman the right to a restraining order.

NATIONAL WOMEN'S CONFERENCE *see* NATIONAL COMMISSION ON THE OBSERVANCE OF INTERNATIONAL WOMEN'S YEAR

NATIONAL WOMEN'S HEALTH NETWORK (NWHN). A feminist health care advocacy group, founded in 1975 as a coalition for the entire women's health movement (q.v.) in the United States. The NWHN provides information to its 12,500 individual and around 500 organizational members and monitors proposed legislation and government regulations affecting women's health. It also serves as a watchdog over the medical profession to expose unsafe and unnecessary medical practices.

NATIONAL WOMEN'S MAILING LIST. A grass-roots US project, begun in 1980, to connect over 60,000 women and 10,000 groups through direct mail. A voluntary registration form, appearing in feminist media, assures that only material on topics of interest will be directed toward each network member.

NATIONAL WOMEN'S POLITICAL CAUCUS (NWPC). A multi-partisan feminist group formed in 1971 to increase the number of women in elected and appointed office in the US government and as delegates at national party conventions. To advance this goal, the Caucus conducts campaign training schools for potential female candidates and recommends qualified women for presidential appointments. The NWPC has over 200 local chapters, a lobbying headquarters in Washington, D. C., and a political action committee. It publishes a newsletter, *The Women's Political Times*.

NATURAL CHILDBIRTH. Prepared childbirth in which the woman and her support person are educated in techniques of relaxation, breathing, and concentration to use during labor. Although the approach does not exclude the use of medications and other procedures to facilitate a safe childbirth, there is an emphasis on the minimal use of drugs and high technology. The revival of interest in natural childbirth began in the 1950's and has been embraced by the feminist movement as a part of a woman-controlled alternative birth movement (q.v.).

NATURE/CULTURE. A Western dichotomy that claims that women are closer to nature and men to culture. Cross-cultural comparisons show that this dichotomy is not universal; many non-Western cultural traditions have a more unitary worldview. In Western societies, women are viewed as closer to nature in the dominance of motherhood over other social roles and men are seen as more bestial.

NEOPAGANISM. Generic term for feminist religious alternatives to male-centered mainstream Western religions. Largely eclectic in nature, neopaganism includes a contemporary version of Goddess (q.v.) religion, witchcraft (q.v.), and earth-centered spirituality. Ties to ancient, pre-patriarchal religious traditions are sought and new myths are brought forth to highlight and ritualize such concepts as egalitarianism and the interconnectedness of all things.

NESTLÉ BOYCOTT *see* "BOTTLE BABY DISEASE"

NETWORKING. Informal social interactions involving individuals or groups. Networks provide information and contacts vital for career advancement and placement. They may also provide support and social functions. Feminists have consciously formed networks to advance the movement's political agenda and to support women. (*See also* Old Boys Club/Old Girls Club.)

NEW FEMINIST MOVEMENT. A term that refers to the resurgence of an organized women's movement in the 1960's. A conventional view of the history of feminism is that first wave feminism (q.v.) died in the 1920s and second wave feminism (q.v.) emerged in the 1960's. Today many women's historians point to the persistence of feminist activity throughout the twentieth century and view the contemporary feminist movement as a part of one continuous movement of different organizations and varying levels of mass support and activity.

NEW FEMINISTS (CANADA) *see* TORONTO WOMEN'S LIBERATION MOVEMENT

NEW FRENCH FEMINISTS. A term used to identify the contemporary French feminists--Julia Kristéva, Luce Irigaray, Hélène Cixous, and Monique Wittig (qq.v.)--who began publishing around 1960, several of them in the semiotic-Marxist journal *Tel Quel*. Although there are several conflicting factions within the Mouvement pour la Libération des Femmes (MLF) (q.v.), in general French feminists believe that Western thought has been based on a systematic repression of women's experiences. Most French feminists assert the claim that there is an "essential" (q.v.) female nature and that it makes sense to begin there as a point from which to deconstruct Western notions of language, philosophy, psychoanalysis, and society. The diversity of positions within this movement can be seen in the anthology *New French Feminisms*, edited by Elaine Marks and Isabelle de Courtivron (1980).

NEW WOMAN NOVEL. A late nineteenth-to early twentieth-century British and American genre developed by Sarah Grand, George Gissing, and others to depict female independence outside traditional romance plots.

NEW YORK FEMALE MORAL REFORM SOCIETY. A group, founded in New York City in 1834, that was concerned with reforming prostitutes and saving fallen women. In 1840 the organization became the American Female Moral Reform Society. (*See also* Moral Reform Feminism.)

NEW YORK RADICAL FEMINISTS (NYRF). Formed in 1969 by Anne Koedt and Shulamith Firestone (qq.v.) as a city-wide mass-based organization that would avoid the ideological and organizational rigidities of the Feminists (q.v.) and the Redstockings (q.v.). A three-stage process of consciousness raising (q.v.) and feminist analysis within small brigades, followed by affiliation with the larger NYRF group, was devised to integrate new members. The founding Stanton-Anthony Brigade disbanded in 1970 after charges of elitism (q.v.), and the three-stage structure was abandoned. The larger group continued until 1972 and in 1971 held the first rape speak-out (qq.v.) and the first feminist conference on prostitution (q.v.).

NEW YORK RADICAL WOMEN (NYRW). New York City's first women's liberation (q.v.) group, formed by Shulamith Firestone (q.v.) and Pam Allen in 1967. The group staged several widely noted demonstrations, including the Miss America Pageant Protest (q.v.) and the anti-war "Burial of Traditional Womanhood," published a journal, *Notes from the First and Second Years*, and attracted many prominent members such as Kate Millett (q.v.), Robin Morgan (q.v.), Ellen Willis, Anne Koedt (q.v.), Kathie Sarachild, Ros Boxandell, and Patricia Mainardi. Deeply divided along politico/feminist (q.v.) lines, the group disbanded in 1969.

NEW YORK STATE CLUB ASSOCIATION V. CITY OF NEW YORK, 108 S. CT. 2225 (1988). A decision of the US Supreme Court that involved clubs with males-only membership policies. New York City's Human Rights Law prohibited discrimination in public accommodations but exempted any institution or club that could prove it was in its nature distinctly private. The association challenged the law as an unconstitutional infringement upon First Amendment protections of private association. The Court concluded that the clubs in the association shared the characteristics of the Jaycees and Rotary Club in terms of size, nonselectivity, and involvement in business transactions; thus, they could not claim a right of private association. (*See also Board of Directors of Rotary International v. Rotary Clubs of Duarte; Roberts v. United States Jaycees*.)

NIGHTINGALE, FLORENCE (1820-1910). The English founder of nursing and a humanist who advocated health and sanitation efforts for all people. Nightingale helped to make nursing a respectable profession for all classes of women and one deserving of a living wage. Her efforts to professionalize nursing were resisted by male physicians, who feared a "dictatorship of women." Nightingale remained aloof from the suffrage movement as a distraction to her health care work.

NINE-TO-FIVE (9TO5, THE NATIONAL ASSOCIATION OF WORKING WOMEN). An organization of women office workers, founded in Boston in 1973. It seeks to assist employees with job problems: improved pay, race and sex discrimination, harassment, health and safety conditions, advancement, and respect by one's peers and supervisors. 9to5 has actively supported state policies to protect video display terminal operators from health hazards. The local groups (13,000 members in 25 chapters) annually honor excellent supervisors and publicize examples of "heartless" behavior by those in positions of power. The group has an education fund that conducts research and has published *The 9to5 Guide to Combating Sexual Harassment* (1992).

NINETEENTH AMENDMENT. An amendment to the US Constitution added in 1920 and stating "the right of the citizens of the United States to vote shall not be denied or abridged by the United States or by any State on account of sex." A woman suffrage amendment was first introduced in Congress in 1878 but was not passed until 1919. (*See also* American Woman Suffrage Association; Anthony, Susan B.; Catt, Carrie Chapman; Mott, Lucretia; National American Woman Suffrage Association; National Woman Suffrage Association; Paul, Alice; Stanton, Elizabeth; Stone, Lucy.)

NO-FAULT DIVORCE. A legal reform adopted in many US states in the 1960's and 1970's that allows dissolution of a marriage without proof of fault or grounds for divorce such as cruelty or adultery. The requirement is only a showing of irreconcilable differences or incompatibility. Although the impetus for these changes did not originate with the feminist movement, there was initial support because of the law's gender-neutral (q.v.) language and lack of assumptions about traditional sex roles in marriage. The impact of no-fault divorce, however, has contributed to the feminization of poverty in that the monetary awards to women have been less generous than under the former system.

NONSEXIST CHILDREN'S LITERATURE. Reading materials for young people that do not reinforce traditional gender roles (q.v.). Prohibited content includes: portrayal of men and women in stereotypical roles and jobs; a preponderance of male characters; passive behavior of female characters; and creative, problem-solving activities only by male protagonists. Under pressure from groups such as Feminists on Children's Media and independent non-profit publishers of nonsexist children's books, both textbook and trade publishers have developed author guidelines that address this critique. The American Library Association's Association for Library Service to Children has also published bibliographies of nonsexist booklists and a list of folktales in which there are active heroines.

NONSEXIST LANGUAGE. Language that is inclusive and does not discriminate against either sex. Examples of such language include "humanity" instead of "mankind," "s/he" instead of "he," "chair" instead of "chairman," and "supervisor" instead of "foreman." Communications studies have found that even when used in the generic sense, the words "he" and "man" do evoke thoughts of males. In 1991 the *Random House Webster's College Dictionary* eliminated sexist language in its definitions.

NONTRADITIONAL OCCUPATIONS, WOMEN IN. The entry of female workers into traditionally male skilled-craft jobs. With the Title VII of the Civil Rights Act of 1964 (q.v.) mandate to employers to adopt sex-neutral hiring practices, there have been large increases in the numbers and percentages of women in blue-collar jobs but their occupational shares remain small. Women workers are especially attracted to these positions on the basis of higher pay, greater challenges, and variability of the tasks.

NORPLANT. A long-term contraceptive method approved for use in the United States in 1990. A specially trained practitioner surgically implants six match-size Silastic rubber capsules in the soft tissue of the woman's upper arm for continuous slow release of a synthetic form of progestin called levornogestrel. The implant remains effective for five years and may be surgically removed at any time. Norplant has been suggested as a method of contraception for sexually active teens and poor women in lieu of sterilization, applications that feminists view as potentially violating women's reproductive freedom (q.v.).

NORTON, CAROLINE SHERIDAN (1808-1877). An English author and activist in the divorce reform and married women's property rights movements. The victim of a bad marriage, Norton wrote *Caroline Norton's Defense: English Laws for Women in the Nineteenth Century* (1854) and other influential pamphlets on the legal status of women and the relation of men and women in England.

-O-

O'CONNOR, SANDRA DAY (1930-). The first woman to be appointed to the US Supreme Court. She formerly served in the Arizona State Senate, where she supported the Equal Rights Amendment (q.v.), and on the Arizona Court of Appeals. Since joining the Court in 1981, O'Connor has generally supported the women's rights position in gender discrimination cases and several of her male colleagues moved toward that position after 1981, possibly because of her influence. She has also developed the "undue burden" test for review of state regulations on abortion (q.v.) that is currently used by the Court and voted to reaffirm the principle of legal abortion contained in *Roe v. Wade* (q.v.) in *Planned Parenthood of Southeastern Pennsylvania v. Casey* (1992).

OCCUPATIONAL SEGREGATION. Employment patterns in the labor force whereby women and men are concentrated in different types of jobs. Female-typed jobs have lower pay and prestige than male-typed jobs, and there are fewer female-typed than male-typed jobs. (*See also* Comparable Worth; Pink-Collar Ghetto.)

OFFICE OF RESEARCH ON WOMEN'S HEALTH, NATIONAL INSTITUTES OF HEALTH *see* WOMEN'S HEALTH INITIATIVE

OLD BOYS CLUB/OLD GIRLS CLUB. Informal social or professional organizations that are limited to individuals of the same sex. These provide significant networking (q.v.) functions involving access to information important for career advancement. Feminists once spoke of the "old boys club" with resentment because of its ability to exclude women. Now feminists use the second term to refer to women in key positions who use their power to include other women.

OLDER BRANCH *see* WOMEN'S RIGHTS MOVEMENT

OLDER WOMEN'S LEAGUE (OWL). A US group founded in 1980 by Laurie Shields and Tish Sommers to address economic equality issues of particular importance to midlife and older women such as pensions, social security (q.v.), and health insurance, and to improve the image and status of women. By the 1990's, OWL had over 120 local chapters in 37 states, a lobbying headquarters in Washington, D.C., and a newsletter, the *Owl Observer*. (*See also* Displaced Homemaker.)

OLSEN, TILLIE (1913-). A US writer, born to a Russian Jewish family that had fled persecution, and well known as the author of a series of feminist essays and short stories that reveal her lower-class and Communist sympathies. Her book *Silences* (1962) collects her earliest essays. These essays meditate on the difficulties facing working-class women who try to find the time and resources to create. Although she did write a novel about her experiences during the Depression, *Yonnondio: From the Thirties* (1974), Olsen's fame rests on her two best-known short stories: "Tell Me A Riddle" (1961) and "I Stand Here Ironing" (1961).

OPERATION RESCUE (OR). A US pro-life (q.v.) organization formed in 1986 and led by fundamentalist Protestant Randall Terry. The group's followers frequently focus on one city and block access to all abortion clinics there to force clinic closings. Demonstrators are often arrested on charges of trespassing or disorderly conduct and are assessed heavy fines. Feminists have responded with local clinic defense and escort services (q.v.), demands for federal and state laws to protect clinic access, such as the National Freedom of Access to Clinic Entrances Act (1994), and litigation charging the group with racketeering, extortion, and anti-trust violations.

OPPOSITE SEX/OTHER SEX. Terms used to refer to the gender other than the one which is the focus of attention or conversation. Since the two genders are not truly opposites, "other sex" has come to be the preferred term.

OPPRESSIONS, INTERSTRUCTURING OF. Term used by feminists to denote the mutually reinforcing yet distinct effects of race, sex, and class oppression. Audre Lorde (q.v.), bell hooks (q.v.), Dorothy Solle, and Barbara Hilkert Andolsen are among those explicitly plumbing the interfacing dynamics and interlocking oppressions of race and class with sexism (q.v.) in Western societies. (*See also* Racism and Feminism.)

ORDINATION OF WOMEN, HISTORICAL EVIDENCE. Archaeological and inscriptional indications of the ministry of women in the early church. Evidence exists from the first century in catacomb frescoes, mosaics, and inscriptions that women served as bishops, priests, and deacons. Inscriptions also refer to women as leaders of synagogues. Such scholarship is used by feminists today to support demands for equality for women within organized religion.

ORGANISATION OF WOMEN OF AFRICAN AND ASIAN DESCENT (OWAAD). A group founded in Great Britain in 1978 by women of color (q.v.), primarily black women, to challenge white domination of the feminist movement. The last annual OWAAD conference was held in 1982; thereafter, women of either Afro-Caribbean or Asian origin met together. Ethnic differences were the major factor in the demise of the OWAAD, but the gay/straight split (q.v.) and tensions between those interested in advancing women within Britain and those stressing global feminism (q.v.) played roles as well.

ORR V. ORR, 440 US 268 (1979). A decision of the US Supreme Court that held that an Alabama statute which made alimony only available to wives was unconstitutional; state laws on alimony had to be gender-neutral (q.v.). The Court specifically rejected the state's view of women as dependent in marriage and its use of sex as a proxy for economic need.

"OTHER" *see* WOMAN AS OTHER

OUR BODIES, OURSELVES see BOSTON WOMEN'S HEALTH
BOOK COLLECTIVE

-P-

PAGLIA, CAMILLE (1947-). Author of *Sexual Personae*
(1990) and the collection of essays *Sex, Art, and American
Culture* (1992), and considered by many feminists to be a tool
of the right-wing anti-feminists (q.v.) for her nontraditional
attitudes. Paglia defends pornography (q.v.), insists that rape
(q.v.) is a type of sex, not violence, and champions motherhood
as the most important role a woman can have. She sees a
connection between art and violence, asserting that "There is no
female Mozart because there is no female Jack the Ripper."
Paglia sees herself as a feminist who is opposed to the current
feminist establishment: "All revolutions start well but go bad.
This one has degenerated into ideology and dogma--groupthink.
They're like the Kremlin. There's only one way to see things."
She also attacks the way feminists have waged war on romance
and women as sexual partners: "This is horrible what they're
doing. What a horrible effect this is having on our best young
women. They're saying: Do not respond with your instincts of
beauty and pleasure. No, no. Be guilty. Be angry. Be
resentful. Find hidden violent meanings. Find conspiracies
against you. Be paranoid. This is evil. What's being done to
young women is evil" (see her collection of essays, *Sex, Art, and
American Culture*).

PALIMONY. The equivalent of spousal support and/or a
property settlement received by an unmarried person after co-
habiting with another. The relationship must be based on an
expressed agreement or quasi-contract unless the contractual
terms explicitly entail "immoral or illicit consideration of
meretricious sexual services." (*See also Marvin v. Marvin.*)

PAN CHAO (c. 45 A.D.). The foremost woman scholar in
China, trained in Han Confucianism and tutor to the Empress.
She is famous for her *Nu Jie* (Precepts for Women), a book of
moral principles addressed to young women in which she
advocates the education of girls and claims women are moral
beings as are men and are capable of becoming wise.

PANKHURSTS, THE. A family that were England's premier women's rights activists beginning in the 1860s: Emmeline (1858-1928) and Richard Marsden (1835-1898) and their daughters Dame Christabel (1880-1956), Sylvia (1882-1956), and Adela (1885-1961). They were the founders in 1903 of the militant Women's Social and Political Union (WSPU). Their use of increasingly disruptive tactics to promote "votes for women" prompted an increasingly heavy-handed response from British authorities, including the Cat and Mouse Bill which authorized the forced feeding of incarcerated suffragists who resorted to hunger strikes. The Pankhursts abruptly terminated their orchestrated mayhem at the onset of World War I and committed their organization to war work, thus providing the government with a face-saving way to give women the vote in 1928 in recognition of their wartime patriotism. Richard Pankhurst, as a member of Parliament, drafted the married women's property bill and the woman suffrage bill and by 1865 had become active in the feminist movement. Both Christabel (in *Unshackled: The Story of How We Won the Vote*) and Sylvia (in *The Life of Emmeline Pankhurst: The Suffragette Struggle for Women's Citizenship*) wrote histories of that period.

PARADIGM. A concept developed by scientist Thomas Kuhn in 1962 and used by feminists to describe frameworks which form women's experiences, roles, and expectations. A "paradigm shift" occurs when a change in consciousness causes a re-envisioning of reality which may be essential for changing views about and roles of women.

PARAGRAPH 218. Part of the German criminal code of 1871 that made abortion (q.v.) illegal in that country. Reform of the code in 1974 by the Federal Republic had made it legal within the first trimester, but a ruling by the constitutional court forced a compromise law in 1976, whereby abortion became criminal except for medical, eugenic, criminological or extraordinary social reasons. In the German Democratic Republic abortion had been legally available within the first trimester. The reunification agreement of 1989 mandated a liberalization of the law and increased emphasis on the right of the unborn. One year after new legislation was passed in 1992 making abortion available after obligatory counseling, a ruling of the constitutional court interpreted "counseling" to mean that the advising physician must urge a woman not to terminate the pregnancy. A second ruling in 1993 declared abortion illegal; however, the court indicated that first-term abortions would not be prosecuted.

PARDO BAZÁN, EMILIA (1851-1921). Spain's greatest novelist, a literary critic, and author of over 50 short stories. She was a militant feminist with a philosophical interest in St. Francis of Assisi, partly because of the high regard in which he held women. She wrote on the subjection of women in Spain and on the life of the philosopher St. Catherine of Alexandria. In 1883 she caused a public furor with a series of articles defending, with reservations, the Naturalism of Émile Zola. She became the acknowledged leader of the new manner reflected in her two most famous works, *Los pazos de Ulloa* (1886), and its sequel, *La madre naturaleza* (Mother Nature) (1887). In 1906 she became the first woman to chair the Literary Section of the Atheneum. Although she was the first woman appointed to a professorial chair at the University of Madrid (1916), her classes were boycotted by the male student body. She is considered a feminist forerunner for her support of women's rights in education and employment.

PARENTAL CONSENT/NOTIFICATION. A requirement of some states that conditions a minor's right to abortion (q.v.) on notification or consent of at least one parent. The constitutionality of notification laws was upheld by the US Supreme Court in *Planned Parenthood of Southeastern Pennsylvania v. Casey*, 112 S.Ct. 2791 (1992). Parental consent laws are permissible only if a judicial bypass is also available so that a young woman can go to court and get a judge's permission instead. Feminists oppose both barriers to reproductive choice, particularly for women from abusive families. (*See also* Bell, Rebecca.)

PARENTAL LEAVE *see* FAMILY LEAVE

PATERSON, EMMA (1848-1886). An English suffragist and women's trade union leader. In 1872 she became the Secretary of the Women's Suffrage Association; in 1874 she formed the

Women's Protective and Provident League and began organizing women in different trades: bookbinding, dressmaking, millinery, and upholstery. She worked for the appointment of women factory inspectors but opposed protective labor legislation (q.v.) because of its potential to jeopardize women's employment. Beginning in 1876 she edited the monthly *Women's Union Journal*, which covered suffrage, educational and legal rights, and dress reform (q.v.).

PATRIA POTESTAD. A concept from Roman law, literally "power of the father." The principle is found in the civil code of many countries, where the husband/father is viewed as the household head with all powers of parental guardianship and authority. Women's rights advocates, particularly in Latin America, have sought legal reforms that would grant mothers a role in their children's guardianship.

PATRIARCHY. The rule by men. The Latin *pater* refers to the social role of a father, not to the biological father, so that a father may be a celibate man (as in the Roman Catholic priesthood). Patriarchal societies exclude women from the exercise of citizens' political responsibilities, although some may have titular women (e.g., Queen Victoria). Patriarchal societies are hierarchical in that, at a minimum, they are a two-class society. A critique of the patriarchy is at the root of most feminist political theory (q.v.).

PAUL, ALICE (1885-1977). Quaker social worker, lawyer, and early leader of the movement for women's equal rights. Deeply influenced by her work with the militant English suffragists, Paul introduced protest marches into the US woman suffrage movement through her group, the Congressional Union (CU), which broke with the National American Woman Suffrage Association (q.v.) over tactical issues. Alice Paul formed the National Woman's Party (q.v.) in 1913 and wrote the first version of the Equal Rights Amendment in 1923.

PAY EQUITY *see* COMPARABLE WORTH

PC *see* POLITICALLY CORRECT

PEARCE, DIANA *see* "FEMINIZATION OF POVERTY"

PENELOPE. According to Greek legend, the long-suffering, faithful wife of Odysseus who for 20 years awaited her husband's return from the Trojan War. Widely celebrated for her cleverness and intelligence, she ruled over Ithaca in her husband's absence, as her son Telemachus grew to manhood. Through the ruse of weaving and unravelling a shroud for her father-in-law Laertes, she managed to put off more than a hundred rowdy suitors for several years. Although there was an alternate tradition which questioned Penelope's faithfulness to Odysseus, she remains the epitome of wifely virtue and one of the few thoroughly admirable women in Greek mythology.

PENIS ENVY *see* FREUD, SIGMUND

PENSIONS *see* EMPLOYEE RETIREMENT INCOME SECURITY ACT

PERÓN, EVA MARIA DUARTE DE (1919-1952). Wife of Argentine President Juan Domingo Perón and considered by many to be an early Argentine feminist. She galvanized popular support, especially among women and workers, for Peronism and her husband during his first term, 1946-52. Known as Evita, she was the first wife to accompany an Argentine political candidate on his electoral campaign. In 1947 her public support for women's suffrage aided its passage through Congress and cemented the political ties between Argentine feminism and Peronism. Two years later she created the Peronist Women's (or Feminist) Party. Although without a formal government portfolio, she acted as the de facto minister of health and labor. In 1948 she established, with government funds, the Eva Perón Foundation, a social welfare agency dedicated to working-class housing, education, employment, and health care. She remained a formidable political and cultural figure after her death, as evidenced by the 1950's effort to have her canonized, her husband's political reemergence in 1973, and her reburial in Argentina in 1976.

PERSONAL-DEVELOPMENT FEMINISM. The strand of the movement, currently associated with Gloria Steinem (q.v.), that focuses on surviving addiction, codependency (q.v.), and abuse and maintaining self-esteem (q.v.). Growing out of a concern with child abuse, violence, and pornography (q.v.), this recovery movement, critics charge, can contribute to women perceiving themselves as "victims" rather than empowered "survivors." (*See also* Victimization of Women.)

PERSONNEL ADMINISTRATOR OF MASSACHUSETTS V. FEENEY, 442 US 256 (1979). A decision by the US Supreme Court that involved an Equal Protection (q.v.) challenge to a Massachusetts law that granted a permanent preference in civil service jobs to military veterans. This policy reduced the employment opportunities available to women, who until 1967 could fill no more than two percent of armed forces positions. However, the Court held that there was no evidence that the state intended to discriminate against women when it instituted the veterans' preference and that demonstration of an adverse impact on women was insufficient to establish a violation of the Equal Protection Clause.

PERSONS CASE OF 1929. A major victory of the first wave feminist (q.v.) movement in Canada. Five suffrage leaders petitioned the federal Senate for an interpretation of the word "persons" in a law. Although the Supreme Court's initial ruling in 1928 was that women were not included, the Judicial Committee of the Privy Council in England reversed that decision in 1929 and permitted qualified women to be appointed to the Senate. The case is viewed as recognizing the "legal personhood" of Canadian women.

PERSUASIBILITY, WOMEN'S. The presumption that women are more easily persuaded than men, a belief linked to traditional gender roles (q.v.) of female submission and male dominance (q.v.). Mid-twentieth-century communication research did find that women audiences of persuasive appeals changed their minds more readily, with less speaker effort, than men. Follow-up studies, however, have shown that when topics are more readily understood by women, men are more persuasible. Current understanding of persuasibility is that *both* women and men are persuaded easily when they know little about the topic.

PETHICK-LAWRENCE, EMMELINE (1867-1954). An English social worker, suffragist, pacifist, and member of the Women's Social and Political Union. In 1907 she founded *Votes for Women* to advocate for the civil and political rights of women. She was active internationally in the Women's International League for Peace and Freedom, the Women's Peace Congress, and the Women's Freedom League. In 1918 she ran unsuccessfully for the House of Commons as a Labour candidate in the first election open to women.

PHALLOCENTRISM. The tendency to conceive of sexuality from a male perspective. Since the penis (phallus) plays a central role both in erotic pleasure and in reproduction in the male, it may be erroneously assumed that vaginal penetration has parallel importance in the female. Feminists have noted that such phallocentrism may lead to disregard of clitoral stimulation and its importance for sexual pleasure in the female. (*See also* "Myth of the Vaginal Orgasm.")

PHALLOGOCENTRIC. A term coined by the French feminists (q.v.) to denote the tyranny of the Symbolic Order, the patriarchy (q.v.), to stabilize, organize, and rationalize all systems of language, thought, and culture around one meaning (represented by the phallus, the symbol of the father's power over all aspects of culture).

PHAN BOI CHAU (1867-1940). A Vietnamese intellectual, reformer, and author of several works on the status of women. The best-known of these, *Van De Phu Nu* (The Women's Question, 1929), not only attacked traditional attitudes and marriages but also encouraged women to become active within movements for their own liberation. He voiced these ideas earlier in a 1926 speech to the opening session of the Women's Labor Study Association.

PHILLIPS V. MARTIN MARIETTA CORPORATION, 400 US 542 (1971). A decision of the US Supreme Court that concluded that an employer's policy which denied employment to women but not men with preschool-age children was unlawful sex discrimination under Title VII of the Civil Rights Act of 1964 (q.v.). The Court rejected a lower court construction of the Act which interpreted the statute to prohibit only discrimination based "solely" on race, sex, or ethnicity. The Court suggested that the bona fide occupational qualification (q.v.) exception might be applied if an employer could prove that family obligations are more relevant to the job performance of a woman than a man; to date, this "sex plus" test has not been met.

PHYLLIS SCHLAFLY REPORT *see* SCHLAFLY, PHYLLIS

PHYSICAL ATTRACTIVENESS. A subjective quality which is determined by comparing an individual's appearance to the prevailing standard of attractiveness as set by social convention. Attractive people are seen to be happier, kinder, more socially competent, and more successful than less attractive people. Feminists have noted that there is also a gender bias in that physical attractiveness is emphasized more in females than in males. Males place greater emphasis on physical attractiveness than do females when picking a mate. However, attractiveness is also a liability for women in professional positions. Attractive women are often seen as not as capable of handling a job, and they are more readily the victims of sexual harassment (q.v.).

PIERCY, MARGE (1936-). An American contemporary novelist, best known among feminists as the author of *Woman on the Edge of Time* (1976), a fictional work that applied the theories about technologizing reproduction that Shulamith Firestone's *Dialectic of Sex* (qq.v.) developed. A prolific poet, Piercy has also published several volumes of poetry, including *Breaking Camp* (1968), *Hard Loving* (1969), *To Be of Use* (1972), and *Living in the Open* (1976). In addition to *Woman on the Edge of Time*, Piercy has also published the novels *Going Down Fast* (1969), *Dance the Eagle to Sleep* (1970), *Small Changes* (1973), and *Vida* (1979).

PILL, THE *see* BIRTH CONTROL PILL

PINK-COLLAR GHETTO. Female-dominated segregated positions involving secretarial and clerical skills. Pink-collar positions are female-typed and have lower status, pay, and prestige than blue- or white-collar, male-typed positions. (*See also* Occupational Segregation.)

PIZAN, CHRISTINE DE (1364-1430). A French poet and the first professional woman writer. In her most famous work, *The Book of the City of Women* (completed 1405), she steps out of a patriarchal frame of reference and the tradition of Aristotelian anti-feminism to construct a reality in which women emerge as powerful and authoritative in all areas of human endeavor. It is modelled partly after Augustine's *City of God* and is a response to the popular misogynist works of the time. Pizan presents philosophical arguments against the oppression of women, maintaining that it is contrary to the goal of improving society as a whole.

PLANNED PARENTHOOD. A social reform group committed to voluntary family planning and access to contraceptive methods, including abortion (q.v.). The Planned Parenthood Federation of America (PPFA) was originally founded by Margaret Sanger (q.v.) in 1921 as the American Birth Control League and adopted its present name in 1942. The PPFA is organized in more than 250 cities, operates about 700 clinics, and recently has begun to directly provide abortion services. The International Planned Parenthood Federation has affiliates in more than 70 nations and concentrates on limiting population growth in developing nations.

POLITICAL LESBIANISM. A conscious adoption of a homosexual orientation in response to peer pressure or personal feminist ideology. Here lesbianism is viewed as primarily a political, not a sexual, choice, and lesbians (q.v.) are hailed as model feminists. Although the pressure within radical feminism (q.v.) to adopt a lesbian orientation has declined since the early 1970's, this period caused a major gay/straight split (q.v.) in the movement as heterosexual women became defensive about their own sexual preferences and roles in the movement and older lesbians expressed distrust of these "instant lesbians" as potential sex partners. (*See also* Lavender Menace; Woman-Identified Woman.)

POLITICALLY CORRECT (PC). A term originally used within the US feminist movement to refer to acceptable behaviors and opinions. Deviations by movement participants from these official doctrines were subject to sanctions and even expulsion. In the 1990's the term was appropriated by political conservatives to discredit feminists as well as others who challenged the status quo and attempted to make society more inclusive. In particular, university policies to diversify the curriculum and to enact codes of unacceptable behavior toward women, gays, and racial and religious minorities have drawn charges of "political correctness." (*See also* Hate Crimes.)

POLITICO/FEMINIST SPLIT. A division within the US women's liberation movement (q.v.), 1967-69, over its relationship with the larger New Left political movement. Politicos (q.v.) viewed women's liberation as a key branch of the Left. Feminists supported an independent movement on the grounds that both capitalism and male supremacy oppressed women; that being so, women's issues would inevitably be peripheral within that male-dominated movement. By 1969 the feminist tendency prevailed as the movement broke from the Left.

POLITICOS. Those who wish feminism to remain a part of the New Left rather than to become an independent women's movement. They believe that women's oppression is rooted in capitalism, racism and/or imperialism and that only a new revolutionary political order can liberate women. Liberal feminist (q.v.) reforms are opposed on the grounds that reform may prevent or retard revolution.

POLITIQUE ET PSYCHANALYSE (POLITICS AND PSYCHOANALYSIS). A small French feminist theory group best known as Psych et Po, founded in 1968 by psychoanalyst Antoinette Fouqué and including prominent theorists Hélène Cixous, Luce Irigaray, and Julia Kristéva (qq.v.). The group's entrepreneurialism and appropriation of the generic term "mouvement pour la libération des femmes" (MLF) (q.v.) is widely resented by other French feminists. Psych et Po conversely considers the rest of the movement bourgeois and insufficiently attendant to its own Lacanian intellectualism and psychosexual linguistic analysis. It does not use the term "feminist" and even calls itself "anti-feminist" (q.v.).

PORNOGRAPHY, FEMINIST DEBATE ON. A divisive issue emerging within the feminist movement in the late 1970's and 1980's concerning responses to the depiction of sexual activity. Anti-pornography feminists and their group Women Against Pornography (WAP), formed in 1979, argue that violence against women (q.v.) is caused by pornography that depicts pain, dominance, and violence. Writer Andrea Dworkin and lawyer Catharine MacKinnon (qq.v.) have written a model ordinance that allows a woman to file a sex discrimination suit against the makers and distributors of pornography. Feminists opposed to this anti-pornography movement formed the Feminist Anti-Censorship Taskforce (FACT) in 1984. FACT members generally support the right to free speech and press but are more concerned with the dangers of a patriarchal legal system's power to prohibit feminist writings and with preserving women's newly acknowledged sexuality and right to sexual expression. Anti-censorship feminists tend to be drawn from the radical, socialist, and liberal (qq.v.) traditions of feminism. Cultural feminists (q.v.), especially lesbian separatists (q.v.), are more often allied with the anti-pornography faction. (*See also* Minneapolis Pornography Ordinance; *Regina v. Butler*.)

POSITIONALITY. The idea that "truth" may be empirical but also contingent because reality and truth depend on the perception of the viewer. Acknowledging "positionality" allows feminists to reconcile apparently inconsistent truths.

POSTFEMINIST. A term used by the US media after the defeat of the Equal Rights Amendment (q.v.) to describe the more conservative environment of the 1980's and the supposed demise and disintegration of the women's movement. It is argued that gender equality has been achieved, and feminism has become an anachronism, irrelevant to and even reviled by women, especially within the younger generation. In fact, the term was first used in 1919 at the height of the suffrage movement.

POSTMODERNISM. A contempory intellectual movement modified and adapted by feminist theory, which rejects traditional assumptions about truth and reality and emphasizes instead the plurality, diversity, and multiplicity of women as distinct from men, who are thought to be unitary and rational. It focuses on expressing the unexpressed through new language (scratching, jotting, scribbling). One faction of feminists is committed to the notion of poststructural analyses, including deconstructionism (q.v.). The purpose of the movement is to unveil the layers of meaning society has attached to certain misogynist beliefs in an effort to reveal the inner core of meanings and make evident their inconsistencies. Some postmodern feminists have an active emancipatory agenda of social reform. Prominent authors, principally New French Feminists (q.v.), include Simone de Beauvoir, Hélène Cixous, Luce Irigaray, and Julia Kristéva (qq.v.).

POSTSTRUCTURALIST FEMINIST CRITICISM. Based on the theories of deconstruction (q.v.) and using the writings of Jacques Derrida (q.v.), Paul de Man, and Michel Foucault (q.v.), among others, to claim a radical decentering of the subject and understanding of history. Most of the New French feminists (q.v.)--Julia Kristéva, Hélène Cixous, and Lucy Irigaray (qq.v.)--would be considered poststructuralist in their visions and philosophical orientations. All of them to some extent believe in an essential (q.v.) female nature, but only as a starting point from which they then go on to deconstruct all intellectual and social traditions--psychoanalysis, philosophy, language, and patriarchal culture. Denise Riley's *"Am I That Name?" Feminism and the Category of "Women" in History* (1988) is an example of a poststructural feminist history that dissects the arbitrary notion of "women" in the history of the feminist movement.

POWER FEMINISM. A tradition advocated by Naomi Wolf in *Fire with Fire* (1993) in reaction against the cult of victimization of women (q.v.) that she believed was dominating the feminist movement in the 1980's and early 1990's. Power feminism emphasizes female strength, ability, and power directed toward positive action and social change. It draws a distinction between hating men and hating sexism (q.v.); it presents itself as pro-men but also tolerant about other women's decisions concerning their own appearance and sexuality. Both men and women are acknowledged as aggressive, self-interested, competitive, individualistic beings interested in money and success. The basis for a women's movement lies in the shared pleasures and strengths of being female rather than common vulnerability, pain, or a constructed fantasy of sisterhood (q.v.).

PREGNANCY DISCRIMINATION ACT. A law enacted by the US Congress in 1978 which amended Title VII of the Civil Rights Act of 1964 (q.v.). Congress defined the Act's prohibition against sex discrimination to include discrimination based on pregnancy, childbirth, or related medical conditions and required that women affected by these conditions be treated the same as other persons who are not pregnant but similar in their ability or inability to work. This mandate extended to "all employment-related purposes, including receipt of fringe benefit programs." (*See also Geduldig v. Aiello; General Electric Co. v. Gilbert.*)

PREMENSTRUAL SYNDROME (PMS). A variety of symptoms that occur in some women in the days before the onset of menstruation. It includes, but is not limited to, nervous tension, irritability, weight gain, edema, bloating, headache, food cravings, fatigue, and depression. British researcher Katherine Dalton is credited with much of the early research on the relationship between a woman's menstrual cycle and her behavior; her research on PMS has been used as a successful defense argument in a murder trial. In 1993 the American Psychiatric Association recommended that severe PMS be included in its manual of mental illnesses as Premenstrual Dysphoric Disorder (PMDD). Some women believed this classification would assure serious treatment of PMS by physicians; others feared child custody or mental competency hearings could be affected by the diagnosis.

PRESIDENT'S COMMISSION ON THE STATUS OF WOMEN (PCSW). A body established in 1961 by US President John F. Kennedy to defuse demands for the Equal Rights Amendment (q.v.). Eleanor Roosevelt was appointed as honorary chair and Esther Peterson, head of the Women's Bureau (q.v.), was chosen as executive vice-chair. The first government body ever to study the status of US women released its report *American*

Women in 1963. Among its 24 recommendations were: equal pay, equal employment opportunities, paid maternity leave, marital property, child care (qq.v.), and a litigation campaign against sex discrimination using the Fifth and Fourteenth Amendments. The mere existence of the Commission is credited with reviving interest in women's issues; more than 64,000 copies of the report were sold in less than a year.

PRIVACY. A US constitutional doctrine deriving from the First, Fourth, Fifth, and Ninth Amendments, as well as the Due Process and Equal Protection (q.v.) Clauses of the Fourteenth Amendment. The Supreme Court has not recognized a comprehensive constitutional right of privacy. Instead, it has preferred to identify "zones of privacy" on a case-by-case basis. In terms of the Fourteenth Amendment, the right to privacy has come to mean a right to engage in certain highly personal activities, such as freedom of choice in marital, sexual and reproductive matters. (*See also Griswold v. Connecticut; Roe v. Wade.*)

PRO-CHOICE MOVEMENT. A coalition organized for the purpose of maintaining a pregnant woman's right to choose among all possible options: having and keeping her baby, adoption, or abortion (q.v.). Efforts include public education, personal counseling, social action, litigation, and lobbying for legislation in many areas. These include maintaining a woman's right to choose abortion and establishing rights to medical care and adequate financial support for those who choose to deliver and keep their babies. The name signals that this is not a "pro-abortion" movement but one about alternatives and options, freely chosen. Since the 1980's these goals have been among the top priorities of the feminist movements in Western nations. (*See also* National Abortion and Reproductive Rights Action League; Planned Parenthood; Reproductive Freedom.)

PRO-FAMILY MOVEMENT. A group coalition formed by US social conservatives in 1977 to coordinate their support of laws reflecting traditional morality and opposition to the Equal Rights Amendment, abortion, child care, comparable worth (qq.v.), and homosexuality. The organization was announced by Phyllis Schlafly at the National Women's Conference (qq.v.), but the label is primarily used to describe the generic anti-feminist movement (q.v.) of the late 1970's and 1980's.

PRO-LIFE MOVEMENT. A movement that seeks to make abortion (q.v.) illegal and places fetal rights above those of the pregnant woman. It encourages adoption as the solution for unwanted pregnancies and uses personal counseling, social action, and the legislative process to prevent abortion. (*See also* Fake Clinics; National Right to Life Committee; Operation Rescue.)

PRO-WOMAN LINE. A feminist argument, developed by the Redstockings (q.v.), that rejects gender role (q.v.) socialization or women's inherent nature as an explanation of women's behavior. Instead of being "brainwashed" or "programmed" into accepting a subordinate status, women consciously acquiesce because they recognize the dangers of noncompliance. Women are thus not responsible for their own oppression; men need to change their behavior, not women. Other feminists charge that this view glorifies victimization (q.v.) and actually rationalizes the status quo in that women's behavior is seen as a rational response to the culture.

PROBLEM PREGNANCY COUNSELING. A service for women (and others, if desired) who have become pregnant at a time when the pregnancy is perceived as a problem. Problem pregnancy counselors help their clients identify all options available to them, including marriage, becoming single parents, adoption, and abortion (q.v.). Each woman is assisted to make her own decision according to her own wants, needs, and circumstances. (*See also* Fake Clinics.)

"PROBLEM THAT HAS NO NAME, THE." Widespread feelings of profound female dissatisfaction identified by Betty Friedan (q.v.) in *The Feminine Mystique* (1963). This discontent did not stem from problems with children, husband, or home but was rooted in the traditional role of women as housewives. Friedan suggested that there was no medical diagnosis for these frequent complaints of unhappiness because such would have challenged existing standards of feminine normality, adjustment, fulfillment, and maturity.

PROSTITUTION. A crime traditionally defined as a female offering her body for intercourse with men, usually for money. More recently, some courts have interpreted the term in a gender neutral (q.v.) fashion to include conduct of any person who engages in sexual activity as a business. First wave feminists (q.v.) were critical of laws such as the Contagious Diseases Acts and the Mann Act (qq.v.) as repressive and reflecting a double standard (q.v.). Second wave feminists (q.v.) were initially split as to whether prostitution could involve free choice or was always economic exploitation of women desperate for money. Today some feminists support punishment of clients and pimps and have organized against sex tours (q.v.) and other types of international traffic in women (q.v.).

PROTECTIVE LABOR LAWS. Late nineteenth- and early twentieth-century laws enacted in a number of US states to protect women working in factories from hardships such as long work days, low pay, and heavy lifting. Initially these laws were invalidated under federal constitutional doctrines which exalted personal liberties and freedom to contract over state legislative efforts to regulate the workplace. However, in 1908 the Supreme Court in *Mueller v. Oregon* (q.v.) upheld one of these protective laws. Although initially supported by the social feminists (q.v.), protective labor legislation is now viewed as having negatively affected the job opportunities that would become available for women. Protective labor legislation increased sexual segregation and stratification in the labor market. Enforcement of Title VII of the Civil Rights Act of 1964 (q.v.) eventually led to the general invalidation of sex-specific state protective labor laws. (*See also Goesaert v. Cleary.*)

PSYCH ET PO *see* POLITIQUE ET PSYCHANALYSE

PSYCHOANALYTIC FEMINIST CRITICISM. The work of a wide-ranging and often disparate group of critics who seek to redefine in feminist terms the basic issues enunciated by Sigmund Freud (q.v.) over one hundred years ago. Those issues center on the nature of gender (q.v.) as a process of sexual maturation, the role of the parents in the formation of gender, the "anatomy is destiny" (q.v.) credo, and the transition a girl makes from identification with her mother to her father or to the patriarchy (q.v.). Contemporary psychoanalytic critics have sought to rethink such Freudian concepts as "the oedipus complex," "penis envy" and "infantile sexuality," rather than merely reject them. The major theorists who have attempted to recast the masculinism (q.v.) of Freud's theories have been Karen Horney (q.v.) and Clara Thompson, and more recently Dorothy Dinnerstein (q.v.), Nancy Chodorow (q.v.), Carol Gilligan (q.v.), and Jane Gallop. Perhaps the most widely known text is Juliet Mitchell's (q.v.) *Psychoanalysis and Feminism*, which argues that patriarchy is no longer crucial for the construction of society because society no longer depends on men exchanging women: "In economically advanced societies, though the kinship-exchange system still operates in a residual way, other forms of exchange--i.e., commodity exchange--dominate and class, not kinship structures, prevail. It would seem that it is against a background of the *remoteness* of a kinship system that the ideology of the biological family comes into its own. In other words, the relationship between two parents and their children assumes a dominant role when the complexity of a class society forces the kinship system to recede" (see Mitchell's *Psychoanalysis and Feminism*).

PUBLIC-PRIVATE DICHOTOMY *see* DOMESTIC SPHERE

-Q-

QUALIFYING LANGUAGE. Words and phrases that modify others and are usually divided into two categories: intensifiers like "so," "very," "quite"; and hedges like "maybe," "kind of," "sort of," "you know," and "somewhat." Semanticist Robin Lakoff argued that women use more qualifying language than men do. Subsequent research in this area tends to confirm Lakoff's claim with regard to intensifiers, but is less conclusive regarding hedges. Researchers have suggested that using qualifying language indicates uncertainty and tentativeness. Feminists note that there are other interpretations that are not so negative to apply to this type of language.

QUEEN BEE SYNDROME. The situation, described by psychologists Graham Staines, Carol Tavris, and Toby Jayaratne, in which a woman who has risen to the top in a male-dominated profession is unconcerned about the plight of other women and may even deny that feminist issues have any substance. Such women are seen as preferring to occupy a position of exclusive female achievement in a world of men. It has been suggested that, with the advance of feminist ideas, the "syndrome" has been less frequently observed.

QUERELLE DES FEMMES (THE WOMEN'S QUESTION). A debate on the nature of women begun in France in the early fifteenth century as a reaction to the blatant misogyny expressed in a current popular novel. The argument raged on in the literary circles of Europe for at least three centuries and centered on the belief in the inherent intellectual and moral equality of women and men versus the age-old and commonly held belief in women's "essential deficiency." (*See also* Pizan, Christine de.)

QUESTIONS FÉMINISTES. A French women's studies (q.v.) journal begun in 1977 by a radical feminist (q.v.) collective (q.v.). In 1981 it underwent a name change (to *Nouvelles Questions Féministes*) and a reorganization that rejected Marxist and neo-feminist intolerance of men and heterosexuality.

QURRAT UL AYN (1815-1851). An Iranian leader of the heretical Babism (later Baha'ism) movement, a religion that supported a higher status for women and limits on polygyny and violence against women (q.v.). She appeared unveiled in 1844 at a time when women had first begun to question Islamic dress. She spoke in public, was a battlefield participant in Babi revolts, and died a martyr.

-R-

RACHEL. In the Hebrew Bible, daughter of Laban, sister of Leah (q.v.), and wife of Jacob. Rachel, whom Jacob wanted as his only wife, pays the price for her father's scheme to have Jacob unknowingly marry her sister Leah. With Leah, she is responsible for her family's return to Canaan, a necessity for the fulfillment of God's promises to Israel. When Jacob unwittingly sentences her to death because of her theft of her father's idols, Rachel uses deception to save her life. Feminists are divided as to whether the account portrays her as a clever, intelligent woman or as a stereotyped idolater who reinforces the image of the untrustworthy woman. After years of childlessness, she bears Benjamin and Joseph, eponymous ancestors of two of the tribes of Israel.

RACISM AND FEMINISM. The recognition by feminists that the systematic devaluation and oppression based on racial and sexual differences (along with classism) are simultaneous and interlocking forms of exploitation. In the United States, bell hooks (q.v.), Audre Lorde (q.v.), and Barbara Hilkert Andolsen have challenged white feminists to address the racism that has corrupted middle-class white women's movements. This has prompted Euro-American feminists to examine and seek theoretical and practical ways to combat their own racism, and to forge genuinely collaborative alliances with African-American, Hispanic-American, and other feminists dedicated to race and gender justice. (*See also* Classism and Feminism; Oppressions, Interstructuring of.)

RADICAL FEMINISM. A dynamic contemporary tradition generated by the women's liberation movement (q.v.) of the 1960's. It is informed by the ideals and politics of the New Left and emphasizes the importance of personal feelings, experiences, and relationships. Women's experiences of oppression are an especially significant impetus in the formation of radical feminist ideals and politics. Radical feminists argue that gender (q.v.) is a system of male dominance (q.v.) and that women's biology is a root cause of patriarchy (q.v.). Women's liberation therefore requires female control over their own sexuality. In terms of theory, radical feminists seek to understand gender as a system of male domination; their political goal is to end it.

RADICALESBIANS *see* LAVENDER MENACE

RAHAB. In the Hebrew Bible, the Canaanite woman who saves Joshua's scouts from the king of Jericho's soldiers, facilitating the Israelites' success at Jericho. Many scholars interpret her as representative of the Canaanite peasants who joined the Israelite movement, redefining the government and religion of Canaan.

RAICHO, HIRATSUKA *see* BLUESTOCKING SOCIETY; ICHIKAWA, FUSAE

RAMABA, PANDITA (1858-1922). A Sanskrit scholar and prominent feminist activist in India. She founded a group of women's organizations, lectured in India and abroad on women, and wrote *Women's Religious Law* and *The High Caste Hindu Woman*, both of which supported women's rights. She founded girls' schools, orphanages, and widows' homes. In 1889 she was one of the delegates to the Indian National Congress.

RANKIN, JEANNETTE (1880-1973). The first woman member of the US House of Representatives, elected in 1916 from the state of Montana. She had been very active in the suffrage movement and had her greatest impact as the leader of the floor debate on the Nineteenth Amendment. She was defeated in her race for the Senate in 1918 but returned to the House in 1941. She is the only member of Congress to have voted against US entry into both world wars and was the sole vote against World War II. Between congressional terms, she lobbied for the National Consumers League (q.v.) and the Women's International League for Peace and Freedom. As a life-long pacifist, she led the Jeannette Rankin Brigade to the Capitol in Washington, D.C., in 1968 to protest the Vietnam War.

RAP GROUP. A method used by participants in the women's liberation (q.v.) branch of the new feminist movement (q.v.) to analyze the political meaning of personal experiences. Women regularly meet in a small group to share personal problems and feelings as women and to gain insight into the commonalities of these experiences.

RAPE. The use of coercion or violence to force a person to engage in sexual activity against her or his will. Under English common law, rape was narrowly defined as penile penetration of a woman's vagina by force and against her will. In the early 1970's the new feminist movement (q.v.) organized around the issue of rape by holding speak-outs (q.v.), founding rape crisis centers (q.v.), and seeking reforms of rape laws. In most US jurisdictions today, rape laws are gender neutral (q.v.) and in some areas the term "sexual assault" is used to encompass different offenses from "unwanted touching" to acts of intercourse (oral, anal, or vaginal) with penetration by an "object." Feminists have succeeded in redefining the nature of rape from an act of sex to an act of violence. Police and court procedures in investigating and prosecuting rape have also undergone major changes: special sexual offense investigative and prosecution units have been established; rules of evidence regarding corroboration and consent have been altered; greater protection is afforded the victim in terms of public testimony and questions about prior sexual history. Health care and social service professionals too have revised their treatment of rape victims to conform with physical evidentiary standards and new mental health knowledge of rape trauma. Because these changes have been most effective in prosecuting rapes by strangers ("real rape"), feminists have begun to define rape as a crime of sexual coercion that occurs between spouses, acquaintances, dates, and strangers. (*See also* Date Rape; Marital Rape; Statutory Rape.)

RAPE CRISIS CENTER. A feminist self-help (q.v.) institution that offers advice and support to the victims of sexual assault by providing persons to accompany victims to hospitals, police stations, and the courts. Typically such centers provide some combination of crisis counseling (with a 24-hour hotline), legal advocacy, medical care, and evidence-gathering services. The first rape crisis centers were established in 1972 and now almost all large US cities and other Western cities have these special services for rape victims.

RAPPORT-TALK *see* REPORT-TALK

RATHBONE, ELEANOR (1872-1946). An Englishwoman selected as the first president of the National Union of Societies for Equal Citizenship (NUSEC, formerly the National Union of Women's Suffrage Societies) in 1919. She was elected to Parliament in 1929 as an Independent Member for the Combined English Universities. During her tenure, Rathbone pushed for equal rights and pay for women at home and relief for women in gender-repressive societies across the Empire, particularly in India.

REALISTIC, EQUAL, ACTIVE, AND FOR LIFE WOMEN
(REAL WOMEN). An organization of New Right Canadian
women, formed in 1982. By 1985 it claimed a membership of
200,000. Adopting the "pro-family" (q.v.) label of their US
counterparts, REAL Women oppose all abortions (q.v.), sex
education, contraception, day-care (q.v.) subsidies, no-fault
divorce (q.v.), comparable worth (q.v.), affirmative action (q.v.),
and homosexuality.

REBEKAH. In the Hebrew Bible, wife of the patriarch Isaac
and mother of Jacob and Esau. God reveals to Rebekah the plan
that her second-born, Jacob, will inherit the ancestral promises.
In response, Rebekah devises the plan to trick Isaac into blessing
Jacob and not Esau, his favorite. Whereas some modern
commentators criticize her deception as cruel to her husband and
unfair to Esau, the first-born, feminists emphasize the use of
trickery as the only means available to people of lesser status
and stress Rebekah's resourcefulness in facilitating God's plan.

RECLAIM THE NIGHT see TAKE BACK THE NIGHT

REDSTOCKINGS. A New York-based radical feminist (q.v.)
group founded by Shulamith Firestone (q.v.) and writer Ellen
Willis in 1969. Although it functioned for less than two years,
the group became nationally known when it disrupted state
legislative hearings on abortion (q.v.) law reform to demand
repeal. It is also credited with: developing the theory of
consciousness raising (q.v.); voicing the "pro-woman line" (q.v.);
and inventing the speak-out (q.v.). Its circulation of the
"Redstockings Manifesto" (1969) and other literature helped to
spread the messages of feminism.

REED V. REED, 404 US 71 (1971). A decision of the US
Supreme Court that marked a new departure in constitutional sex
equality doctrine. Under an Idaho state law where there was a
choice between an equally qualified man and woman, the court
was compelled to select the man for the post of administrator of
an estate. The Supreme Court, however, in a unanimous opinion
invalidated the law as a violation of the Equal Protection (q.v.)
Clause. This opinion represented the first time that the Court
had struck down a law that discriminated on the basis of sex.

REFORM FEMINISM *see* LIBERAL FEMINISM

REFRAMING. A technique to shift the meaning of thoughts, behaviors, feelings, or situations that allows the reframer to think differently (hopefully, more positively) about these. This technique can be useful and therapeutic, but feminists note that women are more often expected to reframe situations to make them work more smoothly than men. For example, if a man is questioning a woman she might resent this and label it a cross-examination. Reframing might have this woman change the label to requests for information.

REGINA V. BUTLER. A ruling by the Canadian Supreme Court in 1992 that permitted the criminalization of pornography (q.v.) when there is harm to women's self-esteem (q.v.), physical safety, and pursuit of equality. The court thus defined obscenity as that which degrades women rather than offends a moral standard. The Women's Legal Education and Action Fund (LEAF), which intervened in the case, and most other Canadian women's groups supported the decision. These guidelines were established: violence, child nudity, and bondage are pornographic; adult erotica is not. In the post-*Butler* era, however, most heterosexual materials have freely circulated and feminist, lesbian, and gay erotica have been suppressed by the Canadian government.

RELATIONAL FEMINISM. A branch of feminism which bases its theories on the assertion that women are essentially "connected" to others through the experiences of pregnancy, intercourse, menstruation, and breast feeding. (*See also* Maternal Thinking; "Mother Right.")

RELIGIOUS COALITION FOR ABORTION RIGHTS (RCAR). A pro-choice (q.v.) group of Protestant and Jewish churches, synagogues, and religious organizations, formed in 1973 to counter the role of the Catholic Church in the pro-life movement (q.v.) and to provide a moral argument for reproductive freedom (q.v.). The United Methodist Board of Church and Society played a key role in the group's formation. The Coalition now has more than 26 state affiliates as well as individual members, including many prominent theologians and religious leaders.

REPORT-TALK. A part of a dichotomy of communications, developed by linguist Deborah Tannen, consisting of two categories: rapport-talk and report-talk. The former deals with feelings and the latter with information exchange. Women are seen as experts in rapport-talk and men in report-talk. However, feminists point out that this distinction reaffirms the "public man-private woman" dichotomy which tends to disempower women in public contexts.

REPRESENTATION, FEMINIST THEORIES OF. Based on the poststructuralist view of the contextual rather than a fixed relationship between sign and signified. Feminist theories of representation analyze the politics of textual representations of gender. Most radically, feminist theorists would argue that all textual representations of women are pornographic as language is phallogocentric (q.v.) and necessarily objectifies women as "the other" (q.v.).

REPRODUCTION. Often viewed as the principal role of women. Feminists distinguish between "biological reproduction," or procreation, and "reproduction of the labor force." Because biological reproduction requires both sexes, the societal attitude that it is the principal role of women is a social construction limiting women's roles and behavior. In patriarchal capitalist societies, reproduction of the labor force is assigned to women ("mothers") who are rewarded with subsistence but not wages. If childbearers and childrearers were given wages, the labor cost to capitalists for commodities production would be greatly raised. Feminists' campaigns for wages for housework (q.v.) are based on this undercompensated labor. In some societies, "reproduction of culture" is also women's role. Women may be seen as innately gifted with the capacity for fine craftwork, better able than men to create beautiful and valued material objects. The Western cultural tradition, however, tends to see men as gifted with the capacity to create material objects and women with the capacity to reproduce organisms and the food and clothing necessary for their nurture.

REPRODUCTION OF MOTHERING see CHODOROW, NANCY

REPRODUCTIVE FREEDOM. A term encompassing a woman's right to control her own fertility, to choose not to become a mother and the right to become one. This includes access to sex education, birth control and family planning (q.v.), abortion (q.v.), and voluntary sterilization.

REPRODUCTIVE TECHNOLOGY. Scientific developments, which enhance the probability of conception through fertility drugs, allow conception of children by means other than intercourse, or permit genetic selection. Radical feminists (q.v.) once viewed these advances as a means to free women from their own biology, and some liberal feminists (q.v.) still support a woman's right to choose these methods. Other feminists view them as the latest examples of male control over women's bodies and argue that these technologies are exploitative, costly, often ineffective and unsafe, and verge on the eugenic search for "perfect babies." (*See also* Amniocentesis; Surrogacy.)

REPUBLICAN MOTHER. A concept that emerged in the aftermath of the American Revolution and during the French Revolution "Reign of Terror." It was argued that the best contribution that a woman could make to the republican cause was to instill republican values in her children and to support her spouse in the performance of his civic duties. Although the concept did not include a political role for women, it did legitimate the charitable work of women and the further education of women to facilitate this new role.

RETRIBUTION, THE LAW OF (*QUASAS*). A penal code passed by the parliament of the Islamic Republic of Iran in 1982. It provides, among other measures, that the value of a woman's life is half that of a man and that two women's testimonies will be equally weighted with that of one man.

REVERSE DISCRIMINATION. A term which refers to allegations of discrimination brought by employees or other individuals, such as US white men, who have not been designated under affirmative action (q.v.) programs as preferred for employment opportunities. The US Supreme Court considers each charge of reverse discrimination on its own merits and has generally accepted the principle of gender or racial preference as a way of redressing past discrimination. (*See also Johnson v. Transportation Agency of Santa Clara County.*)

RICH, ADRIENNE (1929-). A contemporary American feminist poet and theorist and more recently one of the most prominent spokespersons for lesbian feminism (q.v.). In her early books of poetry she reflects her Radcliffe education, which exclusively focused on studying male poets. Her own experience with motherhood produced the more radical later works, "When We Dead Awaken: Writing as Re-Vision" (1972), *Of Woman Born* (1976), the latter a portrait of motherhood compiled through literary, anthropological, political, and medical documents. Her book of poetry, *Diving into the Wreck*, won the National Book Award in 1974, while her *Twenty-One Love Poems* (1976) is a sonnet cycle about lesbian love. In her *It Is the Lesbian in Us* (1976) Rich wrote, "Even before I wholly knew I was a lesbian, it was the lesbian in me who pursued that elusive configuration. And I believe it is the lesbian in every woman who is compelled by female energy, who gravitates toward strong women, who seeks a literature that will express that energy and strength. It is the lesbian in us who drives us to feel imaginatively, render in language, grasp, the full connection between woman and woman" (see her *It Is the Lesbian in Us*).

RIERA, CARMEN (1948-). A professor of Spanish Language at the Universidad Autónoma of Barcelona and a writer in the Catalán language. The theme of sexuality and references to the new feminism are prominent in all her works.

RIGHT TO LIFE *see* NATIONAL RIGHT TO LIFE COMMITTEE (NRLC)

RÍOS CARDENAS, MARIA. A Mexican journalist and founder of the feminist journal *Mujer* (1926-29) in Mexico City. She urged women to join together in one national federation of women to gain equal legal rights to combat street harassment (q.v.), physical assault, and rape (q.v.), and to support children and unmarried mothers. Under her leadership the first Congress of Women Workers and Peasants was held in 1931 in Mexico City and attracted some 600 delegates, most of whom were professional women.   Ríos Cardenas led two more national congresses of women workers, and each failed to create a single unified feminist group. Thereafter Communist women took over the leadership of the women's movement in Mexico.

RIOT GRRRLS MOVEMENT.   A 1990's feminist movement comprised primarily of young women, ages 14-25, who use their sexiness, assertiveness, and loudness to debunk the notions of women as dumb, inferior, or bad. Riot Grrrls use their bodies as art, wear sexually revealing clothes, and use punk rock to convey their message.

ROBERTS V. UNITED STATES JAYCEES, 468 US 609 (1984). A decision of the US Supreme Court that rejected the argument of the male-only Jaycees club that state nondiscrimination laws should not apply to them because of their status as private associations. The Court considered factors such as the size, purpose, policies, selectivity, and congeniality of the organization and concluded that local chapters of the Jaycees were large and basically unselective. Therefore, the organization lacked the distinctive characteristics that might afford constitutional protection to the decision of its members to exclude women.

ROE V. WADE, 410 US 113 (1973).   A US Supreme Court decision that overturned a Texas statute that criminalized procuring or attempting the abortion (q.v.) of a human embryo or fetus except when necessary to save the life of the mother. The Court determined that the statute at issue violated the Fourteenth Amendment's Due Process Clause in that it unnecessarily infringed on a woman's right to privacy (q.v.). With abortion rights now included within the meaning of the Fourteenth Amendment, the state could only act to restrict abortions if necessary to promote a compelling state interest. Such a compelling interest could be found only in two situations: (1) where a restriction was necessary to protect the health or safety of the mother, and (2) where the fetus was viable. Because abortion performed under a doctor's care was as safe as or safer than a completed pregnancy, the majority opinion determined that there could be no significant restriction on a woman's right to choose abortion during the first trimester.

During the second trimester, there was increased risk to the health of a pregnant woman, presenting a compelling state interest in establishing further medical regulations on abortions performed during that stage. With respect to the state's compelling interest in the existence of the fetus, that would exist only when the fetus became viable, typically at the beginning of the third trimester. Thus, after the time of viability, the state could prohibit abortions except where necessary to protect the health or life of the mother. Both the lawyer (Sarah Weddington) who argued the case before the Court and the then-anonymous plaintiff (Norma McCorvey) have been active in the feminist-led movement to preserve the opinion's liberal guidelines. (*See also* O'Connor, Sandra Day; *Webster v. Reproductive Health Services*.)

ROLE MODEL. A person to whom another, usually younger, person can look for inspiration and guidance by example in career planning. Feminists have decried the limited and stereotypical role models available to girls in textbooks, television, films, and (often) their neighborhoods and local institutions. Because women are socialized from an early age to accept certain roles and reject others as "inappropriate," a lack of female role models is a barrier to pursuit of professional and nontraditional careers.

ROMANCE IN THE WORKPLACE. Sexual interest in coworkers that is welcome and reciprocated. The behavior is not coercive and does not constitute sexual harassment (q.v.), although the power differential inherent in relationships between supervisors and subordinates may result in romance turning into harassment.

ROOM OF ONE'S OWN, A (1929). Virginia Woolf's (q.v.) lecture to Girton College on the importance of education and economic independence to the success of women's writing. It is a key document in the history of feminist literary criticism (q.v.).

ROSENBERG, ROSALIND *see EQUAL EMPLOYMENT OPPORTUNITY COMMISSION V. SEARS, ROEBUCK & CO.*

ROSIE THE RIVETER. A World War II era song and media image promoting women's work in undermanned US defense industries. "Rosie" has come to symbolize for feminists the entry of women into heavy industrial jobs traditionally restricted to men and the demonstrated ability of women to perform these duties. After the end of the war, women were encouraged to return to the home. Although most women were pushed out of these nontraditional jobs, they remained in the paid labor force in jobs predominantly held by women.

ROSTKER V. GOLDBERG, 453 US 57 (1981). A decision of the US Supreme Court that upheld the constitutionality of the Military Selective Service Act, which exempted women from the draft registration process. The Court noted that the "constitutional power of Congress to raise and support armies and to make all laws necessary and proper to that end is broad and sweeping." Congress was therefore entitled to focus on the question of military need rather than equity. Since the military registration system was to swiftly move soldiers into combat, and Congress had exempted women from serving in combat, men and women were not similarly situated and therefore the law could distinguish between them. Although feminists were divided on the issue, the dominant view was that of equality feminists (q.v.), that with equal rights must come equal responsibilities and military service is one of those duties. Many feminists recalled that female exclusion from military service had been used as an argument against granting civil rights, including suffrage, to women and that the barriers to female military enlistment had denied women avenues for employment, education, and job training.

ROUDY, YVETTE *see* MINISTÈRE DES DROITS DE LA FEMME

ROY, RAJA RAMMOHAN (1772-1833). A pioneer Bengali advocate for women's rights in India through the reform of Hinduism. Roy supported women's education and property rights and opposed polygamy. In 1818 and 1820 he published pamphlets on suttee (q.v.), which was criminalized in 1829.

ROYAL COMMISSION ON THE STATUS OF WOMEN IN CANADA (RCSW). A body established by Prime Minister Lester B. Pearson on February 16, 1967, at the request of the anglophone women's coalition, the Committee for the Equality of Women (CEW), and its Quebec counterpart, the Fédération des Femmes du Québec (FFQ). In December 1970 its moderate report was tabled in the House of Commons. Even so, during the period of its writing, most Canadian women's organizations developed a feminist perspective, and by 1979 one-third of its reforms had been implemented, including the creation of a federal Advisory Council on the Status of Women on May 31, 1973.

RU 486 (MIFEPRISTONE) An abortifacient pill available since September 1988 in France. It is 96 percent effective in inducing termination of pregnancy during the first nine weeks when used with prostaglandin, another drug. Threatened by a boycott of all their products by the pro-life movement (q.v.), US drug companies have not sought government approval for the marketing of the drug in the United States. Without US Federal Drug Administration approval, the pills cannot be brought into the United States. Because of its many other promising applications in the treatment of other conditions, the drug is welcomed in the medical community. Feminists seek its availability in the United States as an alternative to the surgical procedures that have made abortion clinics the target of anti-abortion activists.

RUKEYSER, MURIEL (1913-1980). A New York feminist poet, raised in a well-to-do Jewish family. Rukeyser's fame rests on her volumes of poetry: *Mediterranean* (1938), *A Turning Wind* (1939), *The Soul and Body of John Brown* (1940), *Wake Island* (1942), *Beast in View* (1944), *The Green Wave* (1948), *Body of Waking* (1958), *The Speed of Darkness* (1968), *Breaking Open* (1973), and *The Gates* (1976). Rukeyser's poetry uses traditional images associated with women, childbirth, fertility, transcendence, and female mythic figures, and transforms these symbols into powerful representations of women's strength.

RUSS, JOANNA (1937-). A contemporary American feminist lesbian author, best known for *The Female Man* (q.v.) and the theoretical work *How to Suppress Women's Writing* (1983). Russ claims that she writes "realism disguised as fantasy, that is, science fiction." Her novels and short story "When It Changed" present a world where men no longer exist, having been exterminated by the superior women who have finally found the ultimate solution to the gender dilemma.

RUTH. Moabite daughter-in-law of Naomi in the book that bears her name in the Hebrew Scriptures. She is usually seen as a model of faithfulness because she agrees to care for her mother-in-law after both are widowed. Some feminists counter that the account shows a desire to suppress the independence of women. Her marriage to Boaz produces the ancestor of King David, striking because Ruth is a foreigner.

-S-

AL-SAADAWI, NAWAL (1931-).   An Egyptian writer, feminist, and psychiatrist, whose explicit 1972 book *al-Mar'ah wa al-Jins* (Women and Sex) cost her her job at the Ministry of Health and caused a controversy comparable to that of Qasim Amin's (q.v.) *Tahrir al-Mar'a.* In denouncing the practice of clitoridectomy and other forms of sexual and commercial exploitation of women's bodies, al-Saadawi politicized the topic of sexuality in Arab society. As the author of six books on Arab women, as well as several novels and short fiction collections, she has received national and international awards. She also served as the first president of the Arab Women's Solidarity Association (q.v.).

SALEM WITCH TRIALS (1692).   Proceedings in Salem, Massachusetts, where 31 people were tried and executed as witches. Twenty-four (or 77 percent) were female, and the men involved were victims of guilt by association. The women were primarily poor widows with no male protector within the society. They were generally accused of crimes against their appropriate female roles: of not loving their families, preying on children, adultery, inspiring fear in men for their lack of deference, or rebellion against an authority figure (usually a magistrate). Any woman who displayed psychological, emotional, or behavioral deviance was labeled a witch throughout the fifteenth to seventeenth centuries. One woman had been married three times and "would not be dominated" by her husbands; another was accused of dressing provocatively.

SAMENESS. A neutral legal standard that prohibits sex discrimination by requiring that like individuals be treated the same. Difference feminists (q.v.) argue that this involves an unstated male norm (i.e.,"same" means "the same as men") which often results in inequities growing out of women's differences such as pregnancy.

SAND, GEORGE (AMANTINE AURORE LUCILE DUPIN) (1804-1876). A French Romantic novelist known for her affectation of a male pseudonym, as well as men's clothing and behaviors such as cigar-smoking. In her often candidly erotic works, she protested the social conventions which locked women in abusive monogamy and denied women the right to romantic love and independent life.

SANDER, HELKE (1937-). A German filmmaker and feminist activist. As a student, she founded the Berlin Action Council for Women's Liberation and presented its program for practical assistance to women at the conference of the Socialist German Students' Federation (SDS) in 1968. She also founded the women's group Brot und Rosen (Bread and Roses) and the journal *Frauen und Film* (Women and Film). Her films include: *Redupers* (1977) and *Der Subjektive Faktor* (The Subjective Factor, 1981).

SANGER, MARGARET (1883-1966). A US pioneer in sex education and "birth control," a term that she originated. Her interest began as a child, when she observed her mother's health weaken with many pregnancies. She began her work with poverty-stricken immigrants on New York's Lower East Side. In 1916 she opened the first birth control clinic in the United States. She founded the American Birth Control League (later, the Planned Parenthood Federation of America), organized the first world population conference, and served as the first president of the International Planned Parenthood Federation. (*See also* Planned Parenthood.)

SAPPHO (c. 600 B. C.). A celebrated Greek poet and the earliest known female writer in Western literature. She was at the center of an intimate circle or school of young women on the Island of Lesbos who studied music and poetry and worshipped Aphrodite (q.v.). Her poetry, which survives only in fragments, is characterized by simplicity, passion, and lyric beauty. Since some of the love poems were dedicated to favorites among her female companions, the word "lesbian" has acquired its current meaning of female homosexual. Her poetry was widely admired in antiquity, and she herself was known as "The Poetess" and "The Tenth Muse."

SARAH. In the Hebrew Bible, wife of the patriarch Abraham and mother of Isaac. Although God announced the covenantal promises to Abraham alone, feminists stress that only the child Sarah bore would receive the inheritance. This makes Sarah crucially important in the literary account of the origin of the Israelite people. Endangered in the harems of Pharaoh and Abimelech by Abraham's fears, God ensures her safety. Scholars are divided on Sarah's treatment of her servant Hagar; some concentrate on the suffering she causes Hagar, and others view their relationship as a metaphor for the conflict between the descendants of Isaac and the descendants of Ishmael, Hagar's son by Abraham.

SATI *see* SUTTEE

SCHLAFLY, PHYLLIS (1924-). An American anti-feminist (q.v.) and conservative spokesperson and author. She was the founder of the Stop ERA movement in 1972 and the Eagle Forum (q.v.) in 1975. Since 1967 she has published the monthly newsletter, *The Phyllis Schlafly Report.* She has long been a conservative activist within the US Republican Party as a speechwriter for Barry Goldwater, a congressional candidate, and vice-president of the National Federation of Republican Women's Clubs. She came to public prominence as the leading opponent of the Equal Rights Amendment (q.v.) and is widely credited with preventing its ratification. Her books include *The Power of the Positive Woman* (1977).

SCHREINER, OLIVE (1855-1920). A South African feminist and writer, best known as the author of *The Story of an African Farm* (1883). A socialist, pacifist, and anti-imperialist, Schreiner also published a wide-ranging history of women's subjugation entitled *Woman and Labour* (1911). Born into a family of missionaries, Schreiner spent her youth travelling across Africa and witnessing injustices and discrimination. Later she served as vice-president of the Women's Enfranchisement League in South Africa, but resigned when it refused to fight for the "colored" woman's right to vote. When she spoke before a meeting of the Women's Political Union in 1914, she demanded "a society in which all women of all races on earth should equally find their place." Perhaps her most provocative contribution to feminism can be found in her essay "Sex-Parasitism" (in *Woman and Labour*). In this essay she compares the modern unemployed female to a large insect that feeds off the body of its mate: "The kept wife, the fine lady, the human female parasite--the most deadly microbe which can make its appearance on the surface of any social organism" (see her *Woman and Labour*).

SCHWARZER, ALICE (1942-). A German activist, writer, and publisher. In 1971 she organized the first public protest against Germany's abortion (q.v.) law, by arranging for the magazine *Stern* to publish names and photographs of 374 women who admitted to having had abortions. Since 1977 she has edited the bi-monthly magazine *EMMA* (q.v.), where she has addressed issues ranging from the theory of sexuality to household politics. She is the author of several books, including *So Fing Es An! Die Nue Frauenbewegung* (That's How It Started! The New Women's Movement, 1983).

SCIENCE, FEMINIST CRITIQUE OF. The assessment of "status quo" scientific research by feminist scientists, who have identified bias in the scientific questions asked, the choice of experimental subjects, the data acquisition process, and the methods of drawing conclusions and postulating theories based on research results.

SEARS CASE *see EQUAL EMPLOYMENT OPPORTUNITY COMMISSION V. SEARS, ROEBUCK & CO.*

SECOND SHIFT *see* DOUBLE SHIFT

SECOND TIER. A term coined by Sheila Tobias to describe college students, a disproportionate number of whom are women, who choose not to pursue studies in science, engineering or mathematics despite considerable demonstrated aptitude and interest. Students in the second tier are often discouraged by the way that science is taught and not by the pursuit of science itself.

SECOND WAVE FEMINISM. The worldwide revival of an organized women's rights movement (q.v.), beginning in the late 1960's in the United States and Western Europe within movements for international peace, racial equality, student power, and socialist politics. Most regions of the Third World also have autonomous groups organized around women's rights issues; women's liberation groups (q.v.) are still primarily found only in Western democracies. (*See also* First Wave Feminism; Third Wave Feminism.)

SELF-DEFENSE (LEGAL DEFENSE) *see* BATTERED WOMAN SYNDROME; INSANITY PLEAS (DEFENSE)

SELF-DEFENSE TRAINING. An early form of anti-rape action adopted by local women's liberation (q.v.) groups. Because rape (q.v.) victims were often blamed for failing to defend themselves, courses in judo, karate, and street-fighting techniques were offered at women's centers (q.v.). By learning to trust her body, a woman could gain self-confidence and self-reliance and reduce the sense of vulnerability and helplessness that comes with dependence on a man for protection. Use of these tactics contributed to the initial militant image of the new feminist movement.

SELF-ESTEEM. How a person perceives the value of the self. A person with low self-esteem is assumed to be more anxious and more willing to respond to pressures to assume a role. Psychologists believe that girls may not utilize all their abilities due to traditional gender role (q.v.) expectations and therefore are less likely to develop an independent sense of self-worth. Instead they depend on others' opinions of them and define themselves in terms of their relationships with others, especially their attractiveness to men. The new feminist movement (q.v.) first focused on the importance of developing a positive self-concept and self-image. With the publication of *Revolution from Within: A Book of Self-Esteem* (1992) by Gloria Steinem (q.v.), the term "self-esteem" came into popular use by feminists.

SELF-HELP. A feminist strategy for empowering women to act together for change in their own lives. Self-help groups have been organized for victims of rape and domestic violence (qq.v.) and in the areas of family law, self-defense (q.v.), and health care. Participants in such groups learn to effect changes in the present system and to create woman-controlled alternative services.

SELF-HELP HEALTH MOVEMENT. Composed of feminist health centers and local groups that diagnose and treat simple gynecological problems. Common services include: pelvic exams, Pap smears, abortions (q.v.), pregnancy tests, menstrual extraction (q.v.) and the treatment of vaginal infections and syphilis. The goal is to demystify medical procedures and to empower women by involving them in their own health care. After peaking at almost 50 centers in the mid-1970's, there are now fewer than 15 women's health centers in the United States due to the rise of abortion clinic violence in the 1980's and the attendant costs of security and insurance.

SEMIOTICS AND FEMINISM *see* BARTHES, ROLAND

SENECA FALLS CONVENTION. The first Woman's Rights Convention in the United States, held in Seneca Falls, New York, in July 1848. It is often used to mark the "official" beginning of the US women's suffrage movement. Under the leadership of Lucretia Mott and Elizabeth Cady Stanton (qq.v.), the convention drafted a Declaration of Sentiments modelled on the Declaration of Independence. It stated that all women and men are created equal and contained 12 resolutions, one of which called for the vote for women.

SENECA WOMEN'S PEACE ENCAMPMENT *see* GREENHAM COMMON WOMEN'S PEACE CAMP

SEPARATISM. A feminist strategy ranging from male exclusion from the women's movement to withdrawal of women into an all-female community and counter-culture (q.v.) in order to learn to trust and value other women. Some women see the withdrawal as temporary, until integration with gender equality is possible. For others, permanent separatism from the patriarchal world and the creation of women's communities is the core goal. Lesbianism (q.v.) is affirmed and heterosexuality is viewed as an institution that favors men and obstructs women's relationships with each other. Early separatist movement groups include the Feminists and the Furies (qq.v.). Prominent theorists of separatism are Charlotte Bunch, Sonia Johnson, Jill Johnston, and Adrienne Rich (q.v.).

SETTLEMENT HOUSE MOVEMENT. A movement that began with Toynbee Hall in London, England, in which concerned persons, usually of above-average means, lived among the poor to improve their conditions. The movement came to the United States in the 1880s and involved teaching self-help (q.v.) skills to the urban poor, largely immigrants. Hull House in Chicago, founded by Jane Addams (q.v.) in 1889, served 19 different nationalities. Staff lived in the settlement houses where they provided child care for working women, facilitated cultural enrichment programs, and became involved in direct political action toward reform, including improving neighborhood conditions, industrial safety laws, and child labor laws. Many social feminists (q.v.) came out of this movement.

SEX ROLE *see* GENDER ROLE

SEX ROLE SOCIALIZATION. The process of learning the culturally prescribed behavioral expectations relevant to our gendered roles in society. Theories of gender socialization differ in the extent to which they view such processes to be rooted in inherent biological processes, psychological processes related to cognitive development, or social (e.g., parental and cultural) processes. While most feminists agree that sex roles are culturally mapped, they differ concerning the relative importance of cognitive development, imitation, and social learning.

SEX ROLE STEREOTYPES. Exaggerated beliefs about appropriate behaviors and traits that relate to gender roles (q.v.). Such stereotypes affect how we see ourselves and others, so that we identify different traits as "naturally" occurring in females or males, rather than viewing "traits" (e.g., "masculinity" or "femininity") as culturally prescribed. Feminists note how stereotypes are used to explain, for example, why women are fulfilled through mothering and caring, while men are rewarded by fighting and working.

SEX SELECTION *see* AMNIOCENTESIS

SEX TOURS. Vacations, booked through travel agencies, in which foreign men are brought in for sex with poor Third-World, often Asian, women who also engage in prostitution (q.v.) near US military bases. Feminists in North America and Western Europe have organized against this international traffic in women (q.v.) and, under this pressure, the sex-tour business has been curtailed.

SEXISM. Discrimination based on sex role stereotypes (q.v.) that cause unfair or inappropriate treatment of one sex. Sexism, like racism, involves a power differential which disadvantages the lower power sex (females) and privileges the higher power sex (males). Sexism is an attitude that results in behaviors such as sexual harassment, street harassment (qq.v.), and unfair hiring practices.

SEXIST LANGUAGE. Language that ignores or objectifies and demeans women. Sexist language is any use of language which reduces the respect due to women as persons. One example is language which assumes words denoting maleness also include women. Communication and linguistic research has shown such assumptions to be false. Other examples include naming women by their body parts or calling women by animal names or names which ridicule women's sexuality. Any language use that assumes male experience is normative for all humans is sexist.

SEXUAL ASSAULT *see* RAPE

SEXUAL CASTE SYSTEM. The view of radical feminists (q.v.) that societies not only have a class system but also classes cross-cut by castes, one of which is based on sex. According to this analysis, the dominant male caste oppresses women in the manner of the dominant economic class over its subordinates.

SEXUAL HARASSMENT. The abuse of or discrimination against a person, usually a woman, because of his or her sex. This behavior may involve verbal abuse, unwanted touching or pushing, seeking to exchange sexual favors for career opportunities, or any unwelcome sexual advances tied to rewards or performance in employment or other situations in which the abuser is in a position of power over another. The action is considered harassment when submission to the conduct is a term or condition of employment or used as a basis for employment decisions (quid pro quo). Harassment may also exist when the action interferes with an individual's work performance or creates a pervasive, intimidating and hostile environment (q.v.). Sexual harassment is illegal under the Civil Rights Act of 1964 (q.v.), but is difficult to prove due to the challenge it presents to the acceptability of behavior between men and women. (*See also Meritor Savings Bank v. Vinson.*)

SEXUAL POLITICS see MILLETT, KATE

"SEXUAL POLITICS OF SICKNESS." A phrase coined by Barbara Ehrenreich and Deirdre English in *Complaints and Disorders: The Sexual Politics of Sickness* (1973). They explored the notion of sickness having both a gender and a class. They concluded that the medical system was a powerful instrument of social control that enforced gender roles (q.v.).

SEXUAL SLAVERY *see* INTERNATIONAL TRAFFIC IN WOMEN

SEXUAL VIOLENCE *see* VIOLENCE AGAINST WOMEN

SHANGE, NTOZAKE (1948-). A contemporary African-American urban playwright, best known for her drama *For Colored Girls Who Have Considered Suicide/ When the Rainbow Is Enuf* (1975). Her other works include *A Daughter's*

Geography (1983), *Nappy Edges* (1978), *Sassafrass* (1977), *From Okra to Greens: Poems* (1984), *Betsey Brown* (1985), *Some Men* (1981), *See No Evil* (1984), and *The Love Space Demands* (1991). Shange's dramas and poetry present the black urban woman's struggle for dignity and self-determination.

SHA'RAWI, HUDA (1879-1947). The founder of the Egyptian Feminist Union (q.v.) and convenor of Arab feminist conferences in 1938 and 1944. At the latter meeting, the Arab Feminist Union was formed, with Sha'rawi as president. Sha'rawi, who had a large inheritance, substantially financed these organizations. Her dramatic gesture of publicly unveiling at the Cairo train station upon returning from an international feminist meeting began a radical activist phase of the movement.

SHAW, ANNA HOWARD (1847-1919). A reformer, physician, and the first woman to be ordained as a minister in the Methodist Church in 1880. In 1885 she became a lecturer for the Massachusetts State Suffrage Association and a year later became superintendent of a branch of the Women's Christian Temperance Union. Shaw also served as president of the National American Woman Suffrage Association (q.v.), 1904-15.

SHELTER MOVEMENT *see* WOMEN'S BATTERY SHELTER

SHEPPARD, KATE (1848-1934). A suffragist organizer and strategist in New Zealand, the first (in 1893) country to enfranchise all women over the age of 21. The Women's Suffrage Campaign grew out of the temperance movement and utilized nationwide petition drives, one of which obtained the signatures of a quarter of all adult women.

SHEPPARD-TOWNER MATERNITY ACT OF 1921. A US program that established grants to the states to provide health care for mothers and children through public health centers and prenatal clinics. The first and perhaps greatest achievement of the post-suffrage coalition, the Women's Joint Congressional Committee (q.v.), the program was attacked by conservatives and the American Medical Association as "socialized medicine" and was allowed to expire in 1929.

SHIELDS, LAURIE *see* DISPLACED HOMEMAKER

SHIKIBU, MURASAKI (970-1031). A Japanese novelist who secretly learned Chinese when this was forbidden to women and wrote the epic novel *Genji Monogatari* (The Tale of Genji). In this, Shikibu questions women's place in Shinto and in Buddhism. The main character is a woman who struggles with the unhappiness of a woman's destiny in a male-oriented society and seeks to be self-determining. Many of the concerns in the book are existentialist from a notably feminine perspective: intentionality, freedom, objectification, and existence.

SHIPHRAH AND PUAH. In the Hebrew Bible, the Hebrew midwives who deceive Pharaoh and avert his order to kill all newly born Hebrew boys. Feminists show the striking contrast of two women without power who defeat Pharaoh, considered divine by the Egyptians. God blesses them with families to reward them for their courage.

SHOWALTER, ELAINE (1941-). A prominent feminist literary theorist and critic, best known as author of *A Literature of Their Own* (1977) and *The Female Malady: Women, Madness, and Culture* (1985). Showalter has also edited major collections of feminist literary criticism (q.v.): *Women's Liberation and Literature* (1971), *These Modern Women: Autobiographies of American Women in the 1920s* (1979), *Feminist Criticism: Essays on Women, Literature, and Theory* (1985), *Speaking of Gender* (1989), *Sexual Anarchy: Gender and Culture at the Fin de Siècle* (1990), and *Sister's Choice: Tradition and Change in American Women's Writing* (1991). (*See also* Gynocriticism.)

SIGNS. One of the first feminist academic journals to publish serious and academically respected scholarship on women's issues. Begun in 1975 by the University of Chicago Press and first edited by Catharine R. Stimpson, *Signs* continues to be the premier academic journal in women's studies, even though in the mid-1990's, it announced that it was shifting to a less academic and more accessible format to promote feminist debate inside and outside the academy. It is credited with helping to legitimize interdisciplinary women's studies as a field of academic research.

SILENCING. Direct and indirect techniques used to discount the discourse and experiences of women. Direct silencing takes place when women are not allowed to speak (as in colonial times, when voluble women were fitted with branks or ducked), are kept from publication (as in very recent times when identical scholarly submissions were accepted under male names and rejected under female names), or when all-male legislatures enact policies that affect women. Indirect silencing occurs when women's experiences lack words to name them, when women's sexuality is named as evil and men's as good, when conversational topics are chosen by men, and when women carry out the relational work in conversations.

SINGLE MOTHERS *see* SINGLE-PARENT FAMILY

SINGLE-PARENT FAMILY. Families headed by a single parent who does not reside with, or is not married to, the children's other parent. A near-majority of single-parent families are headed by women who have incomes below the poverty line. (*See also* Aid to Families with Dependent Children; "Feminization of Poverty.")

SISTERHOOD. A concept stressing female friendship, solidarity, and support, analogous to the term "brotherhood" for male relationships. Feminists believe that women should establish close ties and bonds with other women in recognition that men should not play an exclusive role in women's lives, that women are worth relating to, and that all women share interests.

SISTERHOOD IS POWERFUL. The title of an important collection of early feminist essays (1970), edited by Robin Morgan (q.v.). The volume codified the radical feminist (q.v.) position and the term has passed into general parlance to mean that the united actions of women can effect powerful changes in society.

SMEAL, ELEANOR *see* FUND FOR THE FEMINIST MAJORITY

SMILING. A specific facial expression that generally connotes positivity and is usually exhibited more by adult women than adult men. Feminists suggest that women are pressured by cultural expectations to smile regardless of their inner emotional state and one study reported that children were unable to identify their mothers' emotional state based on smiling alone because mothers smile all the time. This was not the case for fathers. Social class may mediate this finding, however, as middle-class mothers smiled considerably more than their lower-class counterparts.

SOCIAL CONSTRUCTION OF GENDER. An argument, differing markedly from those of reductionists and biological determinists, that roots gender distinctions in social and cultural circumstances and interactions. It is a cultural assumption, not a biological given, that there are two genders, and cultures differ markedly in how these categories are encoded.

SOCIAL FEMINISM. The dominant tradition of US and Canadian feminism during the early 1900s, in competition with equality feminism (q.v.). Social feminists viewed the sexes as having fundamentally different physiological and social roles and therefore supported protective labor laws (q.v.) for women and opposed the Equal Rights Amendment (q.v.). (*See also* Women's Joint Congressional Committee.)

SOCIAL GOSPEL MOVEMENT, WOMEN AND. A late nineteenth- to early twentieth-century movement that sought to relate the Christian message to the problems of labor, economics, and politics. Although the participation of women in this movement has been largely ignored by scholars, the role of social feminist (q.v.) women such as Vida Scudder, Beatrice Webb, and Frances Willard (q.v.) is beginning to be explored.

SOCIAL SECURITY ACT OF 1935. The major piece of US post-Depression social welfare legislation that established the first federal means-tested assistance program to women and their children, Aid to Families with Dependent Children (q.v.), and the current system of social insurance benefits for retirement, disability, and survivors. Although the latter reflected the social reality of the time in which it was passed, the legislation does not reflect the current changing work and childbearing habits of women in its preferential treatment given to married women with children. The act is also inequitable in its treatment of elderly women. Benefit payment levels reflect women's contributions to the program throughout their working lives, yet discrimination, child-rearing responsibilities, and the failure to recognize housework as legitimate employment preclude women from contributing significant amounts to their own retirement funds. Often they receive less in retirement benefits. (*See also Califano v. Goldfarb.*)

SOCIALIST FEMINISM. A tradition of feminist theory that seeks to synthesize radical feminism (q.v.) and Marxism in response to the dominance of liberal feminism (q.v.). Both sexism (q.v.) and classism are used to explain women's oppression; feminist insights into male dominance (q.v.) and the Marxist critique of capitalism are incorporated by contemporary socialist feminists. In contrast to the liberal emphasis on individual rights, there is attention to social relations and the larger community within this tradition.

SOCIALIST WOMEN'S INTERNATIONAL. A group formed in 1907 by Clara Zetkin (q.v.) at the International Socialist Women's Conference, held in conjunction with the Second International. At its founding, it urged that socialist parties work for universal women's suffrage and later endorsed equal pay (q.v.) and maternity insurance. After World War I, Austrian Socialist Adelheid Popp built the group into a major movement of more than 900,000 women.

SOCIÉTÉ FRATERNELLE DES PATRIOTES DE L'UN ET L'AUTRE SEXE (THE FRATERNAL SOCIETY OF PATRIOTS OF BOTH SEXES). A French Revolutionary club to which women were admitted as full members and as officers. Its membership included the Dutchwoman, Etta Palm d'Aelders, who advocated political liberty and equality for both sexes. Another member and advocate of equal rights for women, Théroigne de Méricourt, unsuccessfully attempted to establish a political society and a women's militia company. She urged female participation in patriotic societies dedicated to ferreting out enemies of the Revolution and to performing benevolent works on behalf of women, especially the poor. Still another member of the Société, Pauline Léon, petitioned the National Assembly for the right of women to bear arms. Léon was also a leader with the actress Claire Lacombe of the Club des Citoyennes Républicaines Révolutionnaires (Club of Republican Revolutionary Women Citizens), a radical group associated with those who supported *sans culottes* demands for wage and price controls. Other women's revolutionary clubs included the Club des Femmes de Dijon and the Breteuil Soeurs de la Constitution. All women's clubs and associations were outlawed on October 30, 1793.

SOCIETY FOR THE PROTECTION OF THE UNBORN CHILD (SPUC). A British pro-life (q.v.) group formed in 1967 after passage of the Abortion Act and drawing members from many religions. The SPUC uses public education, often through church sermons, more often than direct contacts with Parliament. The group has a large membership, is well-funded, and has drawn favorable media attention for its exposé of abortion (q.v.) abuses. The publication of *Babies for Burning* (1974) was especially effective, although critics charged that accounts were highly sensationalized.

SOCIOBIOLOGY. A theory of human nature, drawn from studies on animal and insect populations, that suggests that gender differences in behavior are rooted in genetically evolved strategies that promote reproduction of the species. Accordingly, underneath the differing behaviors associated with being male and being female (e.g., promiscuity and aggression in males; domesticity in women) lie genetically based universals. Most feminists reject this theory as another form of biological determinism (q.v.); a few feminist scholars, however, have presented alternative theories of evolution and biological differences that do not accept the male norm and devalue women.

SOMMERS, TISH *see* DISPLACED HOMEMAKER

SOPHIA. The spirit of wisdom, a primordial source of female power, within Christian feminist theology (q.v.). Because Sophia appears in many biblical references, as in the first nine chapters of Proverbs, she is presented as a part of traditional Judeo-Christian worship from its beginnings. (*See also* Woman Wisdom.)

SOPHIA (Pseudonym). The author of *Woman Not Inferior to Man* (1739) that criticized male philosophers who argued for women's inferiority. The tract rejected the view of men as having superior reason and women as being more driven hy the passions. The arguments made by males in favor of men are biased, the author stated, because they are motivated by self-interest, not logic or reason. The writer believed that rationality should be the criterion for evaluation, not the sex of the presenter of the argument.

SOULEY-DARQUE, MARGUERITE. The woman credited with teaching the first women's studies (q.v.) course in Paris from 1900 to 1905. The course was cross-disciplinary and combined philosophical, sociological, and historical approaches to understanding the nature, experience and perceptions of women. Souley-Darque sought to demonstrate that women's social inferiority could be explained as a response to past environmental conditions that industrial capitalism made obsolete.

SPANISH FEMINIST LITERATURE, POST-FRANCO. The participation of a number of women writers in the Spanish literary world after the death of military general Francisco Franco in 1974. The period saw a general lifting of censorship that accompanied his rule of nearly four decades and a simultaneous cultural explosion. Women who had never before been encouraged to create or to exhibit the results of their creative efforts were free to express themselves freely in many different domains. This *apertura* or "opening up" meant a flowering of publications by women, resulting in the rise to fame of now well-known authors such as Gloria Fuertes, Carmen Martín Gaite, Clara Janés, Carmen Laforet, and Ana Maria Matute. This is also evident in Catalonia where a group of successful women writers, all of them interested in women's issues, has emerged. Some of these writers are Montserrat Roig, Carmen Riera, and Esther Tusquets.

SPARE RIB. The best-known of the British new feminist (q.v.) periodicals, founded in 1972 by a collective (q.v.) of women formerly with the alternative press. The nationally circulated monthly magazine, at its height, had 32,000 readers and served as a central focus for all parts of the British women's movement. In 1993 it ceased publication.

SPEAK-OUT. The open discussion through public testimony of personal experiences that women had never previously told to anyone except perhaps a few close friends or family members. Feminist forums on topics such as abortion, rape, sexual harassment, domestic violence (qq.v.), and incest attempt to raise public awareness and to mobilize support for legal changes.

SPENDER, DALE (1943-). An English researcher, writer, and feminist theorist of linguistics. Spender's book, *Man-Made Language*, has set the terms of discussion for feminist communication scholars. Subsequently, Spender has shown the effect of male dominance (q.v.) of publication on women's writing. Her work increases the visibility of women writers and also brings insight into the cultural constraints on women built into the English language.

SPOUSAL RAPE *see* MARITAL RAPE

SPOUSAL SUPPORT. An amount paid to one spouse by the other for financial maintenance upon the dissolution of a marriage. (*See also Orr v. Orr.*)

SPOUSE ABUSE *see* DOMESTIC VIOLENCE

STALKING. A pattern of harassing behavior that terrorizes the victim, usually a woman. Laws making stalking a criminal offense were passed in 48 US states, 1990-93, as a deterrent to domestic violence (q.v.). Ninety percent of women who are murdered by their husbands or boyfriends had previously been stalked. Feminists support these laws but also express concern that they may be ineffective because of vague language and the extensive record of stalking required for conviction and imprisonment.

STANDPOINT THEORY. A feminist critique of traditional scholarship and its claim of neutrality. The view here is that this research involves a nonobjective interpretation of women's lives and renders the experience of women invisible. Standpoint theory suggests that since all research (and knowledge) is produced from a particular standpoint (or social location) and "dominant" (male) standpoints prevail, other perspectives remain hidden. Women's views are less partial and incomplete because their views are shaped by unique experiences within a patriarchal society. Standpoint theory assumes that those who gain most from positions of power and privilege (and who sustain systems that ensure them) are least equipped to see the bias, while those most marginalized (e.g., women) see it most clearly.

STANTON, ELIZABETH CADY (1815-1902). A nineteenth-century US feminist and abolitionist. The first woman to appear as a witness at a congressional hearing, Stanton gave testimony in 1869 in support of suffrage for women. With Lucretia Mott (q.v.), she was one of the organizers of the Seneca Falls Convention (q.v.) and wrote the Declaration of Sentiments adopted there. After the Fifteenth Amendment failed to extend the right to vote to women, she and Susan B. Anthony (q.v.) founded the National Woman Suffrage Association (q.v.) and she served as president, 1869-90. At her request in 1878, the first constitutional amendment to enfranchise women was introduced in Congress. Stanton also opposed the secondary position of women within Christian doctrine and in 1895 published *The Woman's Bible* as a corrective.

STATE COMMISSIONS ON THE STATUS OF WOMEN (SCSW). Organizations created, 1963-67, in every state in the United States, patterned on the President's Commission on the Status of Women (q.v.) and mandated to collect data on women and to suggest changes in discriminatory laws and policies in the states. Linked through the Citizens' Advisory Council on the Status of Women within the Women's Bureau (qq.v.), the state commissions became the core of a national network for women's rights. It was at their third national conference that around two dozen delegates, thwarted in efforts to present a resolution demanding that the Equal Employment Opportunity Commission (q.v.) enforce the sex provision of Title VII of the Civil Rights Act of 1964 (q.v.), formed the National Organization for Women (q.v.). In 1970 the Interstate Association of Commissions on the Status of Women was formed as a private organization that also includes city and county commissions.

STATUTORY RAPE. Any sexual intercourse with a female below the "age of consent." This age has varied from age 7 to 18 years within the United States. In some states, the victim must be below the age of puberty for the offense to be charged; some states require the perpetrator to be a specified number of years older than the victim. (*See also Michael M. v. Superior Court.*)

STEFAN, VERENA (1947-). A German writer and poet, and author of the highly successful book *Häutungen* (Shedding, 1975), which employs linguistic innovation to explore women's understandings of women's experience. The book, while influential in encouraging linguistic experimentation by women writers, was also strongly criticized for its concern with "the image of things ... instead of the things," thus representing an avoidance of a necessary confrontation with patriarchy (q.v.).

STEINEM, GLORIA (1934-). A journalist, editor, and prominent US feminist spokesperson. Steinem was one of the founders of *Ms.* magazine, the National Women's Political Caucus, and the Women's Action Alliance (qq.v.). She is a popular lecturer on women's topics and the author of *Outrageous Acts and Everyday Rebellions* (1983), *Revolution from Within: A Book of Self-Esteem* (1992), and *Moving Beyond Words* (1994). In the mid-1970's Steinem was attacked by the Redstockings (q.v.) for having once been affiliated with a Central Intelligence Agency-funded student group and with using *Ms.* to supplant radical feminism with liberal feminism (qq.v.). Although the trashing (q.v.) of Steinem eventually discredited the Redstockings, radical feminists have never been comfortable with the liberal mainstream *Ms.* or with the media's choice of the formerly unknown Steinem as a movement spokesperson.

STERILIZATION ABUSE. Making women infertile against their will or without their informed consent as a condition for receiving welfare or holding a job believed to be potentially harmful to a fetus. This problem is especially pronounced among disabled and poor women and women of color (q.v.). In 1978, responding to pressure from the women's movement, the US government issued strict regulations on surgical sterilization. The marketing of the long-term birth control device Norplant (q.v.) has again raised fears among feminists that a woman's right to refuse contraception may be endangered.

STERN, WILLIAM AND ELIZABETH see *IN RE BABY M*

STEWART, MARIA W. (1803-1879). An early nineteenth-century US orator, abolitionist, and feminist. She was the first woman, in 1832, to address a mixed gender audience on racial (political) issues and was probably the first black American to lecture in defense of women's rights. Religious, militant, and outspoken, her speeches used arguments drawn from religious sources and were published in a collection of her works in 1835.

STÖCKER, HELENE (1869-1943). A leader in the radical wing of the first German women's movement and an outspoken advocate of the sexual emancipation of women. In 1904 she founded the Federation for the Protection of Mothers and Sexual Reform; its manifesto demanded sexual freedom (including free love as a positive alternative to conventional marriage), the end of the compulsory recognition of marriages by church and registry, and the loosening of divorce laws. Her views were far more radical than those held by the Federation of German Women's Associations.

STONE, LUCY (1818-1893). A founder of the American Woman Suffrage Association (q.v.) in 1869, as well as an early lecturer on abolition and women's rights. In her marriage to Henry Blackwell in 1855, she omitted the word "obey" from her vows and together they pledged to establish an egalitarian relationship. Stone may have been the first woman to retain her birthname, a practice which gave rise to the Lucy Stone League (q.v.). Her husband and her daughter, Alice Stone Blackwell (q.v.), were also active in the women's movement.

STOP ERA see EAGLE FORUM; SCHLAFLY, PHYLLIS

STOPES, MARIE CHARLOTTE CARMICHAEL (1880-1958). A pioneer British advocate of sex education and birth control and founder of the first birth control clinic in England in 1921. Coming out of an unhappy and unconsummated first marriage, Stopes had little knowledge of contraception until her meeting with Margaret Sanger (q.v.) in 1915. In 1918 she published a famous marriage manual, *Married Love: A New Contribution to the Solution of Sex Difficulties*, and a guide to contraception, *Wise Parenthood*.

STORNI, ALFONSINA (1892-1938). An Argentine poet, considered the most prominent feminist writer of her time in Latin America and the first woman to frequent the literary gatherings of Buenos Aires. She was an enemy of social conventions and a defender of more liberty for women. She saw her femininity as an individual and social problem and was among the first feminists to fight male dominance (q.v.). Her lyric poetry reflects a woman with a desire for love and for being loved, but one who does not find that corresponding need in men. She then seems to strike out against men, and her verses are the protest of her tortured soul.

STORYTELLING. A technique of communication which empowers women. Storytelling emphasizes human character, relationships between people, the consequences of actions, and the interconnectedness of human experience. As such, it is a technique well-suited to women's ways of knowing. Women's stories give meaning to family life as well as children's development; further, they help to shape a culture's understanding of itself.

STOWE, EMILY HOWARD (1831-1903). The first woman physician in Canada and founder in 1876 of the first suffrage society, the Toronto Women's Literary Club (later, in 1883, the Toronto Women's Suffrage Association). Stowe and her group also worked for women's educational opportunities and in 1889 formed the first national suffrage group, the Dominion Women's Enfranchisement Association (later, the Canadian Suffrage Association).

STREET HARASSMENT. Abusive, mostly sex-related, language or action directed by male strangers toward women in public places. Such behavior is believed to be especially embedded in the culture of certain occupations, such as truck-driver and construction worker. Existing laws on sexual assault (q.v.) ("touching"), "fighting words," intentional infliction of emotional distress and invasion of privacy (q.v.) offer no effective remedies. A state law or city ordinance to make such harassment a misdemeanor, punishable by a fine, may be in violation of the First Amendment's protection of free speech. (*See also* Hate Crimes.)

STRUCTURELESSNESS *see* TYRANNY OF STRUCTURELESSNESS

SUMMERSKILL, EDITH (1901-1980). A British politician, physician, and active member of the Labour Party who won a seat in Parliament in 1934. A long-time champion of women's causes, she successfully proposed legislation on property rights and financial equality for married women. She also worked to make less painful childbirth procedures available to women, but opposed oral contraceptives on the grounds that their side-effects had not been thoroughly investigated.

SUPERMOM *see* SUPERWOMAN SYNDROME

SUPERWOMAN SYNDROME. A pattern of high achievement by women in both the world of paid labor and in the home as wife and mother. Once viewed as the embodiment of feminism's promise that women can "have it all," these "supermoms" are increasingly seen as stressed-out victims of society's excessive expectations.

SURROGACY. The process by which a woman carries and bears a child, usually conceived through artificial insemination or in vitro fertilization, for an infertile woman and contractually relinquishes all parental rights to the child. Referred to as "womb renting" by some feminists who consider surrogacy a form of female oppression. (*See also* Baby-Selling; *In Re Baby M.*)

SURVIVOR *see* VICTIMIZATION OF WOMEN

SUSANNA. In the Apocrypha, the woman in the book which bears her name who is unjustly accused of immoral sexual relationships after she refuses to submit to scheming, lecherous judges. Susanna remains loyal to God's law and God delivers her through Daniel's intervention. Her faith contrasts with the judges' violation of God's law and she is responsible for the end of their violence against other women. Many feminists lament that she is given little credit because the book ends with praise of Daniel.

SUTTEE. The custom, in Hindu India, of a wife immolating herself on the funeral pyre of her deceased husband. The custom is said to derive from the demand that a bride be a virgin, so that a widow will be unlikely to remarry and may be destitute; to avoid such a fate, the despairing woman was encouraged to depart life with her husband. The practice was criminalized in 1829 and the government of India has recently been more active in enforcement under pressure from contemporary Indian women's groups.

-T-

TAG QUESTIONS. A grammatical construction consisting of a declarative statement followed by a question relating to the statement. For example: "It's hot in here, isn't it?" "This is the restaurant we liked before, right?" "This is a good movie, don't you think?" Woman have been thought to use this construction more than men although the findings are not conclusive. Feminists point out that when women are found to use tag questions more than men, they are seen as unsure and tentative speakers. This interpretation is not applied when men use tag questions more than women, however.

TAHRIR AL-MAR'A see AMIN, QASIM

TAKE BACK THE NIGHT. An annual demonstration held in many Western cities to draw attention to the problem of violence against women (q.v.). As the name implies, the action addresses the inability of women to freely move within the city as do men.

TAKE OUR DAUGHTERS TO WORK DAY. Begun on April 28, 1993, as an annual US public education action designed to introduce girls, ages 9 to 15, to a positive workplace environment. The campaign, sponsored by the Ms. Foundation for Women, was a response to research showing that in adolescence, girls suffer a loss in ambition and self-esteem (q.v.). It is recommended that male classmates receive special sensitivity training on gender issues in their regular classrooms on that day.

TALAQ. Under Islamic law, a man's right to verbally divorce his wife by stating "I divorce thee" three times. A woman has no similar right and, in some interpretations, no right to divorce unless written into the marriage contract. Although the majority of Muslims oppose *talaq*, some Islamic countries retain the practice in legal codes. Feminists in these countries oppose the provision as do non-fundamentalist theologians.

TAMAR. In Genesis 38, the daughter-in-law of Judah. Twice widowed, and denied by Judah her right to marry her dead husband's brother, Shelah, she ensures having descendants by the unwitting Judah himself. Judah sentences her to death, but after she proved his paternity, he declares her more righteous than he. Tamar gives birth to the ancestor of King David. Feminists stress that even though the narrator vindicates her, she still is not given her right to marry Shelah. In 2 Samuel 13, a second Tamar appears as the daughter of King David who is raped by her half-brother Amnon. Feminists stress her innocence and her knowledge of the laws of Israel, in contrast to her despicable brother.

TAYLOR V. LOUISIANA, 419 US 522 (1975). A decision of the US Supreme Court that struck down a provision of the Louisiana Constitution that a woman should not be selected for jury service unless she had previously filed a written declaration of her desire to serve in that capacity. The provision was viewed as a violation of a (male) criminal defendant's Sixth Amendment right to be tried by a jury comprised of a fair cross-section of the community. The Court noted that restricting jury service to only special groups or systematically excluding identifiable segments which played major roles in the community was not consistent with the constitutional concept of a jury trial.

TEMPERANCE *see* WILLARD, FRANCES ELIZABETH

TENDER YEARS DOCTRINE. The invalidated presumption that custody should be granted to the caregiving parent (usually the mother) during the child's early years. Rooted in traditional gender roles (q.v.), this solution was viewed as uniformly in the "best interests of the child." Since 1983, every US state has adopted a gender-neutral (q.v.) doctrine and most allow joint custody (q.v.).

TERRELL, MARY CHURCH (1863-1954). An African-American civil rights activist and co-founder of the National Association of Colored Women (q.v.) in 1896. She addressed the National American Woman Suffrage Association convention with Susan B. Anthony (qq.v.) in 1898. Her attempts to integrate the women's suffrage movement failed, however, and black suffragists worked within their own groups after 1900.

TERRY, RANDALL *see* OPERATION RESCUE

THIRD WAVE FEMINISM. A resurgent involvement of young women in the United States in feminist activism during the post-Reagan era. These new groups consciously seek to include women of color (q.v.) and poor women and to use direct action in order to spread feminism through the media. The best-known of the new groups, the Women's Action Coalition (WAC), has been termed "the National Organization for Women (q.v.) of the 1990's." Formed in 1992, their motto is "WAC is watching. We will take action." (*See also* First Wave Feminism; Second Wave Feminism.)

THOMAS, CLARENCE *see* HILL, ANITA

THOMAS, MARTHA CAREY (1857-1935). American educator, feminist, and advocate for women's equal educational opportunities. She was the first foreigner and the first woman to earn a doctorate from the University of Zurich. She served as president of Bryn Mawr College, 1894-1922, and attempted to make it the equal of the Ivy League men's colleges. Her support for women's entry into the professions was reflected in her comment that "our (Bryn Mawr) failures only marry." She was also active in the suffrage movement and served as president of the National College Women's Equal Suffrage League, 1908-17.

THREE MARIAS, THE. Three Portuguese women (Maria Isabel Barreño, Maria Fatima Velho da Costa and Maria Teresa Horta) known for their book *New Portuguese Letters* (1972). The book was the result of their many meetings and discussions concerning controversial issues common to them as women and writers. They based their work on a seventeenth-century Portuguese classic, *Letters of a Portuguese Nun.* Upon publication, the book was prohibited for its supposed indecency and the three women were arrested. Their case provoked outrage internationally (especially from women's groups) and charges were dropped in 1974. The work is now recognized for its literary value.

TITLE VII *see* CIVIL RIGHTS ACT OF 1964

TITLE IX, EDUCATION AMENDMENTS OF 1972. US legislation that prohibits educational programs or activities receiving federal financial assistance from excluding, denying benefits to, or discriminating against any person based on that person's sex. Title IX also prohibits discrimination against employees as well as students. In 1984 the Supreme Court issued an opinion, *Grove City College v. Bell* (q.v.), which briefly narrowed the application of Title IX until Congress overturned the ruling by legislation. The impact of Title IX has been extensive: vocational and physical education classes, segregated by the separate spheres doctrine, have been integrated; gender-neutral (q.v.) career counseling is required; women's athletic programs have been expanded.

TOBIAS, SHEILA *see* MATH ANXIETY; SECOND TIER

TORONTO WOMEN'S LIBERATION MOVEMENT (TWLM). An organization formed in 1968 by the University of Toronto's Women's Caucus of the peace group, the Student Union for Peace Action. The group was active on the issue of abortion (q.v.), and in 1969 it took over a campus building for use as a day care (q.v.) center and also staged a protest against the scanty attire worn in the Miss Winter Bikini Contest. That same year radical and lesbian feminists (qq.v.), objecting to the lack of attention to sexuality and Marxist class analysis, left to form the New Feminists. In 1970 another faction interested in Third-World issues broke away and formed the Leila Khaled Collective.

TOXIC SHOCK SYNDROME (TSS). A bacterial infection that most commonly occurs in young women who use tampons during menstruation. Symptoms are high temperature, vomiting, diarrhea, low blood pressure, and a rash. Although TSS is rare and readily responds to antibiotics, about four percent of all cases are fatal. Women's health advocates note that TSS became a serious problem at a time when consumer demand for higher absorbency tampons was fueled by use of oral contraceptives that increase menstrual flow and the more hectic lives of women in general.

TRADE UNIONS *see* KNIGHTS OF LABOR, WOMEN; WOMEN'S TRADE UNION LEAGUE (WTUL)

TRAFFIC IN WOMEN *see* INTERNATIONAL TRAFFIC IN WOMEN

TRANSCENDENTAL FEMINISM *see* FULLER, MARGARET

TRANSSEXUALISM. The wish, often present from early childhood, to have the body of the other sex because it seems more congruent with personal experience of gender. Feminists are concerned about those cases of wished-for or actual surgical transsexual change that are motivated by sex role stereotypes (q.v.) or homophobia.

TRASHING. A form of character assassination leveled against feminists by other feminists in which a woman's personality, ideology, or commitment to the movement is questioned. These attacks were particularly common within radical feminist (q.v.) groups, 1969-71, and were directed against women who rose to prominence because of a special talent such as writing or oral communication skills. In a movement committed to nonhierarchical consensual governance, such visibility was viewed as elitist and was strongly sanctioned.

TRISTAN, FLORA (1803-1844). A French socialist and author of various feminist tracts, including "Women's Emancipation, or The Pariah's Testament," in which she termed women "the proletariat of the proletariat." She called for equal education and professional training, the right to free choice of a husband, divorce, and remarriage, and the rights of unwed mothers to respect and equality. Influenced by Fourier, Robert Owen, Chartism, and extensive travels in England, she proposed a Socialist International organization in 1843.

TROPHY WIFE. A derisive term describing the second wife of a successful man. Such women are usually much younger and more attractive than the first wife and often have an interesting career of their own. These women are supposedly symbols that men in their 50s and 60s are still competitive in the bedroom as well as the boardroom.

TRUTH, SOJOURNER (1777-1883). A US evangelist, abolitionist, former slave, reformer, and women's rights activist. In 1850 Truth discovered the new women's rights movement at a conference in Worcester, Massachusetts. Her impassioned "Ain't I a Woman?" (q.v.) speech at an 1851 women's rights convention in Akron, Ohio, challenged "cult of domesticity" (q.v.) stereotypes about feminine frailty.

TSVETAYEVA, MARINA IVANOVNA (1892-1941). A Russian whose work forms the cornerstone of modern feminist poetry in the former Soviet Union. Born in Moscow, she emigrated to Western Europe in 1922 and returned in 1939 to the Soviet Union, where she committed suicide two years later. Tsvetayeva's works did not receive wide recognition during her life because of the extreme individuality of her style and her open opposition to the regime. Among her themes were the special place of women in the world and human passions; her work makes abundant use of materials from Russian folklore, as well as of heroic figures from the Western literary tradition.

Her first collection of poems, *Evening Album*, was published in 1910.

TUSQUET, ESTHER (1936-). A contemporary Spanish author, best known for the first volume of her trilogy *El mismo mar de todo los veranos* (The Same Sea of All Summers, 1978). In these three novels there is always a woman, the main character, who struggles hard to gain maturity and escape from submission. She won the prize *Ciudad de Barcelona* in 1979 for her novel *El amor es un juego solitario* (Love Is a Lonely Game).

TYRANNY OF STRUCTURELESSNESS. A phrase used by political scientist Jo Freeman to describe feminist commitment to a nonhierarchical egalitarian form of organization that often limited the effectiveness and longevity of the group. Small feminist groups of the late 1960's and early 1970's, based on consensus decisionmaking and rotation of all group tasks, found it more difficult to adopt goals and develop strategies for their advancement. Even here, a (less accountable and less democratic) leadership structure did emerge, based on friendship ties and time commitment.

-U-

UKRAINIAN WOMEN'S UNION (SOIUZ UKRAINOK). An organization formed in 1921 to represent all Ukrainian women outside the Soviet Union and seek their cultural, economic, and political advancement. By the 1930's, its mass membership (peasant-dominated) approached 100,000. The Union set up child care centers, offered vocational and domestic arts training courses, and established cooperatives for the sale of women's crafts. The Union also linked Ukrainian women with international feminism as an affiliate of the International Council of Women, the International Woman Suffrage Alliance (qq.v.), and the Women's International League for Peace and Freedom.

UKRAINKA, LESYA (1871-1913). A leading Ukrainian feminist writer and the first to turn people's attention to questions of women's rights and suffrage in Ukraine. Among her better-known works are the poems *On the Wings of Songs*

(1893); the plays *The Blue Rose* (1896) and *Cassandra* (1908); and the novel *The Forest Song* (1912). The Theater of Russian Drama and numerous libraries, schools, and collective farms are named for her.

UNION FOR WOMEN'S EQUALITY (SOIUZ RAVNOPRAVIIA ZHENSHCHIN). The largest of the Russian suffrage societies, formed in 1905. It, with its successor, the All-Russian Union for Women's Equality, supported universal suffrage, representative government, and major societal reforms. The Women's Union was disbanded in 1908 as government moved against radical political movements.

UNION FRANÇAISE CIVIQUE ET SOCIALE (FRENCH CIVIC AND SOCIAL UNION, UFCS). The Catholic wing of the French feminist movement during the suffrage era. Formed in 1925 after the Pope endorsed woman suffrage, the UFCS today is similar to the United States League of Women Voters (q.v.) in its nonpartisanship and dedication to training women for citizenship.

UNION FRANÇAISE POUR LE SUFFRAGE DES FEMMES (FRENCH UNION FOR WOMEN'S SUFFRAGE, UFSF). A group founded in 1909 under the leadership of Madame Braunsching to work for the female vote. Because of a widespread fear by socialists and left-wing Republicans, who were most likely to sponsor a woman suffrage bill, that women would vote as their priests told them and thus strengthen the conservative parties, French women were not enfranchised until 1944.

UNION OF GREEK WOMEN (ENOSIS GYNAIKON ELLADAS, EGE). A socialist feminist (q.v.) organization, formed in 1976, in close association with the Panhellenic Socialist Movement (PASOK) political party. Led after 1982 by Margaret Papandreou, wife of the prime minister, the EGE has a membership of over 10,000 and has won many reforms, including the Family Law of 1983. Greece established a General Secretariat for Sex Equality in 1985, with Equality Bureaus in every local government to implement gender equity policies.

UNION OF HEBREW WOMEN FOR EQUAL RIGHTS. An Israeli women's organization formed in 1919 to obtain suffrage and contest elections. In 1920 14 women were elected as delegates to the Jewish Representative Assembly (the forerunner of the Knesset) and in 1925 the Assembly ratified the principle of woman suffrage. The Union of Hebrew Women ran its own list of female candidates in five national elections, published a feminist magazine called *Woman* and a legal handbook for women, and established domestic relations legal aid services for women. By the end of the 1930's Israeli feminism was supplanted by the crisis of the Holocaust, the World War, and the Arab challenge.

UNISEX. Facilities, materials, and styles of appearance appropriate for both sexes. For feminists, the marketing of such items as clothing, haircuts, toys, and children's books to both sexes is viewed positively as a way to break down rigid and restrictive gender roles (q.v.). Anti-feminists (q.v.) oppose such trends as violating natural differences between the sexes, bringing a boring "sameness" to society, and threatening the physical safety of women with sex-integrated public facilities (e.g., unisex toilets).

UNITED NATIONS COMMISSION ON THE STATUS OF WOMEN. An international body, established in 1947 to prepare recommendations and reports on promoting women's rights in the political, economic, civil, social, and educational fields. The Commission is composed of delegates who represent and speak for governments. The Commission was responsible for many of the activities of the International Women's Year (q.v.) (1975) and the U. N. Decade for Women (1975-85). It also drafted the Convention on the Political Rights of Women (adopted 1953) and the Convention on the Elimination of All Forms of Discrimination Against Women (q.v.) (adopted 1979).

UNITED NATIONS DECADE FOR WOMEN *see* INTERNATIONAL WOMEN'S YEAR

UNITED NATIONS INTERNATIONAL WOMEN'S YEAR *see* INTERNATIONAL WOMEN'S YEAR

UNITED STATES V. ANTHONY, 24 FED. CAS. 829 (1873). A US case in which Susan B. Anthony (q.v.) challenged the denial of voting rights to women. She had voted in an 1872 New York election and was indicted for "knowingly voting without having a lawful right to vote." The court examined the language of the newly ratified Fourteenth and Fifteenth Amendments and held that the State of New York could limit the voting franchise to the male sex. It determined that the right or privilege of voting was not a right of national citizenship under the United States Constitution. Although Anthony was fined $100 for voting illegally, she never paid the fine and no further action was taken. The case signalled that a constitutional amendment would be needed for the national enfranchisement of women.

UNWAGED LABOR *see* WAGES FOR HOUSEWORK

-V-

VAGINAL ORGASM *see* GRAFENBERG AREA; "MYTH OF THE VAGINAL ORGASM"

VAN SCHURMAN, ANNA MARIA (1607-1678). A Dutch philologist who wrote extensively on philosophy and religion. In her *Whether a Maid May Be a Scholar?*, she uses syllogisms to prove her theory that single women should receive scholarly education. In 1637 her *Whether the Study of Letters Is Fitting to a Christian Woman* asserted that education for women was suitable but need not affect traditional social roles.

VETERAN'S PREFERENCE *see* *PERSONNEL ADMINISTRATOR OF MASSACHUSETTS V. FEENEY*

VICTIM BLAMING *see* "BLAMING THE VICTIM"

VICTIMIZATION OF WOMEN. A feminist critique of the vulnerability of women to abuse, violence, and oppression. The portrayal of women as weak and victimized, particularly in sexual relations, has proven effective in creating a feminist consciousness (q.v.). Other feminists, however, believe that the movement should make women feel strong and prefer the term "survivor" (e.g., "rape survivor") not "victim." Katie Roiphe, in her book on "date rape" (q.v.) (*The Morning After*, 1993), has accused feminists of teaching young women to fear all interpersonal relations with men.

VINDICATION OF THE RIGHTS OF WOMAN see WOLLSTONECRAFT, MARY

VIOLENCE AGAINST WOMEN. A term encompassing rape, violent pornography, domestic violence (qq.v.), incest, and crimes against prostitutes (q.v.). Internationally, feminists have spoken out against the cultural practices of female genital mutilation (q.v.), female infanticide, suttee (q.v.), and femicide of women who disgrace their families. Other global issues include selling women into sexual slavery as prostitutes and war crimes against women in Bosnia.

VIRGIN MARY *see* MARY OF NAZARETH

VOICES FROM THE PIPELINE. A term coined by scientist Sheila Widnall to describe the disproportionate number of women who are discouraged from pursuing higher education in science, engineering, and mathematics, or who fail to advance in careers in these areas. Widnall has postulated that this "leakage" from the pipeline is due to a number of factors, including response to educational and career pressures, self-perception and the perception of teachers and mentors, which differs significantly between women and men. (*See also* Second Tier.)

VOLUNTARY ASSOCIATIONS *see* CLUB WOMAN'S MOVEMENT

-W-

WAGE GAP. The disparity existing between salaries earned by men and women. These pay differentials exist in all Western countries and are even larger in developing countries. They were formerly justified by the concept of the "family wage" (q.v.) for the male breadwinner and women's preference for lower-paying jobs that were more compatible with family life. In the United States, the wage gap between full-time, non-seasonal male and female employees has remained fairly stable since World War II; women earn 71 cents for every dollar received by men. The Equal Pay Act of 1963 and Title VII of the Civil Rights Act of 1964 (qq.v.) have had little impact because of occupational segregation (q.v.); men and women hold different jobs. These gap figures undercount the real disparities since only about half of all employed women work full time over 12 months, and a disproportionate number of working women lack fringe benefits such as health care and pensions. (*See also* Comparable Worth; *Equal Employment Opportunity Commission v. Sears, Roebuck & Co.*; Pink-Collar Ghetto.)

WAGES FOR HOUSEWORK. A feminist demand derived from Charlotte Perkins Gilman's (q.v.) analysis of the economic value of childrearing, food preparation, and cleaning. US women's rights groups have recommended that homemakers receive Social Security (q.v.) coverage in their own names, based on their domestic labor (q.v.), not as a dependent of a male wage earner. This would require that the cash value of unpaid housework be calculated and perhaps even be included in the Gross Domestic Product (GDP). Such a policy would lessen the vulnerability and dependency of homemakers. Although these changes in the Social Security system have not been adopted, married women have been given additional rights to participate in their former husbands' retirement benefits and to establish their own Individual Retirement Accounts. The United Nations has recommended that governments count unwaged labor in their GDPs by 1995.

WALKER, ALICE (1944-). A contemporary African-American novelist, poet, and essayist, best known for her novel *The Color Purple* (1982), which won the Pulitzer Prize and the National

Book Award. She is credited with rediscovering the literary achievement of another African-American woman writer, Zora Neale Hurston (q.v.), when she published a collection of Hurston's largely forgotten writings, *I Love Myself When I Am Laughing* (1979). In addition to five collections of poetry, Walker has also published other novels, *The Third Life of Grange Copeland* (1970), *In Love and Trouble* (1973), *Meridian* (1976) and *Possessing the Secret of Joy* (1992)--all of which celebrate the many survival skills black women have developed, not the least of which is the power of a matrilineage, which Walker describes in *In Search of Our Mothers' Gardens* (1983).

WARD, MRS. HUMPHREY (1851-1920). A popular English author and the most prominent anti-suffragist. Although she supported women's entry to Oxford and a role for women in local government, she opposed women's suffrage on the grounds that colonial and foreign policy issues were outside the realm of a woman's experience. In 1889 Mrs. Ward collected the signatures of over 100 distinguished women in opposition to the vote for women and in support of her manifesto.

WATKINS, GLORIA *see* HOOKS, BELL

WEBSTER V. REPRODUCTIVE HEALTH SERVICES, 492 US 490 (1989). A decision by the US Supreme Court that appeared to reject the *Roe v. Wade* (q.v.) "trimester" approach when it upheld a number of restrictive abortion (q.v.) laws. In *Webster*, the Supreme Court examined the constitutionality of four provisions of a Missouri statute which declared in its preamble that "the life of each human being begins at conception," and that "unborn children have protectable interests in life, health, and well-being." It also prohibited public employees and facilities from performing abortions and prohibited public funding of abortion counseling. Finally, it established a set of requirements compelling physicians to perform certain "viability" tests on fetuses of 20 or more weeks gestational age before performing an abortion. Ruling on each, the Supreme Court: (1) concluded that the preamble did not present a ripe constitutional question since there was no indication that a woman's ability to have an abortion would in any way be limited by the language at issue; (2) upheld the prohibition on performance of abortions at public facilities or by public employees since earlier Supreme Court cases had determined that a state's refusal to subsidize abortions did not restrict a woman's right to privacy (q.v.); (3) accepted Missouri's assertion that the statute would not be interpreted to restrict abortion counseling by public employees acting at their own expense during private time; and (4) made no ruling regarding whether a state could establish statutory criteria that would bind individual physicians in a viability determination since the statute only required a physician to exercise reasonable professional judgment in determining whether to use the specified tests in making a viability finding. This case is viewed as a turning point for the pro-choice movement (q.v.) in terms of public demonstrations, mail directed to the Court (over 200,000 pieces before oral arguments were heard), and the large number of Friend of the Court briefs filed on both sides. The implied invitation to the states to enact further restrictions suggested to feminists that recriminalization of abortion was possible. The movement to preserve reproductive freedom (q.v.) became more active in the post-*Webster* period, and the National Abortion and Reproductive Rights Action League (q.v.) greatly expanded its membership.

WEDDINGTON, SARAH *see ROE V. WADE*

WEST, DAME REBECCA (1892-1983). A British essayist and novelist, she once quipped what must be one of the most succinct definitions of feminism: "I myself have never known what feminism is. I only know that people call me a feminist whenever I express sentiments that differentiate me from a doormat." Born Cicily Fairfield, West chose to call herself "Rebecca West" in homage to the feminist character in Henrik Ibsen's drama *Rosmersholm* (1886). After a brief and unsuccessful career on the stage, West turned to writing for the feminist journal *The Freewoman*, and the socialist paper *The Clarion*. In both publications she supported the suffrage, women's trade union, and free love movements. After bearing the illegitimate child of H. G. Wells in 1914, she became active in championing the rights of unwed mothers. Her novels *The Judge* (1922) and *The Return of the Soldier* (1918) expose the hypocrisy of conventional marriage and social proprieties. She is perhaps most widely remembered today as the author of *Black Lamb and Grey Falcon* (1941), generally considered one of the best books on Eastern Europe.

WHEATLEY, PHILLIS (1753?-1784). An African-born slave who became the first African-American woman poet to publish her work. Raised by a supportive white family in Boston, Wheatley was taught to read and write and then exhibited as a "freak," a literate slave, by her masters. Her poetry was published in England, where she was received by and exhibited to London aristocratic circles. There is considerable controversy about the value of her poems: one school of thought holds that the work is derivative and slavish in its imitation of eighteenth-century models; the other claims that the poetry exhibits feminist rage at objectification as both a woman and slave.

WHEELER, ANNA (1785-1848). Nicknamed the "Goddess of Reason," a British utopian and utilitarian who thought that the happiness of women counted equally and was not subsumed under that of men. In response to James Mill's article endorsing coverture (q.v.), she and William Thompson wrote *The Appeal of One Half of the Human Race Against the Pretensions of the Other Half*, which argued that a social system is not utilitarian if it only considers the happiness of half of its members. They concluded that the interests of neither single women nor wives are covered by their male relatives' interests and that the social dependence of women, especially in marriages where the contracts are the moral equivalent of slavery contracts, demeans women and corrupts men.

WHITEHEAD, MARY BETH *see IN RE BABY M*

WICCA. A resurrected Anglo-Saxon word now used for a religion, popular among some feminists, purportedly based on, or surviving from, persecuted pagan European beliefs. Although "wicca" originally meant a male witch, it now refers to a Goddess (q.v.) or cosmic female principle identified with the earth, vegetation and (re)generation. The classical equivalent would be Demeter (q.v.), but this mythic figure is not emphasized because wicca devotees reject classical allusions associated with patriarchal traditions. Instead the religion is based on witches persecuted in the fifteenth through seventeenth centuries who were devotees of an ancient Germanic nature religion. Like Goddess religion, wicca is a contemporary religion fulfilling the spiritual needs of some who reject the patriarchal themes and figures of Judeo-Christian religions. Wicca emphasizes egalitarian relations between persons and between humans and the earth; its vital principle is the generative fertility of the earth. Its devotees organize in local covens, ideally composed of 13 persons, who congregate to hymn and dance in celebration of nature. Where weather permits, this is preferably done outdoors. Wicca covens maintain some secrecy, but seem to be a loose confederation of devotees with a mystical approach to nature as opposed to formal, hierarchical, openly institutionalized Book religions.

WICKEDARY. A gynocentric "metapatriarchal dictionary" by Mary Daly (q.v.) and Jane Caputi (*Webster's First Intergalactic Wickedary of the English Language*, 1987). It creates new words and exposes sexist assumptions in old words by playing with etymological and metaphorical meanings in order to subvert patriarchy (q.v.) through language.

WIFE ABUSE *see* DOMESTIC VIOLENCE

WIFE BATTERING *see* DOMESTIC VIOLENCE

WIFE BEATING *see* DOMESTIC VIOLENCE

WIFE RAPE *see* MARITAL RAPE

WILD WOMAN MOVEMENT. A term coined by Clarissa Pinkola Estes and popularized by her 1992 book *Women Who Run with the Wolves*. The wild woman, analogous to Robert Bly's (q.v.) wild man, represents the woman who attacks society's strictures and rebels against the conformities imposed on her to behave in an acceptable and non-threatening way. The book on which the movement is based consists of folktales, myths, and Jungian analysis about women who assert their sexuality and unique feminine ways of knowledge against the deadening influences of male-dominated society. Estes retells traditional stories with the wild woman twist; when she meditates on the meaning of the Little Match Girl, she writes that the girl wasted her art and was destroyed because she failed to "unresign herself and come out kicking ass. When Wild Woman is cornered, she does not surrender, she comes ahead, claws out and fighting" (see her version of the story of the Little Match Girl in *Women Who Run with the Wolves*). Estes asserts a clear distinction between men and women, based on her essentialist (q.v.) Jungian understanding of the differences between the anima and animus (q.v.).

WILLARD, FRANCES ELIZABETH (1839-1898). A US educator, social reformer, and founder of the Woman's Christian Temperance Union (WCTU) in 1874. The first mass organization of women devoted to social reform, the WCTU viewed alcohol and alcoholism as the causes of poverty and women's subjugation. Willard served as president of the WCTU from 1879 until her death. Under her leadership, the group endorsed woman suffrage, linking the vote to the adoption of prohibition. The involvement of over 200,000 traditional, religious women in the suffrage movement gave the cause a mass base for the first time. Willard also served as president of the Evanston College for Ladies and later as dean of Northwestern University's Woman's College. As a social reformer, she worked for labor legislation, prison reform, early childhood education, and alcohol regulation.

WISH LIST *see* EMILY'S LIST

WITCH BURNING *see* SALEM WITCH TRIALS

WITCH HUNTS *see* SALEM WITCH TRIALS

WITCHCRAFT. Magic employed for malevolent purposes, a form of personal revolt practiced largely by women in virtually every society. Although men and women were both originally involved in covens, women became the focus of witch hunts after the publication in 1487 of *Malleus Maleficarum* (The Hammer Against Witches), commissioned by Pope Innocent VIII. It associated witchcraft with women, particularly elderly and poor women. Just as witchcraft allowed women to rebel against male-dominated societies, the witch hunt and active persecution allowed society to punish such rebellion.

WITTIG, MONIQUE (1935-). A contemporary French novelist and theorist, author of the lesbian epic *Les Guérillères*, the novel *Le Corps lesbien* and "The Straight Mind" (in *Feminist Issues*, 1980). Wittig is suspicious of oppositional thinking that defines woman as the opposite of man, as well as mythical-idealist formulations of *féminité*: "It remains for us to define our oppression in materialist terms, to say that women are a class, which is to say that the category 'woman,' as well as 'man,' is a political and economic category, not an eternal one. Our first task is thoroughly to dissociate 'women' (the class within which we fight) and 'woman,' the myth. For 'woman' does not exist for us; it is only an imaginary formation, while 'women' is the product of a social relationship" (see her "Straight Mind").

WOLF, CHRISTA (1929-). The most prominent of the writers who emerged in the German Democratic Republic. The best-known of her works are the novels *Nachdenken über Christa T.* (The Quest for Christa T., 1968), *Kindheitsmuster* (A Model Childhood, 1977), *Kein Ort, Nirgends* (No Place on Earth, 1979), *Kassandra* (1983), and *Störfall, Nachrichten eines Tages* (Accident, News of the Day, 1987), a reaction to the Chernobyl incident. Prized as much for her literary artistry as for her articulate vision of women's experiences, she has warned that unrestrained subjectivity can become the measure of objective reality when the subject is not merely empty self-observation, but is actively focused on social processes. Since German reunification, there has been much controversy over the nature of her stance when it was discovered that she had cooperated with the Stasi, the East German secret police.

WOLLSTONECRAFT, MARY (1759-1797). A British feminist and author, widely considered the founder of the modern feminist movement. Author of *Mary, A Fiction* (1788), *A Vindication of the Rights of Man* (1790), *A Vindication of the Rights of Woman* (1792), and *The Wrongs of Woman, or Maria* (1798), Wollstonecraft was a mistress, wife, and mother; her lover's infidelity drove her to attempt suicide twice. She later married William Godwin (1797) and died shortly after the birth of her second daughter, Mary, later to become Mary Shelley. Her rich and varied experiences provided the material for her novels, while her novels provided the gothic and melodramatic impetus for her prose works, particularly *A Vindication of the Rights of Woman*. Her writings brilliantly exposed the double standard (q.v.) between men and women in contemporary society. According to Wollstonecraft, this disparity encouraged in men the fullest exercise of their powers of rational autonomy and the development of moral virtue, while imposing social, political, and economic constraints on the development in women of both reason and virtue. Wollstonecraft argued for changes in education which would enable women to become as autonomous as she thought men were. She proposed a theory of human nature, claiming that all humans have reason, and that women and the lower classes are believed to have less only because of the wrongful practices and neglect of patriarchal society. She also argued against Rousseau, who claimed that women should be dependent on men and not utilize their intelligence.

WOMAN AS OTHER. A concept developed in Simone de Beauvoir's (q.v.) *Second Sex* (1953). According to this view, woman is defined by man as everything he is not. If he is culture, she is nature. If he is rational, she is emotional. If he is the mind, she is the body. This endless series of binary oppositions serves to valorize male characteristics and values and objectify and subjugate women in a series of inferior postures. By defining the woman as inherently "other than" man, male-dominated culture is able to define women, keep them in inferior postures, and cause them to view themselves as less than man.

"WOMAN-IDENTIFIED WOMAN, THE." A 1970 Radicalesbian position paper by Rita Mae Brown (q.v.) in which lesbianism (q.v.) is defined as a political choice (in contrast to a sexual alternative) required by feminism. Many heterosexual women felt the paper also suggested that straight women were male-identified, collaborating with the enemy, and untrustworthy. (*See also* Gay/Straight Split; Lavender Menace; Lesbian Feminism; Political Lesbianism.)

WOMAN OF VALOR. In the Book of Proverbs, praised for her prudent running of the household. Feminists point out that she confirms patriarchal values of subservient women, but she also is lauded for her justice and care for the poor. She creates a contrast to the depiction of women as temptresses in the book.

WOMAN SUFFRAGE (CASE LAW) see *CHORLTON V. LINGS; MINOR V. HAPPERSETT; UNITED STATES V. ANTHONY*

WOMAN WISDOM (DAME WISDOM/LADY WISDOM). In the Book of Proverbs, the personification of Wisdom itself. She encourages all to study the laws of God and seek a life of virtue. Woman Wisdom contrasts with other images of women in Proverbs who are depicted as temptresses; she symbolizes the feminine side of the transcendent ("Sophia").

WOMANIST THEOLOGY. A theology of liberation which uses black women's experience as its foundational source. Attention is drawn to the need to encompass race and class, as well as gender, in the movement to transform systems of oppression. Womanists challenge other feminists to acknowledge, deeply integrate, and respond to the reality of differences between and among women. Emphasis is placed on knowledge of black women's history, experiential understanding of the lives of contemporary black women, and ongoing dialogue.

WOMAN'S BIBLE, THE. A collection of essays and commentaries on the Bible, compiled in 1895 by a women's revising committee chaired by Elizabeth Cady Stanton (q.v.). Stanton's avowed purpose was to initiate a critical study of biblical texts which are used to degrade and subject women in order to demonstrate that it is not divine will which humiliates women, but human desire for domination. In "denying divine inspiration for demoralizing ideas," Stanton's committee hoped to exemplify a reverence for a higher Christian "Spirit of All Good." Many women biblical scholars invited to contribute declined because they believed they must put aside their own presuppositions to pursue the author's intention and/or meaning. This tension still exists between feminists who seek to use biblical texts to initiate social change and those whose central allegiance is to historical-critical methods of interpreting the Bible. (*See also* Bible, Feminist Exegesis.)

WOMAN'S CHRISTIAN TEMPERANCE UNION *see* WILLARD, FRANCES ELIZABETH

WOMEN AGAINST PORNOGRAPHY (WAP) *see* PORNOGRAPHY, FEMINIST DEBATE ON

WOMEN AND ECONOMICS see GILMAN, CHARLOTTE PERKINS

WOMEN AND RUSSIA; AN ALMANAC TO WOMEN ABOUT WOMEN. The first feminist samizdat in the Soviet Union, first circulated in 1979 in Leningrad and edited by Marina Oulianova and Tatiana Mamonova. The *Almanac* discussed conditions in maternity hospitals, abortion clinics, and child care centers; rape (q.v.); alcoholism; and the double shift (q.v.). Over time, however, the *Almanac* collective split along political and religious lines, pitting secular feminists who still revered Leninist revolutionary ideals against Russian Orthodox Christian feminists who rejected Marxism and started their own *Maria* journal. In response to the appearance of four issues, the Soviet KGB questioned, searched, arrested, and exiled several authors. Concurrently, the official Soviet press began to examine many of these same women's issues. Mamonova, one of the exiles, subsequently became very visible in the Western feminist movement and in the press.

WOMEN AS JURORS *see HOYT V. FLORIDA; TAYLOR V. LOUISIANA*

WOMEN IN DEVELOPMENT *see* DEVELOPMENT, WOMEN IN

WOMEN OF COLOR *see* COLOR, WOMEN OF

WOMEN WORKERS' COUNCIL (WWC). The feminist arm of the Histadrut labor coalition in Israel, formed in 1921 to promote training and employment for women within agriculture and later in construction and industrial jobs. The movement changed its name to the Organization of Working Mothers in 1930 and became a social service group that addressed the needs of married women rather than its original goals of gender equity in the workforce. The future prime minister Golda Meir served as general-secretary of the WWC, 1927-30.

WOMEN'S ACTION ALLIANCE (WAA). An organization formed in 1972 by Gloria Steinem (q.v.) and Brenda Feigen Fasteau as an information clearinghouse and referral center for local feminists involved in projects. The WAA provides technical and financial assistance to women's groups and facilitates their applications to other foundations.

WOMEN'S ACTION COALITION (WAC) *see* THIRD WAVE FEMINISM

WOMEN'S BATTERY SHELTER. A British term referring to housing available to women and their children when women have been abused by the men in their lives. Services include shelter, food, counseling, legal advice, and eventual return to the community. The women's battery shelter movement began in the early 1970's. (*See also* Battered Woman Syndrome.)

WOMEN'S BUREAU, DEPARTMENT OF LABOR. A US government agency, established in 1920 to serve the interests of working women in industry. Although the Bureau always supported, in principle, equal employment policies, it defended protective labor legislation (q.v.) for women until 1956 and did not endorse the Equal Rights Amendment (q.v.) until 1970. Through much of its history, the agency held the view that mothers and wives should only work out of economic necessity. The Bureau, beginning in 1961 with its major role in the establishment of the President's Commission on the Status of Women (q.v.), has moved into the mainstream of the women's rights movement (q.v.) and has served as a forum, advocacy agency, and data-gathering resource for women's issues.

WOMEN'S BUREAU COALITION *see* SOCIAL FEMINISM

WOMEN'S CAMPAIGN FUND (WCF). The first of the women's political action committees (PACs), formed in 1974, to provide campaign money to feminist women candidates seeking national, state, and local elective offices in the United States. Both Republican and Democratic women are eligible for support.

WOMEN'S CENTER. A meeting place and information center for local feminist movement activists. Typical activities include: classes on women's history (q.v.), self-defense (q.v.), legal rights, and assertiveness (q.v.); a community calendar of women's events; referrals to female professionals and women-run businesses; a job bank; a feminist resource library; consciousness-raising (q.v.) groups; a magazine or newsletter; and targeted services to victims of rape and domestic violence and to displaced homemakers (qq.v.). These institutions often begin as grass-roots, volunteer-run enterprises, funded by donations and minimal program fees, but evolve into complex social service organizations supported by a myriad of government and private foundation grants.

WOMEN'S CLUB MOVEMENT *see* CLUB WOMAN'S MOVEMENT

WOMEN'S CONVENTION *see* CONVENTION ON THE ELIMINATION OF ALL FORMS OF DISCRIMINATION AGAINST WOMEN

WOMEN'S EDUCATIONAL EQUITY ACT (WEEA). A bill passed by the US Congress in 1974 as a part of the larger Special Education Projects Spending Act. The WEEA program receives money for developing curriculum and guidance materials and funding projects that support the Title IX (q.v.) goal of sex equity in education. The program came under attack during the early years of the Reagan administration as a stronghold of feminists. Congress refused to abolish the program, however, and in 1984 rewrote the WEEA authorization to prevent future presidents from ignoring legislative intent.

WOMEN'S EQUALITY DAY. August 26, the anniversary of the passage of the Nineteenth Amendment (q.v.) extending voting rights to US women. Although the day is not an official national holiday, American presidents often issue proclamations marking the day and feminist groups plan major rallies on that date.

WOMEN'S EQUITY ACTION LEAGUE (WEAL). Group founded in Ohio in 1968 by lawyer Dr. Elizabeth Boyer in protest against the support of legalized abortion (q.v.) by the National Organization for Women (q.v.). In the opinion of Boyer, such a radical goal would serve to discredit the newly revitalized feminist movement. WEAL sought to attract the participation of professional women in a more respectable and moderate arm of the new feminist movement (q.v.) by concentrating on educational equity and economic issues affecting women. The group disbanded in 1989.

WOMEN'S HEALTH INITIATIVE. A $625 million study, begun under the sponsorship of the US National Institutes of Health (NIH) in 1993, of major diseases (cancer, heart disease, and osteoporosis) in post-menopausal women. A permanent Office of Research on Women's Health within the NIH has also been established. Women's rights advocates charge that past studies of diseases that occur in both sexes have excluded women from clinical trials and that diseases that only affect women are ignored by researchers. Critics note that even this study does not address the dearth of medical research on women of childbearing years due to researchers' fears of causing birth defects through drug trials.

WOMEN'S HEALTH MOVEMENT. A U.S. feminist challenge to patriarchal male dominance (q.v.) of the medical profession. The first feminist health conference was held in 1971, and in 1975 a coalition group, the National Women's Health Network (q.v.), was formed to coordinate this new movement. Issues of particular interest are: reproduction (q.v.), including childbirth, reproductive technology (q.v.), and abortion (q.v.); drug safety; medical self-help and self-knowledge; unnecessary surgery, such as caesarean births, radical mastectomies, and hysterectomies; fetal protection policies (q.v.); and sterilization abuse (q.v.). (*See also* Self-Help Health Movement.)

WOMEN'S HISTORY MONTH. A period (March) set aside each year in the United States to focus on the effort to reconstruct the female past. Although historians agree that women have rarely been written into history, there is less agreement on the proper approach to addressing this omission. Much attention has been given to women's achievements, the movement for women's legal and political rights, and the changing economic role of women. More recently women's historians have documented the female experience as distinct from that of men and have focused on the family and women's domestic role.

WOMEN'S INTERNATIONAL TERRORIST CONSPIRACY FROM HELL (WITCH). The politico (q.v.) wing of the New York Radical Women (q.v.), founded by (among others) Robin Morgan (q.v.) in 1968 to stage zap actions (q.v.). These included the hexing of the New York Stock Exchange, the release of live white mice at a bridal fair in Madison Square Garden, and a hairy legs demonstration. Covens in other cities emerged with their own guerrilla theater targets and new names to fit the WITCH acronym. These highly visible tactics led to both new recruits and ridicule for the feminist movement. Some feminists also deplored the tactics as too derivative of New Left male counter-cultural politics.

WOMEN'S JOINT CONGRESSIONAL COMMITTEE (WJCC). A post-suffrage US coalition of 14 women's rights groups, formed in 1920 to coordinate lobbying efforts. Members included: the American Association of University Women, the League of Women Voters, the National Consumers League, the National Federation of Business and Professional Women's Clubs, and the Women's Trade Union League (qq.v.). Their social feminist (q.v.) agenda supported education, health care, peace, and protective labor legislation (q.v.). The WJCC remained effective only through the early 1930's, when it became apparent that women did not constitute a cohesive and participatory voting bloc. (*See also* Sheppard-Towner Maternity Act of 1921.)

WOMEN'S LIBERATION MOVEMENT. One of the two major strands in the early history of the contemporary feminist movement in the United States. This sector, also called the revolutionary, radical, or younger branch, was based in numerous local groups spontaneously created as early as 1967 in cities by women formerly active in New Left groups or the African-American civil rights movement (q.v.). These local groups were small, informal, nonhierarchical networks committed to a radical vision of a new society. Well-publicized zap actions (q.v.), protests, and speak-outs (q.v.) were utilized as were consciousness-raising (q.v.) and self-help (q.v.) projects. These groups were often short-lived, having fallen victim to a "tyranny of structurelessness" (q.v.). (*See also* Women's Rights Movement.)

WOMEN'S NATIONAL COALITION. A coalition of 40 South African women's groups, founded in 1992 by the African National Congress (ANC) Women's League, to assure the inclusion of women's rights in the new national constitution. The groups encompassed the entire political spectrum, including the white Conservative and National Parties and the ANC and Inkatha Freedom Movement. The coalition attempted to survey every woman in the country on a Women's Charter for the new document. Topics addressed included property and contract rights, reproductive freedom, comparable worth, domestic violence, and sexual assault (qq.v.)

WOMEN'S NATIONAL COMMISSION (WNC). A British government group, established in 1969, to ensure that women's views are included in government. The commission, by law, is composed of 50 long-established and large national groups. In practice, this eliminates virtually all new feminist (q.v.) groups; member-organizations are primarily women's sections of trade unions and political parties. The WNC studies women's issues and presents position papers.

WOMEN'S ORGANIZATION OF IRAN (WOI). A coalition of women's groups formed in 1966 in the tradition of the High Council of Women's Organizations of Iran, which led the movement for woman suffrage, achieved in 1963. The WOI provided educational and vocational training for women under the guise of modernization, not women's rights. It worked for positive changes in the legal status of women after gaining the support of the Shah and the religious authorities. By 1978 the WOI claimed 400 branches and 51 affiliated groups. After the revolution in 1979, many of these changes were reversed, programs were dropped, and the WOI was labeled "a den of corruption" by the new government.

WOMEN'S RESEARCH AND EDUCATION INSTITUTE (WREI) *see* CONGRESSIONAL CAUCUS FOR WOMEN'S ISSUES

WOMEN'S RIGHTS MOVEMENT. One of the two major strands in the early history of the contemporary feminist movement in the United States. This sector, also called the reform or older branch, began with the founding of the National Organization for Women (q.v.) in 1966 and grew rapidly as many other groups were formed. As a primary proponent of liberal feminism (q.v.), this branch has concentrated on eliminating sex discrimination through the traditional channels of legislative and judicial reforms and has operated through formal, hierarchical, and national organization structures. (*See also* Women's Liberation Movement.)

WOMEN'S ROOM, THE see FRENCH, MARILYN

WOMEN'S SHELTER *see* WOMEN'S BATTERY SHELTER

WOMEN'S SOCIAL AND POLITICAL UNION (WSPU) *see* PANKHURSTS, THE

WOMEN'S STRIKE FOR EQUALITY. A nationwide demonstration, the largest ever for women's rights up to that time, held on August 26, 1970, to commemorate the fiftieth anniversary of US women's suffrage. Women's Strike Day was the idea of Betty Friedan and the National Organization for Women (qq.v.) and was organized by local feminist groups in virtually every major city and some smaller ones in the United States and in several European cities as well. Newspaper and television, in covering the marches, pickets, rallies, and zap actions (q.v.) that marked the day's events, brought the public its first real awareness of the new feminist movement. The strike proved pivotal for the women's movement; many new participants were attracted into active membership as a result of the media coverage.

WOMEN'S STUDIES. An area of research and teaching, often interdisciplinary in nature, which began to develop in the 1960's. It typically includes not only the study of women but also brings a critical feminist perspective to the study of all disciplines. Most US and European universities offer these courses and many also have degree programs or departments. Conservatives and anti-feminists (q.v.) have criticized these curricular developments, charging that women's studies courses are biased and, at a minimum, encourage illiteracy in the standard canons of Western civilization. (*See also* Feminology.)

WOMEN'S TRADE UNION LEAGUE (WTUL). A US organization of female reformers and women in labor formed in 1903 by Progressives and labor officials to help women organize within trade unions, improve workplace conditions for women through protective labor legislation (q.v.), and promote feminism and suffrage. Settlement House (q.v.) workers Lillian Wald and Jane Addams (q.v.) were among the founders, and no trade union women served as WTUL president until 1921. Although the League was active in virtually every strike of women workers, by 1913 it had become primarily a social welfare group devoted to public advocacy and lobbying for legislation through the Women's Joint Congressional Committee (q.v.). By the late 1920s the League had ceased most efforts to unionize women, and in 1950 it closed its small Washington, D. C., office.

WOODHULL, VICTORIA CLAFLIN (1838-1927). An outspoken feminist advocate of suffrage and free love, and the first woman to run for President of the United States, in 1872, on the Equal Rights Party ticket. Throughout much of her early life, Woodhull and her sister Tennessee Celeste Claflin worked as spiritualist physicians. With the assistance of Commodore Vanderbilt, the two opened the first stockbrokerage firm owned by women near Wall Street in New York City in 1870. The assumption that all their advice was from the highly successful financier Vanderbilt brought instant success to the office. Woodhull used this public attention to help her candidacy for the Presidency of the United States. She prepared a memorial on women's rights, arguing that the recently passed Fourteenth and Fifteenth Amendments to the Constitution guaranteed the vote to women as members of races. Representative Benjamin Butler of Massachusetts arranged for her to deliver her statement on January 11, 1871, before the House Judiciary Committee. This brought her to the attention of the National Woman's Suffrage Association (NWSA) and Elizabeth Cady Stanton (qq.v.), who befriended Woodhull, only to be castigated by other NWSA members for associating with a notorious lower-class Free Lover. From 1870 to 1876 the sisters published *Woodhull and Claflin's Weekly*, a newspaper with a printing of 50,000 copies that printed the first English-language American publication of Marx's *Communist Manifesto* and a novel by George Sand (q.v.). After the death of Commodore Vanderbilt, the sisters were provided with passages to England and money to live well there. Woodhull began lecturing on women's rights in England and both women found wealthy husbands. Victoria Claflin Woodhull was a brilliant and forceful woman who worked tirelessly for women's rights, freedom from laws infringing upon private consensual behavior, and the unmasking of hypocrisy and exploitation. The suffrage movement's rejection of her was based on class prejudice. The new feminist movement (q.v.), however, has given her more attention as a feminist pioneer of her day.

WOOLF, ADELINE VIRGINIA (1882-1941). A British novelist, essayist, critic, letter writer, diarist, and pamphleteer who influenced both the Modernist and feminist movements of the twentieth century. Her critical essays in *The Common Reader* (1925) celebrate the canon of English literature while also introducing literary works by women. Woolf's *A Room of One's Own* (q.v.) (1929), and *Three Guineas* (1938) have greatly influenced contemporary feminisms, the former having been especially important in modelling methods of feminist literary criticism (q.v.) and recovery of women's texts. These two feminist essays argue, respectively, that women need intellectual and economic freedom i" they are to be artists and that the patriarchal structures of sexism (q.v.), fascism, and classism, which permeate public and private lives, lead inevitably to war.

WORK-FAMILY CONFLICT. The incompatibility between employment and domestic role demands. This may result in role overload and stress. Such conflict may be reduced by delegation of household activities to paid staff or other household members and by flexible and "family-friendly" organizational practices, such as day care and flexitime (qq.v.).

WORLD PLAN OF ACTION FOR WOMEN *see* INTERNATIONAL WOMEN'S YEAR

WRIGHT, FRANCES (1795-1852). A Scottish-born American journalist and lecturer on controversial topics such as abolition, divorce, birth control, women's education, equality in marriage and economics, and authoritarian religions. "Fanny Wrightism" came to be a demeaning term indicating an amoral and heretical woman. Her travelogue of her visit to America, *Views of Society and Manner in America* (1821), noted the oppression of women here, as in Europe. She was later associated with two US utopian communities, Nashoba, Tennessee, and New Harmony, Indiana.

-X-

X-LINKAGE HYPOTHESIS. An attempt to explain the seemingly different abilities between boys and girls in several areas, including mathematics, visualization, and spatial reasoning, by associating these abilities with sex. There appears to be little valid scientific data to support this hypothesis, yet gender differences in these areas have been widely publicized as facts, possibly leading to lowered parental expectations for girls and correspondingly lower demonstrated abilities by girls. (*See also* Math Anxiety.)

-Y-

"YELLOW WALLPAPER, THE" *see* GILMAN, CHARLOTTE PERKINS

YOUNGER BRANCH *see* WOMEN'S LIBERATION MOVEMENT

"YOU'VE COME A LONG WAY, BABY." An advertising slogan used by a cigarette company to market a product aimed at women. The campaign utilized symbols of the feminist movement in a patronizing manner. Over time the phrase has become associated with attempts to convince women that they have made such great progress that further changes in women's role and status are no longer needed.

-Z-

ZAP ACTION. A form of ad hoc feminist protest designed to deal with a specific issue or a single event through the use of dramatic and often symbolic tactics. One such action was staged on Halloween, 1968, by women dressed as witches who cast a hex upon the New York Stock Exchange, a symbol of male-dominated capitalism.

ZERO POPULATION GROWTH (ZPG). A group formed in 1968 by biologist and environmentalist Paul Ehrlich to advocate for a reduced birthrate in the United States. Goals of the ZPG include a balance between annual births and deaths and a family size that does not exceed natural replacement (i.e., a couple should have no more than two children). The ZPG was one of the first (in 1969) established organizations to endorse legalized abortion (q.v.)

ZETKIN, CLARA (1857-1933). A leading theoretician of the German Social Democratic Party and self-proclaimed feminist who argued in *The Question of Women Workers and Women at the Present Time* (1889) that socialism and feminism were inextricably intertwined. Founder and leader of the Socialist Women's International (q.v.) and editor of the women's newspaper *Equality*, she contended that women's subordination was the consequence of property relations determined by economic conditions. A critic of the feminist Lily Braun (q.v.), Zetkin opposed the socialization of housework and child care and saw contraception as an "easy out." She believed that women should have an equal role in production and equal aspirations with men, while simultaneously functioning as wives and mothers to the highest degree.

BIBLIOGRAPHY

I. REFERENCE MATERIAL
(BIBLIOGRAPHIES, ENCYCLOPEDIAS,
DICTIONARIES, AND ALMANACS)

Bachmann, Donna G. and Piland, Sherry (1978). *Women Artists: An Historical Contemporary and Feminist Bibliography*. Metuchen, NJ: Scarecrow Press.

Carson, Anne (1986). *Feminist Spirituality and the Feminine Divine: An Annotated Bibliography*. Trumansburg, NY: Crossing Press.

Carson, Anne (1992). *Goddesses and Wise Women: The Literature of Feminist Spirituality, 1980-1992: An Annotated Bibliography*. Freedom, CA: Crossing Press.

Clark, Judith Freeman (1987). *Almanac of American Women in the Twentieth Century*. New York: Prentice Hall.

De Coste, F.C., Munro, K.M. and MacPherson, Lillian (1991). *Feminist Legal Literature: A Selective Annotated Bibliography*. New York: Garland.

Dixon, Penelope (1991). *Mothers and Mothering: An Annotated Feminist Bibliography*. New York: Garland.

Driel, Joan, Broidy, Ellen and Searing, Susan (1985). *Women's Legal Rights in the United States: A Selective Bibliography*. Chicago: American Library Association.

Feinberg, Renee (1986). *The Equal Rights Amendment: An Annotated Bibliography of the Issues, 1976-1985*. New York: Greenwood.

Frank, Irene M. (1993). *The Women's Desk Reference*. New York: Viking.

Frost, Wendy and Valiquette, Michele (1986). *Feminist Literary Criticism: A Bibliography of Journal Articles, 1975-1981*. New York: Garland.

Gager, Nancy (1975). *Women's Rights Almanac*. New York: Harper and Row.

Gelfand, Elissa D. and Hules, Virginia Thorndike (1985). *French Feminist Criticism: Women, Language, and Literature: An Annotated Bibliography*. New York: Garland.

Godard, Barbara (1987). *Bibliography of Feminist Criticism*. Toronto: ECW Press.

Greenberg, Hazel (1976). *The Equal Rights Amendment. A Bibliographical Study*. London: Greenwood Press.

Humm, Maggie (1987). *An Annotated Critical Bibliography of Feminist Criticism*. Boston: Hall.

Humm, Maggie (1990). *The Dictionary of Feminist Theory*. Columbus, OH: Ohio State University Press.

Kinnard, Cynthia D.(1986). *Antifeminism in American Thought: An Annotated Bibliography*. Boston: Hall.

Kolin, Philip C. (1991). *Shakespeare and Feminist Criticism: An Annotated Bibliography and Commentary*. New York: Garland.

Kramarae, Cheris and Treichler, Paula (1985). *A Feminist Dictionary*. London: Pandora Press.

Krichmar, Albert (1972). *The Women's Rights Movement in the United States, 1848-1970: A Bibliography and Sourcebook.* Metuchen, NJ: Scarecrow Press.

McPhee, Carol and Fitzgerald, Ann (1979). *Feminist Quotations: Voices of Rebels, Reformers, and Visionaries.* New York: Crowell.

Nordquist, Joan (1992). *The Feminist Movement: A Bibliography.* Santa Cruz, CA: Reference and Research Services.

Sakelliou Schultz, Liana (1994). *American Feminist Criticism: Theory and Practice: An Annotated Bibliography of Critical Texts on Poetry, 1975-1990.* New York: Garland.

Sellen, Betty-Carol and Young, Patricia A. (1987). *Feminists, Pornography and the Law: An Annotated Bibliography of Conflict, 1970-1986.* Hamden, CT: Library Professional Publications.

Steadman, Susan M. (1991). *Dramatic Revisions: An Annotated Bibliography of Feminism and Theatre, 1972-1988.* Chicago: American Library Association.

Tierney, Helen (ed.) (1989-1991). *Women's Studies Encyclopedia.* Three volumes. New York: Greenwood Press.

Tuttle, Lisa (1986). *Encyclopedia of Feminism.* New York: Facts on File Publications.

Watson, G. Llewellyn (1990). *Feminism and Women's Issues: An Annotated Bibliography and Research Guide.* New York: Garland.

Williamson, Jane (1979). *New Feminist Scholarship: A Guide to Bibliographies.* Old Westbury, NY: Feminist Press.

Wright, Elizabeth (ed.) (1992). *Feminism and Psychoanalysis: A Critical Dictionary.* New York: Blackwell.

II. FEMINIST JOURNALS

Affilia: Journal of Women and Social Work, 1986.

The *AHFAD* Journal: Women and Change, 1984.

Atlantis, 1975.

Australian Feminist Studies, 1985.

Belles Lettres, 1985.

Berkeley Women's Law Journal, 1986.

Broadsheet, 1972.

Broomstick, 1978.

CAFRA News/Novedades CAFRA, 1987.

Calyx, 1976.

Camera Obscura, 1976.

Canadian Journal of Women and the Law, 1985.

Canadian Woman Studies/Les Cahiers de la Femme, 1978.

Columbia Journal of Gender and Law, 1991.

Common Lives/Lesbian Lives, 1981.

Concerns: Newsletter of the Women's Caucus of the Modern Languages, 1971.

Connexions: An International Women's Quarterly, 1981.

Daughters of Sarah, 1974.

Differences: A Journal of Feminist Cultural Studies, 1989.

Everywoman, 1985.

Feminism & Psychology: An International Journal, 1991.

Feminist Bookstore News, 1976.

Feminist Collections: A Quarterly of Women's Studies Resources, 1980.

Feminist Issues, 1980.

Feminist Review, 1979.

Feminist Studies, 1972.

Feminist Teacher, 1984.

Feminist Voices, 1987.

Fireweed, 1978.

Frontiers: A Journal of Women Studies, 1975.

Gender and Education, 1989.

Gender and History, 1989.

Gender and Society, 1987.

Genders, 1988.

Harvard Women's Law Journal, 1978.

Health Care for Women International, 1980.

Healthsharing: A Canadian Women's Health Quarterly, 1979.

Hecate: A Women's Interdisciplinary Journal, 1975.

Heresies: A Feminist Publication of Art and Politics, 1977.

Hot Wire, 1984.

Hurricane Alice, 1983.

Hypatia, 1986.

Ikon, 1983/83.

Initiatives: Journal of NAWE, 1937.

Iowa Woman, 1980.

Iris: A Journal About Women, 1980.

Isis International Women's Book Series, 1984.

Isis-WICCE (Women's International Cross-Cultural Exchange), 1983.

Journal of Feminist Family Therapy, 1989.

Journal of Feminist Studies in Religion, 1985.

Journal of Gender Studies, 1991.

Journal of International Feminist Analysis, 1988.

Journal of Women and Aging, 1989.

Journal of Women and Religion, 1989.

Journal of Women's History, 1989.

Kalliope: A Journal of Women's Art, 1979.

Legacy, 1984.

Lesbian Contradiction: A Journal of Irreverent Feminism, 1982-1983.

Lesbian Ethics, 1984.

Lilith, 1976.

Manushi, 1979.

Media Report to Women, 1972.

Minerva: Quarterly Report of Women and the Military, 1983.

Ms. Magazine, The World of Women, 1972 and 1990.

NWSA Journal, 1988.

Off Our Backs, 1970.

On the Issues, 1983.

Peace and Freedom, 1970.

Psychology of Women Quarterly, 1976.

Resources for Feminist Research/Documentation sur la Recherche Feministe, 1979.

Room of One's Own, 1975.

Sage: A Scholarly Journal on Black Women, 1984.

Sagewoman Magazine, 1986.

Sex Roles: A Journal of Research, 1975.

Signs: Journal of Women in Culture and Society, 1975.

Sinister Wisdom: A Journal for the Lesbian Imagination in Arts and Politics, 1976.

Sojourner, 1975.

Tessera, 1983-1984.

13th Moon: A Feminist Literary Magazine, 1973.

Tradeswomen Magazine: A Quarterly Magazine for Women in Blue-Collar Work, 1981.

Trivia: A Journal of Ideas, 1982.

Trouble and Strife: A Radical Feminist Magazine, 1984.

Tulsa Studies in Women's Literature, 1982.

Wisconsin Women's Law Journal, 1985.

The Wise Woman, 1980.

WLW Journal, 1976.

Woman of Power, 1984.

Woman's Art Journal, 1980.

Women: A Cultural Review, 1990.

Women and Criminal Justice, 1989.

Women and Environments, 1976.

Women and Health, 1976.

Women and Language, 1975.

Women and Performance: A Journal of Feminist Theory, 1983.

Women and Politics, 1980.

Women and Therapy, 1982.

Women Artists News, 1975.

Women's Art Magazine, 1983.

Women's Education Des Femmes, 1982.

Women's History Review, 1992.

Women's International Network News (WIN News), 1975.

Women's Research Network News, 1988.

The Women's Review of Books, 1983.

Women's Rights Law Reporter, 1971.

Women's Studies: An Interdisciplinary Journal, 1982.

Women's Studies in Communication, 1977.

Women's Studies International Forum, 1978.

Women's Studies Quarterly, 1972.

Yale Journal of Law and Feminism, 1989.

III. FEMINISM--GENERAL

Barciauskas, Rosemary Curran and Hull, Debra Beery (1989). *Loving and Working: Reweaving Women's Public and Private Lives*. Bloomington, IN: Meyer-Stone Books.

Bernard, Jessie Shirley (1971). *Women and the Public Interest; An Essay on Policy and Protest*. Chicago: Aldine Atherton.

Browne, Alice (1987). *The Eighteenth Century Feminist Mind*. Detroit, MI: Wayne State University Press.

Charvet, John (1982). *Feminism*. London: Dent.

Davaney, Sheila Greeve (ed.) (1981). *Feminism and Process Thought: The Harvard Divinity School/Claremont Center for Process Studies Symposium Papers*. New York: Mellen Press.

Donovan, Josephine (1985). *Feminist Theory: The Intellectual Traditions of American Feminism.* New York: Ungar.

Eisenstein, Hester (1983). *Contemporary Feminist Thought.* Boston: Hall.

Eisenstein, Hester and Jardine, Alice (1980). *The Future of Difference.* Boston: Hall.

Elshtain, Jean Bethke (1990). *Power Trips and Other Journeys: Essays in Feminism as Civic Discourse.* Madison, WI: University of Wisconsin Press.

Ferguson, A. (1984). "Sex War: The Debate Between Radical and Libertarian Feminists." *Signs*, 10, 106-112.

Fox-Genovese, Elizabeth (1991). *Feminism Without Illusions.* Chapel Hill: University of North Carolina Press.

Friedan, Betty (1974). *The Feminine Mystique.* New York: Dell.
Gergen, Mary McCannen (ed.) (1989). *8). Feminist Thought and the Structure of Knowledge.* New York: New York University Press.

Gollancz, Victor (ed.) (1917). *The Making of Women. Oxford Essays in Feminism.* London: Allen and Unwin.

Gornick, Vivian and Moran, Barbara K. (eds.) (1971). *Woman in Sexist Society.* New York: Basic Books.

Grant, Judith (1993). *Fundamental Feminism: Contesting the Core Concepts of Feminism.* New York: Routledge.

Hahn, Emily (1974). *Once Upon a Pedestal.* New York: Crowell.

Hall, C. Margaret (1979). *Woman Unliberated: Difficulties and Limitations in Changing Self.* Washington: Hemisphere Pub. Corp.

Hardee, Maynor and Henry, Freeman G. (eds.) *Feminism.* Columbia, SC: University of South Carolina.

Hawksworth, Mary E. (1990). *Beyond Oppression: Feminist Theory and Political Strategy.* New York: Continuum.

Herrmann, Anne C. and Stewart, Abigail J. (eds.) (1994). *Theorizing Feminism: Parallel Trends in the Humanities and Social Sciences.* Boulder, CO: Westview.

Hirsh, Marianne and Keller, Evelyn Fox (eds.) (1990). *Conflicts in Feminism.* New York: Routledge.

hooks, bell (1984). *Feminist Theory: From Margin to Center.* Boston: South End Press.

Humm, Maggie (ed.) (1992). *Modern Feminisms: Political, Literary, Cultural.* New York: Columbia University Press.

Jaggar, Alison M. and Struhl, Paula Rothenberg (1993). *Feminist Frameworks: Alternative Theoretical Accounts of the Relations Between Women and Men*, 3rd ed. New York: McGraw-Hill.

Janeway, Elizabeth (1971). *Man's World, Woman's Place.* New York: William Morrow.

Jones, Kathleen B. and Jonasdottir, Anna G. (1988). *The Political Interests of Gender: Developing Theory and Research with a Feminist Face.* London: Sage.

Kauffman, Linda S. (1993). *American Feminist Thought at Century's End: A Reader.* Cambridge, MA: Blackwell.

Keohane, Nannerl O., Rosaldo, Michelle Zimbalist and Gelpi, Barbara Charlesworth (1982). *Feminist Theory: A Critique of Ideology.* Chicago: University of Chicago Press.

Kimball, Gayle (1981). *Women's Culture: The Women's Renaissance of the Seventies.* Metuchen, NJ: Scarecrow Press.

Millett, Kate (1970). *Sexual Politics*. Garden City, NY: Doubleday.

Morgan, Robin (1970). *Sisterhood Is Powerful: An Anthology of Writings from the Women's Liberation Movement*. New York: Vintage Books.

Oakley, Ann (1984). *Taking It Like a Woman*. London: Jonathan Cape.

O'Barr, Jean F. and Wyer, Mary (1992). *Engaging Feminism: Students Speak Up and Speak Out.* Charlottesville: University Press of Virginia.

Offen, Karen (1988). "Defining Feminism: A Comparative Historical Approach." *Signs*, 14, 119-157.

Richards, Janet Radcliffe (1980). *The Skeptical Feminist*. London: Routledge and Kegan Paul.

Richardson, Laurel and Taylor, Verta A. (1989). *Feminist Frontiers II: Rethinking Sex, Gender, and Society*. New York: Random House.

Riley, Maria (1989). *Transforming Feminism*. Kansas City, MO: Sheed and Ward.

Rivers, Caryl (1991). *More Joy Than Rage: Crossing Generations with the New Feminism*. Hanover, NH: University Press of New England.

Rowbotham, Sheila (1972). *Women, Resistance and Revolution*. New York: Pantheon Books.

Rowbotham, Sheila (1983). *Dreams and Dilemmas*. London: Virago Press.

Steinem, Gloria (1983). *Outrageous Acts and Everyday Rebellions*. New York: Holt, Rinehart and Winston.

Storkey, Elaine (1986). *What's Right with Feminism.* Grand Rapids, MI: Eerdmans.

Thompson, Mary Lou (ed.) (1970). *Voices of the New Feminism.* Boston: Beacon Press.

Walker, Barbara G. (1987). *The Skeptical Feminist: Discovering the Virgin, Mother, and Crone.* San Francisco: Harper and Row.

IV. AFRICAN-AMERICAN/ HISPANIC FEMINISM

Andolsen, Barbara Hilkert (1986). *"Daughters of Jefferson, Daughters of Bootblacks": Racism and American Feminism.* Macon, GA: Mercer University Press.

Blea, Irene I. (1992). *La Chicana and the Intersection of Race, Class, and Gender.* New York: Praeger.

Caraway, Nancie (1991). *Segregated Sisterhood: Racism and the Politics of American Feminism.* Knoxville: University of Tennessee Press.

Christian, Barbara (1985). *Black Feminist Criticism: Perspectives on Black Women Writers.* New York: Teachers College Press.

Cole, Johnnetta B. (1986). *All American Women: Lines that Divide, Ties that Bind.* New York: Free Press.

Collins, Patricia Hill (1990). *Black Feminist Thought: Knowledge, Consciousness, and the Power of Empowerment.* Boston: Unwin Hyman.

Cornwell, Anita (1983). *Black Lesbian in White America.* Tallahassee, FL: Naiad Press.

Cotera, Marta (1980). "Feminism: The Chicana and the Anglo Versions." In Melville, Margarita B. (ed.), *Twice a Minority: Mexican American Women* (pp. 217-234). St. Louis: Mosby.

Davis, Angela (1971). "The Black Woman's Role in the Community of Slaves." *Black Scholar*, 3(4), 2-15.

Davis, Angela (1981). *Women, Race, and Class*. New York: Random House.

Donaldson, Laura E. (1992). *Decolonizing Feminisms: Race, Gender, and Empire-Building*. Chapel Hill: University of North Carolina Press.

Giddings, Paula (1984). *When and Where I Enter: The Impact of Black Women on Race and Sex in America*. New York: Morrow.

Gonzales, Sylvia (1978). "The White Feminist Movement: The Chicana Perspective." In Johnson, Walter D. and O'Connor, Kathleen Blumhagen (eds.), *Women's Studies: An Interdisciplinary Collection* (pp. 65-74). Westport, CT: Greenwood.

Hersch, Blanche Glassman (1979). " 'Am I Not a Woman and a Sister?' Abolitionist Beginnings of Nineteenth Century Feminism." In Perry, Lewis and Fellman, Michael (eds.), *Anti-Slavery Reconsidered: New Perspectives on the Abolitionists* (pp. 252-283). Baton Rouge: Louisiana State University Press.

hooks, bell (1981). *Ain't I a Woman: Black Women and Feminism*. Boston: South End Press.

hooks, bell (1989). *Talking Back: Thinking Feminist. Thinking Black*. Boston: South End Press.

hooks, bell (1990). *Yearning: Race, Gender, and Cultural Politics*. Boston: South End Press.

Hull, Gloria T., Scott, Patricia Dell and Smith, Barbara (eds.) (1982). *But Some of Us Are Brave.* Old Westbury, NY: Feminist Press.

James, Stanlie M. and Busia, Abana P.A. (eds.) (1993). *Theorizing Black Feminisms: The Visionary Pragmatism of Black Women.* New York: Routledge.

Joseph, Gloria and Lewis, Jill (1981). *Common Differences: Conflicts in Black and White Feminist Perspectives.* New York: Anchor.

Lavender, Abraham D. (1986). *Ethnic Women and Feminist Values: Toward a "New" Value System.* Lanham, MD: University Press of America.

Solomon, Irvin D. (1989). *Feminism and Black Activism in Contemporary America: An Ideological Assessment.* New York: Greenwood Press.

Williams, Patricia J. (1991). *The Alchemy of Race and Rights.* Cambridge: Harvard University Press.

V. ECOFEMINISM

Adams, Carol Jo (ed.) (1992). *Ecofeminism and the Sacred.* New York: Continuum.

Biehl, Janet (1990). *Rethinking Ecofeminist Politics.* Boston: South End Press.

Bigwood, Carol (1993). *Earth Muse: Feminism, Nature, and Art.* Philadelphia: Temple University Press.

Caldecott, Leonie and Leland, Stephanie (eds.) (1983). *Reclaim the Earth.* London: The Women's Press.

Caputi, Jane (1993). *Gossips, Gorgons and Crones: The Fates of the Earth.* Santa Fe, NM: Bear.

Collard, Andree and Contrucci, Joyce (1989). *Rape of the Wild: Man's Violence Against Animals and the Earth.* Bloomington: Indiana University Press.

Diamond, Irene and Wilcox, Helen (eds.) (1990). *Reweaving the World: The Emergence of Ecofeminism.* San Francisco, CA: Sierra Club.

Gaard, Greta (ed.) (1993). *Ecofeminism: Women, Animals, and Nature.* Philadelphia: Temple University Press.

Griffin, Susan (1978). *Woman and Nature: The Roaring Inside Her.* New York: Harper and Row.

Merchant, Carolyn (1980). *The Death of Nature: Women, Ecology, and the Scientific Revolution.* New York: Harper and Row.

Merchant, Carolyn (1992). *Radical Ecology: The Search for a Livable World.* New York: Routledge.

Miess, Marea and Shiva, Vandana (1993). *Ecofeminism.* Halifax, NS: Zed Books.

Plumwood, Val (1993). *Feminism and the Mastery of Nature.* New York: Routledge.

Primavesi, Anne (1991). *The Apocalypse to Genesis: Ecology, Feminism, and Christianity.* Minneapolis: Fortress Press.

Ruether, Rosemary Radford (1992). *Gaia and God: An Ecofeminist Theology of Earth Healing.* San Francisco: Harper San Francisco.

Seager, Joni (1993). *Earth Follies: Coming to Feminist Terms with the Global Environmental Crisis.* New York: Routledge.

Sontheimer, Sally (ed.) (1991). *Women and the Environment: A Reader: Crisis and Development in the Third World.* New York: Monthly Review Press.

VI. EXISTENTIALIST FEMINISM

Ascher, Carol (1981). *Simone de Beauvoir: A Life of Freedom.* Boston: Beacon Press.

Beauvoir, Simone de (1963). *Memoirs of a Dutiful Daughter.* Harmondsworth, England: Penguin Books.

Beauvoir, Simone de (1965). *The Prime of Life.* Harmondsworth, England: Penguin Books.

Beauvoir, Simone de (1967). *The Ethics of Ambiguity.* New York: Citadel Press.

Beauvoir, Simone de (1974). *The Second Sex.* New York: Vintage Books.

Beauvoir, Simone de (1984). *Adieux: A Farewell to Sartre.* New York: Pantheon Books.

Jardine, Alice (1979). "Interview with Simone de Beauvoir." *Signs*, 5, 224-236.

Keefe, Terry (1983). *Simone de Beauvoir.* Totowa, NJ: Barnes and Noble.

Kuykendall, Eleanor H. (1989). "Linguistic Ambivalence in Simone de Beauvoir's Feminist Theory." In Young, Iris and Allen, Jeffner (eds.), *The Thinking Muse* (pp. 1-30). Bloomington: Indiana University Press.

Lloyd, Genevieve (1984). *The Man of Reason: "Male" and "Female" in Western Philosophy.* Minneapolis: University of Minnesota Press.

McCall, Dorothy Kaufmann (1979-1980). "Simone de Beauvoir, *The Second Sex*, and Jean-Paul Sartre." *Signs*, 5, 209-223.

Schwarzer, Alice (1984). *After the Second Sex.* New York: Pantheon Books.

Simons, Margaret A. and Benjamin, Jessica (1979). "Simone de Beauvoir: An Interview." *Feminist Studies,* 5, 330-345.

Whitmarsh, Anne (1981). *Simone de Beauvoir and the Limits of Commitment.* Cambridge: Cambridge University Press.

VII. LIBERAL FEMINISM

Berg, Barbara (1979). *The Remembered Gate: Origins of American Feminism.* New York: Oxford University Press.

Bird, Caroline and Briller, Sara Well (1969). *Born Female: The High Cost of Keeping Women Down.* New York: Pocket Books.

Brennan, Teresa and Pateman, Carole (1979). "'Mere Auxiliaries to the Commonwealth': Women and the Origins of Liberalism." *Political Studies,* 27, 183-200.

Clark, Lorenne M.G. (1979). "Women and Locke: Who Owns the Apples in the Garden of Eden?" In Clark, Lorenne M.G. and Lange, Lydia (eds.), *The Sexism of Social and Political Theory* (pp. 16-40). Toronto: University of Toronto Press.

Dowling, Colette (1981). *The Cinderella Syndrome: Women's Hidden Fear of Independence.* New York: Summit Books.

Eisenstein, Zillah (1982). "The Sexual Politics of the New Right: Understanding the 'Crisis of Liberalism' for the 1980's." *Signs,* 7, 567-588.

Eisenstein, Zillah (1984). *Feminism and Sexual Equality: Crisis in Liberal America.* New York: Monthly Review Press.

Eisenstein, Zillah (1986). *The Radical Future of Liberal Feminism.* Boston: Northeastern University Press.

Eisenstein, Zillah (1994). *The Color of Gender: Reimaging Democracy.* Berkeley: University of California Press.

Elshtain, Jean Bethke (1981). *Public Man, Private Woman.* Princeton, NJ: Princeton University Press.

Elshtain, Jean Bethke (1982). "Feminism, Family, and Community." *Dissent*, 29, 419-441.

Evans, Sara (1983). "The Politics of Liberal Feminism." *Social Science Quarterly*, 64, 880-897.

Ferguson, Kathy E. (1978). "Liberalism and Oppression: Emma Goldman and the Anarchist Feminist Alternative." In McGrath, Michael C.G. (ed.), *Liberalism and the Modern Polity* (pp. 93-118). New York: Marcel Dekker.

Ferguson, Kathy E. (1980). *Self, Society and Womankind: The Dialectic of Liberation.* Westport, CT: Greenwood Press.

Flammang, Janet Angela (1983). "Feminist Theory: The Question of Power." *Current Perspectives on Social Theory*, 4, 37-83.

Guttmann, Amy (1980). *Liberal Equality.* New York: Cambridge University Press.

Jaggar, Alison M. (1977). "On Sexual Equality." In English, Jan (ed.), *Sex Equality.* Englewood Cliffs, NJ: Prentice-Hall.

Krouse, Richard W. (1981). "Patriarchal Liberalism and Beyond: From John Stuart Mill to Harriet Taylor." In Elshtain, Jean Bethke (ed.), *The Family in Political Thought* (pp.145-172). Amherst: University of Massachusetts Press.

McElroy, Wendy (1982). *Freedom, Feminism, and the State: An Overview of Individualist Feminism.* Washington, DC: Cato Institute.

Martin, Jane Roland (1985). *Reclaiming a Conversation: The Ideal of the Educated Woman.* New Haven, CT: Yale University Press.

Nicholson, Linda J. (1980). *Gender and History: The Limits of Social Theory in the Age of the Family.* New York: Columbia University Press.

Pateman, Carole (1979). *The Problem of Political Obligation: A Critique of Liberal Theory.* Berkeley: University of California Press.

Phillips, Anne (1993). *Democracy and Difference.* University Park: Pennsylvania State University Press.

Phillips, Anne (ed.) (1990). *Feminism and Equality.* New York: New York University Press.

Rossi, Alice (1964). "Equality Between the Sexes: An Immodest Proposal." In Lifton, Robert J. (ed.), *The Woman in America* (pp. 98-143). Boston: Beacon Press.

Rossi, Alice S. (ed.) (1970). *Essays on Sex Equality. John Stuart Mill and Harriet Taylor Mill.* Chicago: University of Chicago Press.

Sabrosky, Judith A. (1979). *From Rationality to Liberation: The Evolution of Feminist Ideology.* Westport, CT: Greenwood.

Salper, Roberta (1972). *Female Liberation; History and Current Politics.* New York: Knopf.

Taylor, Joan Kennedy (1992). *Reclaiming the Mainstream: Individualist Feminism Rediscovered.* Buffalo, NY: Prometheus Books.

Trebilcot, Joyce (1982). "Two Forms of Androgyny." In Vetterling-Braggin, Mary (ed.), *"Femininity," "Masculinity,"* and *"Androgyny"* (pp. 161-170). Totowa, NJ: Rowman and Littlefield.

Wollstonecraft, Mary (1983). *A Mary Wollstonecraft Reader.* New York: New American Library.

Zinsser, Judith P. (1993). *History and Feminism: A Glass Half Full.* New York: Twayne Publishers.

VIII. MARXIST FEMINISM

Assiter, Alison (1993). *Althusser and Feminism.* Boulder, CO: Westview.

Barrett, Michele (1980). *Women's Oppression Today: Problems in Marxist Feminist Analysis.* London: Verso.

Bebel, August (1971). *Woman Under Socialism.* New York: Schocken Books.

Beechey, Veronica (1977). "Some Notes on Female Wage Labour in Capitalist Production." *Capital and Class,* 1977, 45-66.

Bell, Susan Groag and Offen, Karen M. (eds.) (1983). *Women, the Family, and Freedom: The Debate in Documents.* Stanford: Stanford University Press.

Benston, Margaret (1969). "The Political Economy of Women's Liberation." *Monthly Review,* 21(4), 13-27.

Boserup, Esther (1970). *Women's Role in Economic Development.* London: George Allen and Unwin.

Brenner, Johanna and Holmstrom, Nancy (1983). "Women's Self-Organization: Theory and Strategy." *Monthly Review,* 34(11), 34-52.

Bridenthal, Renate (1976). "The Dialectics of Production and Reproduction in History." *Radical America,* 10(2), 3-11.

Chao, Paul (1977). *Woman Under Communism: Family in Russia and China.* Bayside, NY: General Hall.

330 Bibliography

Coulson, Margaret, Magas, Branka and Wainwright, Hilary (1975). "The Housewife and Her Labour Under Capitalism: A Critique." *New Left Review,* 89, 59-71.

Cowan, Ruth Schwartz (1976). "The 'Industrial Revolution' in the Home: Household Technology and Social Change in the Twentieth Century." *Technology and Culture,* 17, 1-23.

Dalla Costa, Mariarosa and James, Selma (1972). *The Power of Women and the Subversion of the Community.* Bristol, England: Falling Wall Press.

Davin, Delia (1976). *Woman-Work: Women and the Party in Revolutionary China.* Oxford: Clarendon Press.

Drinnon, Richard (1970). *Rebel in Paradise. A Biography of Emma Goldman.* Boston: Beacon Press.

Dunayevskaya, Raya (1982). *Rosa Luxemburg, Women's Liberation, and Marx's Philosophy of Revolution.* Atlantic Highlands, NJ: Humanities Press.

Eastman, Crystal (1978). *On Women and Revolution.* New York: Oxford University Press.

Engels, Friedrich (1972). *The Origin of the Family, Private Property, and the State.* New York: International Publishers.

Feldberg, Roslyn L. (1984). "Comparable Worth: Toward Theory and Practice in the United States." *Signs,* 10, 311-328.

Flax, Jane (1981). "Do Feminists Need Marxism?" In *Building Feminist Theory: Essays from "Quest," a feminist quarterly* (pp. 174-185). New York: Longman.

Foreman, Ann (1977). *Femininity as Alienation: Women and the Family in Marxism and Psychoanalysis.* London: Pluto Press.

Fox, Bonnie (ed.) (1980). *Hidden in the Household: Women's Domestic Labour Under Capitalism.* Toronto: Women's Educational Press.

Gardiner, Susan (1975). "Women's Domestic Labour." *New Left Review,* 89, 47-58.

Garson, Barbara (1975). *All the Livelong Day: The Meaning and Demeaning of Routine Work.* New York: Penguin Books.

Gerstein, Ira (1973). "Domestic Work and Capitalism." *Radical America,* 7, 101-128.

Glazer-Malbin, Nona (1976). "Housework." *Signs,* 1, 905-922.

Goldman, Emma (1970). *The Traffic in Women and Other Essays on Feminism.* Albion, CA: Times Change Press.

Guettel, Charnie (1974). *Marxism and Feminism.* Toronto: Women's Educational Press.

Hamilton, Roberta (1978). *The Liberation of Women. A Study of Patriarchy and Capitalism.* London: Allen and Unwin.

Hartmann, Heidi (1976). "Capitalism, Patriarchy, and Job Segregation by Sex." *Signs,* 1, 733-776.

Hartmann, Heidi (1981). "The Unhappy Marriage of Marxism and Feminism: Towards a More Progressive Union." In Sargent, Lydia (ed.), *Women and Revolution: A Discussion of the Unhappy Marriage of Marxism and Feminism* (pp. 1-41). Boston: South End Press.

Heilbroner, Robert (1980). *Marxism: For and Against.* New York: Norton.

Holmstrom, Nancy (1982). "'Women's Work,' the Family and Capitalism." *Science and Society,* 45, 186-211.

Holt, Alix (1974). "Marxism and Women's Oppression: Bolshevik Theory and Practice in the 1920s." In Yedlin,

Tova (ed.), *Women in Eastern Europe and the Soviet Union* (pp. 87-114). New York: Free Press.

Holt, Alix (ed.) (1977). *Selected Writings of Alexandra Kollontai.* Westport, CT: Hill.

Humphries, Jane (1977). "The Working Class Family, Women's Liberation and Class Struggle: The Case of Nineteenth Century British History." *Review of Radical Political Economics*, 9(3), 25-41.

Jaggar, Alison M. (1983). *Feminist Politics and Human Nature.* Totowa, NJ: Rowman and Allanheld.

Kuhn, Annette and Wolpe, Ann Marie (eds.) (1978). *Feminism and Materialism: Women and Modes of Production.* Boston: Routledge and Kegan Paul.

Landes, Joan B. (1977). "Women, Labor and Family Life: A Theoretical Perspective." *Science and Society*, 41, 386-409.

Lane, Ann J. (1976). "Woman in Society: A Critique of Friedrich Engels." In Carroll, Bernice A. (ed.), *Liberating Women's History* (pp. 4-26). Champaign: University of Illinois Press.

La Vigna, Claire (1978). "The Marxist Ambivalence toward Women: Between Socialism and Feminism in the Italian Socialist Party." In Boxer, Marilyn J. and Quataert, Jean H. (eds.), *Socialist Women: European Socialist Feminism in the Nineteenth and Early Twentieth Centuries* (pp. 146-181). New York: Elsevier North-Holland.

Lenin, Vladimir Ilich (1975). *The Emancipation of Women: From the Writings of V. I. Lenin.* New York: International Press.

Lopate, Carol (1974). "Pay for Housework." *Social Policy*, 5(3), 27-31.

MacKinnon, Catharine A. (1982). "Feminism, Marxism, Method and the State: An Agenda for Theory." *Signs,* 7, 515-544.

Malos, Ellen (ed.) (1980). *The Politics of Housework.* London: Allison and Busby.

Menon, Usha (1982). "Women and Household Labor." *Social Scientists,* 10(7), 30-42.

Meulenbelt, Anja (1978). "On the Political Economy of Domestic Labor." *Quest: a feminist quarterly,* 4(2),18-31.

Meulenbelt, Anja (ed.)(1984). *A Creative Tension: Key Issues of Socialist Feminism.* Boston: South End Press.

Molyneux, Maxine (1979). "Beyond the Domestic Labour Debate." *New Left Review,* 116, 3-27.

Mullaney, Marie Marmo (1983). *Revolutionary Women: Gender and the Socialist Revolutionary Role.* New York: Praeger.

Quick, Paddy (1977). "The Class Nature of Women's Oppression." *Review of Radical Political Economics,* 9(3), 42-53.

Rapp, Rayna (1977). "Gender and Class: An Archaeology of Knowledge Concerning the Origin of the State." *Dialectical Anthropology,* 2, 309-316.

Reed, Evelyn (1970). *Problems of Woman's Liberation.* New York: Pathfinder Press.

Rowbotham, Sheila (1973). *Woman's Consciousness, Man's World.* Baltimore, MD: Penguin Books.

Sacks, Karen (1975). "Engels Revisited: Women, the Organization of Production and Private Property." In Reiter, Rayna R. (ed.), *Toward an Anthropology of Women* (pp. 211-234). New York: Monthly Review Press.

Saffiote, Heleieth I.B. (1978). *Women in Class Society*. New York: Monthly Review Press.

Sargent, Lydia (ed.) (1981). *Women and Revolution: A Discussion of the Unhappy Marriage of Marxism and Feminism*. Boston: South End Press.

Schwartz, Nancy L. (1979). "Distinction Between Public and Private Life: Marx on the Zoon Politikon." *Political Theory*, 7, 245-266.

Secombe, Wally (1973). "The Housewife and Her Labor Under Capitalism." *New Left Review*, 83, 3-24.

Thorne, Barrie and Yalom, Marilyn (eds.) (1982). *Rethinking the Family: Some Feminist Questions*. New York: Longman.

Vogel, Lise (1983). *Marxism and the Oppression of Women: Towards a Unitary Theory*. New Brunswick, NJ: Rutgers University Press.

Young, Kate, Wolkowitz, Carol and McCullagh, Roslyn (eds.) (1981). *Of Marriage and the Market: Women's Subordination in International Perspective*. London: CSE Books.

Zaretsky, Eli (1974). "Socialism and Feminism III: Socialist Politics and the Family." *Socialist Revolution*, 4, 83-98.

Zaretsky, Eli (1976). *Capitalism, the Family and Personal Life*. London: Pluto Press.

IX. POSTMODERN FEMINIST THOUGHT

Agger, Ben (1993). *Gender, Culture, and Power: Toward a Feminist Postmodern Critical Theory*. Westport, CT: Praeger.

Bree, Germaine (1973). *Women Writers in France.* New Brunswick, NJ: Rutgers University Press.

Brodribb, Somer (1993). *Nothing of Postmodernism.* New York: New York University Press.

Burke, Carolyn Greenstein (1978). "Report from Paris: Women's Writing and the Women's Movement." *Signs,* 4, 843-854.

Cixous, Hélène (1971). "The Laugh of the Medusa." In Marks, Elaine and Courtivron, Isabelle de (eds.), *New French Feminisms* (pp. 245-264). New York: Schocken Books.

Cixous, Hélène (1971). "Sorties." In Marks, Elaine and Courtivron, Isabelle de (eds.), *New French Feminisms* (pp. 90-98). New York: Schocken Books.

Cixous, Hélène (1981). "Castration or Decapitation?" *Signs,* 7, 41-55.

Clement, Catherine (1983). *The Lives and Legends of Jacques Lacan.* New York: Columbia University Press.

Diamond, Irene and Quinby, Lee (eds.) (1988). *Feminism and Foucault: Reflections on Resistance.* Boston: Northeastern University Press.

Fauré, Christine (1981). "The Twilight of the Goddesses, or the Intellectual Crisis of French Feminism." *Signs,* 7, 81-86.

Irigaray, Luce (1980). "When Our Lips Speak Together." *Signs,* 6, 4-28.

Irigaray, Luce (1985). *This Sex Which Is Not One.* Ithaca, NY: Cornell University Press.

Kristéva, Julia (1982). *Desire in Language.* New York: Columbia University Press.

Kristéva, Julia (1982). *Powers of Horror.* New York: Columbia University Press.

Kristéva, Julia (1984). *Revolution in Poetic Languages.* New York: Columbia University Press.

Mitchell, Juliet and Rose, Jacqueline (eds.) (1982). *Feminine Sexuality: Jacques Lacan and the Ecole Freudienne* New York: Norton.

Moi, Toril (ed.) (1987). *French Feminist Thought: A Reader.* New York: Blackwell.

Tristan, Anne and Pisan, Annie de (1977). *Histoires du M.L.F.* Paris: Calmann-Lévy.

X. RADICAL FEMINISM

A. Reproduction

Arditti, Rita, Klein, Renate Duelli and Minden, Shelley (eds.) (1984). *Test-Tube Women: What Future for Motherhood?* London: Pandora Press.

Atwood, Margaret (1985). *The Handmaid's Tale.* New York: Fawcett Crest Books.

Banks, Joseph A. and Banks, Olive (1964). *Feminism and Family Planning in Victorian England.* Liverpool: Liverpool University Press.

Bridenthal, Renate, et al. (eds.) (1984). *When Biology Became Destiny: Women in Weimar and Nazi Germany.* New York: Monthly Review.

Cooey, Paula M., Farmer, Sharon A. and Ross, Mary Ellen (1987). *Embodied Love: Sensuality and Relationship as Feminist Values.* San Francisco: Harper and Row.

Corea, Genea (1985). *The Mother Machine: Reproductive Technologies from Artificial Insemination to Artificial Wombs.* New York: Harper and Row.

Donchin, Anne (1986). "The Future of Mothering: Reproductive Technology and Feminist Theory." *Hypatia,* 1, 130-138.

Dowrick, S. and Grundberg, S. (1980). *Why Children?* London: The Women's Press.

Eisenstein, Zillah R. (1988). *The Female Body and the Law.* Berkeley: University of California Press.

Firestone, Shulamith (1971). *The Dialectic of Sex: The Case for Feminist Revolution.* New York: Bantam Books.

O'Brien, Mary (1981). *The Politics of Reproduction.* Boston: Routledge and Kegan Paul.

Petchesky, Rosalind Pollack (1980). "Reproductive Freedom: Beyond 'A Woman's Right to Choose.'" *Signs,* 5, 661-685.

Piercy, Marge (1976). *Woman on the Edge of Time.* New York: Fawcett Crest Books.

Zak, Michele Wender and Moots, Patricia A. (1983). *Women and the Politics of Culture: Studies in the Sexual Economy.* New York: Longman.

B. Mothering

Allen, Jeffner (1986). "Motherhood: The Annihilation of Women." In Pearsall, Marilyn (ed.), *Women and Values: Readings in Recent Feminist Philosophy* (pp. 91-101). Belmont, CA: Wadsworth.

Chesler, Phyllis (1988). *Sacred Bond: The Legacy of Baby M.* New York: Times Books.

Dornbusch, Sanford M. and Strober, Myra H. (1988). *Feminism, Children, and the New Families.* New York: Guilford Press.

Ferguson, Ann (1986). "Motherhood and Sexuality: Some Feminist Questions." *Hypatia*, 1(2), 3-22.

Koven, Seth and Michel, Sonya (1993). *Mothers of a New World: Maternalist Politics and the Origins of Welfare States.* New York: Routledge.

Lazaro, Reyes (1986). "Feminism and Motherhood: O'Brien vs. Beauvoir." *Hypatia*, 1, 87-102.

Mellown, Mary Ruth (1985). "An Incomplete Picture: The Debate About Surrogate Motherhood." *Harvard Women's Law Journal*, 8, 231-246.

Oakley, Ann (1974). *Woman's Work: The Housewife, Past and Present.* New York: Pantheon Books.

Rich, Adrienne (1976). *Of Woman Born: Motherhood as Experience and Institution.* New York: Norton.

Rossi, Alice S. (1977). "A Biosocial Perspective on Parenting." *Daedalus*, 106(2), 1-32.

Trebilcot, Joyce (ed.) (1984). *Mothering: Essays in Feminist Theory.* Totowa, NJ: Rowman and Allanheld.

C. Gender and Sexuality

Barry, Kathleen (1979). *Female Sexual Slavery.* Englewood Cliffs, NJ: Prentice-Hall.

Bem, Sandra Lipsitz (1993). *The Lenses of Gender: An Essay on the Social Reproduction of Male Power.* New Haven, CT: Yale University Press.

Boston Women's Health Book Collective (1992). *The New Our Bodies, Ourselves.* New York: Simon and Schuster.

Brownmiller, Susan (1975). *Against Our Will: Men, Women and Rape.* New York: Simon and Schuster.

Bunch, Charlotte and Myron, Nancy (eds.) (1974). *Class and Feminism: A Collection of Essays from "The Furies."* Baltimore, MD: Diana Press.

Chafetz, Janet Saltzman (1978). *Masculine/Feminine or Human?* Itasca, IL: Peacock.

Clark, Lorenne and Lewis, Debra (1977). *Rape: The Price of Coercive Sexuality.* Toronto: Women's Educational Press.

Coontz, Stephanie and Henderson, Peta (ed.) (1986). *Women's Work, Men's Property: The Origins of Gender and Class.* New York: Schocken.

Coveney, Lal, Jackson, Margaret, Jeffreys, Sheila, Kay, Leslie and Mahoney, Pat (eds.) (1984). *The Sexuality Papers: Male Sexuality and the Social Control of Women.* London: Hutchinson.

Daly, Mary (1978). *Gyn/Ecology: The Metaethics of Radical Feminism.* Boston: Beacon Press.

Dworkin, Andrea (1974). *Woman Hating: A Radical Look at Sexuality.* New York: E. P. Dutton.

Dworkin, Andrea (1981). *Our Blood: Prophecies and Discourses on Sexual Politics.* New York: G. P. Putnam.

Ferguson, Ann (1984). "The Feminist Sexuality Debates." *Signs*, 10, 106-135.

Frankfort, Ellen (1973). *Vaginal Politics.* New York: Bantam Books.

French, Marilyn (1985). *Beyond Power: On Women, Men, and Morals.* New York: Summit Books.

Frye, Marilyn (1983). *The Politics of Reality: Essays in Feminist Theory.* Trumansburg, NY: Crossing Press.

Gilman, Sander L. (1985). *Difference and Pathology: Stereotypes of Sexuality, Race, and Madness.* Ithaca: Cornell University Press.

Ginsburg, Faye D. Tsing and Lowenhaupt, Anna (1990). *Uncertain Terms: Negotiating Gender in American Culture.* Boston: Beacon Press.

Gordon, Linda (1977). *Woman's Body, Woman's Right: A Social History of Birth Control in America.* New York: Penguin Books.

Griffin, Susan (1979). *Rape: The Power of Consciousness.* San Francisco: Harper and Row.

Heath, Stephen (1982). *The Sexual Fix.* London: Macmillan.

Jeffrays, Sheila (1985). *The Spinster and Her Enemies: Feminism and Sexuality, 1880-1930.* Boston: Pandora Press.

Johnston, Carolyn (1992). *Sexual Power: Feminism and the Family in America.* Tuscaloosa: University of Alabama Press.

Koedt, Anne, Levine, Ellen and Rapone, Anita (eds.) (1973). *Radical Feminism.* New York: Quadrangle Books.

Linden, Robin Ruth, Pagano, Darlene R., Russell, Diana E.H. and Star, Susan Leigh (eds.) (1982). *Against Sadomasochism: A Radical Feminist Analysis.* East Palo Alto, CA: Frog in the Well Press.

Lipman-Blumen, Jean (1984). *Gender Role and Power.* Englewood Cliffs, NJ: Prentice-Hall.

Lorber, Judith and Farrell, Susan A.(1991). *The Social Construction of Gender.* Newbury Park, CA: Sage Publications.

Martin, Del (1976). *Battered Wives.* New York: Pocket Books.

Milan Women's Bookstore Collective (1990). *Sexual Difference: A Theory of Social-Symbolic Practice.* Bloomington: Indiana University Press.

Oakley, Ann (1972). *Sex, Gender and Society.* London: Maurice Temple Smith.

Pateman, Carole (1988). *The Sexual Contract.* Stanford: Stanford University Press.

Rubin, Gayle (1975). "The Traffic in Women: Notes on the Political Economy of Sex." In Reiter, Rayna R. (ed.), *Toward an Anthropology of Women* (pp. 157-210). New York: Monthly Review Press.

Schechter, Susan (1982). *Women and Male Violence.* Boston: South End Press.

Schur, Edwin M. (1984). *Labeling Women Deviant: Gender, Stigma, and Social Control.* New York: Random House.

Shafer, Carolyn M. and Frye, Marilyn. (1986). "Rape and Respect." In Pearsall, Marilyn (ed.), *Women and Values: Readings in Recent Feminist Philosophy* (pp. 188-196). Belmont, CA: Wadsworth.

Shulman, Alix Kates (1980). "Sex and Power: Sexual Bases of Radical Feminism." *Signs,* 5, 590-604.

Snitow, Ann, Stansell, Christine and Thompson, Sharon (eds.) (1983). *Powers of Desire: The Politics of Sexuality.* New York: Monthly Review Press.

Unger, Rhoda Kesler (1989). *Representations: Social Constructions of Gender.* Amityville, NY: Baywood.

Vance, Carole S. (ed.) (1984). *Pleasure and Danger: Exploring Female Sexuality.* Boston: Routledge and Kegan Paul.

Willis, Ellen (1982). "Towards a Feminist Sexual Revolution." *Social Text*, 2(3), 3-71.

D. Pornography

Berger, Ronald J., Searles, Patricia and Cottle, Charles E. (1991). *Feminism and Pornography.* Westport, CT: Praeger.

Caught Looking, Inc. (1988). *Caught Looking: Feminism, Pornography and Censorship.* Seattle: Real Comet Press.

Dworkin, Andrea (1981). *Pornography: Men Possessing Women.* New York: Perigee Books.

Griffin, Susan (1981). *Pornography and Silence.* New York: Harper and Row.

Lederer, Laura (ed.) (1980). *Take Back the Night: Women on Pornography.* New York: William Morrow.

Leidholdt, Dorchen and Raymond, Janice G. (1990). *The Sexual Liberals and the Attack on Feminism.* New York: Pergamon Press.

Linz, Daniel, Turner, Charles W., Hesse, Bradford W. and Penrod, Steven D. (1984). "Bases of Liability for Injuries Produced by Media Portrayals of Violent Pornography." In Malamuth, Neil M. and Donnerstein, Edward (eds.), *Pornography and Sexual Aggression* (pp. 277-282). New York: Academic Press.

McCarthy, Sarah J. (1980). "Pornography, Rape, and the Cult of Macho." *The Humanist*, 40(5), 11-20.

MacKinnon, Catharine A. (1985). "Pornography, Civil Rights, and Speech." *Harvard Civil Rights-Civil Liberties Law Review*, 20, 39-41.

MacKinnon, Catharine A. (1993). *Only Words*. Cambridge, MA: Harvard University Press.

Russell, Diana E.H. (ed.) (1993). *Making Violence Sexy: Feminist Views on Pornography*. New York: Teachers College Press.

Soble, Alan (1986). *Pornography: Marxism, Feminism and the Future of Sexuality*. New Haven, CT: Yale University Press.

US Commission on Obscenity and Pornography (1970). *Report of the Commission on Obscenity and Pornography*. Washington, DC: US Government Printing Office.

E. Lesbianism

Atkinson, Ti-Grace (1973). "Lesbianism and Feminism." In Birkby, Phyllis, et al. (eds.) (1973). *Amazon Expedition: A Lesbian-Feminist Anthology*. Washington, DC: Times Change Press.

Atkinson, Ti-Grace (1974). *Amazon Odyssey*. New York: Links.

Atkinson, Ti-Grace (1986). "Radical Feminism: A Declaration of War." In Pearsall, Marilyn (ed.), *Women and Values: Readings in Recent Feminist Philosophy* (pp. 124-127). Belmont, CA: Wadsworth.

Beck, Evelyn Torton (ed.) (1982). *Nice Jewish Girls: A Lesbian Anthology*. Watertown, MA: Persephone Press.

Brooks, Virginia (1981). *Minority Stress and Lesbian Women*. Lexington, MA: Heath.

Bulkin, Elly, Pratt, Minnie Bruce and Smith, Barbara (1984). *Yours in Struggle.* New York: Long Haul Press.

Bunch, Charlotte (1975). "Lesbians in Revolt." In Myron, Nancy and Bunch, Charlotte (eds.), *Lesbianism and the Women's Movement.* Baltimore, MD: Diana Press.

Bunch, Charlotte (1987). *Passionate Politics: Feminist Theory in Action.* New York: St. Martin's Press.

Califia, Pat (1983). *Sapphistry: The Book of Lesbian Sexuality.* Tallahassee, FL: Naiad Press.

Cockes, Joan (1984). "Wordless Emotions: Some Critical Reflections on Radical Feminism." *Politics and Society,* 13, 27-58.

Ditzinger, Celia and Perkins, Rachel (1993). *Changing Our Minds: Lesbian Feminism and Psychology.* New York: New York University Press.

Goodman, Gerre, Lakey, George, Lashof, Judy and Thorne, Erika (1983). *No Turning Back: Lesbian and Gay Liberation for the '80s.* Philadelphia: New Society Publishers.

Grahn, Judy (1979). *The Work of a Common Woman.* New York: St. Martin's Press.

Grier, Barbara and Reid, Colette (eds.) (1976). *The Lavender Herring: Lesbian Essays from "The Ladder."* Baltimore, MD: Diana Press.

Johnston, Jill (1974). *Lesbian Nation: The Feminist Solution.* New York: Simon and Schuster.

Lorde, Audre (1981). "An Open Letter to Mary Daly." In Moraga, Cherrie and Anzaldúa, Gloria (eds.), *This Bridge Called My Back: Writings of Radical Women of Color* (p. 97). Watertown, MA: Persephone Press.

Myron, Nancy and Bunch, Charlotte (eds.) (1975). *Lesbianism and the Women's Movement*. Baltimore, MD: Diana Press.

Phelan, Shane (1989). *Identity Politics. Lesbian Feminism and the Limits of Community*. Philadelphia: Temple University Press.

Ponse, Barbara (1978). *Identities in the Lesbian World*. Westport, CT: Greenwood Press.

Raymond, Janice (1979). *The Transsexual Empire*. Boston: Beacon Press.

Raymond, Janice (1986). *A Passion for Friends*. Boston: Beacon Press.

Rich, Adrienne (1980). "Compulsory Heterosexuality and Lesbian Existence." *Signs*, 5, 631-690.

Rule, Jane (1982). *Lesbian Images*. Trumansburg, NY: Crossing Press.

Samois (1981). *Coming to Power: Writings and Graphics on Lesbian S/M*. Palo Alto, CA: Up Press.

Wittig, Monique (1971). *Les Guérillères*. New York: Viking.

XI. SOCIALIST FEMINISM

Bartky, Sandra L. (1982). "Narcissism, Femininity and Alienation." *Social Theory and Practice*, 8, 127-144.

Berch, Bettina (1982). *The Endless Day: The Political Economy of Women and Work*. New York: Harcourt Brace Jovanovich.

Boxer, Marilyn J. and Quataert, Jean H. (eds.) (1978). *Socialist Women European Socialist Feminism in the Nineteenth and Early Twentieth Centuries*. New York: Elsevier North-Holland.

Buhle, Mari Jo (1981). *Women and American Socialism, 1870-1920.* Urbana: University of Illinois Press.

Caulfield, Mina Davis (1974). "Imperialism, the Family, and Cultures of Resistance." *Socialist Revolution,* 20(4), 67-85.

Delphy, Christine (1984). *Close to Home: A Materialist Analysis of Women's Oppression.* Amherst: University of Massachusetts Press.

Easton, Barbara (1974). "Socialism and Feminism I: Toward a Unified Movement." *Socialist Revolution,* 4(1), 59-67.

Ehrenreich, Barbara (1981). "Life Without Father: Reconsidering Socialist-Feminist Theory." *Socialist Review,* 14(1), 48-57.

Ehrenreich Barbara, Berkeley-Oakland Women's Union, Russell, Michelle and Dudley, Barbara (1975). "The National Conference on Socialist Feminism." *Socialist Revolution,* 5(4), 85-116.

Ehrenreich, Barbara and English, Deirdre (1975). "Microbes and the Manufacture of Housework." *Socialist Revolution,* 5(4), 5-40.

Eisenstein, Zillah (ed.) (1979). *Capitalist Patriarchy and the Case for Socialist Feminism.* New York: Monthly Review Press.

Ferguson, Ann (1979). "Women as a New Revolutionary Class." In Walker, Pat (ed.), *Between Labor and Capital* (pp. 279-309). Boston: South End Press.

Ferguson, Ann (1991). *Sexual Democracy: Women, Oppression, and Revolution.* Boulder, CO: Westview Press.

Haber, Barbara (1979). "Is Personal Life Still a Political Issue?" *Feminist Studies,* 5, 417-430.

Hansen, Karen V. and Philipson, Ilene J. (eds.) (1990). *Women, Class, and the Feminist Imagination: A Socialist-Feminist Reader.* Philadelphia: Temple University Press.

Hartmann, Heidi (1981). "The Family as the Locus of Gender, Class, and Political Struggle: The Example of Housework." *Signs,* 6, 366-394.

Hartmann, Heidi and Markusen, Ann R. (1980). "Contemporary Marxist Theory and Practice: A Feminist Critique." *Review of Radical Political Economics,* 12(2), 87-93.

Hartsock, Nancy (1985). *Money, Sex, and Power.* Boston: Northeastern University Press.

Martin, Gloria (1978). *Socialist Feminism: The First Decade, 1966-1976.* Seattle: Freedom Socialist Publications.

Meyer, Alfred G. (1985). *The Feminism and Socialism of Lily Braun.* Bloomington: Indiana University Press.

Miller, Sally M. (1981). *Flawed Liberation: Socialism and Feminism.* Westport, CT: Greenwood Press.

Mitchell, Juliet (1966). "Women: The Longest Revolution." *New Left Review,* 40, 11-37.

Mitchell, Juliet (1971). *Woman's Estate.* New York: Pantheon Books.

Nicholson, Linda J. (1986). *Gender and History: The Limits of Social Theory in the Age of the Family.* New York: Columbia University Press.

Phelps, Linda (1975). "Patriarchy and Capitalism." *Quest,* 2(2), 35-48.

Phillips, Anne (1983). *Hidden Hands: Women and Economic Policies.* London: Pluto Press.

Rowbotham, Sheila, Segal, Lynne and Wainwright, Hilary (1979). *Beyond the Fragments: Feminism and the Making of Socialism.* London: Merlin Press.

Slaughter, Jane and Kern, Robert (eds.) (1981). *European Women on the Left: Socialism, Feminism, and the Problems Faced by Political Women.* Westport, CT: Greenwood Press.

Taylor, Barbara (1983). *Eve and the New Jerusalem: Socialism and Feminism in the Nineteenth Century.* New York: Pantheon Books.

Trimberger, Ellen Kay (1979). "Women in the Old and New Left: The Evolution of a Politics of Personal Life." *Feminist Studies,* 5, 432-450.

Vogel, Lise (1973). "The Earthly Family." *Radical America,* 7(4-5), 9-50.

Weinbaum, Batya (1978). *The Curious Courtship of Women's Liberation and Socialism.* Boston: South End Press.

Weinbaum, Batya and Bridges, Amy (1976). "The Other Side of the Paycheck: Monopoly Capital and the Structure of Conscription." *Monthly Review,* 28(3), 88-103.

Weinbaum, Batya and Bridges, Amy (1980). "Socialist Feminism and the Limits of Dual Systems Theory." *Socialist Review,* 10, 169-188.

XII. FEMINIST/WOMEN'S MOVEMENT

Banks, Olive (1981). *Faces of Feminism: A Study of Feminism as a Social Movement.* New York: St. Martin's Press.

Banks, Olive (1987). *Becoming a Feminist: The Social Origins of "First Wave" Feminism.* Athens, GA: University of Georgia Press.

Bassnett, Susan (1986). *Feminist Experiences: The Women's Movement in Four Cultures.* Boston: Allen and Unwin.

Billington, Rosamund (1982). "Ideology and Feminism: Why the Suffragettes Were 'Wild Women.'" *Women's Studies International Forum,* 5(6), 663-674.

Black, Naomi (1989). *Social Feminism.* Ithaca: Cornell University Press.

Bolt, Christine (1993). *The Women's Movements in the United States and Britain from the 1790s to the 1920s.* New York: Harvester Wheatsheaf.

Bouchier, David (1984). *The Feminist Challenge: The Movement for Women's Liberation in Britain and the USA.* New York: Schocken Books.

Burke, Mary P. (1980). *Reaching for Justice: The Women's Movement.* Washington, DC: Center of Concern.

Chafetz, Janet Saltzman (1986). *Female Revolt: Women's Movements in World and Historical Perspective.* Totowa, NJ: Rowman and Allanheld.

Chafetz, Janet Saltzman and Dworkin, Anthony Gary (1983). "Macro and Micro Processes in the Emergence of Feminist Movements: Toward a Unified Theory." *Western Sociological Review,* 14, 27-45.

Dahlerup, Drude (ed.) (1986). *The New Women's Movement: Feminism and Political Power in Europe and the USA.* Beverly Hills, CA: Sage.

Eisenstein, Hester (1991). *Gender Shock: Practicing Feminism on Two Continents.* Boston: Beacon Press.

Evans, Richard J. (1977). *The Feminists: Women's Emancipation Movements in Europe, America, and Australia, 1840-1920.* New York: Barnes and Noble Books.

Gelb, Joyce (1989). *Feminism and Politics.* Berkeley: University of California Press.

Hollis, Patricia (1979). *Women in Public: The Women's Movement, 1850—1900.* London: Allen and Unwin.

Kamm, Josephine (1966). *Rapiers and Battle-axes. The Women's Movement and Its Aftermath.* London: Allen and Unwin.

Katzenstein, Mary Fainsod and Mueller, Carol McClurg (eds.) (1987). *The Women's Movements of the United States and Western Europe: Consciousness, Political Opportunity, and Public Policy.* Philadelphia: Temple University Press.

Kontopoulos, Kyriakos (1972). "Women's Liberation as a Social Movement." In Sanfilios-Rothschild, Constantina (ed.), *Toward a Sociology of Women* (pp. 354- 361). Lexington, MA: Xerox College Pub.

Kuzmack, Linda Gordon (1990). *Woman's Cause: The Jewish Woman's Movement in England and the United States, 1881-1933.* Columbus: Ohio State University Press.

Liddington, Jill and Norris, Jill (1978). *One Hand Tied Behind Us. The Rise of the Women's Suffrage Movement.* London: Virago.

Lowry, Suzanne (1980). *The Guilt Cage: Housewives and a Decade of Liberation.* London: Elm Tree Books.

Meyer, Donald B. (1987). *Sex and Power: The Rise of Women in America, Russia, Sweden and Italy.* Middletown, CT: Wesleyan University Press.

Moghadam, Valentine M. (ed.) (1993). *Identity Politics and Women: Cultural Reassertions and Feminisms in InternationalPerspective.* Boulder, CO: Westview.

Nelson, Barbara J. and Chowdhury, Najma (eds.) (1994). *Women and Politics Worldwide.* New Haven, CT: Yale University Press.

Randall, Jane (1984). *The Origins of Modern Feminism: Women in Britain, France and the United States.* New York: Schocken Books.

Rendal, Jane (1987). *Equal or Different: Women's Politics, 1800-1914.* New York: Basil Blackwell.

Rowbotham, Sheila (1989). *The Past Is Before Us: Feminism in Action Since the 1960's.* London: Pandora.

Rowbotham, Sheila (1992). *Women in Movement: Feminism and Social Action.* New York: Routledge.

Rubinstein, David (1986). *Before the Suffragettes: Women's Emancipation in the 1890's.* New York: St. Martin's Press.

Scharf, Lois and Jensen, Joan M. (1983). *Decades of Discontent: The Women's Movement, 1920-1940.* Westport, CT: Greenwood Press.

Tax, Meredith (1980). *The Rising of the Women: Feminist Solidarity and Class Conflict, 1880-1917.* New York: Monthly Review Press.

Thomis, Malcolm I. and Grimmett, Jennifer (1982). *Women in Protest, 1800-1850.* New York: St. Martin's Press.

Thonnessen, Werner (1973). *The Emancipation of Women: The Rise and Decline of the Women's Movement in Social Democracy, 1863-1933.* Bristol, England: Pluto Press.

West, Guida and Blumberg, Rhoda Lois (eds.) (1990). *Women and Social Protest.* New York: Oxford University Press.

Wortis, Helen and Rabinowitz, Clara (1972). *The Women's Movement: Social and Psychological Perspectives.* New York: Wiley.

Yates, Gayle Graham (1975). *What Women Want. The Ideas of the Movement.* Cambridge, MA: Harvard University Press.

A. Asia/Mideast/Africa

Abdel Kader, Soba (1987). *Egyptian Women in a Changing Society, 1899-1987.* Boulder, CO: Lynne Rienner Publishers.

Accad, Evelyne (1990). *Sexuality and War: Literary Masks of the Middle East.* New York: New York University Press.

Andors, Phyllis (1983). *The Unfinished Liberation of Chinese Women, 1949-1980.* Bloomington: Indiana University Press.

Baig, Tara Ali (1976). *India's Woman Power.* New Delhi, India: S. Chand and Co.

Ballhatchet, Kenneth (1980). *Race, Sex, and Class Under the Raja: Imperial Attitudes and Policies and Their Critics, 1793-1905.* New York: St. Martin's Press.

Bamdad, Badrol-Moluk (1977). *From Darkness into Light: Women's Emancipation in Iran.* Hicksville, NY: Exposition Press.

Beck, Lois and Keddie, Nikki (1978). *Women in the Muslim World.* Cambridge, MA: Harvard University Press.

Bernstein, Gail Lee (ed.) (1991). *Recreating Japanese Women, 1600-1945.* Berkeley: University of California Press.

Calman, Leslie J. (1992). *Toward Empowerment: Women and Movement Politics in India.* Boulder, CO: Westview Press.

Condon, Jane (1985). *A Half Step Behind: Japanese Women of the '80s.* New York: Dodd, Mead.

Croll, Elizabeth J. (1978). *Feminism and Socialism in China.* Boston: Routledge and Kegan Paul.

Everett, Jana Matson (1979). *Women and Social Change in India.* New York: St. Martin's Press.

Everett, Jana Matson (1983). "The Upsurge of Women's Activism in India." *Frontiers*, 7(2), 18-26.

Forbes, Geraldine. (1979). "Votes for Women: The Demand for Women's Franchise in India, 1917-1937." In Muzumbar, V. (ed.), *Symbols of Power*. New Delhi, India: Allied Publications.

Forbes, Geraldine (1982). "Caged Tigers: 'First Wave' Feminism in India." *Women's Studies International Forum*, 5(6), 525-536.

Hazelton, Lesley (1977). *Israeli Women: The Reality Behind the Myths*. New York: Simon and Schuster.

Hijab, Nadia (1988). *Woman-Power: The Arab Debate on Women at Work*. New York: Cambridge University Press.

Jayawardena, Kumari (1986). *Feminism and Nationalism in the Third World*. Atlantic Highlands, NJ: Zed Books.

Johnson, Kay Ann (1978). *Women, the Family and Peasant Revolution in China*. Chicago: University of Chicago Press.

Lateef, Shahida (1990). *Muslim Women in India: Political and Private Realities*. Atlantic Highlands, NJ: Zed Books.

Mernissi, Fatima (1991). *The Veil and the Male Elite: A Feminist Interpretation of Women's Rights in Islam*. Reading, MA: Addison-Wesley.

Minault, Gail (ed.) (1981). *The Extended Family: Women and Political Participation in India and Pakistan*. Columbia, MO: South Asia Books.

Mohanty, Chandra Talpade, Russo, Ann and Torres, Lourdes (eds.) (1991). *Third World Women and the Politics of Feminism*. Bloomington: Indiana University Press.

Nashat, Guity (1983). *Women and Revolution in Iran*. Boulder, CO: Westview Press.

Omvedt, Gail (1980). *We Will Smash This Prison! Indian Women in Struggle*. London: Zed Books.

Omvedt, Gail (1993). *Reinventing Revolution: New Social Movements and the Socialist Tradition in India*. Armonk, NY: M.E. Sharpe.

Robertson, Claire and Benger, Iris (eds.) (1986). *Women and Class in Africa*. New York: Africana Publishing of Holmes and Meier.

Robertson, Claire and Klein, M. (1983). *Women and Slavery in Africa*. Madison: University of Wisconsin Press.

Sievers, Sharon L. (1983). *Flowers in the Salt: The Beginnings of Feminist Consciousness in Modern Japan*. Stanford, CA: Stanford University Press.

Stern, Geraldine (1979). *Israeli Women Speak Out*. Philadelphia: Lippincott.

Strobel, Margaret (1979). *Muslim Women in Mombasa, 1890-1975*. New Haven, CT: Yale University Press.

Swirski, Barbara and Safir, Marilyn P. (eds.) (1991). *Calling the Equality Bluff: Women in Israel*. New York: Pergamon Press.

Wolf, Margery (1985). *Revolution Postponed: Women in Contemporary China*. Stanford, CA: Stanford University Press.

Yao, E. (1983). *Chinese Women: Past and Present*. Mesquite, TX: Ide House.

Young, Marilyn Blatt (1973). *Women in China: Studies in Social Change and Feminism*. Ann Arbor: Center for Chinese Studies, University of Michigan.

B. Australia/New Zealand

Grimshaw, Patricia (1972). *Women's Suffrage in New Zealand.* Wellington, New Zealand: Oxford University Press.

Matthews, Jill Julius (1984). *Good and Mad Women: The Historical Construction of Femininity in Twentieth-Century Australia.* Boston: Allen and Unwin.

C. Europe/Great Britain

Ackelsberg, Martha A. (1991). *Free Women of Spain: Anarchism and the Struggle for Emancipation of Women.* Bloomington: Indiana University Press.

Alberti, Johanna (1989). *Beyond Suffrage: Feminists in War and Peace. 1914-1928.* New York: St. Martin's Press.

Alexander, Sally (1988). *Women's Fabian Tracts.* New York: Routledge.

Allen, Ann Taylor (1991). *Feminism and Motherhood in Germany, 1800-1914.* New Brunswick, NJ: Rutgers University Press.

Anderson, Harriet (1992). *Utopian Feminism: Women's Movements in Fin-de-Siècle Vienna.* New Haven, CT: Yale University Press.

Beale, Jenny (1986). *Women in Ireland: Voices of Change.* Dublin: Gill and Macmillan.

Bidelman, Patrick Kay (1987). *Pariahs Stand Up!: The Founding of the Liberal Feminist Movement in France, 1858-1889.* Westport, CT: Greenwood Press.

Birnbaum, Lucia Chiavola (1986). *Liberazione della donna: Feminism in Italy.* Middletown, CT: Wesleyan University Press.

Birnbaum, Lucia Chiavola (1993). *Black Madonnas: Feminism, Religion, and Politics in Italy.* Boston: Northeastern University Press.

Blackburn, Helen (1971). *Women's Suffrage: A Record of the Women's Suffrage Movement in the British Isles.* New York: Kraus Reprint Co.

Blom, Ida (1982). "A Century of Organized Feminism in Norway." *Women's Studies International Forum*, 5(6), 569-574.

Bohachevsky-Chomiak, Martha (1980). "Socialism and Feminism: The First Stages of Women's Organizations in the Eastern Part of the Austrian Empire." In Yedlin, T. (ed.), *Women in Eastern Europe and the Soviet Union* (pp. 44-64). New York: Praeger.

Bouten, Jacob (1975). *Mary Wollstonecraft and the Beginnings of Female Emancipation in France and England.* Philadelphia: Porcupine Press.

Boxer, Marilyn J. (1982). "'First Wave' Feminism in Nineteenth Century France: Class, Family and Religion." *Women's Studies International Forum,* 5(6).

Brown, Helen (1992). *Women Organizing.* New York: Routledge.

Brunt, Rosalind and Brown, Caroline (eds.) (1987). *Feminism, Culture and Politics.* London: Lawrence and Wishart.

Caine, Barbara (1982). "Feminism, Suffrage and the Nineteenth-Century English Women's Movement." *Women's Studies International Forum*, 5(6), 537-550.

Caine, Barbara (1992). *Victorian Feminists.* New York: Oxford University Press.

Colombo, Daniela (1981). "The Italian Feminist Movement." *Women's Studies International Quarterly*, 4, 461-469.

De Vries, Petra (1981). "Feminism in the Netherlands." *Women's Studies International Quarterly*, 4, 389-407.

Dodds, Dinah (1982)."Extra-Parliamentary Feminism and Social Change in Italy, 1971-1980." *International Journal of Women's Studies*, 5, 148-160.

Duchen, Claire (1986). *Feminism in France: From May '68 to Mitterrand.* Boston: Routledge and Kegan Paul.

Duchen, Claire (ed. and trans.) (1987). *French Connections: Voices from the Women's Movement in France.* Amherst: University of Massachusetts Press.

Ellsworth, Edward W. (1979). *Liberators of the Female Mind: The Shirreff Sisters, Educational Reform, and the Women's Movement.* Westport, CT: Greenwood Press.

Evans, Richard J. (1976). *The Feminist Movement in Germany, 1894-1933.* Beverly Hills, CA: Sage.

Evans, Richard J. (1987). *Comrades and Sisters: Feminism, Socialism, and Pacifism in Europe, 1870-1945.* New York: St. Martin's Press.

Fauré, Christine (1991). *Democracy Without Women: Feminism and the Rise of Liberal Individualism in France.* Bloomington: Indiana University Press.

Fayet-Scribe, Sylvie (1990). *Associations féminines et Catholicisme: XIXe-XXe siècle.* Paris: Editions Ouvrières.

Frank, Miriam (1978). "Feminist Publications in West Germany Today." *New German Critique*, 13, 181-194.

Frevert, Ute (1989). *Women in German History: From Bourgeois Emancipation to Sexual Liberation.* New York: Berg.

Garner, Les (1984). *Stepping Stones to Women's Liberty: Feminist Ideas in the Women's Suffrage Movement,*

1900-1918. Rutherford, NJ: Fairleigh Dickinson University Press.

Gerhard, Ute (1982). "A Hidden and Complex Heritage: Reflections on the History of Germany's Women's Movements." *Women's Studies International Forum*, 5(6).

Halbersleben, Karen I. (1993). *Women's Participation in the British Antislavery Movement, 1824-1865*. Lewiston, NY: E. Mellen Press.

Harrison, Brian (1987). *Prudent Revolutionaries: Portraits of British Feminists Between the Wars*. New York: Clarendon Press of Oxford University Press.

Hause, Steven C. and Kenney, A. (1984). *Women's Suffrage and Social Politics in the French Third Republic*. Princeton, NJ: Princeton University Press.

Hellman, Judith Adler (1987). *Journeys Among Women: Feminism in Five Italian Cities*. New York: Oxford University Press.

Holcombe, Lee (1983). *Wives and Property: Reform of the Married Women's Property Law in Nineteenth-Century England*. Buffalo, NY: University of Toronto Press.

Hollis, Patricia (1979). *Women in Public, 1850-1900: Documents of the Victorian Women's Movement*. Boston: G. Allen and Unwin.

Holton, Sandra Stanley (1986). *Feminism and Democracy: Women's Suffrage and Reform Politics in Britain, 1900-1918*. New York: Cambridge University Press.

Hufton, Oliver (1976). "Women in Revolution, 1789-1796." In Johnson, D. (ed.), *French Society and the Revolution*. Cambridge, England: Cambridge University Press.

Hume, Leslie Parker (1982). *The National Union of Women's Suffrage Societies, 1897-1914*. New York: Garland.

Juusola-Halonen, Elina (1981). "The Women's Liberation Movement—Finland." *Women's Studies International Quarterly,* 4, 453-460.

Kaplan, Gisela (1992). *Contemporary Western European Feminism.* New York: New York University Press.

Kaplan, Marion A. (1979). *The Jewish Feminist Movement in Germany: The Campaigns of the Judischer Frauenbund, 1904-1938.* Westport, CT: Greenwood Press.

Kaufmann-McCall, Dorothy (1983). "Politics of Difference: The Women's Movement in France from May 1968 to Mitterrand." *Signs,* 9, 282-293.

Kawan, Hildegard and Weber, Barbara (1981). "Reflections on a Theme: The German Women's Movement Then and Now." *Women's Studies International Quarterly,* 4, 421-433.

Kent, Susan (1987). *Sex and Suffrage in Britain, 1860-1914.* Princeton, NJ: Princeton University Press.

Lacey, Candida Ann (1987). *Barbara Leigh Smith Bodichon and the Langham Place Group.* New York: Routledge and Kegan Paul.

Lance, Keith Curry (1979). "Strategy Choices of the British Women's Social and Political Union, 1903-18." *Social Science Quarterly,* 60, 51-61.

Leneman, Leah (1991). *A Guid Cause: The Women's Suffrage Movement in Scotland.* Aberdeen, Scotland: Aberdeen University Press.

Levine, Philippa (1987). *Victorian Feminism, 1850-1900.* Tallahassee, FL: Florida State University Press.

Lovenduski, Joni (1986). *Women and European Politics: Contemporary Feminism and Public Policy.* Amherst: University of Massachusetts Press.

Lovenduski, Joni and Randall, Vicky (1993). *Contemporary Feminist Politics: Women and Power in Britain.* Oxford: Oxford University Press.

Morgan, David (1975). *Suffragists and Liberals. The Politics of Woman Suffrage in England.* Oxford: Blackwell.

Moses, Claire Goldberg (1984). *French Feminism in the Nineteenth Century.* Albany: State University of New York Press.

Prelinger, Catherine M. (1987). *Charity, Challenge and Change: Religious Dimensions of the Mid-Nineteenth Century Women's Movement in Germany.* New York: Greenwood Press.

Pugh, Martin (1992). *Women and the Women's Movement in Britain, 1914-1959.* Houndmills, Basingstoke, England: Macmillan Education.

Quataert, Jean H. (1979). *Reluctant Feminists in German Social Democracy, 1885-1917.* Princeton, NJ: Princeton University Press.

Reynolds, Sian (ed.) (1987). *Women, State and Revolution: Essays on Power and Gender in Europe since 1789.* Amherst: University of Massachusetts Press.

Robertson, Priscilla Smith (1987). *An Experience of Women: Pattern and Change in Nineteenth-Century Europe.* Philadelphia: Temple University Press.

Rodgers, Katherine M. (1987). *Feminism in Eighteenth-Century England.* Urbana: University of Illinois Press.

Rosen, Andrew (1974). *Rise Up Women! The Militant Campaign of the Women's Social and Political Union, 1903-1914.* London: Routledge and Kegan Paul.

Rover, Constance (1967). *Women's Suffrage and Party Politics in Britain, 1866-1914*. London: Routledge and Kegan Paul.

Rowbotham, Sheila (1972). "The Beginnings of Women's Liberation in Britain." In Wandor, Micheline (ed.), *The Body Politic. Writings from the Women's Liberation Movement in Britain, 1969-1972*. London: Stage I.

Sanford, Jutta Schroers (1978). *The Origins of German Feminism: German Women, 1789-1870*. Ann Arbor, MI: University Microfilms International.

Shanley, Mary Lyndon (1989). *Feminism, Marriage, and the Law in Victorian England, 1850-1895*. Princeton, NJ: Princeton University Press.

Stetson, Dorothy M. (1982). *A Woman's Issue: The Politics of Family Law Reformism in England*. Westport, CT: Greenwood Press.

Stetson, Dorothy M. (1987). *Women's Rights in France*. New York: Greenwood Press.

Strachey, Ray (1928). *"The Cause": A Short History of the Women's Movement in Great Britain*. London: G. Bell and Sons.

Tickner, Lisa (1988). *The Spectacle of Women: Imagery of the Suffrage Campaign, 1907-14*. Chicago: University of Chicago Press.

Wilson, Elizabeth (1986). *Hidden Agendas: Theory, Politics, and Experience in the Women's Movement*. New York: Tavistock Publications.

Wolchik, Sharon L. and Meyer, Alfred G. (eds.) (1985). *Women, State, and Party in Eastern Europe*. Durham, NC: Duke University Press.

D. Latin America

Acosta-Belen, Edna (1986). *The Puerto Rican Woman: Perspectives on Culture, History, and Society.* New York: Praeger.

Alvarez, Sonia F. (1990). *Engendering Democracy in Brazil: Women's Movements in Transition Politics.* Princeton, NJ: Princeton University Press.

Andreas, Carol (1976). *Nothing Is As It Should Be: A North American Feminist Tells of Her Life in Chile Before and After the Golpe Militar.* Cambridge, MA: Shankman Publishing.

Andreas, Carol (1985). *When Women Rebel: The Rise of Popular Feminism in Peru.* Westport, CT: Hill.

Berbmann, Emile (1990). *Women, Culture, and Politics in Latin America.* Berkeley: University of California Press.

Blachman, Morris (1976). "Selective Omission and Theoretical Distortion in Studying the Political Activity of Women in Brazil." In Nash, Jane and Safa, Helen (eds.), *Sex and Class in Latin America* (pp. 245-264). New York: Praeger.

Carlson, MariFran (1988). *Feminismo! The Woman's Movement in Argentina from Its Beginnings to Eva Perón.* Chicago: Academy Chicago.

Chaney, Elsa (1979). *Supermadre: Women in Politics in Latin America.* Austin: University of Texas Press.

Ferrer, Norma Valle (1979). "Feminism and Its Influence on Women's Organizations in Puerto Rico." In Acosta-Belen, Edna and Christensen, E.H. (ed.), *The Puerto Rican Woman* (pp. 38-50). New York: Praeger.

Hahner, June Edith (1978). "The Nineteenth-Century Feminist Press and Women's Rights in Brazil." In Lavrin, Asuncion (ed.), *Latin American Women: Historical Perspectives* (pp. 254-285). Westport, CT: Greenwood Press.

Hahner, June Edith (1980). "Feminism, Women's Rights, and the Suffrage Movement in Brazil, 1850-1932." *Latin American Research Review*, 15, 65-111.

Hahner, June Edith (1990). *Emancipating the Female Sex: The Struggle for Women's Rights in Brazil.* Durham, NC: Duke University Press.

Jaquette, Jane S. (ed.) (1994). *The Women's Movement in Latin America: Feminism and the Transition to Democracy.* Boulder, CO: Westview Press.

Latin American and Caribbean Women's Collective (1977). *Slaves of Slaves: The Challenge of Latin American Women.* London: Zed Books.

Little, Cynthia Jeffress (1978). "Education, Philanthropy, and Feminism: Components of Argentine Womanhood, 1860-1926." In Lavrin, Asuncion (ed.), *Latin American Women: Historical Perspectives* (pp. 235-253). Westport, CT: Greenwood Press.

Macias, Anna (1978). "Felipe Carrillo Puerto and Women's Liberation in Mexico." In Lavrin, Asuncion (ed.), *Latin American Women: Historical Perspectives* (pp. 286-301). Westport, CT: Greenwood Press.

Macias, Anna (1987). *Against All Odds: The Feminist Movement in Mexico to 1940.* Westport, CT: Greenwood Press.

Miller, Francesca (1991). *Latin American Women and the Search for Social Justice.* Hanover, NH: University Press of New England.

Morton, Ward (1962). *Woman Suffrage in Mexico.* Gainesville: University of Florida Press.

Nash, June, Safa, Helen and Contributors (1986). *Women and Change in Latin America.* South Hadley, MA: Bergin and Garvey Publishers.

Randall, Margaret (1992). *Gathering Rage: The Failure of Twentieth-Century Revolutions to Develop a Feminist Agenda.* New York: Monthly Review Press.

Stob, Barbara and Terrell, Nena (1988). *Confronting the Crisis in Latin America: Women Organizing for Change.* Santiago, Chile: Isis International and Development Alternatives with Women for a New Era.

Stoner, K. Lynn (1991). *From the House to the Streets: The Cuban Women's Movement for Legal Reform, 1898-1940.* Durham, NC: Duke University Press.

Tamez, Elsa and Alves, Rubem A. (1987). *Against Machismo: Rubem Alves, Leonardo Boff, Gustavo Gutierrez, Jose Miguez Bonino, Juan Luis Segundo ... and Others Talk About the Struggle of Women: Interviews.* Yorktown Heights, NY: Meyer-Stone Books.

E. Russia/Soviet Union

Bohachevsky-Chomiak, Martha (1988). *Feminists Despite Themselves: Women in Ukrainian Community Life, 1884-1939.* Edmonton, Alberta: Canadian Institute of Ukrainian Studies; Buffalo, NY: University of Toronto Press.

Buckley, Mary (ed.) (1992). *Perestroika and Soviet Women.* New York: Cambridge University Press.

Clements, Barbara Evans (1979). *Bolshevik Feminist: The Life of Aleksandra Kollontai.* Bloomington: Indiana University Press.

Edmondson, Linda Harriet (1984). *Feminism in Russia, 1900-1917.* Stanford, CA: Stanford University Press.

Engel, Barbara Alpern (1978). "From Separatism to Socialism: Women in the Russian Revolutionary Movement of the 1870's." In Boxer, M. and Quataert, J. (eds.), *Socialist Women: European Socialist Feminism in the Nineteenth and Early Twentieth Centuries* (pp. 51-74). New York: Elsevier North-Holland.

Engel, Barbara Alpern (1980). "Women Revolutionaries: The Personal and the Political." In Yedlin, T. (ed.), *Women in Eastern Europe and the Soviet Union* (pp. 31-43). New York: Praeger

Heitlinger, Alena (1979). *Sex Inequality in the Soviet Union and Czechoslovakia.* London: Macmillan.

Heitlinger, Alena (1979). *Women and State Socialism: Sex Inequality in the Soviet Union and Czechoslovakia.* Montreal: McGill-Queen's University Press.

Holland, Barbara (ed.) (1985). *Soviet Sisterhood.* Bloomington: Indiana University Press.

Jancar, Barbara Wolfe (1978). *Women Under Communism.* Baltimore: Johns Hopkins University Press.

Johanson, Christine (1987). *Women's Struggle for Higher Education in Russia, 1855-1900.* Montreal: McGill-Queen's University Press.

Lapidus, Gail Warshofsky (1977). "Sexual Equality in Soviet Policy: A Developmental Perspective." In Atkinson, D., Dallin, A. and Lapidus, G.W. (eds.), *Women in Russia* (pp. 115-138). Stanford, CA: Stanford University Press.

Lapidus, Gail Warshofsky (1978). *Women in Soviet Society.* Berkeley: University of California Press.

Mamonova, Tatyana (ed.) (1984). *Women and Russia: Feminist Writings from the Soviet Union.* Boston: Beacon Press.

Rosenthal, Bernice Glatzer (1977). "Love on the Tractor: Women in the Russian Revolution and After." In Bridenthal, Renate and Koonz, Claudia (eds.), *Becoming Visible: Women in European History* (pp. 370-399). Boston: Houghton Mifflin.

Stites, Richard (1978). *The Women's Liberation Movement in Russia.* Princeton, NJ: Princeton University Press.

Stites, Richard (1980). "The Women's Liberation Issue in Nineteenth Century Russia." In Yedlin, T. (ed.), *Women in Eastern Europe and the Soviet Union* (pp. 21-31). New York: Praeger.

F. United States/Canada

Adamson, Nancy (1988). *Feminist Organizing for Change: The Contemporary Women's Movement in Canada.* New York: Oxford University Press.

Bacchi, Carol (1983). *Liberation Deferred? The Ideas of the English-Canadian Suffragists, 1877-1918.* Toronto: University of Toronto Press.

Backhouse, Constance and Flaherty, David H. (eds.) (1992). *Challenging Times: The Women's Movement in Canada and the United States.* Buffalo, NY: McGill-Queen's University Press.

Bacon, Margaret Hope (1986). *Mothers of Feminism: Quaker Women in America.* San Francisco: Harper and Row.

Becker, Susan D. (1981). *The Origins of the Equal Rights Amendment: American Feminism Between the Wars.* Westport, CT: Greenwood Press.

Beckwith, Karen (1986). *American Women and Political Participation: The Impacts of Work, Generation, and Feminism.* New York: Greenwood Press.

Beeton, Beverly (1986). *Women Vote in the West: The Woman Suffrage Movement, 1869-1896.* New York: Garland.

Berry, Mary Frances (1986). *Why ERA Failed: Politics, Women's Rights and the Amendment Process of the Constitution.* Bloomington: Indiana University Press.

Boles, Janet K. (1979). *The Politics of the Equal Rights Amendment.* New York: Longman.

Boles, Janet K. (ed.) (1991). *American Feminism: New Issues for a Mature Movement.* Newbury Park, CA: Sage.

Boneparth, Ellen and Stoper, Emily (eds.) (1982). *Women, Power and Policy: Toward the Year 2000.* New York: Pergamon Press.

Bookman, Ann and Morgen, Sandra (1988). *Women and the Politics of Empowerment.* Philadelphia: Temple University Press.

Boydston, Jeanne, et al. (1988). *The Limits of Sisterhood: The Beecher Sisters on Women's Rights and Woman's Sphere.* Chapel Hill: University of North Carolina Press.

Buechler, Steven M. (1990). *Women's Movements in the United States: Woman Suffrage, Equal Rights, and Beyond.* New Brunswick, NJ: Rutgers University Press.

Carden, Maren Lockwood (1974). *The New Feminist Movement.* New York: Russell Sage Foundation.

Cassell, Joan (1977). *A Group Called Women.* New York: McKay.

Castro, Ginette (1990). *American Feminism: A Contemporary History.* New York: New York University Press.

Chafe, William Henry (1977). *Women and Equality: Changing Patterns in American Culture.* New York: Oxford University Press.

Cleverdon, Catherine Lyle (1950). *The Woman Suffrage Movement in Canada.* Toronto: University of Toronto Press.

Clinton, Catherine (1984). *The Other Civil War: American Women in the Nineteenth Century.* New York: Hill and Wang.

Cohen, Marcia (1988). *The Sisterhood: The True Story of the Women Who Changed the World.* New York: Simon and Schuster.

Costain, Anne N. (1992). *Inviting Women's Rebellion: A Political Process Interpretation of the Women's Movement.* Baltimore, MD: Johns Hopkins University Press.

Cummings, Bernice and Schuck, Victoria (eds.) (1979). *Women Organizing: An Anthology.* Metuchen, NJ: Scarecrow Press.

Davis, Flora (1991). *Moving the Mountain: The Women's Movement in America Since 1960.* New York: Simon and Schuster.

Deckard, Barbara (1983). *The Women's Movement: Political, Socioeconomic, and Psychological Issues,* 3rd ed. New York: Harper and Row.

DuBois, Ellen Carol (1975). "The Radicalism of the Women Suffrage Movement: Notes Toward the Reconstruction of Nineteenth-Century Feminism." *Feminist Studies,* 3, 63-71.

DuBois, Ellen Carol (1978). *Feminism and Suffrage: The Emergence of an Independent Women's Movement in America, 1848-1869.* Ithaca, NY: Cornell University Press.

DuBois, Ellen Carol (1979). "Women's Rights and Abolition: The Nature of the Connection." In Perry, L. and Fellman, M. (eds.), *Anti-Slavery Reconsidered: New Perspectives on the Abolitionists* (pp. 238-251). Baton Rouge: Louisiana State University Press.

Echols, Alice (1989). *Daring to Be Bad: Radical Feminism in America, 1967-1975.* Minneapolis: University of Minnesota Press.

Evans, Sara M. (1979). *Personal Politics: The Roots of Women's Liberation in the Civil Rights Movement and the New Left.* New York: Knopf.

Faludi, Susan (1991). *Backlash: The Undeclared War Against American Women.* New York: Crown.

Feree, Myra Marx and Hess, Beth B. (1985). *Controversy and Coalition: The New Feminist Movement.* Boston, MA: Twayne.

Firestone, Shulamith (1971). "On American Feminism." In Gornick, V. and Moran, Barbara K. (eds.), *Woman in Sexist Society* (pp. 665-686). New York: Basic Books.

Fishman, Sylvia Barack (1993). *A Breath of Life: Feminism in the American Jewish Community.* New York: Free Press.

Flexner, Eleanor (1974). *Century of Struggle. The Woman's Rights Movement in the United States.* New York: Atheneum.

Forster, Margaret (1985). *Significant Sisters: The Grassroots of Active Feminism, 1839-1939.* New York: Knopf.

Freeman, Jo (1975). *The Politics of Women's Liberation: A Case Study of an Emerging Social Movement and Its Relation to the Political Process.* New York: McKay.

Friedan, Betty (1976). *It Changed My Life: Writings on the Women's Movement.* New York: Random House.

Friedan, Betty (1981). *The Second Stage.* New York: Summit Books.

Friedl, Bettina (ed.) (1987). *On to Victory: Propaganda Plays of the Women's Suffrage Movement*. Boston, MA: Northeastern University Press.

Fritz, Leah (1979). *Dreamers and Dealers: An Intimate Appraisal of the Women's Movement*. Boston, MA: Beacon Press.

Fulenwider, Claire Knoche (1980). *Feminism in American Politics: A Study of Ideological Influence*. New York: Praeger.

Gelb, Joyce and Klein, Ethel (1988). *Women's Movements: Organizing for Change*. Washington, DC: American Political Science Association.

Gelb, Joyce and Palley, Marian Leaf (1987). *Women and Public Policies*, rev. & expanded ed. Princeton, NJ: Princeton University Press.

Gordon, Suzanne (1991). *Prisoners of Men's Dreams: Striking Out for a New Feminine Future*. Boston, MA: Little, Brown.

Gorham, Deborah (1976). "The Canadian Suffragists." In Matheson, Gwen (ed.), *Women in the Canadian Mosaic* (pp. 23-55). Toronto: Peter Martin Associates.

Grimes, Alan P. (1967). *The Puritan Ethic and Woman Suffrage*. New York: Oxford University Press.

Harrison, Cynthia Ellen (1988). *On Account of Sex: The Politics of Women's Issues, 1945-1968*. Berkeley: University of California Press.

Hartmann, Susan M. (1989). *From Margin to Mainstream: American Women and Politics Since 1960*. New York: Knopf.

Hawkes, Ellen (1986). *Feminism on Trial: the Ginny Foat Case and Its Meaning for the Future of the Women's Movement.* New York: Morrow.

Hersh, Blanche Glassman (1978). *The Slavery of Sex: Feminist-Abolitionists in America.* Urbana: University of Illinois Press.

Hole, Judith and Levine, Ellen (1971). *Rebirth of Feminism.* New York: Quadrangle Books.

Howell, Sharon (1990). *Reflections of Ourselves: The Mass Media and the Women's Movement, 1963 to the Present.* New York: Lang.

Jensen, Joan (1983). "All Pink Sisters: The War Department and the Feminist Movement in the 1920s." In Scharf, L. and Jensen, J. (eds.), *Decades of Discontent: The Women's Movement, 1920-1940* (pp. 199-222). Westport, CT: Greenwood Press.

Justice, Betty and Pore, Renate (1981). *Toward the Second Decade: The Impact of the Women's Movement on American Institutions.* Westport, CT: Greenwood Press.

Kamen, Paula (1991). *Feminist Fatale: Voices from the "Twentysomething" Generation Explore the Future of the Women's Movement.* New York: Fine.

Kimball, Gayle (ed.) (1981). *Women's Culture: The Women's Renaissance of the Seventies.* Metuchen, NJ: Scarecrow Press.

Klein, Ethel (1984). *Gender Politics: From Consciousness to Mass Politics.* Cambridge, MA: Harvard University Press.

Kraditor, Aileen (1965). *The Ideas of the Woman Suffrage Movement, 1890-1920.* New York: Columbia University Press.

Lemons, Stanley J. (1973). *The Woman Citizen: Social Feminism in the 1920s.* Urbana: University of Illinois Press.

Linkugel, Wil A. and Shaw, Anna Howard (1991). *Anna Howard Shaw: Suffrage Orator and Social Reformer.* New York: Greenwood Press.

Luker, Kristin (1984). *Abortion and the Politics of Motherhood.* Berkeley: University of California Press.

Lunardini, Christine A. (1986). *From Equal Suffrage to Equal Rights: Alice Paul and the National Woman's Party, 1910-1928.* New York: New York University Press.

McGlen, Nancy E. and O'Connor, Karen (1995). *Women, Politics, and American Society.* Englewood Cliffs, NJ: Prentice-Hall.

Mandle, Joan D. (1978). *Women and Social Change in America.* Princeton, NJ: Princeton Book Co.

Mansbridge, Jane J. (1986). *Why We Lost the ERA.* Chicago: University of Chicago Press.

Mathews, Donald G. and Dehart, Jane Sherron (1990). *Sex, Gender, and the Politics of ERA: A State and the Nation.* New York: Oxford University Press.

Matthews, Glenna (1992). *The Rise of Public Woman: Woman's Power and Woman's Place in the United States, 1630-1970.* New York: Oxford University Press.

Melder, Keith E. (1977). *Beginnings of Sisterhood. The American Woman's Rights Movement, 1800-1850.* New York: Schocken Books.

Morgan, David (1972). *Suffragists and Democrats: The Politics of Woman Suffrage in America.* East Lansing: Michigan State University Press.

Morgan, Robin (1978). *Going Too Far: The Personal Chronicle of a Feminist.* New York: Vintage Books.

O'Neill, William L. (1969). *Everyone Was Brave: A History of Feminism in America.* Chicago: Quadrangle Books.

O'Neill, William L. (1989). *Feminism in America: A History.* New Brunswick, NJ: Transaction Books.

Riegel, Robert E. (1963). *American Feminists.* Lawrence: University of Kansas Press.

Rivers, Caryl (1991). *More Joy Than Rage: Crossing Generations with the New Feminism.* Hanover, NH: University Press of New England.

Rossi, Alice S. (1982). *Feminists in Politics: A Panel Analysis of the First National Women's Conference.* New York: Academic Press.

Rowland, R. (ed.) (1984). *Women Who Do and Women Who Don't (Join the Feminist Movement).* London: Routledge and Kegan Paul.

Rupp, Leila J. and Taylor, Verta A. (1987). *Survival in the Doldrums: The American Women's Rights Movement, 1945 to the 1960's.* New York: Oxford University Press.

Ryan, Barbara (1992). *Feminism and the Women's Movement: Dynamics of Change in Social Movement, Ideology, and Activism.* New York: Routledge.

Sangster, Joan (1988). *Dreams of Equality: Women on the Canadian Left, 1920-1950.* Toronto: McClelland and Stewart.

Schramm, Sarah Slavin (1979). *Plow Women Rather Than Reapers: An Intellectual History of Feminism in the United States.* Metuchen, NJ: Scarecrow Press.

Shanley, Mary Lyndon (1988). *Women's Rights, Feminism, and Politics in the United States.* Washington, DC: American Political Science Association.

Simon, Rita James (1991). *Women's Movements in America: Their Successes, Disappointments, and Aspirations.* New York: Praeger.

Sinclair, Andrew (1966). *The Emancipation of the American Woman.* New York: Harper and Row.

Siu, Bobby (1975). *A Sociology of American Feminism: The Rise of Women's Consciousness in Nineteenth-Century America.* Hong Kong: Revomen Publications Co.

Sochen, June (1971). *The New Feminism in Twentieth-Century America.* Lexington, MA: Heath.

Sochen, June (1972). *The New Woman. Feminism in Greenwich Village, 1910-1920.* New York: Quadrangle.

Sochen, June (1973). *Movers and Shakers: American Women Thinkers and Activists, 1900-1970.* New York: Quadrangle/New York Times Book Co.

Staggenborg, Suzanne (1991). *The Pro-Choice Movement: Organization and Activism in the Abortion Conflict.* New York: Oxford University Press.

Steiner, Gilbert Y. (1985). *Constitutional Inequality: The Political Fortunes of the Equal Rights Amendment.* Washington, DC: Brookings Institution.

Stewart, Debra W. (1980). *The Women's Movement in Community Politics in the US* New York: Pergamon Press.

Tingley, Elizabeth and Tingley, Donald Fred (1981). *Women and Feminism in American History: A Guide to Information Sources.* Detroit, MI: Gale Research Co.

Vickers, Jill, Appelle, Christine and Rangin, Pauline (1993). *Politics As If Women Mattered: A Political Analysis of the Action Committee on the Status of Women.* Toronto: University of Toronto Press.

Wandersee, Winifred D. (1988). *On the Move: American Women in the 1970's.* Boston, MA: Twayne.

Welter, Barbara (1976). *Dimity Convictions: The American Woman in the Nineteenth Century.* Athens, OH: Ohio University Press.

Wheeler, Marjorie Spruill (1993). *New Women of the New South: The Leaders of the Woman Suffrage Movement in the Southern States.* New York: Oxford University Press.

Wortis, Helen and Rabinhowitz, Clara (eds.) (1972). *The Women's Movement: Social and Psychological Perspectives.* New York: Wiley.

Yates, Gayle Graham (1975). *What Women Want: The Ideas of the Movement.* Cambridge, MA: Harvard University Press.

Yellin, Jean Fagan (1989). *Women and Sisters: The Antislavery Feminists in American Culture.* New Haven, CT: Yale University Press.

G. Men and Feminism/The Men's Movement

Barzm, Helmut (1991). *For Men Too: A Grateful Critique of Feminism.* Wilmette, IL: Chiron Publications.

Bly, Robert (1990). *Iron John.* Reading, MA: Addison-Wesley.

Boone, Joseph A. and Gadden, Michael (eds.) (1990). *Engendering Men: The Question of Male Feminist Criticism.* New York: Routledge.

Farrell, Warren (1974). *The Liberated Man.* New York: Random House.

Farrell, Warren (1986). *Why Men Are the Way They Are: The Male-Female Dynamic.* New York: McGraw-Hill.

Farrell, Warren (1993). *The Myth of Male Power: Why Men Are the Disposable Sex.* New York: Simon and Schuster.

Hagen, Kay Leigh (1992). *Women Respond to the Men's Movement.* San Francisco, CA: Pandora.

Jardine, Alice and Smith, Paul, (eds.) (1987). *Men in Feminism.* New York: Routledge.

Keen, Sam (1991). *Fire in the Belly: On Being a Man.* New York: Bantam.

Levin, Michael E. (1987). *Feminism and Freedom.* New Brunswick, NJ: Transaction Books.

Marine, Gene (1972). *A Male Guide to Women's Liberation.* New York: Holt, Rinehart and Winston.

May, Larry and Strikwerda, Robert A. (eds.) (1992). *Rethinking Masculinity: Philosophical Explorations in Light of Feminism.* Totowa, NJ: Rowman and Littlefield.

Porter, David (ed.) (1993). *Between Men and Feminism.* New York: Routledge.

Rowan, John (1987). *The Horned God: Feminism and Men as Wounding and Healing.* New York: Routledge.

Seidler, Victor J. (1991). *Recreating Sexual Politics: Men, Feminism, and Politics.* New York: Routledge.

Seidler, Victor J. (ed.) (1991). *Achilles Heel Reader: Men, Sexual Politics, and Socialism.* New York: Routledge.

H. Anti-Feminism

Abbott, Pamela and Wallace, Clare (1993). *The Family and the New Right*. Boulder, CO: Westview.

Amneus, Daniel (1979). *Back to Patriarchy*. New Rochelle, NY: Arlington House.

Aubert, Jean Marie (1988). *L'Exil Féminin: Antiféminisme et Christianisme*. Paris: Cerf.

Baumert, Norbert (1992). *Antifeminismus bei Paulus?: Einzel Studien*. Würzburg: Echten.

Bax, Ernest Belfort (1913). *The Fraud of Feminism*. London: Grant Richards.

Conover, Pamela Johnston and Gray, Virginia (1983). *Feminism and the New Right: Conflict Over the American Family*. New York: Praeger.

Davidson, Nicholas (1988). *The Failure of Feminism*. Buffalo, NY: Prometheus Books.

Decter, Midge (1972). *The New Chastity and Other Arguments Against Women's Liberation*. New York: Coward, McCann and Geoghegan.

Dworkin, Andrea (1983). *Right-Wing Women*. New York: Coward-McCann.

Harrison, Brian (1978). *Separate Spheres: The Opposition to Women's Suffrage in Britain*. London: Helm.

Hewlett, Sylvia Ann (1986). *A Lesser Life: The Myth of Women's Liberation in America*. New York: Morrow.

Hudson, Kenneth (1968). *Men and Women: Feminism and Anti-Feminism Today*. Newton Abbot, England: David and Charles.

Jepsen, Dee (1984). *Women: Beyond Equal Rights.* Waco, TX: Word Books.

Klatch, Rebecca G. (1987). *Women of the New Right.* Philadelphia: Temple University Press.

LaHaye, Beverly (1993). *The Desires of a Woman's Heart: Encouragement for Women When Traditional Values Are Challenged.* Wheaton, IL: Tyndale House.

Mason, Mary Ann (1988). *The Equality Trap.* New York: Simon and Schuster.

Paglia, Camille (1990). *Sexual Personae: Art and Decadence from Nefertiti to Emily Dickinson.* New Haven, CT: Yale University Press.

Schlafly, Phyllis (1978). *The Power of the Positive Woman.* New York: Jove Publications.

Sommers, Christina Hoff (1994). *Who Stole Feminism?* New York: Simon and Schuster.

Wolf, Naomi (1993). *Fire with Fire.* New York: Random House.

XIII. ANTHROPOLOGY AND SOCIOLOGY

Andersen, Margaret L. (1988). *Thinking About Women: Sociological and Feminist Perspectives.* New York: Macmillan.

Ardener, Shirley (ed.) (1978). *Perceiving Women.* London: Malaby.

Conkey, Margaret W. (1991). "Original Narratives." In di Leonardo, Micaela (ed.), *Gender at the Crossroads of Knowledge* (pp. 102-139). Berkeley: University of California Press.

Etienne, Mona and Leacock, Eleanor (eds.) (1980). *Women and Colonialization.* New York: Praeger.

Gero, Joan M. and Conkey, Margaret W. (eds.) (1991). *Engendering Archaeology.* Oxford: Basil Blackwell.

Goodale, Jane C. (1971). *Tiwi Wives.* Seattle: University of Washington Press.

Haraway, Donna J. (1991). *Simians, Cyborgs, and Women.* New York: Routledge.

Helm, J. (1991). "The Weaver's Wraith." In Wald, Dale and Willows, Noreen D. (eds.), *The Archaeology of Gender* (pp. 430-435). Calgary: University of Calgary Press.

Kehoe, Alice B. (1981). "Revisionist Anthropology: Aboriginal North America." *Current Anthropology,* 22(5), 503-509, 515-517.

Kehoe, Alice B. (1983). "The Shackles of Tradition." In Albers, P. and Medicine, B. (eds.), *The Hidden Half* (pp. 53-73). Washington, DC: University Press of America.

Kornfeld, Marcel (ed.) (1991). *Approaches to Gender Processes on the Great Plains.* Lincoln, NE: Plains Anthropological Society, Memoir 26.

Nelson, Sarah M. and Kehoe, Alice B. (eds.) (1990). *Powers of Observation: Alternative Views in Archaeology.* Washington, DC: Archaeological Papers of the American Anthropological Association, Number 2.

Oakley, Ann (1974). *The Sociology of Housework.* New York: Pantheon Books.

Oakley, Ann (1981). *Subject Women.* New York: Pantheon Books.

Spector, Janet D. and Whelan, Mary K. (1989). "Incorporating Gender into Archaeology Courses." In Morgen, S. (ed.),

Gender and Anthropology (pp. 65-94). Washington, DC: American Anthropological Association.

Stanley, Liz (1990). *Feminist Praxis: Research, Theory, and Epistemology in Feminist Sociology.* New York: Routledge.

Zalk, Sue Rosenberg and Gordon-Kelter, Janice (1992). *Revolutions in Knowledge: Feminism in the Social Sciences.* Boulder, CO: Westview Press.

XIV. ARTS, ARCHITECTURE, AND AESTHETICS

Battersby, Christine (1989). *Gender and Genius: Towards a Feminist Aesthetics.* Bloomington: Indiana University Press.

Broude, Norma (1991). *Impressionism: A Feminist Reading.* New York: Rizzoli.

Broude, Norma and Garrard, Mary D. (eds.) (1982). *Feminism and Art History: Questioning the Litany.* New York: Harper and Row.

Broude, Norma and Garrard, Mary D. (eds.) (1992). *The Expanding Discourse: Feminism and Art History.* New York: Icon Editions.

Case, Sue-Ellen (1988). *Feminism and Theatre.* New York: Routledge.

Clover, Carol J. (1992). *Men, Women, and Chainsaws: Gender in the Modern Horror Film.* Princeton, NJ: Princeton University Press.

Cook, Susan C. and Tsou, Judy S. (eds.) (1994). *Cecilia Reclaimed: Feminist Perspectives on Gender and Music.* Urbana: University of Illinois Press.

Creed, Barbara (1993). *The Monstrous-Feminine: Film, Feminism, Psychoanalysis.* New York: Routledge.

Doane, Mary Ann (1991). *Femmes Fatales: Feminism, Film Theory, Psychoanalysis.* New York: Routledge.

Doane, Mary Ann, Mellencamp, Patricia and Williams, Linda (eds.) (1984). *Re-vision: Essays in Feminist Film Criticism.* Frederick, MD: University Publications of America.

Dolan, Jill (1988). *The Feminist Spectator as Critic.* Ann Arbor, MI: UMI Research Press.

Dotterer, Ronald and Bowers, Susan (1992). *Politics, Gender, and the Arts: Women, the Arts, and Society.* Selinsgrove, PA: Susquehanna University Press.

Ecker, Gisela (ed.) (1985). *Feminist Aesthetics.* London: The Women's Press.

Erens, Patricia (ed.) (1990). *Issues in Feminist Film Criticism.* Bloomington: Indiana University Press.

Friedan, Sandra, et al. (1993). *Gender and German Cinema: Feminist Interventions.* New York: St. Martin's Press.

Gentile, Mary C. (1985). *Film Feminisms: Theory and Practice.* Westport, CT: Greenwood Press.

Goodman, Lizbeth (1993). *Contemporary Feminist Theatres.* New York: Routledge.

Hayden, Dolores (1982). *The Grand Domestic Revolution: Feminist Designs for American Homes, Neighborhoods and Cities.* Cambridge, MA: MIT Press.

Hayden, Dolores (1984). *Redesigning the American Dream: The Future of Housing, Work, Family Life.* New York: Norton.

Hein, Hilde and Korsmeyer, Carolyn (eds.) (1993). *Aesthetics in Feminist Perspective*. Bloomington: Indiana University Press.

Kipnis, Laura (1993). *Ecstasy Unlimited: On Sex, Capital, Gender, and Aesthetics*. Minneapolis: University of Minnesota Press.

Kuhn, Annette (1993). *Women's Pictures: Feminism and Cinema*. New York: Routledge.

McCormick, Richard W. (1991). *Politics of the Self: Feminism and the Postmodern in West German Literature and Film*. Princeton, NJ: Princeton University Press.

Manning, Susan A. (1993). *Ecstasy and the Demon: Feminism and Nationalism in the Dances of Mary Wigman*. Berkeley: University of California Press.

Mayne, Judith (1990). *The Woman at the Keyhole: Feminism and Women's Cinema*. Bloomington: Indiana University Press.

Mellencamp, Patricia (1990). *Indiscretions: Avant-Garde Film, Video, and Feminism*. Bloomington: Indiana University Press.

Nead, Lynda (1992). *The Female Nude: Art, Obscenity, and Sexuality*. New York: Routledge.

Parker, Rozsika and Pollack, Griselda (eds.) (1987). *Framing Feminism: Art and the Women's Movement, 1970-1985*. New York: Routledge.

Penley, Constance (1989). *The Future of an Illusion: Film, Feminism, and Psychoanalysis*. Minneapolis: University of Minnesota Press.

Penley, Constance (ed.) (1988). *Feminism and Film Theory*. New York: Routledge.

Penley, Constance, et al. (eds.) (1990). *Close Encounters: Film, Feminism, and Science Fiction.* Minneapolis: University of Minnesota Press.

Pollack, Griselda (1988). *Vision and Difference: Femininity, Feminism, and Histories of Art.* New York: Routledge.

Raven, Ariene (1988). *Crossing Over: Feminism and Art of Social Concern.* Ann Arbor, MI: UMI Research Press.

Rodowick, David (1990). *The Difficulty of Difference: Psychoanalysis, Sexual Difference, and Film Theory.* New York: Routledge.

Rosenberg, Jan (1983). *Women's Reflections: The Feminist Film Movement.* Ann Arbor, MI: UMI Research Press.

Rothblatt, Donald N., Carr, David J. and Sprague, Jo (1979). *The Suburban Environment and Women.* New York: Praeger.

Silverman, Kaja (1988). *The Acoustic Mirror: The Female Voice in Psychoanalysis and Cinema.* Bloomington: Indiana University Press.

Solie, Ruth A. (ed.) (1993). *Musicology and Difference: Gender and Sexuality in Music Scholarship.* Berkeley: University of California Press.

Spain, Daphne (1992). *Gendered Spaces.* Chapel Hill: University of North Carolina Press.

Tasker, Yvonne (1993). *Spectacular Bodies: Gender, Genre, and the Action Cinema.* New York: Routledge.

Todd, Janet (1993). *Gender, Art, and Death.* New York: Continuum.

Walser, Robert (1993). *Running with the Devil: Power, Gender, and Madness in Heavy Metal Music.* Hanover, NH: University Press of New England.

Wekerle, Gerda R., Peterson, Rebecca and Morley, David (eds.) (1980). *New Space for Women.* Boulder, CO: Westview.

XV. COMMUNICATION

Campbell, Karlyn Kohrs (1989). *Man Cannot Speak for Her.* Two volumes. New York: Praeger.

Carter, Katheryn and Spitzack, Carole (1989). *Doing Research on Women's Communication: Perspectives on Theory and Method.* Norwood, NJ: Ablex.

Eakins, Barbara W. and Eakins, Gene R. (1978). *Sex Differences in Human Communication.* Boston, MA: Houghton Mifflin.

Ferguson, Marjorie (1985). *Forever Feminine: Women's Magazines and the Cult of Femininity.* Brookfield, VT: Gower.

Foss, Karen A. and Foss, Sonja K. (1991). *Women Speak: The Eloquence of Women's Lives.* Prospect Heights, IL: Waveland Press.

Graddol, David and Swann, Joan (1989). *Gender Voices.* New York: Blackwell.

Hady, Maureen E. (1982). *Women's Periodicals and Newspapers from the 18th Century to 1981.* Boston, MA: Hall.

Hardesty, Nancy (1987). *Inclusive Language in the Church.* Philadelphia: John Knox Press.

Henley, Nancy (1986). *Body Politics: Power, Sex and Nonverbal Communication.* New York: Touchstone Press.

Howell, Sharon (1990). *Reflections of Ourselves: the Mass Media and the Women's Movement, 1963 to the Present.* New York: Lang.

Kramerae, Cheris (1981). *Women and Men Speaking: Frameworks for Analysis.* Rowley, MA: Newbury House.

Martyna, Wendy (1983). "Beyond the He/Man Approach: The Case for Nonsexist Language." In Thorne, Barrie et al. (eds.), *Language, Gender and Society* (pp. 25-37). Rowley, MA: Newbury House.

Miller, Casey and Swift, Kate (1977). *Words and Women: New Language in New Times.* Garden City, NY: Doubleday/Anchor Books.

Miller, Casey and Swift, Kate (1988). *The Handbook of Nonsexist Writing,* 2nd ed. New York: Harper and Row.

Pearson, Judy C., Turner, Lynn H. and Todd-Mancillas, William (1991). *Gender and Communication.* Dubuque IA: Brown.

Penfield, Joyce (1987). *Women and Language in Transition.* Albany, NY: State University of New York Press.

Perry, Linda A.M., Turner, Lynn H. and Sterk, Helen M. (1992). *Constructing and Reconstructing Gender.* Albany, NY: State University of New York Press.

Rapping, Elayne (1994). *Mediations: Forays into the Culture and Gender Wars.* Boston, MA: South End Press.

Spender, Dale (1980). *Man Made Language.* London: Routledge and Kegan Paul.

Thorne, Barrie and Henley, Nancy (eds.) (1975). *Language and Sex: Difference and Dominance.* Rowley, MA: Newbury House.

Van Leeuwen, Stewart, Koch, Mary, Kroppurs, Margaret, Schuurman, Annelies Douglas and Sterk, Helen (1993). *After Eden: Facing the Challenge of Gender Relations.* Grand Rapids, IA: Erdmand.

Van Zoonen, Liesbet (1994). *Feminist Media Studies.* Thousand Oaks, CA: Sage.

XVI. ECONOMICS/LABOR MOVEMENT

Balser, Diane (1987). *Sisterhood and Solidarity: Feminism and Labor in Modern Times.* Boston, MA: South End Press.

Blum, Linda (1991). *Between Feminism and Labor: The Significance of the Comparable Worth Movement.* Berkeley: University of California Press.

Boyd, Marilyn S. (1981). *Women's Liberation Ideology and Union Participation: A Study.* Saratoga, CA: Century Twenty One.

Briskin, Linda and McDermott, Patricia (eds.) (1993). *Women Challenging Unions: Feminism, Democracy, and Militancy.* Toronto: University of Toronto Press.

Cuneo, Carl J. (1990). *Pay Equity: The Labour-Feminist Challenge.* New York: Oxford University Press.

Dye, Nancy Shrom (1980). *As Equals and As Sisters: Feminism, the Labor Movement, and the Women's Trade Union League of New York.* Columbia: University of Missouri Press.

Ferber, Marianne and Nelson, Julie A. (eds.) (1993). *Beyond Economic Man: Feminist Theory and Economics.* Chicago: University of Chicago Press.

Foner, Philip S. (1979). *Women and the American Labor Movement: From Colonial Times to the Eve of World War I.* New York: Free Press.

Fudge, Judy and McDermott, Patricia (eds.) (1991). *Just Wages: A Feminist Assessment of Pay Equity.* Toronto: University of Toronto Press.

Gabin, Nancy F. (1990). *Feminism in the Labor Movement: Women and the United Auto Workers, 1935-1975.* Ithaca, NY: Cornell University Press.

Gilman, Charlotte Perkins (1966). *Women and Economics.* New York: Harper and Row.

Gilman, Charlotte Perkins (1972). *The Home, Its Work and Influence.* Urbana: University of Illinois Press.

Hill, Mary A. (1980). *Charlotte Perkins Gilman: The Making of a Radical Feminist, 1860-1896.* Philadelphia: Temple University Press.

Parker, Kathy and Leghorn, Lisa (1981). *Woman's Worth: Sexual Economics and the World of Women.* London: Routledge and Kegan Paul.

Pujol, Michele A. (1992). *Feminism and Anti-Feminism in Early Economic Thought.* Brookfield, VT: Elgar.

Venkatesh, Allandi (1985). *The Significance of the Women's Movement to Marketing: A Life Style Analysis.* New York: Praeger.

XVII. HISTORY

Amussen, Susan Dwyer (1988). *An Ordered Society: Gender and Class in Early Modern England.* New York: Blackwell.

Anderson, Bonnie S. and Zinsser, Judith P. (1988). *A History of Their Own: Women in Europe from Pre-History to the Present.* New York: Harper and Row.

Aptheker, Bettina (1982). *Woman's Legacy: Essays on Race, Sex, and Class in American History.* Amherst: University of Massachusetts Press.

Arrom, Silvia Marina (1985). *The Women of Mexico City, 1790-1857.* Stanford: Stanford University Press.

Bacchi, C. (1983). *Liberation Deferred? The Ideas of the English-Canadian Suffragists, 1877-1918.* Buffalo, NY: University of Toronto Press.

Banta, Martha (1987). *Imaging American Women: Idea and Ideals in Cultural History.* New York: Columbia University Press.

Bauer, Carol and Ritt, Lawrence (1979). *Free and Ennobled: Source Readings in the Development of Victorian Feminism.* New York: Pergamon Press.

Blair, Karen J. (1980). *The Clubwoman as Feminist: True Womanhood Redefined, 1868-1914.* New York: Holmes and Meier.

Blake, Nelson Manfred and George, Carol V. R. (1975). *"Remember the Ladies": New Perspectives on Women in American History: Essays in Honor of Nelson Manfred Blake.* Syracuse, NY: Syracuse University Press.

Blocker, Jack S. Jr. (1984). *Give to the Winds Thy Fears: Women's Temperance Crusade, 1873-1874.* Westport, CT: Greenwood Press.

Bordin, Ruth (1981). *Woman and Temperance: The Quest for Power and Liberty, 1873-1900.* Philadelphia: Temple University Press.

Boulding, Elise (1992). *The Underside of History: A View of Women Through Time.* Two volumes. Thousand Oaks, CA: Sage.

Boxer, Marilyn J. and Quataert, Jean H. (1987). *Connecting Spheres: Women in the Western World, 1500 to the Present.* New York: Oxford University Press.

Braybon, Gail (1981). *Women Workers in the First World War: The British Experience.* Totowa, NJ: Barnes and Noble.

Braybon, Gail and Summerfield, Penay (1987). *Out of the Cage: Women's Experiences in Two World Wars.* New York: Pandora.

Burstyn, Joan N. (1980). *Victorian Education and the Ideal of Womanhood.* Totowa, NJ: Barnes and Noble.

Campbell, D'Ann (1984). *Women at War with America: Private Lives in a Patriotic Era.* Cambridge, MA: Harvard University Press.

Clark, Anna (1987). *Women's Silence, Men's Violence: Sexual Assault in England, 1770-1845.* New York: Pandora.

Clark, Elizabeth A. (1971). *Religion, Rights and Difference: The Origins of American Feminism, 1848-1860.* Madison, WI: Institute for Legal Studies.

Cogan, Frances B. (1989). *All-American Girl: The Ideal of Real Womanhood in Mid-Nineteenth Century America.* Athens, GA: University of Georgia Press.

Conrad, Susan Phinney (1976). *Perish the Thought: Intellectual Women in Romantic America, 1830-1860.* New York: Oxford University Press.

Cott, Nancy F. (1977). *The Bonds of Womanhood. "Woman's Sphere" in New England, 1780-1835.* New Haven, CT: Yale University Press.

Cott, Nancy F. (1987). *The Grounding of Modern Feminism.* New Haven, CT: Yale University Press.

Davidoff, Leonore and Hall, Catherine (1987). *Family Fortunes: Men and Women of the English Middle Class, 1780-1850.* Chicago: University of Chicago Press.

Degler, Carl N. (1980). *At Odds: Women and the Family in America from the Revolution to the Present.* New York: Oxford University Press.

DuBois, Ellen Carol (1981). *Elizabeth Cady Stanton, Susan B. Anthony: Correspondence, Writings, Speeches.* New York: Schocken Books.

Epstein, Barbara Leslie (1981). *The Politics of Domesticity: Women, Evangelism and Temperance in Nineteenth-Century America.* Middletown, CT: Wesleyan University Press.

Fletcher, Sheila (1980). *Feminists and Bureaucrats: A Study in the Development of Girls' Education in the Nineteenth Century.* New York: Cambridge University Press.

Fout, John C. (1984). *German Women in the Nineteenth Century: A Social History.* New York: Holmes and Meier.

Franzol, Barbara (1985). *At the Very Least She Pays the Rent: Women and German Industrialization, 1871-1914.* Westport, CT: Greenwood Press.

Glazer, Penina Midgal and Slater, Miriam (1987). *Unequal Colleagues: The Entrance of Women into the Professions, 1890-1940.* New Brunswick, NJ: Rutgers University Press.

Gluck, Sherna Berger (1987). *Rosie the Riveter Revisited; Women, the War, and Social Change.* Boston, MA: Hall.

Gorham, Deborah (1982). *The Victorian Girl and the Feminine Ideal.* Bloomington: Indiana University Press.

Grimké, Sarah (1970). *Letters on the Equality of the Sexes and the Condition of Woman.* New York: Franklin.

Hanawalt, Barbara A. (1986). *Women and Work in Preindustrial Europe.* Bloomington: Indiana University Press.

Harris, Barbara J. (1978). *Beyond Her Sphere: Women and the Professions in American History.* Westport, CT: Greenwood Press.

Heeney, Brian (1988). *The Women's Movement in the Church of England, 1850-1930.* New York: Clarendon Press of Oxford University Press.

Hellerstein, Erna Olafson, et al. (eds.) (1981). *Victorian Women: A Documentary Account of Women's Lives in Nineteenth-Century England, France, and the United States.* Stanford, CA: Stanford University Press.

Herstein, Sheila R. (1985). *A Mid-Victorian Feminist: Barbara Leigh Smith Bodichon.* New Haven, CT: Yale University Press.

Higonnet, Margaret Randolph, et al. (eds.) (1987). *Behind the Lines: Gender and the Two World Wars.* New Haven, CT: Yale University Press.

Hilden, Patricia (1986). *Working Women and Socialist Politics in France, 1880-1914: A Regional Study.* New York: Clarendon Press of Oxford University Press.

Hollis, Patricia (1987). *Ladies Elect: Women in English Local Government, 1865-1914.* New York: Clarendon Press of Oxford University Press.

Honey, Maureen (1984). *Creating Rosie the Riveter: Class, Gender, and Propaganda During World War II.* Amherst: University of Massachusetts Press.

Jalland, Pat (1986). *Women, Marriage, and Politics, 1860-1914.* New York: Clarendon Press of Oxford University Press.

Joeres, Ruth-Ellen B. and Maynes, MaryJo (1986). *German Women in the Eighteenth and the Nineteenth Centuries: A Social and Literary History.* Bloomington: Indiana University Press.

John, Angela V. (1986). *Unequal Opportunities: Women's Employment in England, 1800-1918.* New York: Blackwell.

Kava, Beth Millstein and Bodin, Jeanne (1977). *We, the American Women: A Documentary History*. New York: Ozer.

Kelly, Joan (1984). *Women, History, and Theory; The Essays of Joan Kelly*. Chicago: University of Chicago Press.

Kennedy, Susan Estabrook (1979). *If All We Did Was to Weep at Home: A History of White Working-Class Women in America*. Bloomington: Indiana University Press.

Kerber, Linda K. (1980). *Women of the Republic: Intellect and Ideology in Revolutionary America*. Chapel Hill: University of North Carolina Press.

Kerber, Linda K. and De Hart-Matthews, Jane (1987). *Women's America: Refocusing the Past*. New York: Oxford University Press.

Kern, Louis J. (1981). *An Ordered Love: Sex Roles and Sexuality in Victorian Utopias--The Shakers, the Mormons and the Oneida Community*. Chapel Hill: University of North Carolina Press.

Kessler-Harris, Alice (1982). *Out to Work: A History of Wage-Earning Women in the United States*. New York: Oxford University Press.

Koonz, Claudia (1987). *Mothers in the Fatherland: Women, the Family, and Nazi Politics*. New York: St. Martin's Press.

Kraditor, Aileen S. (1968). *Up from the Pedestal: Selected Writings in the History of American Feminism*. Chicago: Quadrangle Books.

Lamphere, Louise (1987). *From Working Daughters to Working Mothers: Immigrant Women in a New England Industrial Community*. Ithaca, NY: Cornell University Press.

Laubier, Claire (1990). *The Condition of Women in France: 1945 to the Present: A Documentary Anthology.* London, New York: Routledge.

Leach, William (1980). *True Love and Perfect Union: The Feminist Reform of Sex and Society.* New York: Basic Books.

Lerner, Gerda (1979). *The Majority Finds Its Past: Placing Women in History.* New York: Oxford University Press.

Lerner, Gerda (1986). *The Creation of Patriarchy.* New York: Oxford University Press.

Lerner, Gerda (1993). *The Creation of Feminist Consciousness: From the Middle Ages to Eighteen-Seventy.* New York: Oxford University Press.

Lewis, Jane (1984). *Women in England, 1870-1950: Sexual Divisions and Social Change.* Bloomington: Indiana University Press.

McMillan, James F. (1981). *Housewife or Harlot? The Place of Women in French Society, 1870-1940.* New York: St. Martin's Press.

Marcus, Jacob R. (1981). *The American-Jewish Woman, 1654-1980.* New York: American Jewish Archives.

Martin, Wendy (1972). *The American Sisterhood: Writings of the Feminist Movement from Colonial Times to the Present.* New York: Harper and Row.

Martineau, Harriet and Yates, Gayle G. (1985). *Harriet Martineau on Women.* New Brunswick, NJ: Rutgers University Press.

Matthaei, Julie A. (1982). *An Economic History of Women in America: Women's Work, the Sexual Division of Labor, and the Development of Capitalism.* New York: Schocken Books.

Menefee, Samuel Pyeatt (1981). *Wives for Sale: An Ethnographic Study of British Popular Divorce.* New York: St. Martin's Press.

Milkman, Ruth (1987). *Gender at Work: The Dynamics of Job Segregation by Sex During World War II.* Urbana: University of Illinois Press.

Mullaney, Marie Marmo (1983). *Revolutionary Women: Gender and the Socialist Revolutionary Role.* New York: Praeger.

Newton, Judith R., Ryan, Mary P. and Walkowitz, Judith R. (1983). *Sex and Class in Women's History.* Boston, MA: Routledge and Kegan Paul.

Norton, Mary Beth (1980). *Liberty's Daughters: The Revolutionary Experience of American Women, 1750-1800.* Boston, MA: Little, Brown.

Ogden, Annegret S. (1986). *The Great American Housewife: From Helpmate to Wage-Earner, 1776-1986.* Westport, CT: Greenwood.

Papachristou, Judith (1976). *Women Together: A History in Documents of the Women's Movement in the United States.* New York: Knopf.

Prior, Mary (ed.) (1985). *Women in English Society, 1500-1800.* New York: Methuen.

Reynolds, Sian (ed.) (1986). *Women, State, and Revolution: Essays on Power and Gender in Europe Since 1789.* Amherst: University of Massachusetts Press.

Riley, Glenda (1981). *Frontierswomen: The Iowa Experience.* Ames: Iowa State University Press.

Riley, Glenda (1984). *Women and Indians on the Frontier: 1825-1915.* Albuquerque: University of New Mexico Press.

Riley, Glenda (1988). *The Female Frontier: A Comparative View of Women on the Prairie and the Plains.* Lawrence: University of Kansas.

Roberts, Elizabeth (1985). *A Woman's Place: An Oral History of Working Class Women, 1890-1940.* New York: Blackwell.

Rohrlich, Ruby and Hoffman Baruch, E. (ed.) (1984). *Women in Search of Utopia: Mavericks and Mythmakers.* New York: Schocken Books.

Romero, Patricia W. (1987). *E. Sylvia Pankhurst: Portrait of a Radical.* New Haven, CT: Yale University Press.

Rosenberg, Rosalind (1982). *Beyond Separate Spheres: Intellectual Roots of Modern Feminism.* New Haven, CT: Yale University Press.

Rossi, Alice (ed.) (1973). *The Feminist Papers: From Adams to de Beauvoir.* New York: Columbia University Press.

Rossiter, Margaret L. (1986). *Women in the Resistance.* New York: Praeger.

Rotella, Elyce (1981). *From Home to Office: US Women at Work, 1870-1930.* Ann Arbor, MI: UMI Research.

Rowbotham, Sheila (1976). *Hidden from History: Rediscovering Women in History from the 17th Century to the Present.* New York: Vintage Books.

Scharf, Lois (1980). *To Work and to Wed: Female Employment, Feminism, and the Great Depression.* Westport, CT: Greenwood Press.

Schneir, Miriam (1972). *Feminism: The Essential Historical Writings.* New York: Random House.

Scott, Joan Wallach (1988). *Gender and the Politics of History.* New York: Columbia University Press.

Sealander, Judith (1983). *As Minority Becomes Majority: Federal Reaction to the Phenomenon of Women in the Work Force, 1920-1963.* Westport, CT: Greenwood Press.

Smith, Bonnie G. (1989). *Changing Lives: Women in European History Since 1700.* Lexington, MA: Heath.

Smith-Rosenberg, Carol (1985). *Disorderly Conduct: Visions of Gender in Victorian America.* New York: Knopf.

Soldon, Norbert C. (1978). *Women in British Trade Unions, 1874-1976.* Dublin: Gill and Macmillan.

Solomon, Barbara Miller (1985). *In the Company of Educated Women: A History of Women and Higher Education in America.* New Haven, CT: Yale University Press.

Sowerwine, Charles (1982). *Sisters or Citizens?: Women and Socialism in France Since 1876.* New York: Cambridge University Press.

Stansell, Christine (1986). *City of Women: Sex and Class in New York, 1789-1860.* New York: Knopf.

Stephenson, Jill (1981). *The Nazi Organization of Women.* Totowa, NJ: Barnes and Noble.

Stewart, Mary Lynn (1989). *Women, Work, and the French State: Labor Protection and Social Patriarchy, 1879-1919.* Buffalo, NY: McGill-Queen's University Press.

Stratton, Joanna L. (1981). *Pioneer Women: Voices from the Kansas Frontier.* New York: Simon and Schuster.

Summerfield, Penny (1984). *Women Workers in the Second World War: Production and Patriarchy in Conflict.* Dover, NH: Helm.

Tilly, Louise A. and Scott, Joan W. (1978). *Women, Work, and Family.* New York: Holt, Rinehart and Winston.

Trustram, Myna (1984). *Women of the Regiment: Marriage and the Victorian Army.* New York: Cambridge University Press.

Ulrich, Laurel Thatcher (1982). *Good Wives: Image and Reality in the Lives of Women in Northern New England, 1650-1750.* New York: Knopf.

Van Horn, Susan Householder (1988). *Women, Work, and Fertility, 1900-1986.* New York: New York University Press.

Vicinus, Martha (1977). *A Widening Sphere: Changing Roles of Victorian Women.* Bloomington: Indiana University Press.

Vicinus, Martha (1985). *Independent Women: Work and Community for Single Women, 1850-1920.* Chicago: University of Chicago Press.

Wandersee, Winifred D. (1981). *Women's Work and Family Values, 1920-1940.* Cambridge, MA: Harvard University Press.

Ware, Susan (1981). *Beyond Suffrage: Women in the New Deal.* Cambridge, MA: Harvard University Press.

Ware, Susan (1987). *Partner and I: Molly Dewson, Feminism, and New Deal Politics.* New Haven, CT: Yale University Press.

Weinberg, Sydney Stahl (1988). *The World of Our Mothers: The Lives of Jewish Immigrant Women.* Chapel Hill: University of North Carolina Press.

Weiner, Lynn Y. (1985). *From Working Girl to Working Mother: The Female Labor Force in the United States, 1820-1980.* Chapel Hill: University of North Carolina Press.

Wilson, Margaret Gibbons (1979). *The American Woman in Transition: The Urban Influence, 1870-1920.* Westport, CT: Greenwood Press.

XVIII. LAW/FEMINIST JURISPRUDENCE

Baer, Judith A. (1991). *Women in American Law: The Struggle Toward Equality from the New Deal to the Present.* New York: Holmes and Meier.

Bartlett, Katharine T. and Kennedy, Rosanne (eds.) (1991). *Feminist Legal Theory: Readings in Law and Gender.* Boulder, CO: Westview Press.

Bottomley, Anne and Conaghan, Joanne (eds.) (1993). *Feminist Theory and Legal Strategy.* Cambridge, MA: Blackwell.

Dahl, Tove Stang (1988). *Women's Law: An Introduction to Feminist Jurisprudence.* New York: Oxford University Press.

Fineman, Martha Albertson and Thomadsen, Mary Sweet (eds.) (1991). *At the Boundaries of Law: Feminism and Legal Theory.* New York: Routledge.

Frug, Mary Joe (1992). *Postmodern Legal Feminism.* New York: Routledge.

Goldstein, Leslie Friedman (1988). *The Constitutional Rights of Women: Cases in Law and Social Change.* Madison, WI: University of Wisconsin Press.

Goldstein, Leslie Friedman (1992). *Feminist Jurisprudence: The Difference Debate.* Lanham, MD: Rowman and Littlefield Publishers.

Hoff, Joan (1992). *Law, Gender, and Injustice: A Legal History of US Women.* New York: New York University Press.

Kanowitz, Lee (1969). *Women and the Law: The Unfinished Revolution.* Albuquerque: University of New Mexico Press.

Kingdom, Elizabeth (1990). *What's Wrong with Rights?: Problems for Feminist Politics of Law.* Edinburgh: Edinburgh University Press.

Kirp, David L. (1986). *Gender Justice.* Chicago: University of Chicago Press.

MacKinnon, Catharine A. (1987). *Feminism Unmodified: Discourses of Life and Law.* Cambridge, MA: Harvard University Press.

Mezey, Susan Gluck (1992). *In Pursuit of Equality: Women, Public Policy, and the Federal Courts.* New York: St. Martin's Press.

Minow, Martha (1990). *Making All the Difference: Inclusion, Exclusion, and American Law.* Ithaca, NY: Cornell University Press.

Naffine, Ngaire (1990). *Law and the Sexes: Explorations in Feminist Jurisprudence.* Boston, MA: Allen and Unwin.

Rhode, Deborah L. (1989). *Justice and Gender: Sex Discrimination and the Law.* Cambridge, MA: Harvard University Press.

Sachs, Albie and Wilson, Joan Hoff (1978). *Sexism and the Law: A Study of Male Beliefs and Legal Bias in Britain and the United States.* New York: Free Press.

Smart, Carol (1989). *Feminism and the Power of Law.* New York: Routledge.

Smith, Patricia (ed.) (1993). *Feminist Jurisprudence.* New York: Oxford University Press.

Weisberg, D. Kelly (ed.) (1993). *Feminist Legal Theory: Foundations.* Philadelphia: Temple University Press.

XIX. LITERATURE

Anger, Jane (1974). "Jane Anger, Her Protection for Women..." In Goulianos, Joan Susan (ed.), *By a Woman Writ, Literature from Six Centuries By and About Women.* Baltimore: Penguin Books.

Ardis, Ann L. (1990). *New Women, New Novels: Feminism and Early Modernism.* New Brunswick, NJ: Rutgers University Press.

Atkinson, Clarissa W. (1983). *Mystic and Pilgrim: The Book and the World of Margery Kempe.* Ithaca, NY: Cornell University Press.

Barr, Marleen S. (1987). *Alien to Femininity: Speculative Fiction and Feminist Theory.* New York: Greenwood Press.

Barr, Marleen S. (1992). *Feminist Fabulation: Space/Postmodern Fiction.* Iowa City: University of Iowa Press.

Basham, Diana (1992). *The Trial of Woman: Feminism and the Occult Sciences in Victorian Literature and Society.* New York: New York University Press.

Berkman, Joyce Avrech (1979). *Olive Schreiner: Feminism on the Frontier.* St. Albans, VT: Eden Press Women's Publications.

Brown, Janet (1979). *Feminist Drama: Definition and Critical Analysis.* Metuchen, NJ: Scarecrow Press.

Brown, Nathaniel (1979). *Sexuality and Feminism in Shelley.* Cambridge, MA: Harvard University Press.

Browne, Alice (1987). *The Eighteenth Century Feminist Mind.* Detroit: Wayne State University Press.

Carby, Hazel V. (1987). *Reconstructing Womanhood: The Emergence of the Afro-American Woman Novelist.* New York: Oxford University Press.

Clark, Veve A., et al. (1993). *Revising the Word and the World: Essays in Feminist Literary Criticism.* Chicago: University of Chicago Press.

Cocalis, Susan L. (1986). *German Feminist Poems from the Middle Ages to the Present: A Bilingual Anthology.* New York: Feminist Press at the City University of New York.

Cunningham, Gail (1978). *The New Woman and the Victorian Novel.* New York: Barnes and Noble Books.

Cunningham, Lucia Guerra (1990). *Splintering Darkness: Latin American Women Writers in Search of Themselves.* Pittsburgh, PA: Latin American Literary Review Press.

David, Deirdre (1987). *Intellectual Women and Victorian Patriarchy: Harriet Martineau, Elizabeth Barrett Browning, George Eliot.* Ithaca, NY: Cornell University Press.

Donovan, Josephine (1989). *Feminist Literary Criticism: Explorations on Theory.* Lexington: University Press of Kentucky.

Felski, Rita (1989). *Beyond Feminist Aesthetics: Feminist Literature and Social Changes.* Cambridge, MA: Harvard University Press.

Ferguson, Moira (1985). *First Feminists: British Women Writers, 1578-1799.* Bloomington: Indiana University Press.

Fernando, Lloyd (1977). *"New Women" in the Late Victorian Novel.* University Park: Pennsylvania State University Press.

Fleischman, Fritz (1982). *American Novelists Revisited: Essays in Feminist Criticism.* Boston, MA: Hall.

Fuller, Margaret (1971). *Woman in the Nineteenth Century.* New York: Norton.

Hirsch, Marianne (1989). *The Mother/Daughter Plot: Narrative, Psychoanalysis, Feminism.* Bloomington: Indiana University Press.

Hoeveler, Diane Long (1990). *Romantic Androgyny: The Women Within.* University Park, PA: Penn State University Press.

Howells, Carol Ann and Hunter, Lynette (1991). *Narrative Strategies in Canadian Literature: Feminism and Postcolonialism.* Philadelphia: Open University Press.

Jones, Libby Falk and Goodwin, Sarah Webster (1990). *Feminism, Utopia, and Narrative.* Knoxville: University of Tennessee Press.

Jordan, Constance (1990). *Renaissance Feminism: Literary Texts and Political Models.* Ithaca, NY: Cornell University Press.

Kaplan, Cora (1986). *Sea Changes: Essays on Culture and Feminism.* New York: Verso.

Lefanu, Sarah (1988). *Feminism and Science Fiction.* Bloomington: Indiana University Press.

Lefanu, Sarah (1988). *In the Chinks of the World Machine: Feminism and Science Fiction.* London: Women's Press.

Little, Judy (1983). *Comedy and the Woman Writer: Woolf, Spark, and Feminism.* Lincoln: University of Nebraska Press.

Markey, Janice (1985). *A New Tradition?: The Poetry of Sylvia Plath, Anne Sexton, and Adrienne Rich, a Study of Feminism and Poetry.* New York: Lang.

Meese, Elizabeth (1986). *Crossing the Double-Cross: The Practice of Feminist Criticism.* Chapel Hill: University of North Carolina Press.

Moi, Toril (1985). *Sexual/Textual Politics: Feminist Literary Theory.* New York: Methuen.

Moraga, Cherrie and Castallo, Ana (1988). *Este Puente, Mi Espalda: Voces de Mujeres Tercermundistas en los Estados Unidos.* San Francisco: ISM Press.

Perry, Ruth (1986). *The Celebrated Mary Astell: An Early English Feminist.* Chicago: University of Chicago Press.

Poovey, Mary (1988). *Uneven Developments: The Ideological Work of Gender in Mid-Victorian England.* Chicago: University of Chicago Press.

Reddy, Maureen T. (1988). *Sisters in Crime: Feminism and the Crime Novel.* New York: Continuum.

Rich, Adrienne (1980). *On Lies, Secrets and Silence: Selected Prose, 1966-1978.* London: Virago.

Richards, Earl Jeffrey, et al. (1992). *Reinterpreting Christine De Pizan.* Athens: University of Georgia Press.

Roller, Judi M. (1986). *The Politics of the Feminist Novel.* New York: Greenwood Press.

Rosinsky, Natalie M. (1984). *Feminist Futures--Contemporary Women's Speculative Fiction.* Ann Arbor, MI: UMI Research Press.

Salmonson, Jessica Amanda (1989). *What Did Miss Darrington See?: An Anthology of Feminist Supernatural Fiction.* New York: Feminist Press at the City University of New York.

Showalter, Elaine (1971). *Women's Liberation and Literature.* New York: Harcourt.

Showalter, Elaine (1977). *A Literature of Their Own. British Women Novelists from Brontë to Lessing.* Princeton, NJ: Princeton University Press.

Showalter, Elaine (1985). *The Female Malady: Women Madness and English Culture, 1830-1980.* New York: Pantheon.

Stanley, Liz (1992). *The Autobiographical I: The Theory and Practice of Autobiography.* New York: Manchester University Press.

Stanton, Domna C. (1986). *French Feminist Poems from the Middle Ages to the Present: A Bilingual Anthology.* New York: Feminist Press.

Wagner, Geoffrey Atheling (1972). *Five for Freedom: A Study of Feminism in Fiction.* London: Allen and Unwin.

Woolf, Virginia (1929). *A Room of One's Own.* London: The Women's Press.

Woolf, Virginia (1938). *Three Guineas.* London: The Women's Press.

Woolf, Virginia (1979). *Women and Writing.* London: The Women's Press.

XX. MYTHOLOGY

Bachofen, Jacob J. (1967). *Myth, Religion, and Mother Right.* Princeton, NJ: Princeton University Press.

Bell, Robert E. (1991). *Women of Classical Mythology: A Bibliographical Dictionary.* Santa Barbara, CA: ABC-CLIO.

Berger, Pamela (1985). *The Goddess Obscured: Transformation of the Grain Protectress from Goddess to Saint.* Boston, MA: Beacon.

Bolen, Jean Shinoda (1984). *Goddesses in Every Woman.* San Francisco, CA: Harper and Row.

Dexter, Mirian Robbins (1990). *Whence the Goddess: A Sourcebook.* Elmsford, NY: Pergamon.

Downing, Christine (1981). *The Goddess: Mythological Images of the Feminine.* New York: Crossroad.

Gadon, Elinor W. (1989). *The Once and Future Goddess: A Sweeping Visual Chronicle of the Sacred Female and Her Reemergence in the Cultural Mythology of Our Time.* San Francisco: Harper and Row.

Gimbutas, Marija (1982). *The Goddesses and Gods of Old Europe: 6500-3500 BC,* 2nd ed. Berkeley: University of California Press.

Goodrich, Norma Lorre (1989). *Priestesses.* New York: Harper Collins.

Hays, H. R. (1966). *The Dangerous Sex. The Myth of Feminine Evil.* New York: Pocket Books.

Johnson, Buffie (1988). *Lady of the Beasts: Ancient Images of the Goddess and Her Sacred Animals.* San Francisco: Harper and Row.

Kinsley, David (1989). *The Goddess' Mirror: Visions of the Divine from East and West.* Albany: State University of New York.

Kraemer, Ross S. (ed.) (1988). *Maenads, Martyrs, Matrons, Monastics: A Sourcebook on Women's Religions in the Greco-Roman World.* Philadelphia: Fortress.

Larrington, Carolyne (ed.) (1992). *The Feminist Companion to Mythology*. London: Pandora.

Lederer, Wolfgang (1968). *The Fear of Women*. New York: Grune and Stratton.

Lefkowitz, Mary R. (1986). *Women in Greek Myth*. Baltimore: Johns Hopkins University Press.

Neumann, Erich (1963). *Women in Greek Myth*, 2nd ed. Princeton, NJ: Princeton University Press.

O'Brien, Joan (1993). *The Transformation of Hera: A Study of Ritual, Hero, and the Goddess in the Iliad*. Lanham, MD: University Press of America.

Orenstein, Gloria (1990). *The Reflowering of the Goddess*. Elmsford, NY: Pergamon.

Pomeroy, Sarah B. (1975). *Goddesses, Whores, Wives, and Slaves: Women in Classical Antiquity*. New York: Schocken Books.

Pomeroy, Sarah B. (1984). *Women in Hellenistic Egypt: From Alexander to Cleopatra*. New York: Schocken Books.

Slater, P. E. (1968). *The Glory of Hera: Greek Mythology and the Greek Family*. Boston, MA: Beacon.

Stone, Merlin (1979). *Ancient Mirrors of Womanhood: Our Goddess and Heroine Heritage*. Two volumes. New York: Sibylline Books.

Woolger, Jennifer Barker and Woolger, Roger J. (1989). *The Goddess Within: A Guide to the Eternal Myths That Shape Women's Lives*. New York: Fawcett Columbine.

XXI. PEDAGOGY AND RESEARCH

Brock-Utne, Brigit (1985). *Educating for Peace: A Feminist Perspective.* New York: Pergamon.

Gabriel, Susan L. and Smithson, Isaiah (1990). *Gender in the Classroom: Power and Pedagogy.* Urbana: University of Illinois Press.

Giroux, Henry A. (ed.) (1991). *Postmodernism, Feminism and Cultural Politics: Redrawing Educational Boundaries.* Albany: State University of New York Press.

Gore, Jennifer M. (1992). *The Struggle for Pedagogies: Critical and Feminist Discourses as Regimes of Truth.* New York: Routledge.

Griffin, Gabriele (1994). *Changing Our Lives: Women into Women's Studies.* Boulder, CO: Westview.

Kramarae, Cheris and Spender, Dale (1992). *The Knowledge Explosion: Generations of Feminist Scholarship.* New York: Teachers College Press.

Lather, Patricia Ann (1991). *Getting Smart: Feminist Research and Pedagogy within the Postmodern.* New York: Routledge.

Lauretis, Teresa de (ed.) (1986). *Feminist Studies. Critical Studies.* Bloomington: Indiana University Press.

Luke, Carmen and Gore, Jennifer (eds.) (1992). *Feminisms and Critical Pedagogy.* New York: Routledge.

Middleton, Sue (1993). *Educating Feminists: Life Histories and Pedagogy.* New York: Teachers College Press.

Peterson, Spike V. (ed.) (1992). *Gendered States: Feminist Revisions of International Relations Theory.* Boulder, CO: Lynne Rienner Publishers.

Reinharz, Shulamith (1992). *Feminist Methods in Social Research.* New York: Oxford University Press.

Spender, Dale (ed.) (1981). *Men's Studies Modified: The Impact of Feminism on the Academic Disciplines.* New York: Pergamon.

Stacey, Judith, Bereaud, Susan and Daniels, Joan (1974). *And Jill Came Tumbling After: Sexism in American Education.* New York: Dell.

Stanley, Liz and Wise, Sue (1993). *Breaking Out: Feminist Consciousness and Feminist Research,* 2nd ed. London: Routledge and Kegan Paul.

Stone, Lynda (ed.) (1993). *The Education Feminism Reader: Developments in a Field of Study.* New York: Routledge.

Weiler, Kathleen (1988). *Women Teaching for Change: Gender, Class and Power.* Westport, CT: Bergin and Garvey.

XXII. PHILOSOPHY

Baker, Robert and Elliston, Frederick (1975). *Philosophy and Sex.* Buffalo, NY: Prometheus Books.

Bartky, Sandra L. (1979). "On Psychological Oppression." In Bishop, Sharon and Weinzweig, Marjorie (eds.), *Philosophy and Women* (pp. 11-33). Belmont, CA: Wadsworth.

Bryson, Valeria (1987). *Feminist Political Theory: An Introduction.* Houndmills, Basingstoke, England: Macmillan.

Butler, Judith (1993). *Bodies That Matter.* New York: Routledge.

Card, Claudia (1991). *Feminist Ethics.* Lawrence, KS: University Press of Kansas.

Clark, L. and Lange, L. (1979). *The Sexism of Social and Political Theory.* Toronto: University of Toronto Press.

Cole, Eve Browning and Coultrap-McQuin, Susan (1992). *Explorations in Feminist Ethics: Theory and Practice.* Bloomington: Indiana University Press.

Coole, Diana (1988). *Women in Political Theory: From Ancient Misogyny to Contempory Feminism.* Boulder, CO: Lynne Rienner Publishers.

Daly, Mary (1984). *Pure Lust: Elemental Feminist Philosophy.* Boston, MA: Beacon Press.

Elshtain, Jean Bethke (1987). *Women and War.* New York: Basic Books.

Fargains, Sondra (1994). *Situating Feminist Theory.* Thousand Oaks, CA: Sage.

Flax, Jane (1993). *Disputed Subjects: Essays on Psychoanalysis, Politics and Philosophy.* New York: Routledge.

Frazer, Elizabeth, Hornsby, Jennifer and Lovibond, Sabina (1992). *Ethics: A Feminist Reader.* Cambridge, MA: Blackwell.

Gould, Carol C. (1984). *Beyond Domination: New Perspectives on Women and Philosophy.* Totowa, NJ: Rowman and Littlefield Pub.

Gould, Carol C. and Wartofsky, Marx W. (1976) *Women and Philosophy: Toward a Theory of Liberation.* New York: Putnam.

Grimshaw, Jean (1986). *Philosophy and Feminist Thinking.* Minneapolis: University of Minnesota Press.

Gunew, Sneja (ed.) (1991). *A Reader in Feminist Knowledge.* New York: Routledge.

Harding, Sandra and Hintikka, Merrill (1983). *Discovering Reality: Feminist Perspectives on Epistemology, Metaphysics, Methodology, and Philosophy of Science.* Boston, MA: Reidel.

Held, Virginia (1993). *Feminist Morality: Transforming Culture, Society, and Politics.* Chicago: University of Chicago Press.

Jaggar, Alison M. (ed.) (1994). *Living with Contradictions: Controversies in Feminist Social Ethics.* Boulder, CO: Westview.

Johnson, Pauline (1994). *Feminism as Radical Humanism.* Boulder, CO: Westview.

Kennedy, Ellen and Mendus, Susan (eds.) (1987). *Women in Western Political Philosophy: Kant to Nietzsche.* New York: St. Martin's Press.

Landes, Joan B. (1988). *Women and the Public Sphere in the Age of the French Revolution.* Ithaca, NY: Cornell University Press.

Lloyd, Genevieve (1984). *The Man of Reason: Male and Female in Western Philosophy.* London: Methuen.

Lugones, Maria and Spelman, Elizabeth V. (1986). "Have We Got a Theory for You! Feminist Theory, Cultural Imperialism, and the Demand for 'The Woman's Voice.'" In Pearsall, Marilyn (ed.), *Women and Values: Readings in Recent Feminist Philosophy* (pp. 19-32). Belmont, CA: Wadsworth.

Mahowald, Mary (ed.) (1978). *Philosophy of Woman: Classical to Current Concepts.* Indianapolis, IN: Hackett.

Nicol, Iain G. (1992). *Schleiermacher and Feminism: Sources, Evaluations, and Responses.* Lewiston, NY: Mellen Press.

Noddings, Nel (1984). *Caring: A Feminine Approach to Ethics and Moral Education.* Berkeley: University of California Press.

Okin, Susan (1980). *Women in Western Political Thought.* London: Virago.

Pateman, Carole and Gross, Elizabeth (eds.) (1986). *Feminist Challenges: Social and Political Theory.* Boston, MA: Northeastern University Press.

Rhode, Deborah L. (ed.) (1990). *Theoretical Perspectives on Sexual Difference.* New Haven, CT: Yale University Press.

Roszak, Theodore (1969). "The Hard and the Soft: The Force of Feminism in Modern Times." In Roszak, Betty and Roszak, Theodore (eds.), *Masculine/Feminine: Readings in Sexual Mythology and the Liberation of Women.* New York: Harper and Row.

Rover, Constance (1970). *Love, Morals, and the Feminists.* London: Routledge and Kegan Paul.

Rowbotham, Sheila (1977). *A New World for Women.* London: Pluto Press.

Royden, A. Maude (1917). "Modern Love." In Gollancz, Victor (ed.), *The Making of Women. Oxford Essays in Feminism.* London: Allen and Unwin.

Segal, Lynne (1987). *Is the Future Female? Troubled Thoughts on Contemporary Feminism.* London: Virago.

Spender, Dale (1982). *Women of Ideas (and What Men Have Done to Them).* London: Routledge and Kegan Paul.

Spender, Dale (1985). *For the Record: The Making and Meaning of Feminist Knowledge.* London: The Women's Press.

Stern, Karl (1966). *The Flight from Woman.* London: Allen and Unwin.

Sunstein, Cass R. (1990). *Feminism and Political Theory.* Chicago: University of Chicago Press.

Tronto, Joan C. (1993). *Moral Boundaries: A Political Argument for an Ethic of Care.* New York: Routledge.

Weiss, Penny A. (1994). *Gendered Community: Rousseau, Sex, and Politics.* New York: New York University Press.

XXIII. PSYCHOANALYTIC FEMINISM

Barr, Marleen S. and Feldstein, Richard (1989). *Discontented Discourses: Feminism/Textual Intervention/ Psychoanalysis.* Urbana: University of Illinois Press.

Bernheimer, Charles and Kahane, Claire (eds.) (1985). *In Dora's Case: Freud - Hysteria - Feminism.* New York: Columbia University Press.

Burack, Cynthia (1994). *The Problem of the Passions: Feminism, Psychoanalysis and Social Theory.* New York: New York University Press.

Chodorow, Nancy (1974). "Family Structure and Feminine Personality." In Rosaldo, Michelle Zimbalist and Lamphere, Louise (eds.), *Women, Culture, and Society.* Stanford, CA: Stanford University Press.

Chodorow, Nancy (1978). *The Reproduction of Mothering: Psychoanalysis and the Sociology of Gender.* Berkeley: University of California Press.

Clement, Catherine (1987). *Les Fils de Freud Sont Fatigués.* (The Weary Sons of Freud). New York: Verso.

Deutsch, Helene (1944). *The Psychology of Women: A Psychoanalytic Interpretation.* New York: Grune and Stratten.

Dinnerstein, Dorothy (1977). *The Mermaid and the Minotaur: Sexual Arrangements and Human Malaise.* New York: Harper Colophon Books.

DuBois, Page (1988). *Sowing the Body: Psychoanalysis and Ancient Representations of Women.* Chicago: University of Chicago Press.

Elliot, Patricia (1991). *From Mastery to Analysis: Theories of Gender in Psychoanalytic Feminism.* Ithaca, NY: Cornell University Press.

Engel, Stephanie (1980). "Femininity as Tragedy: Re-examining the 'New Narcissism.'" *Socialist Review,* 10(5), 77-104.

Freud, Sigmund (1938). "The Sexual Aberrations." In Brill, A.A. (ed.), *The Basic Writings of Sigmund Freud* (pp. 135-172). New York: Modern Library.

Freud, Sigmund (1963). *Dora: An Analysis of a Case of Hysteria.* New York: Collier Books.

Freud, Sigmund (1963). "On Narcissism: An Introduction." In Freud, Sigmund, *General Psychological Theory* (pp. 56-82). New York: Collier Books.

Freud, Sigmund (1966). "Femininity." In Freud, Sigmund, *The Complete Introductory Lectures on Psychoanalysis* (pp. 576-599). New York: Norton.

Freud, Sigmund (1968). "The Passing of the Oedipus Complex." In Freud, Sigmund, *Sexuality and the Psychology of Love* (pp. 176-182). New York: Collier Books.

Freud, Sigmund (1974). "Some Psychical Consequences of the Anatomical Distinction Between the Sexes." In Strouse, Jean (ed.), *Women and Analysis* (pp. 27-38). New York: Grossman.

Gallop, Jane (1982). *The Daughter's Seduction: Feminism and Psychoanalysis.* Ithaca, NY: Cornell University Press.

Garrison, Dee (1981). "Karen Horney and Feminism." *Signs,* 6, 672-691.

Klein, Viola (1971). *The Feminine Character.* London: Routledge and Kegan Paul.

Kofman, Sarah (1985). *The Enigma of Woman: Woman in Freud's Writings.* Ithaca, NY: Cornell University Press.

Kurzweil, Edith (1994). *Freudians and Feminists.* Boulder, CO: Westview.

Mead, Margaret (1974). "On Freud's View of Female Psychology." In Strouse, Jean (ed.), *Women and Analysis* (pp. 116-128). New York: Grossman.

Miller, Jean Baker (ed.) (1978). *Psychoanalysis and Women.* Baltimore, MD: Penguin Books.

Mitchell, Juliet (1974). *Psychoanalysis and Feminism.* New York: Vintage Books.

Mitchell, Juliet and Rose, Jacqueline (eds.) (1982). *Feminine Sexuality, Jacques Lacan à l'École Freudienne.* London: Routledge and Kegan Paul.

Person, Ethel Spector (1980). "Sexuality as the Mainstay of Identity: Psychoanalytic Perspectives." *Signs,* 5, 605-630.

Ross, Cheryl Lynn and Ross, Mary Ellen (1983). "Mothers, Infants, and the Psychoanalytic Study of Ritual." *Signs,* 9, 76-139.

Thompson, Clara (1964). *Interpersonal Psychoanalysis: The Selected Papers of Clara Thompson.* New York: Basic Books.

Van Herik, Judith (1982). *Freud on Femininity and Faith.* Berkeley: University of California Press.

Webster Brenda S. (1985). "Helene Deutsch: A New Look." *Signs,* 10, 553-571.

Weisstein, Naomi (1971). "Psychology Constructs the Female." In Gornick, Vivian and Moran, Barbara (eds.), *Woman in Sexist Society: Studies in Power and Powerlessness* (pp. 207-224). New York: Basic Books.

XXIV. PSYCHOLOGY

Aguirre, B. E. (1985). "Why Do They Return? Abused Wives in Shelters." *Social Work,* 3, 350-354.

Allen, P. (1970). *Free Choice: A Perspective on the Small Group in Women's Liberation.* Washington, NJ: Times Change Press.

Baker Miller, J. (1978), *Toward a New Psychology of Women,* Boston, MA: Beacon Press.

Baruch, G., Barnett, R. and Rivers, C. (1983). *Lifeprints: New Patterns of Love and Work for Today's Women.* New York: New American Library.

Belenky, Mary Field (1986). *Women's Ways of Knowing: The Development of Self, Voice, and Mind.* New York: Basic Books.

Bem, Sandra L. (1974). "The Measurement of Psychological Androgyny." *Journal of Consulting and Clinical Psychology,* 42, 155-162.

Bernard, Jessie (1971). "The Paradox of the Happy Marriage." In Gornick, Vivian and Moran, Barbara (eds.), Woman in Sexist Society (pp. 145-161). New York: Basic Books.

Brownmiller, Susan (1980). "The Mass Psychology of Rape." In Ruth, Sheila (ed.), Issues in Feminism (pp. 232-234). Boston, MA: Houghton Mifflin.

Chasseguet-Smirgel, J. (ed.) (1970). *Female Sexuality*. Ann Arbor, MI: University of Michigan Press.

Chesler, Phyllis (1971). "Patient and Patriarch: Women in the Psychotherapeutic Relationship." In Gornick, Vivian and Moran, Barbara (eds.), *Woman in Sexist Society* (pp. 362-392). New York: Basic Books.

Chesler, Phyllis (1972). *Women and Madness*. Garden City, NY: Doubleday.

Cook, E. P. (1985). *Psychological Androgyny*. New York: Pergamon.

Crocker, P. L. (1983). "An Analysis of University Definitions of Sexual Harassment." *Signs*, 8, 696-707.

Dickinson, R. L. and Beam, L. (1934). *The Single Woman*. Baltimore: Williams and Wilkins.

Doherty, M. A. (1973). "Sexual Bias in Personality Theory." *The Counseling Psychologist*, 4, 67-74.

Erikson, Eric H. (1964). "Inner and Outer Space: Reflections on Womanhood." *Daedalus*, Spring, 582-606.

Fennema, E. H. and Sherman, J. (1978). "Sex-Related Differences in Mathematics Achievement and Related Factors: A Further Study." *Journal for Research in Mathematics Education*, 9, 189-203.

Gilligan, Carol (1982). *In a Different Voice: Psychological Theory and Women's Development*. Cambridge, MA: Harvard University Press.

Henley, N. M. (1985). "Psychology and Gender." *Signs*, 11, 101-119.

Hite, Shere (1981). *The Hite Report on Female Sexuality*. New York: Corgi.

Hite, Shere (1981). *The Hite Report on Male Sexuality*. New York: Knopf.

Hite, Shere (1995). *The Hite Report on the Family: Growing Up Under Patriarchy*. New York: Grove Press.

Horner, Matina S. (1970). "Femininity and Successful Achievement: A Basic Inconsistency." In Bardwick, J.M. et al. (eds.), *Feminine Personality and Conflict*. Belmont, CA: Brooks/Cole.

Horner, Matina S. (1974). "Toward an Understanding of Achievement-Related Conflicts in Women." In Stacey, J., Bereaud, S., and Daniels, J. (eds.), *And Jill Came Tumbling After: Sexism in American Education*. New York: Dell.

Horney, Karen (1973). *Feminine Psychology*. New York: Norton.

Howell, Elizabeth and Bayes, Marjorie (1981). *Women and Mental Health*. New York: Basic Books.

Kelman, H. (1967). "Karen Horney on Feminine Psychology." *American Journal of Psychoanalysis, 27*, 163-183.

Maccoby, Eleanor E. and Jacklin, C. (1974). *The Psychology of Sex Differences*. Stanford, CA: Stanford University Press.

Mariechild, Diane (1986). *Mother Wit: A Feminist Guide to Psychic Development*. Trumansburg, NY: Crossing Press.

Masters, William and Johnson, Virginia (1968). "Human Sexual Response: The Aging Female and the Aging Male." In Neugarten, B. (ed.), *Middle Age and Aging*. Chicago: University of Chicago Press.

Mitchell, Juliet (1974). "On Freud and the Distinction Between the Sexes." In Strouse, J. (ed.), *Women and Analysis*. New York: Grossman.

Parlee, Mary B. (1979). "Psychology and Women." *Signs,* 5, 121-133.

Rheingold, Joseph C. (1964). *The Fear of Being a Woman.* New York: Grune and Stratton.

Sherman, Julia (1971). *On the Psychology of Woman.* Springfield, IL: Thomas.

Tresemer, David W. (1977). *Fear of Success.* New York: Plenum.

Unger, Rhoda Kesler and Crawford, Mary (1992). *Women and Gender: A Feminist Psychology.* New York: McGraw-Hill.

Wilkinson, Sue (1986). *Feminist Social Psychology: Developing Theory and Practice.* Philadelphia: Open University Press.

Woolley, Helen Thompson (1910). "Psychological Literature: A Review of the Recent Literature on the Psychology of Sex." *Psychological Bulletin,* 1, 335-342.

Woolley, Helen Thompson (1914). "The Psychology of Sex." *Psychological Bulletin,* 2, 353-379.

XXV. RELIGION

Atkinson, Clarissa W., Buchanan, Constance and Miles, Margaret R. (1985). *Immaculate and Powerful: The Female in Sacred Image and Social Reality.* Boston, MA: Beacon Press.

Behnke, Donna A. (1982). *Religious Issues in Nineteenth Century Feminism.* Troy, NY: Whitston Pub. Co.

Bird, Phyllis (1974). "Images of Women in the Old Testament." In Ruether, Rosemary (ed.), *Religion and Sexism.* New York: Simon and Schuster.

Brenner, Athalya (1985). *The Israelite Woman: Social Role and Literary Type in Biblical Narrative--The Biblical Seminar.* Sheffield, England: JSOT Press.

Cady, Susan, Ronan, Marian and Taussig, Hal. (1986). *Sophia: The Future of Feminist Spirituality.* San Francisco, CA: Harper and Row.

Carson, Anne (1992). *Goddesses and Wise Women: The Literature of Feminist Spirituality, 1980-1992: An Annotated Bibliography.* Freedom, CA: Crossing Press.

Christ, Carol P. (1979). "Why Women Need the Goddess: Phenomenological, Psychological, and Political Reflections." In Christ, Carol and Plaskow, Judith (eds.), *Woman's Spirit Rising* (pp. 273-287). New York: Harper and Row.

Christ, Carol P. (1980). *Diving Deep and Surfacing: Women Writers on Spiritual Quest.* Boston, MA: Beacon Press.

Christ, Carol P. (1987). *Laughter of Aphrodite: Reflections on a Journey to the Goddess.* San Francisco, CA: Harper and Row.

Collins, Adela Yarbro (ed.) (1985). *Feminist Perspectives on Biblical Scholarship.* Chico, CA: Scholars Press.

Daly, Mary (1973). *Beyond God the Father: Toward a Philosophy of Women's Liberation.* Boston, MA: Beacon Press.

Darr, Katheryn Pfisterer (1991). *Far More Precious Than Jewels: Perspectives on Biblical Women, Gender and the Biblical Tradition.* Louisville, KY: Westminster/ Knox Press.

Erickson, Victoria Lee (1993). *Where Silence Speaks: Feminism, Social Theory, and Religion.* Minneapolis, MN: Fortress Press.

Ferraro, Barbara, Hussey, Patricia and O'Reilly, Jane (1990). *No Turning Back: Two Nuns' Battle with the Vatican Over Women's Right to Choose.* New York: Poseidon Press.

Field-Bibb, Jacqueline (1991). *Women Towards Priesthood.* New York: Cambridge University Press.

Fischer, Kathleen R. (1988). *Women at the Well: Feminist Perspectives on Spiritual Direction.* New York: Paulist Press.

Garrett, Clarke (1977). "Women and Witches: Patterns of Analysis." *Signs,* 3, 461-470.

Goldenberg, Naomi R. (1979). *Changing of the Gods: Feminism and the End of Traditional Religions.* Boston, MA: Beacon Press.

Gray, J. Patrick (1979). "The Universality of the Female Witch." *International Journal of Women's Studies,* 2, 541-550.

Greaves, Richard L. (1985). *Triumph Over Silence: Women in Protestant History.* Westport, CT: Greenwood Press.

Grob, Leonard, Hassan, Riffot and Gordon, Haim (eds.) (1991). *Women's and Men's Liberation: Testimonies of Spirit.* New York: Greenwood Press.

Gross, Rita M. (1993). *Buddhism After Patriarchy: A Feminist History, Analysis, and Reconstruction of Buddhism.* Albany: State University of New York Press.

Heine, Susanne (1988). *Christianity and the Goddesses: Systematic Criticism of a Feminist Theology.* London: SCM Press.

Hurtado, Larry W. (1990). *Goddesses in Religions and Modern Debate.* Atlanta, GA: Scholars Press.

Jeansonne, Sharon Pace (1990). *The Women of Genesis: From Sarah to Potiphar's Wife.* Minneapolis, MN: Fortress Press.

Kassian, Mary A. (1992). *The Feminist Gospel: The Movement to Unite Feminism with the Church.* Wheaton, IL: Crossway Books.

Lacocque, André (1990). *The Feminine Unconventional: Four Subversive Figures in Israel's Tradition.* Minneapolis, MN: Fortress.

Laffey, Alice L. (1988). *An Introduction to the Old Testament: A Feminist Perspective.* Philadelphia: Fortress.

McIntyre, Marie (1986). *Female and Catholic: A Journal of Mind and Heart.* Mystic, CT: Twenty-Third Publications.

Merrim, Stephanie (1991). *Feminist Perspectives on Sor Juana Ines de la Cruz.* Detroit: Wayne State University.

Newsom, Carol A. and Ringe, Sharon H. (eds.). (1992). *The Women's Bible Commentary.* Louisville, KY: Westminster/John Knox Press.

Ochshorn, Judith (1981). *The Female Experience and the Nature of the Divine.* Bloomington: Indiana University Press.

Orr, Elaine Neil (1987). *Tillie Olsen and a Feminist Spiritual Vision.* Jackson: University Press of Mississippi.

Ostriker, Alicia (1993). *Feminist Revision and the Bible.* Cambridge, MA: Blackwell.

Pagels, Elaine (1976). "What Became of God the Mother? Conflicting Images of God in Early Christianity." *Signs* 2, 293-315.

Plaskow, Judith (1990). *Standing Again at Sinai: Judaism from a Feminist Perspective.* New York: Harper and Row.

Plaskow, Judith and Christ, Carol P. (1989). *Weaving the Visions: New Patterns in Feminist Spirituality.* San Francisco: Harper and Row.

Porterfield, Amanda (1989). *Feminine Spirituality in America: From Sarah Edwards to Martha Graham.* Philadelphia: Temple University Press.

Ruether, Rosemary (ed.) (1974). *Religion and Sexism: Images of Woman in Jewish and Christian Traditions.* New York: Simon and Schuster.

Ruether, Rosemary Radford (1985). *Womanguides: Readings Toward a Feminist Theology.* Boston, MA: Beacon Press.

Russell, Letty M. (ed.) (1985). *Feminist Interpretation of the Bible.* Philadelphia: Westminster Press.

Schneiders, Sandra Marie (1991). *Beyond Patching: Faith and Feminism in the Catholic Church.* New York: Paulist Press.

Spretnak, Charlene (1982). *The Politics of Women's Spirituality: Essays on the Rise of Spiritual Power within the Feminist Movement.* Garden City, NY: Anchor Books.

Steichen, Donna (1991). *Ungodly Rage: The Hidden Face of Catholic Feminism.* San Francisco: Ignatius Press.

Trible, Phyllis (1984). *Texts of Terror: Literary-Feminist Readings of Biblical Narratives. Overtures to Biblical Theology.* Philadelphia: Fortress Press.

VanDyke, Annette (1992). *The Search for a Woman-Centered Spirituality.* New York: New York University Press.

Weaver, Mary Jo (1985). *New Catholic Women: A Contemporary Challenge to Traditional Religious Authority.* San Francisco: Harper and Row.

Wren, Brian (1990). *What Language Shall I Borrow? God Talk in Worship: A Male Response to Feminist Theology.* New York: Crossroad.

XXVI. SCIENCE/MEDICINE

Bleier, Ruth (1984). *Science and Gender: A Critique of Biology and Its Theories on Women.* New York: Teachers College Press.

Bleier, Ruth (ed.) (1986). *Feminist Approaches to Science.* New York: Teachers College Press.

Daniels, Cynthia (1993). *At Women's Expense: State Power and the Politics of Fetal Rights.* Cambridge, MA: Harvard University Press.

Donnison, Jean (1977). *Midwives and Medical Men. A History of Inter-Professional Rivalries and Women's Rights.* London: Heinemann.

Drachman, Virginia (1984). *Hospital with a Heart: Women Doctors and the Paradox of Separatism at the New England Hospital, 1862-1869.* Ithaca, NY: Cornell University Press.

Ehrenreich, Barbara and English, Deirdre (1973). *Witches, Midwives, and Nurses: A History of Women Healers.* Old Westbury, NY: Feminist Press.

Fausto-Sterling, Anne (1985). *Myths of Gender: Biological Theories about Men and Women.* New York: Basic Books.

Fennema, Elizabeth and Leder, Gilah C. (eds.) (1990). *Mathematics and Gender.* New York: Teachers College Press.

Fins, Alice (1979). *Women in Science.* Skokie, IL: National Textbook Company.

Fox, Lynn H. (1981). *The Problem of Women and Mathematics: A Report to the Ford Foundation.* New York: Ford Foundation.

Haas, Violet B. and Perucci, Carolyn C. (1984). *Women in Scientific and Engineering Professions.* Ann Arbor, MI: University of Michigan Press.

Haber, Louis (1979). *Women Pioneers of Science.* New York: Harcourt.

Haller, John S. and Haller, Robin M. (1974). *The Physician and Sexuality in Victorian America.* Urbana: University of Illinois Press.

Harding, Jan (ed.) (1986). *Perspectives on Gender and Science.* New York: Falmer Press.

Harding, Sandra (1986). *The Science Question in Feminism.* Ithaca, NY: Cornell University Press.

Hillyer, Barbara (1993). *Feminism and Disability.* Norman: University of Oklahoma.

Holmes, Bequaert and Purdy, Laura M. (1992). *Feminist Perspectives in Medical Ethics.* Bloomington: Indiana University Press.

Kahle, Jane Butler (1982). *Double Dilemma: Minorities and Women in Science Education.* West Lafayette, IN: Purdue University.

Kammer, Ann E. (1979). *Science, Sex and Society.* Newton, MA: Educational Development Center.

Keller, Evelyn Fox (1984). *Reflections on Gender and Science.* New Haven, CT: Yale University Press.

Kimball, M. M. (1981). "Women and Science: A Critique of Biological Theories." *International Journal of Women's Studies,* 4, 318-388.

Mattfeld, Jacquelyn and Van Aken, Carolyn G. (eds.) (1965). *Women and the Scientific Professions.* Cambridge, MA: MIT Press.

Moldow, Gloria (1987). *Women Doctors in Gilded Age Washington: Race, Gender, and Professionalization.* Urbana: University of Illinois Press.

Morantz-Sanchez, Regina Markell (1985). *Sympathy and Science: Women Physicians in American Medicine.* New York: Oxford University Press.

Muff, Janet (1982). *Socialization, Sexism, and Stereotyping: Women's Issues in Nursing.* St. Louis, MO: Mosby.

Newman, Louise Michele (1985). *Men's Ideas/Women's Realities: Popular Science, 1870-1915.* New York: Pergamon Press.

Rose, Steven, Kamin, Leon, and Lewontin, R.C. (1984). *Not in Our Genes: Biology, Ideology and Human Nature.* Harmondsworth, England: Pelican.

Rosser, Sue Vilhauer (1985). *Teaching Science and Health from a Feminist Perspective.* New York: Pergamon Press.

Rosser, Sue Vilhauer (1990). *Female Friendly Science: Applying Women's Studies Methods and Theories to Attract Students.* New York: Pergamon Press.

Rosser, Sue Vilhauer (ed.) (1988). *Feminism within the Science and Health Care Professions.* New York: Teachers College Press.

Rothschild, Joan (1986). *Teaching Technology from a Feminist Perspective.* New York: Pergamon.

Rothschild, Joan (ed.) (1983). *Machina Ex Dea.* New York: Teachers College Press.

Ruzek, Sheryl Burt (1978). *The Women's Health Movement: Feminist Alternatives to Medical Control.* New York: Praeger.

Sazers, Janet (1982). *Biological Politics: Feminist and Anti-Feminist Perspectives.* Totowa, NJ: Rowman and Allanheld.

Schiebinger, Londa L. (1989). *The Mind Has No Sex?: Women in the Origins of Modern Science.* Cambridge, MA: Harvard University Press.

Sherwin, Susan (1992). *No Longer Patient: Feminist Ethics and Health Care.* Philadelphia: Temple University Press.

Smith, Dorothy E. (1975). "Women and Psychiatry." In Smith, D. and David, S. (eds.), *Women Look at Psychiatry.* Vancouver: Press Gang Publishers.

Stage, Sarah (1979). *Female Complaints: Lydia Pinkham and the Business of Women's Medicine.* New York: Norton.

Tobias, Sheila (1990). *They're Not Dumb, They're Different: Stalking the Second Tier.* Tucson, AZ: Research Corporation.

Tuana, Nancy (1989). *Feminism and Science.* Bloomington, IN: Indiana University Press.

Verbragge, Martha H. (1988). *Able-Bodied Womanhood: Personal Health and Social Change in 19th-Century Boston.* New York: Oxford University Press.

XXVII. SOCIAL WORK AND FEMINIST THERAPY

Bricker-Jenkins, Mary and Hooyman, Nancy (1983). *Not for Women Only: Social Work Practice for a Feminist Future.* Silver Spring, MD: National Association of Social Workers.

Bricker-Jenkins, Mary, Hooyman, Nancy R. and Gottlieb, Naomi (1991). *Feminist Social Work Practice in Clinical Settings*. Newbury Park, CA: Sage.

Burstow, Bonnie (1992). *Radical Feminist Therapy*. Thousand Oaks, CA: Sage.

Davis, Allen F. (1967). *Spearheads for Reform. The Social Settlements and the Progressive Movement 1890-1914*. New York: Oxford University Press.

Davis, Allen F. (1973). *American Heroine: The Life and Legend of Jane Addams*. New York: Oxford University Press.

Gordon, Linda (1990). *Women, the State, and Welfare*. Madison, WI: University of Wisconsin Press.

Gottlieb, Naomi (ed.) (1980). *Alternative Social Services for Women*. New York: Columbia University Press.

McHugh, Paul (1980). *Prostitution and Victorian Social Reform*. New York: St. Martin's Press.

Masi, Dale A. (1981). *Organizing for Women: Issues, Strategies, and Services*. Lexington, MA: Lexington Books.

Miller, Dorothy C. (1990). *Women and Social Welfare: A Feminist Analysis*. New York: Praeger.

Pascall, Gillian (1986). *Social Policy: A Feminist Analysis*. New York: Tavistock Publications.

Valentich, Mary and Gripton, James (1985). *Feminist Perspectives on Social Work and Human Sexuality*. New York: Haworth Press.

Van Den Bergh, Nan and Cooper, Lynn B. (1986). *Feminist Visions for Social Work*. Silver Spring, MD: National Association of Social Workers.

Walton, Ronald G. (1975). *Women in Social Work*. London: Routledge and Kegan Paul.

West, Guida (1981). *The National Welfare Rights Movement: The Social Protest of Poor Women*. New York: Praeger.

Wilson, Elizabeth (1977). *Women and the Welfare State*. London: Tavistock.

ABOUT THE AUTHORS

JANET K. BOLES (Ph.D., University of Texas at Austin), Associate Professor of Political Science, Marquette University, has taught and written on the United States feminist movement, including *The Politics of the Equal Rights Amendment* and *American Feminism: New Issues for a Mature Movement*. She was president of the American Political Science Association Organized Section on Women and Politics Research, 1994-95, and has served on editorial boards for *Women and Politics*, the *Women's Studies Encyclopedia*, and *Ms*. Her current research involves the impact of local elected women on public policy and women's groups.

DIANE LONG HOEVELER (Ph.D., University of Illinois-Urbana), Associate Professor of English, Marquette University. She is author of *Romantic Androgyny: The Women Within* (1990), *Approaches to Teaching "Jane Eyre"* (1993), *Milwaukee Women Yesterday* (1979), and *Milwaukee Women Today* (1979). One of the original contributors to Ungar's *Guide to American Women Writers*, she has also published over two dozen articles and reviews on women's literature and literary criticism. She is Coordinator of MU's Women's Studies program, and is currently in the process of completing two books on gothic feminism.

REBECCA BARDWELL (Ph.D., University of Iowa), Associate Professor of Educational and Counseling Psychology, Marquette University, has done research on gender differences in motivation and achievement. She served as Coordinator of the Women's Studies program at Marquette University from 1990 to 1994. Presently she is doing research on women in midlife.